Turner's First Century

A HISTORY OF TURNER CONSTRUCTION COMPANY

Turner's First Century

A HISTORY OF TURNER CONSTRUCTION COMPANY

Donald E. Wolf

GREENWICH PUBLISHING GROUP, INC.

Library of Congress Cataloging-in-Publication Data

Wolf, Donald E., 1927-
  Turner's first century : a history of Turner Construction Company /
Donald E. Wolf.
      p. cm.
Includes index.
  ISBN 0-944641-56-3
  1. Turner Construction Company–History. 2. Construction
industry–United States–History. I. Title.
  HD9715.U54 T879 2002
  338.7'624'0973–dc21
                                          2002006052

Produced and published by Greenwich Publishing Group, Inc.
Lyme, Connecticut

Design by Clare Cunningham Graphic Design

First Printing: May 2002

10 9 8 7 6 5 4 3 2 1

Page one: The first *Turner City*, illustrated all the work Turner had done between 1902 and 1910 as if it had all been built in a single city. It was published in 1911, and since then a new *Turner City* has been published each year.

Henry C. Turner (left) and DeForest H. Dixon, who had previously worked together as engineers for Ernest L. Ransome, were the only construction men on Turner's first board. Henry C. Turner became president of the new company, and he brought in DeForest H. Dixon as its general superintendent. The two men are shown here in 1932, at St. Andrew's Golf Club, Hastings-on-Hudson, New York, where a golf competition was held as part of the company's celebration of its 30th anniversary.

Table of Contents

Preface

I t's unlikely that anyone could complete a serious study of Turner's history without a feeling of having been privy to something extraordinary. It's a history that spans a hundred years and has played out in a setting fraught with challenge and risk. The company has worked on almost 10,000 jobs, employed as many as 25,000 workers at one time, and from its earliest years has been able to develop and sustain a glorious reputation and a position of industry leadership.

After four years of my own research, I've confirmed an early sense that a study of Turner's history was bound to reveal something genuinely exceptional. That was an idea that began as a general impression within a few days of my starting the project, when I was given absolutely free and unrestricted access to all the company's records, and was encouraged to talk at length with any of its present or retired staff. It intensified after that, when I realized that no one had sought (or was seeking) to influence anything I wrote. In time it became clear to me that this approach of Turner's was itself an expression of its own rigorous commitment to my being able to write the history exactly as I saw it, without interference. What struck me as extraordinary was the idea that the managers of this great, 100-year-old company were so sure there was nothing to hide that they could safely allow a complete stranger unlimited access to all the company's records.

Now, of course, I've come to understand why that was so easy for them. They knew they had nothing to worry about. They understood and took for granted the permanence and inviolability of the ethical commitment that had been at the core of everything the company had been doing since its founding, in 1902. In all my research, I never found a single instance in which the company failed to perform in just the way its Quaker founders would have expected it to perform.

A hundred years is a long time, and the research required for writing a history of such a period is extensive. I needed plenty of help, and I was fortunate enough to get it.

In acknowledging the contributions of persons who were important in that process, I'll start with Bud Gravette. He was the company's ninth chairman, and it was he who initiated the plan for writing a history and set the stage for how it would be done. Bud Gravette deserves special credit here, because he was the first chairman who hadn't been either a family member or a career Turner executive, and he might have been expected to have a less serious interest than the others in seeing the company's history recorded.

Tom Turner, one of four members of the Turner family working in the company today, took time from his duties as director of marketing to manage the history project. I'm indebted to this quiet and capable man for shepherding the project through its long course.

Because there had never been anything written about Turner that was more than a short history of a selected period, I had to rely a great deal on personal interviews, at least for the period since the Second World War. About seventy-five interviews were conducted, many of them extremely productive. Among those, there were a few that were exceptionally good, and at this point I'll acknowledge (in alphabetical order) the persons who provided them.

One was Jim Allaire, now in his eighties and living in Iowa. He had spent much of his Turner career in the Far West, and his recollections of projects and personalities there were exceptionally clear and relevant.

Another was Doug Bennett, an alumnus of Harvard's Graduate School of Business Administration. After a few years with Turner in the Midwest, he had joined the corporate staff in New York. He was able to provide excellent and extremely useful material about the personalities and events of the late 1970s, the 1980s, and the early 1990s.

Roger Lang, who was educated in architecture, was close to the seat of corporate management during the late 1980s and the 1990s. His intelligence and his perspectives on some of the transitions the company underwent during those years were extremely helpful.

Dick Manteuffel, a longtime veteran of Turner's work in the Midwest, is an exceptionally reflective engineer-executive who was able to provide sensitive insights into some of the persons and events that had figured in his own long career in the company.

Bernie Newton is one of those Turner loyalists whose passion for the company knows few limits, and his intelligent recollections of his own long history with Turner were especially helpful.

There were lots of other good interviews, of course. Each one brought something new to the story, but limitations of space prevent my describing each of these persons individually. Instead, I've listed alphabetically the names of those additional Turner persons whose interviews were especially helpful. They are Karl Almstead, Bill Altom, Bill Arnold, Anton Bajuk, Ralph Beck, Nick Billotti, Don Burbrink, Ed Clarke, Herb Conant, Dick Corry, Peter Davoren, Paul DeMange, Don Denman, Dick Dorais, Charlie Enscoe, Bob Fee, George Frost, Tom Gerlach Jr., Tom Gerlach Sr., Jack Greenip, Lou Hall, John Hanft, Chuck Harger, Bob Hettema, Myron Hinckley, Wells Jarboe, Ralph Johnson, Don Kerstetter, Charlie Koch, Bob Kupfer, Tom Leppert, Rick Lombardi, Jerry Mandel, Bob Marshall, Al McNeill, Bob Meyer, Doug Meyer, Rod Michalka, Andy Miller, George Morrison, Bob Nilsson, Frank O'Connor, Hal Parmelee, Ed Quimby, Jack Quinn, Shelby Reaves, Ted Rhoades, Tony Sanfillipo, Barry Sibson, Don Sleeman, Howard Turner, Jeb Turner, Jerry Turner, Roger Turnier, Rod Wille, and Jack Woolf.

Turner City, the wonderfully detailed drawing that's produced annually to illustrate all the work the company has completed during the year, has been prepared by six artists, over the years. I'm indebted to Katherine C. Palagonia for information about those artists, as it was presented in her Profile of Turner City Artists.

Historical research requires a good deal more than interviews and archival study. It needs persons who can facilitate access to other people and information, and no one was more helpful in those areas than Pat Knowles. Iris Stuart, another longtime Turner person, was also invaluable in the business of trying to make everything come together. And of course Barbara McAllister, whose many responsibilities include the management of the database in which critical information about Turner projects exists, was always helpful as well. Indexing of research materials during the preparation of the manuscript was especially valuable, and for that well-done work I'm indebted to Rachel Wahl. Drew Martin and Chris Drummond helped in many ways along the way, especially when the time came to collect pictures and process them electronically for use in the book.

After all the research is done, and after the author has organized and converted it into what he sees as a good story, it's the editor who has the task of ensuring that everything the author has written is consistent with everything else he has written, that it's all been spelled and punctuated correctly, and that its syntax is rigorous. The editor's task is formidable, normally requiring at least the skills of a scholar and a diplomat. In rare cases a good editor might have the perspective of a sensitive writer, too, and perhaps a sense of humor. Ursula Smith combines all four qualities, and her help has been critical and is immensely appreciated.

The least-acknowledged contributor to the process is the unsung, unpaid person who reads or listens to often-rewritten passages and suffers more than a small number of late or missed dinners while the manuscript is taking shape. My wife, Ellen, had that job here, and her help is gratefully acknowledged.

Foreword

Writing a foreword to precede the very professional work done by Donald Wolf is an awesome assignment, but my special qualification is that at the age of ninety I have the retrospect to have known the founder and many who followed him in the life of this great company. A few personal reminiscences about some of the Turners who have led the company might be useful in a foreword to its written history.

The character and competence of Turner Construction Company were defined by the founder, Henry C. Turner, who led the company for thirty-nine years. Henry was succeeded by my father, J. Archer Turner, his youngest brother and fourteen years his junior. After my father's death in 1946 — and after the brief Moreell hiatus — Henry's son Chan followed, from 1947 to 1968. I succeeded Chan in 1968, and served until 1978.

I'm indebted to Bob Turner, Henry's son, for his recollections of his own youth in the Turner household. He would occasionally go along for the ride when the chauffeur drove his father from the family home in Brooklyn to the Turner office in lower Manhattan. It was always Henry's preference to walk back, at the end of the day, across the Brooklyn Bridge.

Henry was always interested in and proud of his family, even when two of his sons, Bob and Haines, chose careers unrelated to construction. Bob, an artist, became a highly respected potter and teacher, and Haines became a university professor of economics and an educator of labor leaders. The youngest son, James, became successful on his own as a consultant/development manager in construction.

According to Bob, his father always retained a warm recollection of his own childhood on the family farm near Betterton, on the upper Eastern Shore of

Maryland. In season, the farm produced peaches and tomatoes, to be sailed across the Chesapeake Bay to markets in Baltimore, often with one of the six Turner brothers aboard. Henry would never acknowledge that any peaches or tomatoes from "up north" could match those he recalled from his youth.

Henry was the first of the Turner brothers to attend Swarthmore College, from which he graduated in 1893, and by 1902 he had established his new company. Not many years later, memories of his youth and his desire for a summer "getaway" where his wife Charlotte's asthma could be alleviated led to Skyland Farm at Buck Hill Falls in the Poconos. He built a home and guest house there, and with a farmer grew corn, garden vegetables, and flowers, and maintained cows, chickens, and riding horses. It was a great place for Henry and Charlotte's growing children and within reasonable reach of New York by train. The children, however, were required to earn their allowances by doing chores and by maintaining the tennis court that father and sons enjoyed. Bob tells of the time he rushed to tell his mother after he had defeated his father for the first time, but his excitement was dampened as she inquired whether he had left his father to take down the net alone.

Among his brothers, Henry developed a special fondness and respect for his youngest brother, J. Archer, but it would be the end of the First World War before J. Archer would begin working for Henry's company. Until that time, the two brothers most closely allied would be J. Archer and his next-older brother, William W. The two of them would work together in their own Philadelphia-based construction company until its absorption by Turner in 1919. In 1930, William W. would retire, leaving J. Archer to lead Turner's Philadelphia office until succeeded there by Chan in 1938.

In 1901 it was J. Archer's turn to enter Swarthmore College. Like the two brothers who preceded him, he chose a civil engineering major, and the record confirms that he was a good student despite the competing demands of his participation in athletics, in which he excelled. While president of his class, he was captain of the lacrosse team for two years when it won the intercollegiate championship while playing against all the Ivy League teams and Johns Hopkins. He maintained his interest in athletics, following college sports and his favorite game of golf. He, Henry, and Chan were the ones to beat in contests at Buck Hill.

J. Archer remained close to his alma mater all his life. He succeeded Henry on the board of managers, and served as treasurer of the corporation. His allegiance was further cemented by his marriage to Helen Carré, a college class-mate. Of his three sons, the oldest, Donald, and the youngest, J. Archer Jr. (Jerry), chose Turner for their careers, and this pleased their father. Nevertheless, he encouraged my own early interest in chemistry and later supported me beyond college as I earned my Ph.D. at MIT. J. Archer was always interested in the national political scene and always good for an argument at a Sunday family dinner, which was always adjusted in timing to accommodate his golfing schedule for the day.

In 1940, Henry Turner designated his brother J. Archer to be executive vice-president in New York. In 1941, Henry assumed the newly created position of chairman, and J. Archer became president, serving in that capacity until 1946.

After the demanding years of the war, J. Archer, not in good health, sought a reduction in his responsibilities. It was in response to that request that Henry, J. Archer, and R. C. Wilson, with full board support, reached out to retiring Adm. Ben Moreell in 1946 with a successful invitation to become president of Turner. On September 18, 1946, Henry retired as chairman, to be succeeded by J. Archer, and Moreell became president on October 1. Regrettably, J. Archer died unex-pectedly on November 1, 1946, soon after Admiral Moreell's arrival. Even more unexpectedly, two months later Admiral Moreell was offered and accepted the positions of chairman and president of the country's fourth-largest steel company, Jones & Laughlin in Pittsburgh. The board pulled itself together, and with relief and cheers welcomed Henry Chandlee Turner Jr. to the presidency.

In 1947, I left DuPont and moved my family to Pittsburgh, where I was given senior responsibility for creating a research center for the country's largest com-mercial coal company, Pittsburgh Consolidation, a 1946 merger of Mellon and Rockefeller interests. Turner was just starting construction of a new headquarters building in Pittsburgh for U.S. Steel, and during the inspection visits that Chan Turner made to Pittsburgh he regularly included visits to my home. We came to know each other better, and in 1952 I accepted his invitation to join the Turner board to fill the vacancy created by Henry's retirement.

Henry Turner has written of Chan's boyhood as a model of youthful industry, exemplified by his operating a chicken business at Skyland Farm, caddying during his adolescent years, and working summers for construction contractors during his college years. As soon as he graduated from Swarthmore in 1923, Chan began his career with Turner, working nine-and-a-half-hour days, six days a week, rebuilding the Inn at Buck Hill Falls.

In 1926, he was assigned to build the Breakers Hotel in Palm Beach, where a career-long association began with F. B. (Joe) Warren. On a brief 1928 vacation, Chan met Virginia Melick in March and they were married in August. It was a marriage of talents. She was a beautiful Phi Beta Kappa Swarthmore graduate of 1927, accomplished in many campus activities, articulate, and socially vigorous. In personality, she complemented the equally social but more low-keyed personality of Chan. She was helpful in her husband's career. Together they had two attractive daughters, Ann and Marlee.

Chan was handsome, even as a young boy. As an adult, he was soft-spoken, socially confident, graceful in his movements, always well dressed, and a comfortable conversationalist. I saw his relationships with Turner people at all levels as uniformly friendly, but he was intimate with few beyond his confidant and adviser, Joe Warren, and me. He was never brusque and left the less pleasant but necessary aspects of management to his immediate subordinates. He avoided confrontation. If angered, his face gave no sign, as if his feelings were behind a mask.

Chan's very valuable contributions to the growth of Turner rested on his competitive desire to increase the company's business. It was an objective toward which he used his considerable skills in developing relationships with architects and among leaders who represented business opportunities for Turner. A significant number of contracts acquired by Turner had their origins in critical contacts made by Chan. From its earliest days, the company's success has been inextricably linked to the work of architects and engineers whose designs it converts to brick and mortar, and to the vision of owners and developers who conceive and pay for them.

The company prospered under Chan's leadership as he continued the direct line relationship between the business unit managers and the president. In other respects there were changes, e.g. entertainment at the annual black-tie dinner for staff members at the level of superintendent and higher, changed. A men's chorus that previously had served as entertainment was replaced, for at least one such dinner, by an exotic dancer. At another annual dinner, a distinguished-looking actor was seated at the head table and allowed to present himself as a potential client, inducing eager Turner salespeople to exhaust themselves trying to secure his business.

Meanwhile, in 1954, my own career had taken a surprising turn. Unknown to me, Dr. J. C. Warner, then president of the Carnegie Institute of Technology in Pittsburgh and a director of Jones & Laughlin Steel Corporation, had recommended that I be offered the soon-to-be-vacated position of corporate vice president for research and development for J & L. I accepted and gained valuable experience in problems of corporate management. But my surprise at the Jones & Laughlin development paled alongside my reaction to Chan's suggestion, ten years later, that I terminate my successful career in Pittsburgh in favor of accepting his offer to move to New York and become president of Turner. Chan and Joe Warren had often discussed with me the matter of succession at Turner, but until the 1964 offer I had never considered the possibility of taking on the presidency myself.

The prospect of heading the great company that had, in one way or another, been part of my life since boyhood, was extremely attractive. I accepted the offer and became president in March 1965 and chief executive officer in 1968. When Chan retired at the end of 1970, I succeeded him as chairman. During these years, the company continued to grow. I retired in 1978, the last Turner to head the company. Its growth since my retirement is a compelling testament to the ability and character of the men who have managed it since. Despite stresses imposed by occasional failed strategies and difficult economic conditions, the company at its hundredth anniversary is stronger than ever, producing annual volumes that, when expressed in constant dollars, are almost three times what they were when I retired, with proportionately increased earnings. Its continued role as the country's No. 1 builder seems assured.

— *Howard S. Turner*

1.

Before

en who survive the country's great political wars tend to be a wily and tireless lot, and Michigan-born Thomas E. Dewey was no exception. He was a tough and ambitious lawyer who had first captured national attention before the Second World War as a spectacular crime-fighting district attorney in New York, and during the 1940s he had come close to winning the presidency in a couple of bruising campaigns, most recently in the 1948 election in which Harry Truman had taken everyone, including his own supporters, by surprise. But by the early weeks of December 1949, well into his second term as governor of New York, Dewey was beginning to tire. He was looking forward with even more relish than usual to a peaceful Christmas respite at the home he had built in upstate Pawling.

It wasn't to be. A few weeks before Christmas, bids were opened for building the superstructure of a huge new bus terminal in the heart of New York City, where the crush of traffic was threatening to choke off the vital flow of people and goods that was the city's lifeline. Because both New York and New Jersey relied heavily on the transportation systems of New York City, responsibility for building such a facility had been delegated to the Port of New York Authority, whose architects had designed a single, $25 million building to replace the randomly scattered terminals that had been servicing the 2,500 buses that entered and left the city every day. Contracts had been signed with the thirty-six companies that operated the buses, guaranteeing in no uncertain terms that space in the splendid new terminal would be ready for their vehicles by the end of 1950, and all that remained now was the task of getting the place built in a little less than one year.

That would be no easy job, as everyone who knew anything about building in New York knew very well. When the bids were opened, the lowest of the ten competing bidders proved to be Merritt-Chapman & Scott, a big, well-established firm with a long history and a decent reputation for building large civil works. The second bidder, higher by about $200,000 (the end-of-century equivalent of almost $2 million) was Turner Construction Company, a privately held, New York–based building firm that had been in business there since 1902. Turner was among the country's most eminent builders by 1949, a big, strong contracting firm immensely well regarded as a builder of high-quality structures. But in the arena in which big construction firms compete with one another for public contracts, a miss is about as good as a mile, and Turner's second-place bid on the bus terminal job was a clear miss.

The compelling importance of getting the job done properly and within the prescribed single year was well understood by just about everyone concerned, and almost as soon as the bids had been opened evidence began to grow that the port authority was unlikely to be comfortable with anyone but Turner. The potential consequences of ending up with a building that was anything less than what they had designed or of missing the critical target date for completion were so serious that the port authority resolved to do everything it could to obtain approval for awarding the job to Turner.

The project had been the subject of political argument for years, even before the bids were taken, and awarding a contract to the second bidder, a dangerous course on any public project, was bound to be a formidable task on so highly visible and politically sensitive a job as this one. No one knew that better than the political appointees who ran the port authority or their chief of staff, Austin Tobin. The low bidder was a big and well-known firm, with powerful friends in Albany, and there would have to be plenty of convincing evidence that selecting the second bidder was absolutely critical to the City's interest before anyone in authority would dare to risk the protests that were bound to follow.

Time was critical, of course, and by the twelfth of December the port authority had referred the matter to the six-man Independent Board of Consulting Engineers on whom it had come to rely for recommendations in such special circumstances. By the thirteenth the board had deliberated and submitted its findings to the port authority: a unanimous recommendation that the low bidder be passed over and that the award be made to Turner.

When Merritt-Chapman & Scott's people learned about the port authority's inclination to reject its bid in favor of Turner's, they proposed an effort to join forces on the job with Turner, and as a result of the port authority's urging, a discussion toward that end followed. But although Chan Turner proved to be entirely willing to share the administration and the profits of the job with his competitor, he wanted no part of a plan to share responsibility for its management. If Turner's name was going to be on the job, Turner would have to make all the decisions, and it was after that position had been established by Turner that the plan for joining forces with Merritt-Chapman & Scott collapsed.

That was when any plans that Governor Dewey might have had for a few weeks of Christmas holiday in the country collapsed too. Without delay, port authority chairman Howard Cullman forwarded to him the board's vigorous recommendation that the award be made to Turner, requesting the governor's earliest possible approval. Clearly this would be a tough call for Dewey, who was being hounded by powerful political colleagues advocating for Merritt-Chapman & Scott while the port authority argued that the unusual and unforgiving schedule and quality demands of the job militated for a contractor like Turner. Dewey called in Gov. Alfred Driscoll of New Jersey, with whom he shared control of the port authority, and the two of them mulled over the port authority's potentially controversial recommendation for a couple of days, but they weren't convinced. The two seasoned politicians weren't able to find enough merit in their arguments to justify exposing themselves to criticism for departing from the lowest- responsible-bidder tradition, and they directed the port authority to award the job to Merritt-Chapman & Scott.

But the port authority wouldn't give up. A week later, the commissioners themselves and their director went up to Albany to plead their case directly to the two governors, emphasizing Turner's extraordinary reputation and the special importance of having such a contractor on this especially sensitive job. It worked. The governors agreed not to do anything to prevent the award to Turner and by the twenty-ninth of December their decision had been made public.

Of course, that didn't end the controversy. January brought recriminations and accusations in the state legislature and threats of litigation. But by then a blue-and-white Turner Construction Company sign had announced the first signs of work along the west side of Eighth Avenue, and Turner had started the work of building the big superstructure with a force that would within a few months exceed 2,000 men.

No single, detailed rationale for the decision to pass over Merritt-Chapman & Scott in favor of Turner was ever really made public. Some contemporaneous reports attributed the port authority's strong preference for Turner to the company's performance on an earlier job for the organization, and to its superior experience in major building projects, vis-à-vis the low bidder's historical emphasis on marine construction and other nonbuilding projects. But although Merritt-Chapman & Scott had indeed concentrated on civil works and the like (not buildings), it had done its share of major building work too, probably enough to qualify it for this job. In fact, they were finishing at least two big hospitals and a number of other buildings in the New York area at the time that bids for the bus terminal were taken, so the argument that they weren't qualified as building contractors might have been hard to support. The press gave some attention as well to Turner's long history of good relations with organized labor, suggesting that the City's interests might best be served by a firm that was highly regarded by the New York trade unions, but the truth is that it would have been difficult to fault Merritt-Chapman's own respectable labor relations history. And there were other explanations: At least one newspaper mentioned Turner's financial strength as a factor, even though Merritt-Chapman & Scott was itself a very large and well-financed construction firm, clearly strong enough for this job.

To some insiders who appeared to know and understand the thinking of the port authority best, it seemed that there was something more compelling in the agency's insistence on Turner. They spoke, and later wrote, of the extremely fine reputation of this company that had been started by Quakers almost fifty years earlier and that had continued to do business in the style of its founders, producing buildings of uniformly high quality and maintaining an extraordinary reputation for a level of ethical behavior that was difficult to match in the rough-and-tumble of the contemporaneous construction marketplace. There was apparently a widely held view within the port authority that a promise given by Turner that the building would be completed during 1950 was a promise in which they could place their full and certain confidence. That was a powerful incentive, given the very high stakes, and the port authority's managers didn't feel they wanted to take a chance on anyone else.

Within the promised year their judgment was vindicated. In spite of labor shortages, design changes, and most of the other factors that would have been expected to hinder progress on such a job in the postwar environment, the terminal became fully operational on December 15, 1950.

This extraordinary reputation of Turner's, powerful enough to sweep aside political forces that could normally be expected to be in control, was clearly something that had been a long time in the making. Determining just what circumstances and events were responsible for it isn't simple, but there's certainly reason to believe that there must have been something about the personalities of the men who founded the company, something in the patterns they established early on, that had profoundly influenced the culture and style of everything that followed.

The first Turners had come to America from England almost 300 years earlier, settling along the Eastern Shore of Maryland as early as 1653. That was a full three years before Mary Fisher and Ann Austin, the first Quakers to arrive on American soil, had landed in what was then the twenty-six-year-old port of Boston, where they had been tormented for their religious views and imprisoned by Puritans before being deported to Barbados. It wasn't until 1657 that settlements of newly "convinced" Quakers began to appear in Maryland, where they fared much better than their brothers and sisters in New England, but where their radically different style of worship, their rejection of an ordained ministry, their acceptance of the full equality of women and men, and their refusal to swear oaths or bear arms still set them apart from what they called "the world" and encouraged its hostility.

The first American Turner had already been in Maryland for a few years when Elizabeth Harris, a charismatic Englishwoman, arrived in 1657 to spread the gospel of the Society of Friends to new settlers; William Turner, liking what he heard, became the first of a long line of Quaker Turners. They increased in numbers and prosperity over the generations that followed, settling later in Baltimore, where a descendant named Richard Townsend Turner established a business.

By the middle of the nineteenth century this vigorous young Turner (the ice skating champion of Baltimore) had found prosperity, but he also found himself drawn to the rural life. An accomplished sailor and outdoorsman, he abandoned Baltimore for the Eastern Shore, where in 1851 he acquired 180 acres in Kent County, only a few hundred yards from the shoreline of Chesapeake Bay and not far from where other Turners had been living for almost 150 years. He was married to Elizabeth ("Lizzie") Betterton Turner, a Quaker woman whose own forebears had originally settled near Philadelphia around 1700, where her great-grandfather had been a prosperous merchant and a signer of banknotes that financed the American Revolution.

Starting life over in their middle years was a radical and risky undertaking for the Turners, but it proved to be an entirely worthwhile one for these grandparents of Henry C. Turner, the still-unborn founder of Turner Construction Company. Richard Townsend Turner named the Eastern Shore hamlet in which he settled Betterton, after his wife's family, and he named the gracious Victorian house he built on his land there Ellwood. He soon established a general merchandise business in town, and within a few years it had expanded to include a sawmill, a granary, and a substantial fleet of vessels for transporting materials to and from other bay ports, including Baltimore. Not much later he acquired at least a dozen other farms in the area, on which cows were kept and wheat, corn, and other crops were grown, but where the primary emphasis appears to have been on growing fruit —

mainly peaches, but including cherries and pears as well — for commercial marketing. The prosperity that Richard Townsend Turner had enjoyed in Baltimore had clearly not diminished a bit when he shifted his base to the Eastern Shore, and it fairly quickly increased.

At Ellwood, the Turners raised six children of their own and at least as many more from other families, including some who had been orphaned when their mother, Richard Turner's sister Cassandra and her husband, Dr. Edwin Chandlee, died within a few years of each other, and some who came from the families of other relatives or neighbors.

It was a time when rural living was simple and sometimes, by later standards, primitive, but life at Ellwood appears to have been good. The house, a large one approached by a long, two-lane, tree-lined driveway, had a good many rooms, including two servants' rooms. There was plenty of help on the farms and enough income to allow all the children to go off to Quaker boarding schools and to college. In spite of the rural setting, there was even a certain amount of society in the area, with several Turner relatives living nearby and others, including the forebears of the actress Katherine Hepburn, living within a few miles.

No Quaker family has been known to have owned slaves after about 1800, and the Turners were no exception. Because they were vigorously sympathetic to the Quaker humanism of the period, Ellwood became a station along the Underground Railway that provided refuge for runaway slaves on their way north, generating antagonism from some Turner neighbors and occasionally causing Richard Townsend Turner to have to leave the area for short periods. But except for that, and except for the naturally occurring problems that beset most families, the senior Turners and their children lived a comfortable life in Betterton.

One of the six children born to them at Ellwood, and one who enjoyed and doubtless benefited from the nurturing life there, was Richard Townsend Turner Jr. Described by some who knew him later as "a good and kind man," he married Martha Ellen Birch, one of the orphans who had been raised alongside her future husband and his siblings at Ellwood. In 1870, just a year after his marriage to Mary Ellen, Richard Townsend Turner Jr. formed a partnership called Turner Brothers with his brother Joseph, and they advertised their new firm as "manufacturers of lumber, peach baskets, fruit crates, etc., dealers in lumber, coal, lime, salt, flour, grain, fertilizers, etc." Too early for a Betterton post office, the new firm listed its address as Still Pond, Maryland, and it expanded and prospered along the Betterton waterfront for a good many years. To make life even sweeter, young Turner's father deeded over to his son 119 acres of the original Ellwood land. Here the young couple built a modest Victorian house they called Maple Lawn. In that comfortable setting they raised six boys: Howard, Henry C., James R., Richard Sinclair, William W., and Joseph Archer.

It was the second oldest, Henry Chandlee Turner, born October 16, 1871, who would go on to study engineering at Swarthmore College, to found Turner Construction Company, and to be followed at Swarthmore and at Turner Construction Company by three of his younger brothers, James R. (called J. R.), William W. (called W. W.), and Joseph Archer (called Archie), and still later by his own son Henry Chandlee Turner Jr. (called Chan). Like his father, Henry Chandlee Turner enjoyed a nineteenth-century Eastern Shore upbringing that was exemplified in much of the period's literature: a primary school education in a one-room schoolhouse attended by his siblings, a few cousins, and the children of the few other families who had settled in the area and the support and guidance of an educated and loving family. Ever energetic and inquisitive, he learned something about the ways of nature in the still-unspoiled countryside of nineteenth-century eastern Maryland, something about ethical behavior in the Friends meeting house, and doubtless quite a little about commerce in the orchards and shops of his father and grandfather. And living on the edge of Chesapeake Bay he learned enough about swimming, crabbing, fishing, duck and goose hunting, and sailing skipjacks to ensure that recreation would continue to figure in his life as an adult. It was a setting that wasn't wasted on the young Henry C. Turner.

In 1885, when he was fourteen years old, he was packed off to the Abington Friends School in Jenkintown, near Philadelphia, where he continued his education in Quaker religious and ethical thinking and prepared for study at Swarthmore College. By 1889 he had entered Swarthmore, one of the few schools in the country where a student could concentrate on science or engineering within a liberal arts framework. Young Henry opted for civil engineering.

Henry Turner's years at Swarthmore College were defining ones for him. When he started there in 1889, it had been barely twenty years since his own great-grandmother, Rebecca Sinclair Turner, together with a group of other Quakers, had founded the school, and although it would later abandon its formal connection with the Society of Friends, in 1889 Swarthmore was still a Quaker college. Later in his own life Henry Turner would serve as a longtime member of the college's board of managers.

When Henry Turner entered Swarthmore, it was a small college with only 189 undergraduates, struggling to establish a clear direction for itself somewhere between the conservatism of its Quaker board and the relative liberalism of its increasingly modernist students. Its peaceful, rural setting a few miles southwest of Philadelphia was understood to have a beneficent effect on its students, but it was an effect that the management of the school ensured would be imposed on the males and females separately: They were forbidden to walk together unless they were brother and sister, although they did take meals together in small groups at chaperoned tables. Football, which had been introduced earlier, was slowly increasing in popularity on campus after a brief decline that the student editors of the Phoenix attributed more to student laziness than to anything else. By the time Henry Turner entered, there had been some liberalizing of conditions and attitudes, and there was increasing student interest in such things as athletics and other forms of recreation, but Swarthmore was for the most part concerned with the life of the mind and the spirit and was on its way to achieving the academic prominence that would characterize its later years.

Henry Turner was the ideal undergraduate: popular among his classmates, academically successful, and excelling at just about everything except athletics, though he was still able to get himself appointed manager of the track team during his senior year. He was an honor student, class president as a senior, winner of a number of academic awards, assistant business manager of the school's newspaper and of its yearbook, a member of the school's literary society, and a speaker at his commencement exercises. In 1892 he was elected to Book and Key, an elite and secret undergraduate honor society in which membership, like candidacy for Rhodes scholarships, was restricted to a small number of students who had not only distinguished themselves academically but also in some nonacademic way, most often but not always as athletes. In a gentle memoir written about Turner by a fellow student who had roomed with him at Swarthmore for two and a half years, he is described as a "good all-round man, handsome, endowed with considerable talent and executive ability, an honor student and no slouch of an engineer." The former roommate went on to praise Turner's singing voice and to identify his strong preference for the color blue, a portent of the company's later emphasis on that color in its graphics.

The senior class of Swarthmore College in 1893, when Henry Turner graduated, had only twenty-four members, divided about equally between liberal arts and science students, of which about half, including Henry Turner, were majoring in engineering. The school's early advocacy for women's rights was evident from the gender mix of the class of 1893, in which ten of the twenty-four graduates were women.

It's difficult to find a meaningful pattern in the array of jobs that Henry Turner took on during the first half-dozen years that followed his graduation from college, but the absence of a pattern itself say something about where the new graduate was heading. The period was a kind of heyday for civil engineering, with railroad, bridge, and tunnel work still abundant and new construction sprouting everywhere to accommodate the impact of burgeoning immigration. More often than not, newly minted young civil engineers of the day headed for the established engineering firms and started their careers at a drafting board, doing most of the hands-on work of their superiors and many of the routine, sometimes tedious calculations needed to support their designs. While Turner had certainly done well enough in his undergraduate engineering studies to have qualified for any of those tasks, he had distinguished himself in liberal arts work too, winning awards there and gaining admission to the school's exclusive literary society. It's not unreasonable to think that the newly graduated Henry Turner wasn't entirely sure that a traditional engineering career was what he wanted and that he might have been casting about for something that would blend several of his skills and talents.

Henry Turner's first job after graduation was for the Franklin Printing Company of Philadelphia, and although there are few clues today as to just what his duties there were, it is probably relevant to note that the firm's principal was E. Lawrence Fell, a Quaker entrepreneur who had preceded Turner at Swarthmore by about five years. Franklin Printing Company had been founded by Benjamin Franklin himself, in 1728, and the Fells were a prominent and well respected Philadelphia family, linear descendants of the founders of the Society of Friends and active and successful in the city's commerce. Although young Turner might have seen a commercially viable opportunity in the Franklin Press organization, it may also be that he saw an association with the Fell interests as a step toward other opportunities. In any event, he had only been at Franklin Printing for a little over a year when an old Swarthmore friend named Frederick C. Hicks came along.

Fred Hicks was something of a maverick. Born Frederick C. Cocks, he was the scion of two very old and prosperous New York Quaker families. At the age of seventeen, just before entering Swarthmore, Fred Cocks had been adopted by his father's cousin, another well-known Quaker named Benjamin D. Hicks, and he had taken his surname. Young Hicks, who would later become a congressman, a successful investment banker, and a national figure in the field of naval affairs, had left Swarthmore in 1892, before graduating, and had gone on to Harvard Law School. By 1895, when he renewed his friendship with Turner, he had joined a prominent and substantial New York firm called U.S. Leather Company, and he induced his old school friend to join its real estate department. That change of jobs had the effect of bringing Henry Turner to New York, where he would ultimately make his career, but the job itself apparently held no more lasting interest for the young engineer than had the Franklin Press job, and within a few years he had made another change, this one to the Brooklyn Wharf and Warehouse Company.

At Brooklyn Wharf and Warehouse, which had land development and shipping interests, Turner moved comfortably closer to his engineering roots and might well have made a career for himself there if not for a radical change in the firm's management that sent him looking for still another job before the end of 1899. That was an unanticipated and unsettling turn of events for the twenty-eight-year-old Turner. It came less than a year after he had married Charlotte Wright Chapman, an Ohio-born girl whose Quaker parents had brought her to Brooklyn as a small child, and the young couple had just moved into an apartment on Pineapple Street in Brooklyn. But as often happens in such unanticipated detours in the careers of young people, losing his job at Brooklyn Wharf and Warehouse may have been one of the best things that ever happened to Henry C. Turner.

His search for still another position led him to one of the engineering visionaries of the period, Ernest L. Ransome. There's reason to believe that Turner and Ransome met through the Pratt family of Brooklyn, survivors of the deceased Charles Pratt, a wealthy and influential principal in Rockefeller's Standard Oil Company and benefactor of Pratt Institute in Brooklyn. The Pratts, having become interested in Ransome's innovative new approach to the design of concrete structures, had provided the capital for his Ransome Concrete Company, and young George Pratt lived in and was active in the Brooklyn community in which the Turners were living. George Pratt and Standard Oil itself would surface often, always helpfully, during the early years of the career that still lay ahead for young Turner.

Ernest Ransome was one of those restless souls of the nineteenth century who energized the Industrial Revolution by simply inventing most things they felt they needed but didn't have. He had come by his talent naturally enough, inheriting it from a father who had run the venerable Ransome and Sim's Iron Works in Ipswich, England, and who had invented (among other things) the rotary kiln that facilitated and encouraged the manufacture of portland cement. It was probably the elder Ransome's ongoing interest in the possibilities offered by portland cement that inspired his son's extensive and extremely productive work in the field of reinforced concrete.

For a good many centuries before the days of Ernest Ransome and a handful of other, mostly French, thinkers, concrete had performed superbly as a foundation material. Its great durability in almost all environments, its resistance to fire, and the plasticity that enabled it to be formed into almost any shape that a designer could imagine had interested architects and builders for years, but well into the nineteenth century no one had yet figured out a way to make it work where the forces imposed on it were trying to pull it apart rather than to crush it. It was a material that had great value in compression, but very little in tension, and young Ransome resolved to address that weakness.

After apprenticing in his father's factory (but without any formal engineering education), Ransome emigrated to America, where for a few years he managed a San Francisco plant that manufactured a product pioneered by his father and later called "cast stone": The material was used mostly in decorative precast concrete elements that did in fact have to resist small tensile forces, a problem that hadn't previously been given much attention in concrete design. Ransome began to experiment with the notion of reinforcing the concrete with metal elements, and by the 1880s he had moved on to designing modest structures in which he was casting concrete beams and slabs with integral tie-bolts and then threading nuts and washers onto their ends to take even greater tensile forces than he'd faced with his cast stone. It was a precursor to the pre-stressing and post-tensioning technologies that would surface almost a century later, but in 1888 it was simply an important step toward the practical objective of providing a tension element in the concrete itself. Within a few years Ransome was able to demonstrate that integrating square iron bars, twisted to enhance bond, would effectively resist substantial tensile and shearing forces in concrete structures, and he had designed and built several important buildings that relied on such an approach. In 1889 he designed and built the Alvord Lake Bridge in San Francisco, the first reinforced concrete bridge in the United States.

As the end of the century approached, Ransome sensed that the leading edge of a vast national expansion was being honed in the northeastern part of the United States and that such growth was bound to favor this new technology. Rapidly accelerating immigration was intensifying the demand for new structures there, and conditions in the urban centers argued for building them of reinforced concrete: Fire was still the formidable enemy of the city, use of structural steel meant long waiting times, and a great wave of immigration was bringing in plenty of low-cost labor. When Pacific Coast Borax Company asked Ransome to design and build a new facility for them in Bayonne, New Jersey, in 1897, he moved east and used that job as a starting base for setting up shop in New York. By 1900, when Henry Turner applied to him for a job, Ransome had added the new St. James Church in Brooklyn to his list of completed concrete buildings, and he was in the market for a bright young civil engineer to deal with the abundance of other work that was on the horizon.

Going to work for Ransome was a critical milestone in Henry Turner's career. After almost seven years in jobs that never quite demanded the full measure of his engineering capability, nor what his former roommate had identified as his executive talent, he would now be able to concentrate all his energies in a single setting. Ransome Concrete Company was in the business of engineering and constructing reinforced concrete buildings for people and companies who saw the newly patented technology as the wave of the future.

There was a bonus at Ransome Concrete too. DeForest H. Dixon, another young civil engineer just four years out of Cornell, would become his colleague and good friend there. Unlike Turner, who was gravitating toward the engineering and cost-estimating side of construction, the Wisconsin-bred Dixon was an "outside" man, someone whose talents and interests drew him to the construction site itself. He was a man who had gone right to the job site as soon as he had his engineering degree, staying behind at Cornell long enough to work on construction of the concrete dam and hydraulics laboratory in which generations of civil engineering students after him would study. Then, after brief service with the U.S. Army Corps of Engineers during the Spanish-American War, Dixon had returned to work as a field engineer on concrete projects in New York and Pennsylvania and on one as far off as Pueblo, Colorado, before joining Ransome in New York.

Working for Ransome, who was an eccentric and sometimes difficult personality, provided a postgraduate education for Henry Turner. The use of reinforcing steel was so new that there was almost no literature to guide a young engineer in its use, no handy tables from which to establish designs, so he had to rely on the considerable body of experience that Ransome himself had accumulated. There had been so little reinforced concrete construction done that there were few guidelines for estimating its cost either, so Turner was obliged to make his own observations and to establish his own cost algorithms as he went along. And, of course, the whole business of selling the new idea to a potential client was new as well, and Turner was to learn from Ransome just how it could best be done.

Some of what was done under Ransome's direction was actual construction, but much of it was design and supervision of reinforced concrete work for buildings in which the rest of the design work was done by others. In Mineola, Long Island, not far from where the Pratts maintained a summer home, the Pratt family was able to convince county officials to build their new, state-of-the-art courthouse and jail of reinforced concrete, using Ransome's design, and the job became something of a trial by fire and a further education for Henry Turner. The building's complex architectural design, which included a thin concrete dome, was poorly suited to execution in concrete, a material clearly more useful where the formwork was simpler. The general contractor who was unfortunate enough to land the job soon found that he had bitten off more than he could chew, and it wasn't long before the fellow lost any tolerance he might have had for the sometimes imperious behavior of Ernest Ransome. Relations between the two deteriorated quickly, and it became necessary to schedule site visits by Ransome and the contractor at times that would ensure that they would never be on the job at the same time.

Management of that delicate scheduling and the resulting complicated business of supervising the fieldwork fell to young Turner, who was apparently able to complete those tasks without losing the goodwill of either Ransome or the contractor, suggesting management skills that would become increasingly useful and important during the years to follow. The courthouse and jail buildings themselves, complete with painted dome (the original plan for applying gold leaf to the dome was abandoned when the job ran over its budget) was still providing good service to the County of Nassau at the beginning of the twenty-first century.

By 1902, Ransome Concrete Company was providing valuable experience for its young engineers, but it wasn't proving to be the source of profit for the Pratts that they had expected when they invested their capital in it. Like many creative people, Ernest Ransome was much better at solving design problems than he was at managing a business, and only two years after Henry Turner had come to work for him the Pratts decided to withdraw their financial support, shutting down the company and leaving Ransome to continue with his consulting work, but leaving Turner and his friend Dixon to shift for themselves. Dixon was only twenty-eight years old and unmarried, so such a change of employment at this juncture was unlikely to be an especially serious matter for him, but Henry Turner was thirty-one years old in 1902 and his wife was pregnant with their first child. The decision about what to do next was a critical one for him.

For the first time Turner now seriously considered establishing his own business instead of seeking further employment with others. He had seen enough to convince him that there was a real need for reinforced concrete construction, albeit in a marketplace that was slightly different from the one that Ernest Ransome had addressed, and he felt that he was ready to establish a firm that would fill the need. He saw the new material as a sound structural solution, not usually well suited for churches and courthouses but ideal for factories and warehouses, buildings that required lots of simple, fireproof space that could be produced inexpensively and quickly. The Ransome years had added to his education just the combination of technical and commercial experience he needed to launch a firm to do such work, and all he needed in 1902 was the courage to launch the venture, the money to fund it, and some good people to help him implement it.

The courage, of course, he could provide himself.

The money wasn't as easy. Turning to his family wasn't an option he wanted to exercise because things in Betterton, while certainly stable and comfortable, were less good than they had been a decade or two earlier. Competition and the traditional vagaries of agriculture and commerce had weakened the family's economic base somewhat, and when Richard Turner Sr. had died in 1891, the family had sold off some of their own properties and tightened their belts a bit to raise the cash needed to pay his debts. But by 1902 Henry Turner had established a professional reputation of his own, and it stood him in good stead: He called on his former boss at U.S. Leather, Gurdon B. Horton, to invest in his new venture, and Horton's response set the tone for what was to follow. "I'm in favor of investing in anything you personally have to do with," Horton wrote to his former engineering assistant, and it was agreed that he would provide most of the money the fledgling company would require to get started.

As to people, it was DeForest H. Dixon that Henry Turner wanted for getting underway. Dixon had gone back to work temporarily for an old boss who had a contract to build a section of the new subway tunnel in New York, with the understanding that just as soon as Henry Turner had put his venture in order he would return to become general superintendent in the new firm.

By spring 1902, Turner Construction Company was beginning to take shape.

2.

Beginning

T he timing of Henry Turner's move into the mainstream of New York City's commerce couldn't have been much better. Before about 1902, he really hadn't broadened his experience enough to go off on his own, and only a few years later he'd probably have missed some of the wondrously promising opportunities that abounded in the exploding commercial and industrial environment that characterized the city in 1902.

It was a time when New York was itself moving from an exuberant adolescence into a glorious young adulthood. Having only a few years earlier absorbed the neighboring communities of Brooklyn, Richmond, and Queens and those parts of the Bronx that it didn't already include, what came to be thought of as Greater New York was, with about 3.4 million residents, the largest and richest city in the United States. It accounted for 40 percent of the country's exports and 64 percent of its imports, and it produced more than half of New York State's manufactured goods. There were already almost a thousand millionaires among the city's residents, and there were plenty more in the making. Theodore Roosevelt, recently returned to national adulation from his military service against the Spanish in Cuba, was president of the United States, while his young cousin Franklin Delano Roosevelt was just finishing his freshman year at Harvard. A political reformer named Seth Low, who had earlier been president of Columbia University, was mayor. And the glorious Brooklyn Bridge, which had been completed almost twenty years earlier to connect the island of Manhattan to Brooklyn, was about to be joined by a sister span, the Williamsburg Bridge.

Of course, with all its vitality, New York was still very young in comparison with the great cities of the old world. A quarter of its land was still agricultural at the turn of the century, and 2,000 farms still produced crops and maintained cattle within the city limits. Fourteenth Street, New York's principal commercial thoroughfare, was generally regarded as being uptown, although Twenty-third Street was beginning to compete for its shops and offices. It would be another four years before the New York Times would be praised for its courage in building its new headquarters as far north as Forty-second Street, at what would be called Times Square. Just days before Henry Turner and Gurdon Horton were scheduled to formalize the incorporation of their new venture, a team of carriage horses, apparently frightened by the unfamiliar sight and sound of an automobile on Broadway, had taken its terrified passengers for a wild and uncontrolled ride through town that ended only when an agile policeman managed to mount one of the horses just off Fifth Avenue and bring the team to a stop. The passengers were described as shaken but unharmed and were comforted at the nearby Waldorf-Astoria Hotel, where the newly completed Astoria had been merged with its neighbor, the Waldorf, to provide a thousand of the city's finest and, at an average nightly rate of about five dollars, its most expensive hotel rooms. About thirty years later the Waldorf-Astoria would move even farther uptown, displaced from its Thirty-third and Fifth location by the brand new Empire State Building.

Dinner, in 1902, could be purchased at a decent New York restaurant for well under a dollar, and the physical culturist Bernarr MacFadden had opened a place on Pearl Street in which most items on the menu sold for one cent. It wasn't unusual for people to work ten hours a day, often seven days a week, generally for wages that averaged less than twenty-five cents an hour. Children were permitted by law to work if they attended school for at least eighty days each year, but of the city's estimated 500,000 children, fewer than 15,000 reached the eighth grade.

What made Turner's timing so good wasn't simply what New York was in 1902, it was what it was in the process of becoming. Fueled by an unprecedented surge of immigration, its population was soaring and would reach 4.7 million by 1910, adding dramatically to the demand for goods and services and contributing significantly to the pool of inexpensive labor that would be needed to satisfy such a demand. Within a few years, New York's horses would be finding the sights and sounds of an increasing number of automobiles less unsettling, but the human population of the city would view the horseless carriage with increasing terror until 1919, when a law requiring the licensing of all drivers was enacted. In 1902 the New York Telephone Company, whose predecessor had established its system only twenty-two years earlier, with 252 subscribers, was serving almost 50,000 telephone customers in New York City.

It was into this dynamic setting that Henry C. Turner was to bring his new construction company in the spring of 1902. They were exciting times for the thirty-one-year-old Turner: Only a month earlier, Charlotte Turner had borne the couple's first son, Henry Chandlee Turner Jr., who would be called Chan and who would years later succeed to his father's leadership in the firm, and the young family was getting ready to move into larger quarters on Emerson Place, where they had purchased a house in a community being developed by the Pratt family. By May 1902, Henry Turner was prepared to stake the family's future on an idea whose time seemed to have come: an organization of skilled and well-educated managers and competent workmen specializing in the new field of reinforced concrete construction. He had entered into an agreement with Ernest Ransome that gave him the patent rights to the Ransome System for most of New York City and for several adjacent and growing counties, in exchange for payment of a future royalty of 5 percent of the cost of the Ransome System construction they would do. Having calculated that $25,000 in operating capital would be needed, and that most of it would come from Horton, Henry Turner made a modest cash investment in the venture and then brought in his old Swarthmore friend Fred Hicks and his former Ransome colleague DeForest Dixon to supplement it with small investments of their own.

Even in those days before the birth of the new firm, it's clear that Henry Turner never thought of his new venture as anything less than a grand undertaking. The Certificate of Incorporation that was filed on the sixth of May, 1902, authorized Turner Construction Company to engage not simply in the business of general contracting but in the engineering and design of buildings and other facilities as well, and in the acquisition and sale of all kinds of properties; the sale, rental, and repair of equipment and materials; and in almost any activity that might reasonably relate to or grow out of the business of general contracting. A capital structure for the fledgling firm was designed to accommodate the needs of the much larger company it would become: All the shares acquired for cash by the initial investors were $100 par value preferred shares whose 6 percent dividend had to be paid before any income could accrue to later owners of Turner common stock. Gurdon Horton's investment of $18,000 was the largest, of course, and provided him with 180 of the 250 preferred shares that were issued. Of the remaining 70 preferred shares, Henry C. Turner paid $3,500 for 35 of them, Frederick C. Hicks paid $3,000 for 30, and DeForest H. Dixon paid $500 for the other 5. All but Hicks became directors of Turner Construction Company, and the first meeting of the new board was set for three days later, the ninth of May, at a small office on Gold Street in Manhattan. At that meeting, Henry Turner turned over to the new corporation his rights to use the Ransome System in exchange for all 250 shares of the new company's common stock, and he became Turner Construction Company's first president, at $2,000 per year, with Horton as its unsalaried vice president and treasurer and DeForest Dixon as its secretary at $1,800 per year.

There was apparently some suspicion at that time that Gurdon Horton's health was fragile, and the new board members used the May 9 meeting to elect Horton's son-in-law, Frederick Knapp, as a fourth director. Horton did die a few months later, and when a financial associate named Oscar B. Grant succeeded him on the board, Fred Knapp succeeded his father-in-law as vice president and treasurer of the company. Neither Knapp nor Grant ever became directly involved in the operations of the firm itself.

By the end of May, the company had settled into a one-room office at 11 Broadway, where its first significant prospect for construction work provided a useful test of the young firm's skills and prudence. An earlier letter from the Sewerage and Water Board of the City of New Orleans, probing Ernest Ransome's interest in submitting a proposal for building its new water treatment plant, had been forwarded by Ransome to Henry Turner with a note urging him to follow the job. Mindful that young Turner had supervised design of the facility's structural systems when he had been in his employ, Ransome apparently hoped that having Turner's new company build the plant would ensure that his designs would be properly executed. For his part, Turner was inclined to favor the idea of bidding on the work, although — at what he estimated to be a cost of about $500,000 — it must have seemed large for his relatively small firm. His approach was to send DeForest Dixon down to New Orleans to investigate. Dixon's report, submitted at the next board meeting, revealed something about its author's skill and about the disciplined methodology that would become characteristic of the firm's future planning and work. In just a few days, Dixon was able to investigate everything from the quality of the bidding documents to the annual rainfall in New Orleans. He evaluated subsurface data, the extent of drainage infrastructure available at the site to facilitate dewatering, the local labor pool, the experience and probable competitiveness of local contractors, and the validity of the cost estimate that the owner's staff had prepared. When he completed his investigation, Dixon didn't like what he saw, and he reported to the board accordingly. He anticipated that the bidding documents would be too loose to avoid serious disputes; his own analysis of the subsurface data suggested the probability of quicksand; he predicted that dewatering would be extraordinarily difficult, a problem intensified by heavy annual rainfall; he warned that there were capable and aggressive local contractors whose bids would be difficult to beat; and, worst of all, he estimated that the cost of the job would probably be closer to $1.5 million than to the $500,000 estimated by Henry Turner. Once the board heard what Dixon had to say, the exhilaration of taking on such a large and potentially prestigious contract so early in the new company's life receded, and they declined to bid.

The grand scale of Henry Turner's vision notwithstanding, the new company had, of course, to start off with at least a few small jobs. One of the first of these was a reinforced concrete vault for the Thrift Bank, a Brooklyn enterprise of the Pratt family, at a contract price of $690. The Pratts, friends of Henry Turner and former sponsors of the Ransome Company, were best known as partners of the Rockefellers, and the executive in charge of the Thrift contract was A. C. Bedford, who would later become president of Standard Oil Company. Bedford was only the first of a good many important figures whose confidence in young Turner would nurture the company's growth over the years that followed.

Among the very early jobs, it was probably the concrete staircases for the new subway system being built from the southern tip of Manhattan to the Bronx that were destined to have the greatest impact on the company's fortunes. The staircases were originally designed to be built of steel with cast iron treads and risers, and because virtually all such fireproof staircases of that period were built in about the same way, there was no reliable model for estimating the cost to build them in reinforced concrete. But Henry Turner had seen enough of what it took to build steel staircases to convince him that building them in concrete had to be cheaper. He made it his business to find out the costs of the steel version and then simply submitted an alternative price that was low enough to induce the authorities to award him a contract to build a few staircases in concrete. It was a risky estimating approach but it worked, and Turner Construction Company was launched on a specialty that would serve the firm well for a few years. Once they had built the first few, of course, they had learned enough about the cost of building concrete staircases to enable them to bid comfortably for additional ones, and the company went on to secure contracts for almost all the staircases on the new subway system. The staircases were especially important to Turner at the time because such jobs not only produced revenue but they generated a need to hire and develop a capable early force of mechanics and superintendents.

As soon as the subway work was started, T. Arthur Smith, a Swarthmore graduate who'd been working for U.S. Steel's construction department, was hired to run the fieldwork. He'd later go on to become general superintendent, vice president, and a member of the Turner board. As the work became more spread out, more field supervision was needed, and within another few months Joseph C. Grady, Albert Larson, and Otto Lindberg, all of whom went on to become superintendents, were hired to help Smith run the fieldwork. Soon the administration of the increasing number of subway projects became substantial, and Henry Turner hired as an office boy a red-haired young fourteen-year-old who'd been sent over by the local YMCA. He was S. W. Johnson, who years later would become the company's assistant treasurer.

Before long, the stair contracts broadened to include subway platform contracts too, and by 1904, when the first subway system went into operation, Turner had built almost all its stairs and platforms. At the same time, the Long Island Railroad had begun to develop its own network of tracks and stations in Brooklyn and eastward into Long Island; similar work for them became an extension of the work the company had been doing on the first subway system.

There was a growing number of other jobs during those first few years too, most of the early ones costing less that $20,000, and if there was a single unifying thread that tied them all to Turner, it was that they were all built of concrete. The technology of fire fighting was still fairly crude, relying largely on cumbersome steam-driven pumping equipment and horse-drawn vehicles, so architects and owners were looking with increasing interest at the idea of using a material that appeared to combine fire resistance with economy.

On Staten Island, where the J. B. King & Company manufactured water pails, plaster, and other building materials, the need to reduce the cost of fire insurance first led King's architect to concrete and then to Turner for a construction program that started with a small cooper shop and then went on to include another twenty-six buildings over a period of more than twenty-five years. Concrete began to be considered in more and more places, and there seemed to be no end to its possibilities. In a time when the horse still dominated the transportation of products, concrete seemed natural for use in the construction of large stables, offering safety and an easily maintained sanitary environment for the animals. Between 1903 and 1907, Turner built at least half a dozen large reinforced concrete stables, most of them for the big merchants of the area, some costing as much as $70,000 and one rising to six stories, with ramps covered by used fire hose to provide traction for the horses. And there was hardly a time in this period when the company wasn't working on at least one or two big reinforced concrete reservoirs or tanks designed to hold large quantities of water needed for fire fighting.

Fire wasn't the only factor, of course. The architect for the new Vanderbilt mansion on Fifth Avenue recognized the potential for exploiting the inherent plasticity of concrete to produce complex shapes, so he engaged Turner to build the mansion's main staircase of reinforced concrete. The design was so elaborate that the architect required the forms be built by a cabinetmaker. When J. P. Morgan wanted a concrete barn for his cows in Highland Falls, a few miles up the Hudson, he hired Turner to build it.

It was all good for Turner, as there were few contractors able and willing to risk using concrete for anything except foundation work. On one occasion, early on, Turner did some concrete stair work and built a concrete water tank as a subcontractor for a well-established New York general contractor, but Henry Turner failed to convince the fellow to consider substituting a reinforced concrete frame for its masonry and timber superstructure. The contractor admitted that he'd like to produce the promised savings in cost and time, but he told Henry Turner that he just couldn't afford to endanger his reputation with such a risky experiment as reinforced concrete. Ten years later the contractor was out of business, and Turner was taking over some of his work. Even major general contractors like the George A. Fuller Company and the William L. Crow Company, both of which were well established before the turn of the century and would go on to national prominence, were subcontracting reinforced concrete work to Turner during the early years rather than trying to build with it themselves.

Not every contracting firm was so timid, and even that proved to be good for the new company, because Henry Turner had acquired the exclusive right to fabricate and distribute in his own operating area the twisted-steel reinforcing bars that were at the heart of the Ransome System. During its early years, the company did a thriving business fabricating and selling such bars to contractors who integrated them into reinforced concrete designs of their own, and after only a little more than two years, annual sales of twisted bars were approaching 1,600 tons and annual revenues of over $60,000. In later years Turner would abandon the Ransome bar in favor of using and selling other patented reinforcing bars, but eventually all the relevant patents (including Ransome's) expired or were held by the courts to be invalid, and the company phased out what had continued for some years as a profitable, virtually independent element in its business plan.

By the end of 1904, Turner Construction Company had reached a sustained and powerful stride and was lengthening it. It was busy and growing, with new work coming increasingly frequently from such distinguished customers as Standard Oil Company and Pratt Institute, and it wouldn't be long before the Turner Construction Company of Henry Turner's grand vision would begin to appear. The company had systematized its efforts to secure new work, advertising in trade journals like *Engineering News* and *Engineering Record* (predecessors of the trade publication *Engineering News-Record*) and spending what was in those years considered to be the substantial sum of $200 a year for Dodge Reports, a trade service that reported potential construction contracts over an area for which similar reports at the end of the century would cost about $10,000 a year.

The company's own unique style was being defined in those very early days. Few engineering firms had yet developed any solid knowledge of reinforced concrete design, so Turner's was as much the role of the consulting engineer as it was the role of the contractor when it came to concrete work, and a well-educated staff was essential. In a time when fewer than about twenty-five adults in every thousand had graduated from college, all five of the men who provided Turner's senior management during the start-up years were graduates of distinguished colleges or universities. It was a pattern that would establish a style at Turner that would for many years set it apart from most of its competitors.

Significant profits were still elusive at the end of 1904, although Turner had by then put in place almost $400,000 worth of work, an amount of construction that would be valued at almost $15 million at the beginning of the twenty-first century. But even after the costs of starting up had been considered, the company was already beginning to show a modest surplus. If there was ever a company that could be described as being well positioned in terms of capability and markets, at a time when opportunities abounded, it was Turner in 1904.

3.

Growth

B y late 1904, nourished on a diet of progressively larger concrete subcontracts and contracts, including an abundance of subway stair and
platform work, the new company was emerging from its infancy. Across
the river in New Jersey, it had taken on a $27,000 contract to build a warehouse
and had subcontracted almost half the work to a local masonry contractor, effectively beginning to define itself as a general contractor prepared not only to do the
required concrete work but to manage the whole process of construction as well.

Henry Turner himself was emerging as a man whose talents probably exceeded
even his own expectations. Of course, he proved to be a competent engineer, as
might have been expected, and the correspondence and detailed instructional
documents that have survived from those early days make that clear, but evidence
of his talents and skills in dealing with and inspiring the confidence of a broad
range of colleagues, subordinates, and others suggests something more than technical competence. Henry Turner was clearly a cultivated young man, well bred and
educated, attractive and articulate. Years later he'd be described by a reporter from
Time Magazine as looking more like a Groton schoolmaster than a construction
contractor, so it's little wonder that he was comfortable and effective in dealing
with powerful industrialists like Pratt and Bedford of Standard Oil and with
Eastman of Eastman Kodak, who tried to induce him to build a new plant for him
in Rochester. What suggests something extraordinary is his clear ability to deal just
as effectively with the laborers and carpenters who worked for him as he did with

the freewheeling, often uneducated, newly rich industrial and financial barons who had accumulated wealth during the booming years of the late nineteenth century and were ready to spend some of it on new construction during the twentieth.

There was a succession of such tycoons, and they would be a critical element in the growth of the Turner Company. One especially important and talented one was Robert Gair, an inordinately successful and colorful Scot who became an early believer in concrete construction in general and in young Henry Turner in particular and who would become a powerful force in Turner Construction Company's early growth and success. Born in Edinburgh in 1839, Gair had worked as a boy in paper mills there before immigrating to the United States and settling in New York. After a brief, unsatisfying stint as a plumber's apprentice, he was drawn to the paper trade he had begun to learn back in Edinburgh, and he began buying bags and boxes from manufacturers and selling them at a small profit to commercial consumers.

Gair prospered modestly, lived with some gusto the life of a handsome young bachelor in New York, and occupied some of his time with service in New York's Seventy-ninth Highlanders, a colorful national guard unit comprising about a thousand transplanted Scots like himself and apparently devoted more or less equally to military drill and vigorous social drinking. It was a spirited unit, regularly drilling and parading in tartan kilts, accompanied by its own pipers, celebrating every American holiday and as many Scottish holidays as its members could think of, and occasionally providing some help to the New York police in putting down social disturbances of one sort or another. Gair had risen to the level of sergeant in the Seventy-ninth by 1860, when Abraham Lincoln sounded a call for 50,000 volunteers from the New York area to fight the rebels in the South. Within twenty-four hours the Seventy-ninth had volunteered to go to war as a single unit.

Although most such volunteer units served for periods of less than a year, the bloody tour of the Seventy-ninth would last a full three years and would end, finally, at the battle of Spottsylvania. About 200 of its original number survived, including Bvt. Maj. Robert Gair, who had by then become its commanding officer. He returned home a hero, relieved and happy to learn that the savings he had been sending home to his sister had been wisely invested by her at the soaring interest rates that obtained during the war and that they now amounted to enough to fund resumption and expansion of his old business. It was the beginning of his own spirited campaign for fortune.

That was a campaign in which Gair was eminently successful. He combined his considerable knowledge of paper with his instincts for mechanizing the production process and with a prodigious capacity for hard work, and within a dozen years he had become an important figure in the industry. He improved the quality of paper bags and boxes, moving into the use of cotton-based materials as well, and invented a practical technique for producing folding cartons with just a few mechanical steps, making the folding carton economically feasible for the first time. He improved the process of corrugating paper board too, moved into the new business of producing paper cups, and was able to refine a system of distribution that ensured his getting a large share of markets that were emerging in the new age of grocery distribution and sales. Coffee and sugar, long sold in barrels, were now being sold in bags and cartons, as were seed and other products, and Gair was providing much of the needed packaging. By the end of the nineteenth century, he had become a very rich man and had outgrown the manufacturing and distribution facilities that the firm had occupied in downtown Manhattan.

Gair began construction of some new buildings along the Brooklyn waterfront around the turn of the century, but even at the new location he feared an enemy that could still terrify: fire. Commercial and industrial structures were, generally, still being built of masonry and wood, a system that was extremely vulnerable to fire damage. It was a time when buildings and sometimes whole neighborhoods burned to the ground with unsettling regularity, and that was a serious cause of concern to Gair.

Although Gair's first Brooklyn building was among the earliest in the country to include an automatic fire-sprinkler system, he didn't take much comfort from it since its design was still primitive and the level of protection it afforded was modest. And besides, the accidental discharge of a sprinkler head, not infrequent, could probably do almost as much damage in a building filled with paper products as a fire could do.

Almost as soon as his first building in Brooklyn was finished, Gair was ready for another one, even larger than the first. Something he thought might address his fire concerns in this next building would be the use of heavy timbers, the kind that would burn slowly enough to allow firefighters time to do their work before damage to the structure became devastating. Finding the long, heavy timbers he needed was going to require an exhaustive national search, and for that purpose he enlisted the help of his nephew, James Beattie, early in 1904.

Beattie's search for suitable timbers took him across half the country, but he didn't really get anywhere until he had spent a few days in Jacksonville, Florida. Even there, it wasn't big timber that caught Beattie's eye, it was concrete. Most of downtown Jacksonville had itself been recently destroyed by fire and a Florida grocery magnate named John Christopher was leading the redevelopment program by rebuilding his own warehouse using concrete. Once Beattie spotted the material being poured into forms on the Christopher project, he knew it was a material with the potential for solving the Gair problem, and his search for big timbers ended. Just as soon as he was able to get some of the details from Christopher and from the local contractor who was doing his work, he headed back to New York to report his finding to Robert Gair and his son, George, who was assuming an increasing share of his father's responsibilities at the firm.

Acceptance of a new material like concrete, Beattie quickly discovered, wasn't going to be quite as easy to get as he had expected. William Higginson, a conservative, London-born architect who had been doing the Gairs' design work, didn't think much of the idea, and he let his clients know it in no uncertain terms. Too radical an experiment, Higginson argued, for the buildings they were planning for the Brooklyn waterfront. And Higginson properly worried that he had no experience of his own in the design of such buildings and that he really didn't know anyone who did.

Higginson's objections were frustrating to Beattie, of course, but they weren't entirely unfounded, and young George Gair was inclined to go along with them. The elder Gair, on the other hand, hadn't risen to command the Seventy-ninth

Highlanders or built his business with a faint heart, and at sixty-five, he was still entirely ready to explore what struck him as a promising new idea. He wanted to know everything there was to know about concrete, more about its properties and cost, and it didn't take much probing of his commercial sources in New York to lead him to Henry Turner, who was, of course, well prepared for him. He convinced the Gairs that concrete was here to stay, that it was well suited to their objectives, and that the Turner Construction Company was up to the task of applying the new technology to the construction of Gair's next building.

Something in what Turner had to say and perhaps something about the confident but self-effacing, Quaker-influenced style in which he said it apparently struck a responsive chord in Gair, and the die was cast. A decision was made to go ahead with concrete and with Turner, at a price for the first building that would be worked out between the two of them. It was agreed that Turner would teach Higginson all he needed to know about this new application for an old material and that Henry Turner would do the required structural engineering for him as well. What Turner would build, an eight-story building aggregating 180,000 gross square feet, would cost less than $200,000, only a shade more than one dollar per square foot, and it would be the largest reinforced concrete building in the United States. With the Gair contract, Turner would enter the ranks of major American contractors, its days in the minor leagues having ended before its second birthday.

Breaking new ground is rarely easy, and the Gair work was no exception. The engineers at the New York Building Department had, before 1904, been relatively casual about the few low-rise concrete buildings they had approved, although they had required a limited amount of testing. But for buildings of this size they wanted no part of any abstractions about fire resistance or structural integrity. What they wanted was to test a small reinforced concrete building as a prototype before a permit for the main building would be granted. Turner built a prototype at the site, and the whole structure was subjected to four hours of fire that raised the ambient temperature to 1,800 degrees Fahrenheit before cold water was applied under high pressure for five minutes to suppress it. Then they loaded the slabs with pig iron and measured the resulting deflections. Only after deflections were shown to be well within allowable values and that the condition of the concrete remained perfect except for minor spalling was the permit issued. The tests were additionally useful in providing empirical validation for some of the design assumptions that Henry Turner had inherited from Ernest Ransome, reassurance that would be helpful in the extensive structural design work that still lay ahead.

Turner's first Gair building, completed within a year, was a defining milestone in the company's history. In some ways it was an ideal vehicle for the young construction firm: big enough to attract widespread attention but simple enough in its architecture to accommodate the still-limited capability of a committed group of young engineers who were honing their skills in a new technology. Its size attracted a great deal of attention, of course, although it wasn't actually the tallest concrete building in the country: That distinction went to the fifteen-story Ingalls Building, built in Cincinnati a year earlier by the Ferro Concrete Company, a firm that Turner would acquire in 1953 and that would become its Cincinnati branch office. More importantly, the first Gair building demonstrated in a thriving industrial and commercial marketplace the availability of a material that could provide economically all the fire resistance offered by fireproofed steel and that could be put in place just as quickly, when compared with steel that normally had to be rolled and then fabricated in remote locations. In addition, the Gair building announced to a broad population of potential customers the special capability of the Turner Construction Company. It put Turner on the map.

Turner went on to build another sixteen buildings in Brooklyn for Gair, and the industrial enclave that was created in the process was called Gairville. Almost a hundred years later the Gairville buildings, still in first-class condition, were being converted by New York entrepreneurs for mixed uses, including housing and commerce. The Gair Company itself continued to increase its prominence and importance in the industry, with factories in several states, eventually merging with the Continental Can Company in the 1950s.

Robert Gair himself didn't settle for simply awarding Turner more contracts or for giving glowing references to persons who asked about it. He thought extremely highly of the company, and he became its vigorous advocate. Before his first

Turner building was completed, Gair had sold a nearby Brooklyn waterfront property to his friend and kindred spirit John Arbuckle, principal of one of the period's leading coffee-roasting firms and a pioneer in the mass production (and national marketing in Gair bags) of ground coffee. Gair convinced Arbuckle to engage Turner to build an even larger concrete building than his own for Arbuckle Brothers Coffee Company. And there were many others too, most notably the Great Atlantic and Pacific Tea Company, another Gair customer, for whom Turner would build twenty-three large buildings during the early years of the century.

These were good years for Turner, but, of course, they weren't perfect. A few years later, the structural steel and hollow-tile interests in New York, both of them understandably unhappy with the impact that concrete construction was having on their businesses, lobbied the New York City fathers to revise the building code to impose potentially crippling restrictions on concrete construction, including one that would limit the height of concrete buildings to seventy-five feet. Robert Gair, his hair white by now but his big frame still imposing and his Scottish speech as resonant and compelling as ever, personally appeared before the board of aldermen and cautioned them to resist the forces of special interest by rejecting the code changes. He didn't quite turn the tide; although his arguments narrowed the vote, a revised code still passed, threatening the future of concrete in New York and certainly posing a potential threat to Turner's prosperity.

But Gair didn't let that stop him. As soon as he got word of the board's vote, he dispatched a courier to go out and find New York mayor George McLellan, son of the Civil War general, who was vacationing in a remote corner of the Adirondacks and who had veto power over the board's resolutions. The mayor, who was unsympathetic to the steel and tile lobbyists, was found and brought back to repel the attack on the code, and there was temporary relief. But the old code had to weather still another attack a few years later, when the steel and tile lobby struck again. Once again, though, forces that recognized the solid reliability of the existing code prevailed, and the future of concrete in New York was assured.

Once the Gair project became widely known, Turner's own volume of business soared. Between 1904 and 1905 it doubled, and it doubled again during the next few years. It wasn't just the jobs that Gair himself was awarding or referring to Turner, it was a broad mixture of projects, some from companies reacting to destructive fires or trying to protect against the potential for future fires, others from companies that were simply seeking to expand in the best and most economical way and were inclined to see Turner as a rising new star that was likely to do well by them. More than a few of the early jobs were designed by Howard Chapman, a brother of Charlotte Chapman Turner, who had a beginning architectural practice in New York. Early on, Chapman was probably able to refer an occasional job to his brother-in-law, but the evidence is that later it tended to work the other way: Turner was getting work on which an architect hadn't yet been selected, and he was able to recommend Chapman.

Many of the firms for which Turner was building in those days were historically important and some were developing in about the same way (and had reached about the same stage) as Turner itself. Some that prospered are still well known at the beginning of the twenty-first century, including the Great Atlantic and Pacific Tea Company (later simply A&P), Keuffel and Esser, Murphy Paint and Varnish Company, McCall's Publishing Company, Schirmer Music Publishers, Austin Nichols Distilleries, Vacuum Oil Company (later Standard Vacuum and then Mobil) and, of course, many of the subsidiaries and affiliates of the original Standard Oil Company. Even the names of once-prominent firms no longer extant say something about the type of company that was looking to Turner for construction early in the century: the Pierce-Arrow Motor Car Company, the Biograph Motion Picture Company, and the American Snuff Company, to name a few — virtually all formidable names for a young firm only a few years old.

Although Robert Gair was probably the most important of the powerful industrialists whose early confidence in Turner influenced the company's course, he wasn't the only one. Irving T. Bush was another. Bush was probably every bit as rich and powerful as Gair, but he had reached that state of well-being by a route that was radically different from Gair's and probably a good deal easier: He was born into it. His father, Rufus Bush, had been president of an oil refining company when John D. Rockefeller was developing Standard Oil, and when the Bush firm was acquired by Standard Oil, Rufus Bush, already rich, became even richer. He and his wife raised their children in a luxurious setting that included splendid homes, servants, and cruises to Europe on the family's yacht. When Rufus Bush died in 1890 he left to his twenty-one-year-old son, who was by then an executive in Standard Oil Company himself, a considerable share of the family's fortune and a couple of empty lots on the Brooklyn waterfront. The two lots had originally been acquired by the elder Bush as a convenient dumping ground for ash produced in the refining process, and they adjoined the abandoned refinery.

Bush's high social station notwithstanding, he was an energetic and imaginative entrepreneur, and he wisely saw those two waterfront lots as the potential beginning of a profitable enterprise. His idea was to develop the area as a vast transportation terminal that would connect the great and growing seaport of Brooklyn to the developing network of railroads that would be hauling goods into and out of the metropolitan area burgeoning all around him. He quit his job at Standard Oil, admitting years later that he had found it too dull for his tastes anyway, and began development of what would come to be called Bush Terminal. Starting slowly, he first established a small retail coal plant on the property to generate revenues for filling the lots and rendering them suitable for the construction of buildings and then proceeded with the construction of a few warehouses. By 1904, his relationship with the contractor who was building them had soured, and it ended in an unsatisfying legal battle in which Bush was represented by Charles Evans Hughes, then a young lawyer but destined to become chief justice of the United States Supreme Court.

Bush wasn't easily discouraged. By early 1905, he owned a few completed warehouses and had begun to lease space in them to the cotton industry, and he had started construction of a couple of new piers that would reach out into the bay in anticipation of connecting to some of the port's shipping traffic. He had a tremendous vision of what he wanted to build at Bush Terminal and had engaged the architect William Higginson to design a huge complex: It was the same Higginson who had a year earlier opposed Robert Gair's plan to engage Turner. But by 1905 Higginson had learned a good deal about reinforced concrete work and about

Henry Turner personally, and he liked everything he saw. Like many converted unbelievers, Higginson had become Turner's passionate advocate, and he brought Turner and Bush together.

By this time Bush was already moving ahead with plans to expand his holdings to what would ultimately become a 200-acre complex on which he would build his own complete system of electric power, twenty-one miles of his own railroad, and eight of the largest piers in the world, to say nothing of dozens of concrete and masonry buildings. His meeting with Turner came along at just the right time. The two men hit it off, and almost immediately they entered into an arrangement in which Turner would become the principal building contractor at the terminal.

Over a period of the succeeding approximately thirteen years, Turner would build twenty-one huge buildings at Bush Terminal, with an aggregate floor area of more than 5 million square feet. Unlike the Gair work, for which a fixed price had to be hammered out directly between Robert Gair and Henry Turner before the start of each building, the Bush Terminal work introduced Turner to the agency arrangement, in which Turner was paid a fixed fee for each project (defined to include the salary of the superintendent and the cost of such tools and equipment as might be required), all other costs being reimbursed. The fixed fee on the first job, which cost less than $200,000, was $10,000.

The company was prospering in every way. In 1907 its annual volume exceeded a million dollars for the first time (almost $38 million when indexed for turn-of-the-century dollars) and the implications of such spectacular growth were broad. Not only was its financial capital growing, but Turner's technical and professional capital was growing apace too. An unusually large number of bright young men entered the firm during the years between 1902 and about 1907, and they became a powerful force in its development.

Henry Heywood Fox came in 1904. He had graduated from Harvard in 1900, worked in a variety of construction jobs afterward, and returned to Harvard for an advanced degree in 1904 before joining Turner as an assistant superintendent later that year. Like T. Arthur Smith, who had come the first year to run the subway work, Fox would later become a vice president. Arthur C. Tozzer came in 1905, a few years after receiving a second degree at Dartmouth, and he brought along some strong experience in building and tunnel work. Tozzer, a big, lumbering man well over six feet tall with a powerful, sometimes intimidating voice, would later become general superintendent and the first manager of a new Boston office. He would manage the construction of some of the largest buildings in the world during World War I and would eventually become a member of the Turner board.

Allen Whitmore Stephens, William E. Lyle, and Egbert Jessup Moore all joined the company in 1905 too. Stephens, a Mainer, was a man whose early experience had been at the American Bridge Company before he came into Turner's drafting room, and he would later become chief engineer. Lyle came from Kentucky, where he had been working in railroad construction, and he would later run an office for the company in Buffalo and manage construction of some of its largest projects. Moore, another Cornell man, had spent a few years in steel construction and had worked on the Pennsylvania Railroad's East River Tunnel in New York before coming to Turner. He was another who would go on to become chief engineer, vice president, and director.

John Prince Hazen Perry had graduated from Harvard in 1903, worked for a few years in railroad construction, and came to Turner in 1906 from the New York Board of Water Supply. Starting as an estimator, he worked for a few years as an assistant superintendent and then as a superintendent before becoming a vice president. Robert Clifford Wilson, a Columbia graduate, started with Turner in 1907 after a few years in heavy construction and went on to become one of the most important figures in the company's history, finally retiring in 1953 as chairman of its board of directors.

These were the bright, extraordinarily well-educated young men who formed the core of the company's middle and upper management during the earliest years of the twentieth century, and there wasn't a single one of them out of his twenties.

The high quality that characterized Turner's management from the start was no accident. Certainly it owed something to Henry Turner's own standards and preferences, but to a great extent it was something that was made necessary by the evolving nature of the firm's work, which was significantly different from the work of the traditional general contractor of the period. A construction firm specializing in reinforced concrete work during the early 1900s was plying uncharted waters and needed to be able to go beyond traditional construction tasks. It had to be able to design the required structural systems of its projects, not just put them in place, and it had to be able to design the complex forming and temporary shoring systems that were required for them as well. Every square foot of formwork done by Turner in those days and every reinforcing bar had to be fully designed and detailed in the Turner office before any fieldwork could be done, and many of the devices used in building the forms or in fabricating the reinforcing steel were developed in Turner's own engineering department. Many were patented. In addition, occasional design commissions that were not associated with construction contracts, especially from locations that were far from the company's New York base, continued to come into the office well into the 1920s. These weren't responsibilities that could be given to or supervised by casually trained persons, and it was by no means a deception that the company advertised itself, in those days, as a firm of engineers and contractors.

By 1907, the firm's growth was itself producing changes. There were departmental changes intended to ensure that senior management in the expanded firm would remain directly involved in every project, and there was modest expansion into additional, rented space at the home office at 11 Broadway. That same year, dividends that had been deferred to give the young company some time to grow were paid, and a little over $100,000 was distributed to the original investors. By 1907 the company had established and was relying on a line of bank credit, but now it was decided that the time had come to enlarge the actual capital base of the company.

Henry Turner saw the need for more capital as a chance to broaden the ownership base of the company, so he and his fellow directors voted in 1907 to reorganize along lines that would facilitate acquisition of shares by selected employees. Under the new arrangement, the original investors exchanged their preferred shares for common shares and voted to convert the cash surplus that the company had accumulated to additional common shares. Seven of the firm's most senior employees were offered (and accepted) the right to acquire a total of 150 shares of the newly issued common stock, an allocation that represented almost 10 percent of the company's value. This established a precedent for later, significant acquisitions of the company's shares by its employees.

Opening up to senior employees the right to acquire shares in a closely held firm like Turner was a radical departure from traditional corporate practice in 1907, but even such an enlightened move paled alongside the profit-sharing plan the company initiated three years later. Henry Turner made it clear to the board that he wanted to ensure that employee participation in the company's prosperity wouldn't be limited to those key employees who owned shares, so in 1910 two profit-sharing plans were ratified by the Turner board: One applied to officers, heads of departments, and other key employees; the second applied to the company's field superintendents. They were landmark plans by any standard, generous and forward-looking in their provisions, and extraordinary in their timing, originating as they did only eight years into the life of the new firm, many years before most corporate employers began to consider such plans and even a few years before the enactment of a federal income tax law would make them less expensive for the company to implement.

The plan for officers, heads of departments, and selected others stipulated that a percentage of the firm's net earnings, after deduction of expenses and after allocation of eight dollars per share of common stock, would be distributed to designated employees in accordance with a formula that reflected their positions, performance, and length of service. For the first year of operation the board established 30 percent as the employees' share, but that was increased in subsequent years to 35 percent and sometimes to 50 percent. The second plan, the one that provided for additional compensation for superintendents (later expanded to include assistant superintendents and certain other field personnel) was designed to give persons who were managing the company's fieldwork a share in profits generated directly by the work they managed. Its structure was less rigid, simply laying down ground rules and leaving to a committee the task of assigning the actual amount of each bonus, instructing the committee to be guided by a comparison of anticipated costs with actual costs but taking pains to emphasize in forceful terms that adequate attention must be paid to preserving "quality of workmanship, and . . . the relationship maintained by the superintendent between the company and its employees and between the company and the owner, the architect and others." Those were guidelines that were clearly designed to ensure that the eagerness of field staff to enhance profits wouldn't be allowed to compromise quality. The details of both plans would vary through the years that followed, but the essential conceptual bases of the 1910 plans would survive.

Once recapitalization and profit sharing had been put in place, the company shook off most of the growing pains that had attended its earliest years. By 1912, when it had been in business ten years, Turner had completed almost $12 million worth of work, a volume which, adjusted to reflect inflation in costs through the end of the twentieth century, would be equivalent to almost $500 million. In 1912 the value of construction put in place by Turner was about $2.5 million, and except during the worst of the depression years the company's annual production would never fall below that amount in the years that followed.

The number of people running the company's departments and supervising its field forces was bound to increase as the number and size of jobs grew. By 1912, James L. Bruff, H. C. Paddock, W. T. Anderson, W. T. Baker, A. D. Mellor, F. E. Schilling, and E. L. Ford had been added to what can, from a historical perspective, be considered the firm's first management group.

There were a few Turners and Turner relatives among the executives in those days too. A. Wright Chapman, one of Charlotte Chapman Turner's brothers, was one. He was about the same age as Henry Turner and, like his sister, had been born in Ohio and raised in New York, where he had studied at Columbia, graduating in 1894 and going on to earn a master's degree in electrical engineering. He'd already spent a couple of years practicing engineering in Maryland and another nine years in an unrelated commercial enterprise in New York when he joined Turner in 1905, opting for the administrative side of the business in preference to its production side, and becoming over the years a financial officer, secretary of the company, and later a director. From all appearances he was a quiet man with what may have been a scholarly side, and his *Brief History of the Company*, written in 1927, provides more than a few subtle insights into the company's early years. A serious sailor, Wright Chapman served for a while as commodore of the Manhasset Yacht Club in Long Island and retired fairly early from his career at Turner.

William Webb Turner, Henry's younger brother by ten years, came along in 1905. He'd been working for O'Rourke Engineering and Construction Company on the new tunnel that the New York Central Railroad was building under Park Avenue. Only two years out of Swarthmore, he started with the company as a time-keeper on the first Gair building, where future Turner chairman Cliff Wilson was in charge, and within a few months he had become a superintendent on other Turner work himself. But after a couple of years in New York, W. W., as he was called, decided he'd like to try doing something on his own back in the Philadelphia area, where he'd gone to college, and he joined with another Swarthmore alumnus named Joseph Forman to form Turner Forman Concrete Steel Company. Forman acquired about 18 percent of the stock of the new firm, W. W.'s older brother Henry took a token 3 percent, and W. W. took the rest. They recruited the youngest Turner brother, Archie, who had only a few years earlier graduated from Swarthmore, where he had distinguished himself as an honor stu-dent and as an athlete. Archie had been accumulating some useful field experi-ence working for a Ransome affiliate. Together, they entered the still-young busi-ness of concrete construction in Philadelphia.

There's some evidence that earlier family connections in the business commu-nity there (and perhaps an occasional boost from brother Henry in New York) were helpful in getting the new company underway, as much of the early work was done for prominent Philadelphia-area commercial and industrial firms, but the partners apparently acquitted themselves extremely well. Within a few years the Philadelphia operation was producing modest profits and taking on sizable con-tracts and subcontracts from large general contractors, including at least one for the W. J. McShane Company and another for the George A. Fuller Company, two firms that later rose to national prominence in the industry. In 1912 Forman's health brought about his early retirement, but the firm continued and prospered as Turner Concrete Steel Company, under the management of W. W. and Archie Turner, continuing until about 1919 to do a substantial amount of concrete construction in the Philadelphia area.

During these years in which Turner was growing and restructuring itself, establishing plans to bring its employees into the ownership of its stock, and sharing with them its increasing profitability, other changes were occurring that would significantly affect the company's course. Among the more important of these was its growing awareness that it was going to have to move beyond the relatively confining limits of the New York metropolitan area if it was going to exploit fully the considerable professional and commercial advantages it had acquired for itself during its early years. Ironically, it was a judicial decision that was at first thought to be antagonistic to such an expansion that actually facilitated it: In 1908, a court held Ransome's patents to be invalid, that is, it held that the use of the Ransome System of reinforced concrete construction was no longer protected by patents and that anyone who wanted to use the technology was free to do so. What seemed like a decision that was bound to damage the company in the area around New York, where Turner held the patent rights, turned out to have little effect. By the time of the decision, Turner was so closely identified with the Ransome System in the New York area that potential competitors simply failed to materialize, and the impact of the decision proved to be minimal. In fact, the decision's real effect on Turner was positive: It opened up the rest of the country to Turner just when the company was considering strategies for a major expansion.

The first two of the company's earliest forays into out-of-town work owed their origins to the same powerful force: fire. In 1907, the plant and offices of the Phelps Publishing Company, which had been built twenty-seven years earlier in Springfield, Massachusetts, had burned to the ground. Phelps, the prominent and successful firm that published *Good Housekeeping* and *American Farm Journal*, was headed by a canny New Englander named Edward Phelps, who resolved as soon as the fire was out that he would replace his Springfield plant immediately with a state-of-the-art facility that most assuredly would never burn down, a resolution that led him to Henry Turner in New York. What emerged from their negotiation in 1908 was a cost-plus-fixed-fee contract. Turner would build an approximately $250,000 reinforced concrete building in Springfield that would provide just about everything a modern publisher could want, including superior fire resistance, the capacity to support unusually heavy loads and to accommodate excessive vibration, an open plan with large spaces, and even a self-contained power plant that would supply electrical energy to the publishing plant itself and to its Springfield neighbors. It was Turner's first out-of-town contract, and Arthur Tozzer went out to Springfield to manage it.

A few years before the Springfield move, the downtown area of Jacksonville, Florida, had been destroyed by fire too. It had been during the reconstruction of his grocery warehouse there, in the aftermath of that fire, that John Christopher had first begun to use the concrete that caught the eye of Robert Gair's nephew when he was in Jacksonville in 1904 searching for heavy timbers. In 1908, Christopher, by then unhappy with his local contractor, was ready to do more construction, and his broad commercial interests, increasingly centered around his coastal shipping activities between Jacksonville and New York, had given him some knowledge of what Turner had been doing for Gair and, more recently, for Irving T. Bush in New York.

Christopher, born in Missouri but raised in New York, was another turn-of-the-century figure cast in the mold of Gair and Bush: rich, smart, and not afraid to exploit whatever the new technologies had to offer. A few years before the downtown Jacksonville fire destroyed his property, he had built and operated in a Jacksonville suburb the first and largest of the spectacular new Florida oceanfront resort hotels, the Murray Hall, an exclusive 350-room Mediterranean-style palace complete with sweeping terraces, Venetian architecture, and its own electric generating plant. Only a few years after it opened, the Murray Hall had burned to the ground, as did the four almost equally spectacular resort hotels that other investors had built, one after another, as replacements. John Christopher was a man who didn't need to be reminded about the importance of fire resistance, and when it was time to for him to build again in 1908 he wanted concrete and he wanted Turner. He awarded an approximately $200,000 cost-plus-fee contract to Turner for the first of his new buildings, a concrete warehouse, and followed it over a period of a few years with a series of other concrete buildings that included a 650,000-square-foot complex that was patterned after the Bush Terminal and designed to facilitate the surging industrial and commercial growth of Jacksonville. The Christopher work, relatively large and profitable, brought a good deal of experience and public notice to Turner, but by 1913 it had absorbed what was thought to be a disproportionate share of the company's attention, at a great distance from the home base, as well as five years of the full attention of T. Arthur Smith, who had run the work in the field. In spite of the success and profitability of the Jacksonville work, a decision was made not to take on any more of it.

Although Turner's management encouraged and supported the idea of out-of-town work and was ready to support it whenever it showed enough promise, there was evidence that the company's enthusiasm for a permanent Turner presence anywhere but in New York was still fairly limited. Neither Springfield nor Jacksonville passed muster, but western New York State looked good for a while. Buffalo and the area around it had been gaining as an industrial center since the beginning of the century, and for a few years, beginning about 1908, Turner sought and secured several jobs in and near Buffalo, including a major plant for Pierce-Arrow. That was a project that impressed the local skeptics with the company's ability to maintain concrete operations through a winter in which ten feet of snow fell in the area. In 1910 the company dispatched James L. Bruff to Buffalo to establish and manage a branch office, and he was followed by H. E. Plumer as engineer and W. E. Lyle as field superintendent. But management also sent along a strict set of rules that suggested that enthusiasm for a new branch office was still modest. While authorizing the new office to "obtain and manage contracts for the construction of reinforced concrete work in the western part of New York State and vicinity," the rules emphasized that general supervision would still be provided by the main office and that all financial work, including payment of bills and preparation of payrolls, would continue to be done by the main office in New York.

While it lasted, the Buffalo office would do some big and important work, including plants for Alcoa, Vacuum Oil, the Carborundum Company, and others, but a few years later the company decided, once again, that the special demands of maintaining a remote branch office simply weren't offset by its advantages, and all the work of the Buffalo branch was absorbed by New York. The out-of-town forays were important, of course, and they were precursors of a time when Turner business units would be distributed across the whole country, and some of the rest of the world as well, but during this early period in the company's history they certainly weren't critical to its prosperity.

By 1914 Turner had become a recognized presence in the construction industry of the region. It had started a modest advertising campaign that began to feature the slogan "Turner for Concrete," later abandoned as being too limiting, and it was estimated that the company had built 70 percent of the concrete buildings that then existed in New York City. The company's good friend William Higginson had designed a new building for Loose-Wiles Baking Company, predecessor of Sunshine Biscuits, and Turner's contract to build it would be its first exceeding $1 million. Annual sales by then exceeded $4 million, and the company was well along in developing an enviably solid, well-trained management. These were good times for the young firm, with more and bigger jobs for prestigious companies coming along every year, facilitating the essential recruitment of good staff and encouraging new business as well.

This was all work that required substantial operating capital, especially in a time when Turner's modus operandi demanded performing most of the fieldwork with forces in its own direct employ, without many subcontractors. It was work that required a large workforce in the field and competent supervision at every level, and of course it produced some very large payrolls. In 1913, only a few years after its most recent recapitalization, the company again increased its capital base by selling an additional $100,000 worth of shares to its own stockholders and to additional selected employees, buttressing its operating capability and further broadening its base of employee shareholders.

Of course, life wasn't all work, even during the early days of the twentieth century. Henry Turner was a man of many parts, and although organizing and managing Turner Construction Company certainly engaged him intensely, he was able to nourish a wide variety of other interests as well. In 1909, the company held the first of what would become the annual dinners to which senior management and selected employees, as well as clients and important persons from the community, would be invited. The 1909 affair appears to have given the tradition a modest start, attended by only ten persons and costing a total of only thirty dollars, but it was held in an elegant setting: the Crescent Club of Brooklyn, which had been founded before the turn of the century by the almost legendary Walter Camp, a widely admired former Yale football hero (and originator of the All-American concept for football players) who had established it as a private club for Yale men and their guests, and apparently for others who appeared to be socially and economically qualified.

The personal living style of the Turners had kept pace with the company's success. In 1914, when the family had grown to include four children, the Turners moved into a gracious eleven-room house on Monroe Place in Brooklyn, with five bathrooms and with a fourth floor given over to servants' quarters. What had been built as a stable on the property in 1857 had been converted by the previous owner to a garage, one of the few in the neighborhood, and the Turners' second Cadillac, one of the first to have a self-starter, was parked and maintained there by the family chauffeur. Summers were hot in the city, and starting about 1909 the family had been escaping some of the city's heat in the Pocono Mountain village of Buck Hill Falls, at first for only a few weeks at a time, in rooms they rented at the Inn at Buck Hill Falls for about thirty-five dollars per week (including meals) and a little later in a small cottage they rented in a largely Quaker settlement near the inn. By 1914 they were beginning to think about building something for themselves in Buck Hill Falls, but it still would be a couple of years before they would buy the approximately forty-four-acre farm on which they'd build the beautiful and restrained compound they'd call Skyland Farm. For many years Skyland Farm would be a comfortable vacation home for the family and a periodic retreat for company executives.

War in Europe was a long way from Buck Hill Falls in those days, and it probably seemed as academic to Henry Turner as it did to most Americans. But by the
spring of 1914, when antagonisms that had been festering in the Balkans for centuries began to erupt into open conflict, the sounds of rattling sabers began to be
heard in the United States. In June of that year, the assassination of an Austrian
archduke marked the beginning of a five-year period in which Turner
Construction Company would do more than five times the volume of construction
it had done during all the years that had gone before.

4.

War

B y the summer of 1914, when the cauldron of ancient hatreds in Europe boiled over into the bloodiest war in history, Turner Construction Company had come of age.

Its youth had been brief, by most standards. Like any starting company, Turner had endured some early days of relatively limited business, but by any measure those days were few in number: Even the $40,000 worth of work it had done during its first year corresponds to almost $1.6 million when expressed in the currency of the early twenty-first century. By 1914, when the Great War started in Europe, twelve-year-old Turner Construction Company was completing more than $4 million worth of work a year, an amount that would be the equivalent of almost $165 million a year at the time of the company's hundredth anniversary. It was a substantial level of production for any builder and enough to place the company in the first tier of building contractors during the second decade of the 1900s. Turner was by then well staffed and comfortably accustomed to working on more than fifty jobs at a time, mostly in the Northeast but in some cases as far from its home base as Maryland and Florida, and it regularly employed a workforce of more than a thousand, including more than a hundred superintendents, assistant superintendents, foremen, and engineers. If the first few years are ignored, it's reasonable to say that Turner was never really a small company. By 1914 it was a big company, as construction companies go, and well on its way to getting bigger.

Work for two or three of the largest oil companies, especially for Standard Oil and its future partner Vacuum Oil, came along every few months (between 1911 and 1915 alone Turner did twenty jobs for these two companies) and for a while giant warehouse projects for A&P were almost an annual event. There was still a steady stream of big jobs for Gair and Bush as well, all part of a rapidly expanding workload that by 1914 had reached an annual value of $4.2 million, more than six times what it had averaged during the company's first five years and almost three times what it had been averaging during the second five years. The list of major industrial firms who were contracting with Turner to do their construction, a distinguished list from the beginning, had lengthened to include names like U.S. Rubber, Pratt and Lambert, L. E. Waterman, American Can, General Electric, Hooker Chemical, and Firestone Rubber. It had become clear that Henry Turner's original idea of designing the form and structure of his new company as if it were a much larger one, even before he had hired its first employee or contracted with its first customer, had been a good one.

Of course, Turner wasn't the only successful builder in the Northeast by any means. The William L. Crow Company and the James Stewart Company were a couple of contracting firms that had been in business in the New York area since before the Civil War, and by the early twentieth century both were building major structures that already included some of the skyscrapers that would define the emerging New York skyline. Marc Eidlitz & Sons, founded in the nineteenth century and eventually to be succeeded by the Vermilya-Brown Company, was typical of the firms that were doing the region's big institutional construction and building the elegant residences of the Vanderbilts and the Whitneys as well. The George A. Fuller Company, later in the century Turner's arch-competitor and its occasional joint venture partner, had moved its headquarters from Chicago to New York in 1900, and by 1904 had completed construction of New York's famous Flatiron Building.

In New England, where the new century had brought the same promise that was fueling New York's growth, Boston firms like Walsh Brothers and Macomber had been established and were prospering, and in Philadelphia Irons and Reynolds was doing much of the larger work. But most of these firms tended to favor highly finished urban buildings that relied on cast iron or structural steel frames clad in elaborate masonry exteriors, elegant and expensive projects for which they were well suited. For the most part, they were firms that had neither experience nor interest in the new and demanding technology of reinforced concrete, so they pretty much ignored it or, when it was required, subcontracted it to firms like Turner. It was in such a setting, just when American industry was entering its period of greatest growth, that Henry Turner had brought his own leadership and his young staff into the marketplace, equipped with a new technology that was made to order for aggressive and enlightened industrial consumers.

Almost all the young men who had provided the company's early field and office management during the start-up years were still working for Turner in 1914 when war broke out in Europe, and by then they had begun to mature into seasoned executives. Henry C. Turner and DeForest H. Dixon remained in charge, of course, but by 1914 the company hadn't just become bigger, it had achieved a level of commercial sophistication that was appropriate to its size and to the broad scope of work it was doing. The emerging management staff centered on Fox, Lyle, Moore, Perry, Smith, Stephens, Tozzer, and Wilson, all skilled and well-educated men whose long subsequent careers with the company attest to their commitment to it. W. W. and young Archie, the two Turners who had followed their older brother into careers in construction, were now well established in Philadelphia, where they were prospering as Turner Concrete Steel Company, the firm that had succeeded Turner Forman in 1912 when Joseph Forman retired. New starters at Turner Construction Company were coming aboard in New York every year: more bright young men hired by Henry Turner during the years before the war and destined to become senior executives and company directors as well. William Nye, a Harvard graduate, came in 1906. Fred Schilling and Elmer L. Ford came in 1908 and 1909, respectively, and Harry A. Ward came in 1910, all three educated at schools like Harvard and Dartmouth. In 1913 three additional future managers and directors were hired: George Horr from Lafayette and William B. Ball and Walter K. Shaw, both from Cornell. Shaw would eventually become a vice president and treasurer at Turner, and years later his son, Walter B. Shaw, would become chairman of the Turner board.

The company had plenty to show for itself by 1914, and the increasing vigor of its advertising reflected its pride in what it had been doing. It regularly advertised in publications like *Engineering News* and *Engineering Record* and in *American Architect* and the *Journal of the AIA*. What they were seeking at this stage was the attention of the architects and engineers who were designing the country's most important buildings, but they extended their advertising to regional newspapers whenever Turner landed a contract to build something important in the area served by the newspaper. Almost all the advertising included a good photograph of a recently completed building and a few lines of text that offered, in language that was usually understated and quaintly reserved, a list of reasons why Turner should be considered if and when construction was being planned. In addition, the company published and distributed to a mailing list of design professionals and to selected potential owners several series of glossy periodicals telling about the company itself and displaying photographs of work in progress or recently completed.

Not all the marketing was so soft. In 1913, Turner sent penny postcards to everyone on its several mailing lists featuring on one side of each card a photograph of one of its recently completed buildings and on the other side a message stating that "such buildings as this can be built of concrete more economically than they can be built of any other material" and suggesting that the reader contact Turner for more information at the address given.

Henry Turner's idea of engaging an artist to illustrate all the buildings the company had completed before and during 1910 and then to combine all of them in a single picture, as if they had been built contemporaneously as a single city, may have been the company's most daring advertising in these early years and perhaps its most effective as well. In that year, he is said to have seen tourists photographing sections of the New York skyline from the gallery at the top of the Woolworth Building, and to have conceived the idea of the composite drawing. He commissioned an artist named Richard Rummel to prepare such a drawing, showing all the buildings the company had built through 1910, and the black-and-white print that was produced from Rummel's painting was distributed in 1911. It was initially called *Turner for Concrete*, after the company slogan that was appearing with increasing frequency on construction signs around New York and elsewhere.

Rummel's drawing was an instant success, and production of what during the 1920s would begin to be called Turner City became an annual event. Rummel was succeeded in 1925 by a commercial artist named Edward W. Spofford, who produced Turner City until he retired in 1929. In that year, Edwin Mott was engaged to produce the annual composite drawing. He was a talented illustrator who'd been apprenticed to an architect, and he would continue to produce Turner City every year until his death, thirty-two years later. His nephew, Herbert Mott, who had learned illustration from his uncle, succeeded him for a few years, but in 1966 Ben Palagonia was engaged to take over the project. Palagonia brought to the task the combined skills of a gifted artist and an experienced architectural renderer. He'd already been doing architectural drafting and rendering for some of the country's most outstanding architects, and producing Turner City every year after 1966 became his career. Over time he would add his own refinements, including more detailed landscaping and, in 1989, including color. Palgonia's son John, who had earned a degree in fine arts in 1992, joined his father during 1994, and by 1998 principal responsibility for producing Turner City had passed to him.

The years just before the outbreak of the First World War in Europe had been very good ones for American industry, and Turner's history, for all practical purposes, was intimately linked to that pattern. New manufacturers were appearing and expanding at a furious rate in those years in a frantic effort to keep pace with a population whose growth in numbers and whose appetite for manufactured goods were nothing short of spectacular. During the twenty years preceding 1914 American exports had increased by 500 percent, and the country's mills were producing more steel than her two nearest competitors, Germany and England, combined.

Like Turner, many of the companies that would later rise to the leadership of their own industries were in their most vital years of growth in 1914. American Can Company was typical: Recently organized, it had offices at 11 Broadway, just a few floors below Turner's. Of course, although a Turner contemporary in age, Canco, as it was also called, was much farther along in its commercial life than Turner. Through its absorption of many small tinplate manufacturing companies, it already controlled 90 percent of the flourishing tin can industry in the United States and was in hot pursuit of the other 10 percent. Between the vigor of the few fiercely independent manufacturers who refused to be absorbed and the later resistance of the U.S. attorney general, Canco had achieved less-than-satisfactory results from its efforts at complete national monopoly. But things had turned up for them in 1908, when they acquired a small, poorly financed competitor who had developed a method for completing the manufacture of tin cans after they had been filled with food, vastly simplifying the manufacturing process and reducing the cost of the product. By 1914 their business had doubled, and when they needed extensive new manufacturing space at their plant in Maryland, they engaged Turner to build it. It was the first of twelve such big projects that Turner would build for American Can between 1914 and 1927, and the beginning of a long and profitable relationship between the two companies.

There were literally dozens of firms like American Can, all growing exuberantly in the favorable economic climate that preceded America's involvement in the European war and all of them seeking new manufacturing space. Another Turner neighbor, already well established but destined to become an even larger presence in American industry, produced something as popular and deceptively simple as Canco's tin cans. Just a few blocks from Turner's office, the five Colgate brothers, all direct descendants of the men who had started Colgate and Company almost a century earlier, presided over one of the largest soap-making businesses in the country. By the time Colgate and Company celebrated its one hundredth anniversary in 1906, the family-owned firm that had four generations earlier been producing tiny quantities of soap and delivering them by handcart throughout lower Manhattan had expanded its product line to include 160 varieties of soap, 625 perfumes, and 2,000 other related products. In 1914 they engaged Turner to build a vast addition to their Jersey City plant. Again, it was a beginning: Turner would build four more plants for Colgate before it merged with Palmolive in the 1920s to form Colgate-Palmolive.

Of all the factors that attracted buyers of construction to concrete and to Turner in those years, fire was still the principal one. For some owners, like Robert Gair, it was simply the fear of fire and a determination to protect employees and property from it; for others, like Keuffel and Esser, the great scientific and engineering instrument company that engaged Turner to replace its Hoboken buildings after a terrible fire in 1907 had destroyed its entire plant, it was a response to a real disaster. For the Naumkeag Steam Cotton Mills of Salem, Massachusetts, it was another terrible fire.

When the Great Salem Fire struck in 1914, Naumkeag had already been manufacturing textiles there, mainly bedsheets, for seventy-five years, and with a workforce of almost 6,000 the company employed almost one-third of the working residents of Salem. The fire started in the early afternoon of a summer workday, in a factory about a mile away that manufactured patent leather shoes. Within minutes, a freshening breeze had spread the fire to adjacent workshops and tenements, and when volunteer firemen and horse-drawn fire-fighting equipment arrived half an hour after the fire had started it was already well beyond anything they could control. A wind now gusting to twenty knots carried the fire through the town and across the railroad tracks toward Naumkeag's sprawling plant, destroying everything in its path. Within a couple of hours, eight fire companies from four surrounding towns had joined the fight, but the power of the fire was so great and its heat so searing that within five hours of its start it had burned a raging swath through the town, leapt across the narrow South River, and was licking at the sixteen buildings of Naumkeag Steam Cotton. Naumkeag's own firemen, many of whom had seen their own homes destroyed earlier in the afternoon, joined the battle, but it was futile from the beginning: three hours after the fire had roared onto the Naumkeag grounds, it had burned fifteen of its sixteen buildings to the ground. There was only one death, but more than 10,000 residents of the town had been made homeless, and the town's principal employer was shut down.

Naumkeag's single surviving building, not surprisingly, was a concrete structure with wire glass windows, designed to resist fire. As soon as the fire had reached the building, interior metal shutters held open by fusible links had closed down over the inside face of the windows, sealing the concrete building so thoroughly that even the fabrics stored inside were found entirely undamaged after the fire had been extinguished.

Such a stark lesson wasn't lost on Naumkeag's management, who almost immediately engaged the firm of Lockwood, Greene and Company of Boston, which had been practicing engineering in New England since 1832, to design all the required replacement structures in reinforced concrete. It was no casual choice: Lockwood, Greene had a few years earlier designed the country's first reinforced concrete cotton mill in nearby East Boston and — as far as Naumkeag's managers were concerned — the days of timber construction for mills like theirs were over.

It would be a busy summer for Lockwood, Greene. By the time the season ended, they were well along on documents for almost a million square feet of new manufacturing and storage space, all to be contained in three state-of-the-art buildings: spacious, well lighted, well heated, and — of course — built of reinforced concrete. During September and October, eleven of the best-qualified construction firms in the country were interviewed and invited to submit competitive cost estimates for the new plant. By the end of October Turner Construction Company, whose estimate wasn't the lowest one received, had been selected for the work. Naumkeag, desperate to get back into production, had elected to bet on Turner's promise and ability to complete the work by December 1915, just slightly over a year from the date on which it would be possible to start construction.

It was to be no easy task. Existing foundations would be used for some areas of the new buildings, but the usual deviations from anticipated conditions made even that entirely reasonable economy less simple than expected. Because subsurface conditions and depths to firm bearing varied widely across the site, some of the foundations that were to be built new were designed as shallow footings; some as deep, pedestal piers with footings reaching down to rock; and some as piles with concrete pile caps. The deep, pedestal footings would prove the most difficult, as their construction required working twenty-four feet below the level of adjacent tidal water, during periods calculated to exploit low tides. Worst of all, a November start in Massachusetts meant that most of the foundation work and some of the superstructure work would have to be driven through a New England winter.

Turner organized a broad attack on the problems. As soon as foundation work was substantially advanced in April 1915, leaving only eight months before the December completion deadline, work on the superstructure went forward and was prosecuted vigorously. Two entirely separate construction crews worked independently, one completing about 37,000 square feet of concrete floor per week and the other completing about 23,000 square feet per week, in spite of low temperatures in the beginning of the period and a rainy period later. By mid-summer, with superstructure concrete work substantially advanced and masonry work moving along well, the December completion goal began to look realistic, although considerable mechanical and electrical work was still to be done and several hundred thousand square feet of maple flooring were still to be laid down over wood sleepers to provide the required surface for the factory floor itself. By Christmas, Naumkeag Steam Cotton was beginning to move its equipment and personnel into its new quarters. It was an enormous achievement, thoroughly appreciated by Naumkeag's management and by the production force that began returning to its jobs in the spring of 1916.

The Naumkeag job was Turner's largest New England job, but it was far from the only one. The company had been taking on more and more work in the area, much of it for other big textile mills that were at the core of New England's economy before they all began to move south, later in the century, in search of cheap labor. Toward the end of the Naumkeag job, Henry Turner and his board recognized the momentum of the New England market and, accepting the likelihood of its durability, established a Turner office in Boston.

It was during this period of extraordinary growth in the company's business that what came to be called the Great War started in Europe, and the bitter irony of that brutal and destructive war is that it replaced fire as the great generator of work for Turner Construction Company. The belligerents had voracious appetites for products that were being manufactured (or could be manufactured) in the United States, and that meant a massive volume of construction work, including the expansion of existing plants, the construction of new ones, even the construction of the buildings the government would need to manage the distribution of such goods and eventually buildings for the management and deployment of the country's own military forces. The terrible events in Europe ushered in a period of unprecedented prosperity and growth for Turner.

That period of growth had started a little before hostilities in Europe actually broke out. Just the prospect of war had been enough to influence the U.S. economy as early as 1913, when some of the potential belligerents began to feel strains on their own domestic production capability and when the first echoes of what came to be called "preparedness" began to be heard in Washington. General Electric's 1913 decision to expand its transformer plant in Pittsfield, Massachusetts, doubtless owed much to these roots.

GE was still a young company in 1913, only about twenty years old, but the exuberant growth of electric power had already made the company of Thomas Edison and Charles Steinmetz one to reckon with. During the late nineteenth century, electric lighting in the cities had been provided mostly by small firms that generated and delivered direct current to local clusters of electrified buildings and streetlights, but by 1903 that pattern had begun to give way to one in which electric power was produced and distributed to larger areas by the predecessors of modern electric utility companies. Such centralized power generation meant longer transmission distances, and high voltages were needed to make such transmission economical. Producing such high voltages required transformers, and transformers, in 1903, were the business of the Stanley Electrical Manufacturing Company of Pittsfield, Massachusetts.

Stanley had been making transformers in Pittsfield since about 1891, when William Stanley, a pioneer in the field, had built his small factory there. He had actually started his career working for Thomas Edison a dozen years earlier, but when Edison refused to accept Stanley's view that alternating-current power would eventually dominate the industry (a view that Thomas Edison would maintain until his death) Stanley left Edison to work for his competitor, George Westinghouse, in Pittsburgh. Westinghouse was apparently a difficult man to work for, and although he backed Stanley in the work he was doing in the field, he insisted on taking all the credit for himself. Stanley quit and set up his own plant in Pittsfield. Ironically, by about that time the Morgan banking interests had acquired control of Thomas Edison's firm, combining it with the Thompson-Houston Company, an important early player in the field of alternating-current power, and the company produced by that merger bought Stanley Electrical Manufacturing Company in Pittsfield. Within a few years all the transformer manufacturing capability of what was by then called the General Electric Company had been centralized in the old Stanley works in Pittsfield.

During the early years, General Electric was able to limp along with the plant it had acquired from Stanley, patching and buttressing it from time to time, but by the middle of 1913 things had begun to change. Signs of war in Europe were unmistakable, and both the military and civilian uses of electric power were increasing fast, bringing an unprecedented surge in transformer orders to General Electric. GE needed new space quickly for research and manufacturing, and at a time when transformers still used oil that burned easily, they needed space that was fireproof. Concrete was a material that would meet all those needs, and early in 1913 they brought Turner up from New York to build the first of several big new concrete buildings for them in Pittsfield.

Of course, GE was only one of many firms whose need for bigger and better facilities would be generated by the developing war economy. Once the likelihood of a European war became clear, the center of gravity of Turner's clientele began to shift from manufacturers of paper boxes, food products, and other consumer goods to manufacturers whose products would be needed in a wartime economy.

Sperry Gyroscope was typical. Elmer Sperry, a gifted inventor born in upstate New York in 1860, had already distinguished himself as a pioneer in the new field of electrical technology by the turn of the century, having developed and produced a wide variety of equipment, ranging from arc lighting systems to streetcar motors and electric cars, much of which was eventually acquired and produced by General Electric. But during the early 1900s Sperry had become absorbed with the extraordinary behavior of spinning masses like children's tops, and he was among the earliest scientists to recognize and harness their special properties for much more serious applications. By about 1909 Sperry's work had the attention of the expanding U.S. Navy, whose budget had been generously increased during the administration of defense-minded Theodore Roosevelt, and by 1912 the British, wary about German military expenditures, were knocking on Sperry's door too. He had developed gyrostabilizers that increased the effectiveness of naval warships operating in heavy seas, and he was close to production of gyrocompasses that would make such vessels, and the U.S. Navy's increasingly important submarine fleet, invulnerable to the distortions imposed on their old magnetic compasses by steel hulls and shipboard electrical equipment. But Sperry was still doing his work in a few thousand square feet of loft space he had carved out of an old building in Brooklyn, and just after war broke out in Europe he engaged Turner to build a state-of-the-art, 350,000-square-foot reinforced concrete plant near the Brooklyn Navy Yard. In that building, Sperry developed the great firm that would produce a vast range of technologically advanced products during and between the two great wars and that would later become Sperry Rand and eventually become Litton Industries. Elmer Sperry's own diaries attest to his special appreciation of the work that Turner did for him in Brooklyn.

Dozens of such firms came to Turner as the European war intensified the needs of the belligerents and as the United States itself became increasingly aware that Woodrow Wilson's 1916 campaign promise to keep the country out of war was going to be extremely difficult to keep. Scovill Manufacturing Company in Waterbury, Connecticut, was one. Scovill had specialized in manufacturing brass products in Waterbury since the middle of the nineteenth century, producing shrapnel cases and a whole range of products required aboard naval vessels, and the press of new orders demanded increased manufacturing and administration space. Scovill had gone to Turner for the first of its new buildings as early as 1915 and by the end of the war Turner had built five more for them. The Carborundum Company, which manufactured the abrasives that were essential to virtually every machining process involved in heavy manufacturing, was another firm whose work increased radically as the European war continued and the industrial demands of the United States expanded. Carborundum started in Pennsylvania before the turn of the century and in 1894 had relocated to a plant in Niagara Falls, New York, to which it had moved in search of low-cost power. It was then only the second customer of Niagara Mohawk Power Company, whose first customer had been another young firm called Pittsburgh Reduction Company, later to become the Aluminum Company of America, another firm for which Turner would later do a great deal of construction. Turner started doing work for Carborundum as early as 1909, and during the few years just before the United States was drawn into the war, the company would build half a dozen more buildings for them, surprising almost everyone with the speed with which reinforced concrete work could be done and winning the admiration of an upstate population who had never seen such work driven through the fierce winters of western New York State.

For American industry, these were the early days of what is now thought of as the American century. It was bursting at the seams, with luxuriant growth encouraged in almost every sector by a confluence of rapidly developing technology, expanding markets, and an abundance of skilled labor. And they were certainly good days for Turner Construction Company too.

As the business of provisioning Allied forces in Europe became increasingly the central preoccupation of American industry, the impact of the war began to be felt almost everywhere in the economy, and Turner's business surged even further. In 1916 the company's completed work volume exceeded its previous high by two-thirds, reaching $6.6 million, and in 1917 it almost doubled to $11.6 million. Such an annual volume of business was extraordinary for a firm only fifteen years old. There were more projects than ever, many of them larger than most of the earlier ones, and the list of firms for which Turner was regularly doing work had grown longer, now including, in addition to many of the earlier names, Bristol-Myers, National Biscuit, Bausch & Lomb, and Hudson Motor Car. More architects and engineers had accepted reinforced concrete as a safe and workable option and many were now able to do the required design work themselves, so the number of jobs on which Turner assumed any significant design responsibility decreased as the volume of construction increased. The construction itself was still largely industrial, almost always involving a concrete structure, but the fraction of work represented by subcontracted specialties like mechanical and electrical work, elevators, and ornamental iron work increased as the complexity and sophistication of the jobs increased.

By 1916, with the United States still technically neutral, the war in Europe had intensified and showed no sign of resolution. After two years of fierce fighting and almost 5 million casualties, the two sides were continuing to inflict punishing losses on one another without significantly moving the lines of battle that separated them. The likelihood that the United States might be drawn into the conflict as a trump card against the Central Powers was increasing.

The Turks had long since joined the Germans and the Austrians, and more recently the Italians, Greeks, and Portuguese had come in on the side of the British, French, and Russians. American neutrality had been seriously imperiled as early as May 1915, when the Germans' sinking of the British passenger vessel *Lusitania* had cost more than a hundred American lives, but Wilson's strong protest had convinced the Germans to pledge that such vessels, properly identified, would not be attacked again.

By early 1917 that pledge had been violated several times, and what had earlier been a modest American bias in favor of the Allies was becoming a strong American preference to support them. When the Germans announced, on January 31, 1917, that they were abandoning all restraint in favor of a policy of unrestricted submarine warfare against any vessels suspected of complicity with their enemy, Wilson's campaign commitment to "keep America out of war" lost all meaning and in April, after a last effort at compromise, he sought and obtained from Congress a declaration of war against the Central Powers.

Although the declaration of war formalized the end of a neutrality that had been waning for some time, there was lingering concern that dissident elements opposed to war with Germany might obstruct the war effort. One in three Americans still had at least one parent living in Europe in 1917, many of them in Germany or Austria, and German was the most widely spoken non-English language in the United States, so such apprehension in Washington appeared to have a strong basis. But the concern proved to be unfounded: When the first draft call was issued in June 1917, there were patriotic celebrations all over the country and almost 10 million men between the ages of twenty-one and thirty registered without a single incident or protest. A year later a second registration, widening the age group, brought in another 12 million registrants, and eventually about 2 million were actually drafted from the two registrations. A national Committee on Public Information flooded the country with patriotic and anti-German propaganda, inspiring people to accept what quickly became an almost repressively regulated economy and occasionally encouraging the kind of excessive chauvinism that caused the firing of the distinguished German-born conductor of the Chicago Symphony Orchestra and the suspension of German language instruction in many schools and even in some universities. But despite its excesses, the campaign served to inspire widespread, useful, war-related efforts and to infuse the population with a sense of patriotic urgency that would later prove critical to the successful prosecution of the war.

During the first few months of 1917, the Germans had been sinking Allied shipping at a monthly rate of about 500,000 tons, depriving the British and French of supplies and equipment they desperately needed to resist a well-equipped, relentlessly advancing enemy and convincing some highly placed officials on the Allied side that the war was going to be lost. As soon as the United States entered the war, it moved quickly and effectively to increase domestic production and to increase its own badly needed shipping capability, seizing and pressing into service German vessels that were in U.S. ports, commandeering many private ships and accelerating a large shipbuilding program already underway. At the same time, the British developed an effective convoy system that would slowly reduce their loss rate, but not before a good many additional vessels were sent to the bottom. A deteriorating situation was made worse in the fall of 1917 when the Italians were overrun by the Austrians, and the Russians, preoccupied with their own revolution, began to sue for a separate peace, relieving pressure on the Germans in the East and facilitating the release of German troops for duty against the Allies in the West. What was needed was a large, well-trained American fighting force that would arrive in Europe with its own equipment and its own provisions and bring new vigor to the war against the Germans. The overriding question was whether or not it would be possible to get such a force there in time.

It was that urgency that was at the heart of the role played by Turner in the American war effort. The company was superbly suited to the critical problem of building, quickly and well, the huge structures that the government and the military were going to need. There's been a story around for years that early in 1917, when war fear had reached a fever pitch, someone in Brooklyn reported to a government agency that suspicious-looking gun emplacements were being built on the premises of a local factory. It's said that an officer from the nearby Brooklyn Navy Yard was dispatched to investigate and that he found that the suspected gun emplacements were nothing more threatening than equipment foundations being built by a Turner crew. The story has it that the officer was struck by the good quality of the work being done and by what appeared to be the high character of the workforce, and that when he reported all this back to his commanding officer Turner became a candidate to build a major facility that the navy was designing and wanted built right away. The Brooklyn yard was a key location for the Atlantic fleet, and the navy was gearing up for the task of protecting and provisioning troop movements to Europe.

In fact, Turner had already been providing consulting services for the design of the building, and there's not much evidence to support the details of the gun-emplacement story. But some element of the story could well have been a factor in the navy's decision to select Turner to build a 722,000-square-foot, eleven-story reinforced concrete warehouse at the Brooklyn Navy Yard in the first days of the war. What made the job extraordinary was that it had to be completed within what would normally have been regarded as the outrageously short period of six months.

An award was made on the April 29, 1918, on a cost-plus-percentage basis, from completed structural drawings but with only preliminary architectural, mechanical, and electrical drawings. Turner quickly fielded a team that included Cliff Wilson as engineer-in-charge, and within four days Raymond Concrete Pile Company had been brought in to drive the first of about 4,000 of its patented concrete piles. A month later, the formwork for the first elevated floor slab was started and eleven weeks after that, with almost 25,000 cubic yards of concrete in place, the last concrete for the roof was being placed and steel windows were being unloaded at the site. By early December, three weeks ahead of schedule, the navy had begun moving into its first new building and was so pleased that it had already engaged Turner to build two more buildings at the yard.

This was still a time when concrete was king for Turner, but it wasn't the company's only business. A month before the navy warehouse in Brooklyn was finished, the army notified Turner that it had selected the company to build 200 wood-frame barracks at five locations to accommodate the forces of the coast artillery, who until the proposed barracks were completed would be living in tents. Again the issue was speed. The notification came on November 3, and the contract stipulated that the government wanted the men housed in the new buildings before snow, a provision that in New York meant completion in about six weeks. Within a few days Turner had superintendents on all five sites, all reporting to general superintendent G. F. Floyd, and by the middle of November almost 1,500 men were working. By Christmas Day 1917, the job had been completed, but with the war well underway by this time, there was little rest for some of the Turner crew. They were spirited off to build a similar but smaller barracks complex for the Portsmouth Naval Prison at Kittery Point, Maine, where a harsh, seaborne wind blew relentlessly across the construction site and regularly drove temperatures down to twenty degrees below zero.

Oddly enough, not everything the government hired Turner to do during the war was construction. In the fall of 1917, six months into the war, the navy found itself overwhelmed by the complexity and extent of work required to identify, follow, and expedite the production and transportation of materials it desperately needed. As the war widened and the problem intensified, some of its senior officers began to recognize that the ability to manage such complex processes was in fact at the core of what the navy liked best about Turner, and they turned to the company for help. At first only half a dozen men were involved, headed by W. T. Anderson, but by the time the war ended Turner would be providing 167 men to manage navy processes in dozens of locations around the country.

All these difficult and urgent tasks and many smaller ones gradually crowded out anything Turner was doing that wasn't related to the war effort, and by 1918 the company was, for all practical purposes, entirely committed to war work. There were many projects, more than a few of them bigger than anything the company had ever done before, but everything that had been built before 1918 paled alongside what was to come along during 1918. During that year and 1919, Turner would put in place some of the largest buildings in the world and would complete almost twice as much work as the company had built in all fifteen years that had come before.

And it was ready for such an explosion of work. In 1913 it had increased its working capital again by selling additional shares to its employees, and it would do that again in 1917 and 1919. Its work volume had been increasing vigorously every year, and the size of individual projects it was doing had grown regularly larger. With plenty of big work under its belt, the company's leadership had come to the view that no job was too big for it, that once the concept and the mechanics of organizing effectively for very large work were properly understood there was no limit.

The very large jobs of the war years started with the Navy and War Office Building project in Washington, D.C., a job that would become, by the time it was finished, the largest office building in the world. The navy had for years been operating in twenty-one buildings at widely separated locations around Washington, but once the urgency of war replaced the relatively forgiving pace of peace, a decision was made that it would have to consolidate everything in a single location to speed up its work. The navy wasn't the only department to face that problem, of course, and many other agencies had already started work on temporary new quarters around Washington: New wood-frame buildings with lath-and-plaster partitions were beginning to be seen everywhere by the end of 1917. But the navy felt it had too many critical materials like maps, charts, codes, and other vital papers to risk wood-frame construction, and it may even have had unspoken philosophical reservations about sheltering its highest-ranking officers in buildings that could be regarded as less than permanent. When the navy brass learned that it could build in concrete for not much more than wood frame and plaster it decided to call in Turner. How it happened to pick Turner, a fifteen-year-old firm with no experience or presence in Washington, isn't clear, but there's certainly basis for speculating that Turner's performance in the Brooklyn yard must have been a factor.

By January 1918, the plan for the navy's huge Washington office building project had already almost doubled in size when it was decided to consolidate it with a similar facility for the War Department, which ran the army, increasing the gross required area to about 2 million square feet. The idea was to build everything on three levels, along a spine that would be a third of a mile long, and to extend seventeen 500-foot-long office wings from its side, separated from one another by courtyards but joined by connecting bridges. Nine of the wings were to be for the navy and the other eight, across the street, were to be for the War Department. The whole structure was to be built of reinforced concrete, about 80,000 cubic yards of it, and everything was to be completed within seven months.

Franklin D. Roosevelt, who was the thirty-six-year-old assistant secretary of the navy in 1918, signed the cost-plus-percentage contract that the government awarded Turner on February 25, 1918, and project executive Bill Lyle of Turner Construction Company started work on an 8,000-square-foot field office the following morning.

This was to be a job that would draw on all the experience that this capable young company had been accumulating, and then some. Things didn't start off well: In the rush to finish the design work quickly, the navy's engineers had opted to risk doing without borings, and the first few shovels of dirt revealed subsurface material that couldn't be relied on to support even the relatively light loads of the three-story structure that had been designed. They did some quick calculations and began revising foundation drawings to require about 5,000 friction piles expected to fetch up at somewhere between twenty-five and fifty feet, and Turner brought its friends from Raymond Concrete Pile Company in New York down to Washington for what proved to be nine consecutive weeks of uninterrupted pile driving: four rigs working three shifts a day, seven days a week. Bill Lyle protested the government's ungenerous addition of only two weeks to the seven-month schedule for this added work, but the restrained tone of the protest may have reflected Lyle's own awareness that the added pile-driving requirement might have had a good side. It gave Turner some time for addressing a problem that was every bit as severe as the substructure: an inadequacy of available local labor.

Washington wasn't an industrial town where manufacturers were regularly building new plants and where there would almost always be construction jobs starting and finishing. Rather, it was a fairly static government town in which there was only a relatively small pool of construction labor. Now the unprecedented flood of new construction that attended the start of the war had used up whatever local labor had been available, and this was a huge job that was going to require an average of 3,500 men to meet the schedule that the government had established. Most of that labor force would have to come from out of town, and Turner would have to find the people, induce them to come, facilitate their finding places to live in a town where housing was already tight, and then make the most of a largely untested labor force. From the beginning it was a matter of scouring the Northeast for men, transporting them to Washington in buses, building temporary housing at the site to accommodate them, and even providing meals for them while they were looking for their own housing. It even meant seeing to some of their social needs as the job went on: Band concerts and sporting events — including inter-craft boxing bouts — were sponsored, motion pictures were shown, and a whole array of diversions was provided to encourage their sticking with the job. This was certainly not much like the peacetime work that Turner was accustomed to, where there were almost always former Turner men around who wanted to get back onto a Turner crew and others who wanted to become Turner men.

It all worked out, of course, but not without a struggle. Many of the men who came were poorly qualified, and some just didn't like the conditions. Turner paid for bringing them all to Washington and paid to send them home too, providing they stayed with the job for as long as they were needed. Wages in some trades were raised by as much as 50 percent during the course of the job, but the turnover was so great that an average of about three men had to be hired for each position.

The shortage of labor challenged Turner to do everything possible to reduce the amount of on-site labor that was needed, and the company acquitted itself well. All the concrete was mixed on the job, of course, but to accommodate the steady stream of dump trucks delivering sand, gravel, and cement Turner built an elevated truck road the entire length of the job. At eight equally spaced locations in the road, openings were left for dumping into hoppers at stations below, where the concrete was mixed, and from those mixing stations a narrow-gauge railway allowed completely mechanized distribution of concrete to every location on the site. Forms and rebars were fabricated in large sheds mechanized for efficient material handling, and the whole job took on a futuristic look as it was pressed forward.

The navy had never seen anything quite like it, and its senior officers were unanimously admiring. They began moving into their new building on August 23, with the army following on September 8. By the middle of October, to the delight of the government, the last of the building's 15,000 occupants were moving in. A few weeks later, the chairman of the House Committee on Appropriations, addressing the House of Representatives, took a few minutes to tell his colleagues what an extraordinary thing these Turner people had accomplished over near the Potomac, and how much it meant to the efforts of the people who were prosecuting the war.

Even the Washington job, huge as it was, paled alongside the mammoth war construction that Turner was to do in Brooklyn during 1918. The Brooklyn work started early in the year, just after Turner had begun the Washington job. The navy started by selecting the company to build its fleet supply base, comprising more than 2 million square feet of buildings, ten miles of railroad, floating bridge connections, and piers out into New York Bay. Two months later Gen. George Goethals, of Panama Canal fame, came along with another contract, this one to build more than twice that much square footage for the army, together with more piers and another seventeen miles of railroad. The two projects, both of which would be well along before the end of 1918, represented more than $40 million in

1918 costs and would regularly employ more than 8,000 men simultaneously. During one period in 1918, when the two Brooklyn jobs and the Washington job were all at their height, Turner employed a total of almost 15,000 men in its work.

The navy job in Brooklyn was started before the army job, and here the reason for the award is apparent: The navy had become convinced, at its earlier Brooklyn Navy Yard job, that building the fleet supply base in seven and a half months was a job for Turner. Cliff Wilson came over from the navy yard job to become project executive, with H. C. Paddock as his engineer and John Nelson, R. E. Fall, and N. L. Kennedy as superintendents. This was a job on which the workforce was bound to be exceptionally large, and Wilson dispatched an additional superintendent, A. E. Hansen, just to manage the subcontracted work. All the purchasing and record keeping would be done at the site, making the job staff entirely self-sufficient.

By this time the United States had been at war for almost a year, and with troop shipments to Europe in full swing, the navy's need to enlarge its capacity to service and provision its fleet was imposing huge pressures and demanding the earliest possible availability of this new facility in Brooklyn. The job aggregated about 2.3 million square feet and would include a couple of gigantic, eight-story reinforced concrete storehouses as well as a couple of heavy-timber-and-masonry warehouses, a central heating plant, and an administration building, all adjacent to the Bush Terminal buildings that Turner had built a few years earlier. The piers would reach almost half a mile out into the bay, and it would take more than 12,000 piles to support everything that was to be built.

The army's job followed a couple of months later and, just when the company's management must have thought it had seen the limit of what it would be asked to do, proved to be much bigger even than the navy job. One building of the five to be constructed at what was called the U.S. Army Supply Base at Brooklyn would be, at about 2.3 million square feet, the largest building in the world. The army had engaged the nationally prominent Cass Gilbert, who had earlier designed the Woolworth Building in New York, to design it.

Turner brought Arthur Tozzer down from Boston to run the job. His general superintendent would be Albert Larson, who would have four superintendents working under him: G. E. Larson, W. T. Quinn, W. W. Roberts, and G. H. Smith. In addition, Larson would have a separate superintendent for each of the major specialties: one for dredging and pier construction (C. E. Trout), one for mechanical work (T. I. Coe), one for railroad work (J. P. Patterson), one for reinforcing steel (L. H. Usilton), one for elevator work (E. R. Bear), and several others for special areas. When concrete work hit its stride, later in 1918, new concrete construction was being completed at a rate of an acre per day, and by the end of the job about 285,000 cubic yards had been put in place. Between formwork and timber construction, almost 20 million board feet of lumber and timber had been used. During one forty-day period, 1.6 million square feet of floor area was formed and floored, and the cry "40 acres in 40 days" became part of Turner lore. Even during the wars that came after the Great War, production to match the scale and intensity of what was achieved on these 1918 projects of Turner's is difficult to find.

The demands of the work were nothing short of monumental. Recruiting and maintaining the workforce in Brooklyn was every bit the task it had been in Washington, here exacerbated by an occasional strike. As in Washington, the company regularly staged patriotic mass meetings, complete with marching bands, often punctuated by spirited singing of popular and patriotic songs, and occasionally addressed by returning war heroes who assured the men that their work was every bit as vital to the country's security as the work of the soldiers themselves. Honors and awards were publicly announced and presented for production records set in heated competitions that pitted crew against crew and that were said to have increased productivity markedly. A Turner-published weekly newspaper, the *Mixer* reported all the goings on, featuring stories about Turner men who had produced exceptionally well, reporting on the families of workers, and relieving the long hours of work (workdays usually ran to ten and a half hours) with some of the innocent humor of the times.

As it turned out, although both the gigantic Brooklyn projects were brought to completion and occupied during 1919, neither would ever contribute to the war effort they were designed to support. By the middle of July 1918, before either building was completed, the tide in the European war had begun to turn in favor of the Allies after the American First and Second Armies joined ranks with French troops to stop the German advance. By August of 1918 a self-contained American army had engaged the Germans for the first time as a unit, overwhelming them at St. Mihiel and taking 16,000 prisoners. In September, a million-man American force attacked the Germans along a front that extended from the Meuse River to the Argonne Forest and, after a fierce forty-day battle in which it suffered 120,000 casualties, broke through the Hindenburg Line, drove the Germans back, and, for all practical purposes, began the end of the war. By early October the Germans had floated peace initiatives that led to the signing of an armistice on November 11, and seven months later the former belligerents met at Versailles to sign what one observer described as an agreement that was so punitive it was less a peace treaty than a preamble to the next war.

Both the big Brooklyn complexes would see service again in World War II, but after that war ended, the navy component would be demolished (with a difficulty that reflected the good concrete work Turner had done building it) to make room for a landfill. The Army Supply Base, on the other hand, has survived, and after serving its military function during three wars, it passed into the hands of the City of New York during the 1970s. Later, during the 1980s, the city's Economic Development Corporation (EDC) brought Turner back to what has come to be called the Brooklyn Army Terminal to manage three big renovation programs in which $100 million worth of renovation was done to upgrade large areas for industrial use. New York's printing industry, which was about to abandon the city for new quarters elsewhere, moved into one big section of the army terminal to take advantage of the heavy-duty floors and new power systems, and other industrial tenants followed suit. The old World War I building that Cass Gilbert had designed and Turner had built sixty years earlier was given a new life. In Washington, the Navy and War Office complex continued a healthy and useful life well after its wood-frame contemporaries in the region had been demolished, but by 1970 "Old Navy" and "Munitions," as its two components had come to be called, had succumbed to the wrecking ball.

Most of the subcontractors who worked for Turner on these vast projects have long since gone out of business or lost their identities after mergers with other firms, but some survive. L. K. Comstock and Hatzel and Buehler are two firms that did electrical work on the jobs, and they are still going strong in the New York area. J. I. Hass did most of the painting work, New York Roofing Company did most of the flat roofing, and the Otis Elevator Company built and installed the elevators, and all those firms are still extant. Globe Automatic Sprinkler Company, which did much of the fire-sprinkler work, is still active, but the Automatic Sprinkler Company of America, which also did a good deal of the fire-sprinkler work now only manufactures devices for the industry and is no longer a fire-sprinkler contractor. New England Dredge and Drydock Company, which did the dredging work, is still around, and the George B. Spearin Company, which built the substructure for a couple of the piers, has become Spearin, Preston and Burrows. Raymond Concrete Pile Company, which went on to do millions of dollars' worth of piling for Turner on many jobs and which co-ventured with Turner during the Second World War, became Raymond International and continued to be an important force in substructure work until just a few years ago, when it terminated its activities.

Turner Construction Company itself emerged from the Great War strengthened both professionally and financially. Its leadership and many of its intermediate and junior managers had been tempered in the crucible of a unique national emergency, working on extraordinarily large jobs under conditions that they'd have been unlikely to see for a good many years, if ever. And although the company did the work for modest fees, it earned some profits too. For work in which so large a component would be put in place by the company's own forces, Turner's fee of less than 3 percent was unusually low, but the total cost of what was done was so large and the economic risks were so small that it was thought to be adequate. In fact, it was an arrangement that proved to be entirely reasonable, and Turner emerged from the war years even stronger financially than it had entered them.

The war itself didn't really have any widespread, lasting impact on the personnel of the company. Among its salaried staff, 128 men entered military service, and of those 49 went overseas. Two men died in service: J. D. Cook was killed in action and J. P. Uhlinger died in camp. There doesn't appear to be any reliable account of the impact of the war on Turner's hourly employees.

Turner Concrete Steel Company of Philadelphia might be considered a casualty of the war, although its senior management survived as the Philadelphia office of Turner Construction Company. There's a basis for thinking that the cause of the company's demise was a combination of the war and the superior ethical style of its principals. Until and during 1916, Turner Concrete Steel had been a small, prospering Philadelphia contracting firm, specializing in concrete work and doing enough of it to pay W. W. and Archie Turner respectable salaries and to pay its shareholders regular dividends. In 1917, TCS took a subcontract from a general contractor called Chester Construction and Contracting Company to do the reinforced concrete work on the new Chester Waterside Power Plant Chester was building for Beacon Light Company. At $650,000, the subcontract was about twice the size of most of the jobs TCS had been doing, and the company addressed the work with a vengeance. By the middle of 1918 its work was well advanced when Chester Construction and Contracting Company revealed that it would be unable to pay TCS its current invoice of more than $200,000. The power company had apparently run into problems in its own financing plan and was unable to pay Chester's bill. TCS withdrew its workforce from the site, pending receipt of payment, struggling meanwhile to meet cash obligations that were accumulating on its other jobs, all labor-intensive concrete contracts on which wages and material bills had to be paid on demand.

Although TCS was able to raise some capital through short-term bank borrowing and from its own shareholders, W. W. and Archie Turner worried about the longer-term implications of the suspension of the Chester job. The very industrial expansion that had induced Beacon to enlarge its power plant in the first place was already off to a furious start, with almost every Chester-area worker who hadn't already left for military service signing on to one of a flurry of new construction jobs. As the availability of workers shrank, wages rose, and the prospect of TCS's being able to hire skilled mechanics when work resumed on the power plant job, at a wage that would accord with the fixed-price subcontract that TCS had with

Chester, became smaller and smaller. There were rumors that Beacon would soon resolve its problems, but there was no clear evidence of when such resolution would allow payment of money due TCS and when, if ever, TCS would be able to resume its work.

In a later day, a different contractor might have thought in terms of a lawsuit and damages, but the Turners simply weren't so inclined. They opted to relinquish their subcontract, finish up all their other work, pay their bills, and liquidate their young firm. Eighty-three years later Archie's son Howard S. Turner, himself by then long retired from his own service as Turner's president and chairman, would remember his father's 1918 lament that it looked like he'd have to restore the mortgage he'd already paid off on his home. By 1919, Turner Concrete Steel Company of Philadelphia was gone, and W. W. and Archie Turner had established a new Philadelphia office for Turner Construction Company.

5.

Peace

By the time the country began to turn its attention away from the Great War, 3 million American men and almost half a million American women who had served or worked in places or under conditions that they never could have imagined had gone home, many of them changed forever. Arrangements for returning control of the railroads to private industry were underway, a constitutional amendment giving women the right to vote was being drafted, and another one prohibiting the sale of liquor was in the process of being ratified. Automobiles (only 10 percent of them enclosed) were beginning to appear on the country's still-primitive roads, and radio had entered the culture and was starting to entertain and inform people in even the country's most remote areas. It was the new world of the 1920s.

The good years that followed would be spectacular ones, while they lasted, for the country's businesses and for most of its population, but they were destined to be relatively few in number. The United States had emerged from the war as the single creditor nation among the major powers, with almost $11 billion owed to it by its wartime allies, and while the Europeans labored to rebuild their manufacturing and commercial infrastructure, the United States grew and prospered as the world's most prolific producer and exporter. Warren G. Harding, swept into the presidency on a groundswell of conservative public support, promised a "return to normalcy" that would be achieved by policies designed "to get government out of business and to get business into government." To a great extent he succeeded, preserving and expanding a period of high tariffs and low taxes, encouraging the virtually unrestricted expansion of business, and providing a setting in which a general feeling of well-being raised consumer spending to levels rarely seen in years past. When Harding died in office three years after his election, Calvin Coolidge followed him with more of the same.

Henry Turner was forty-nine years old when the twenties began, eighteen years along in his leadership of one of the country's most successful construction companies and justifiably content with the way things were working out. The Turners were enjoying the good life of a family of means, dividing their time between a large, well-appointed and well-staffed home on Monroe Place in Brooklyn and Skyland Farm, the property they had purchased in Buck Hill Falls, Pennsylvania, in 1916, and on which they had built a gracious house. Skyland Farm would become a treasured country retreat for the family over the years and the site of annual social events to which only the most senior or most promising of the company's executives would be invited for a few days of golf and camaraderie. By the twenties the Turners were well into the enjoyment of some of the material fruits of their increasing professional and commercial successes, and Henry Turner was honing his already well-established horsemanship skills at the Brooklyn Riding Club and playing an increasingly excellent game of golf. Young Chan Turner was entering his second year at Swarthmore College and three of the four other Turner children were being educated in Quaker schools in Brooklyn: In 1920 Katherine was sixteen, Haines was eleven, and Bob was seven. The youngest, Jim, had just turned three.

W. W. and Archie Turner, having made the transition from Turner Concrete Steel Company to the management of Turner Construction Company's new Philadelphia office, were doing very well in 1920, their already well-established local reputation enhanced by the strength and reputation of the parent company. Having acquired modest blocks of Turner Company stock, both brothers would eventually join Henry on the company's board, but another Turner brother, J. R., who had worked for Turner during the war years, would succumb to illness in 1923. Two other brothers, Howard and Richard Sinclair, stayed on in Maryland to run the farms and the family's business and never became associated with the con-struction company.

Henry C. Turner and DeForest Dixon were still in charge of things, with Henry continuing to exert a powerful influence in virtually every aspect of the work and DeForest managing what by 1920 had become a considerable and increasingly far-flung field force. But Turner's emerging leaders were beginning to influence the course of events in serious ways. Arthur Tozzer, finished with his work at the Brooklyn army terminal project and now a Turner director, had returned to his Boston base to manage the New England District. Two others, both destined to join Tozzer on the board within a few years, were running the company's business in other remote regions: Cliff Wilson, fresh from his navy work, had become gen-eral manager of the promising new Southern District, headquartered in Atlanta; and Bill Lyle, the Turner executive who had run the Navy and War Office Building project in Washington, had returned to manage what was left of the Buffalo office after a 1917 company decision to bring all Buffalo's estimating, purchasing, and engineering work back into New York City.

At the time of the 1920 annual dinner, many years before Turner had begun to include directors from outside the company on its board, all seven of the board members were active in Turner's management. All but Tozzer were based in attrac-tive new offices the company had acquired in 1917, at 244 Madison Avenue, to replace what it had outgrown at 11 Broadway. In addition to Henry C. Turner, DeForest Dixon, and Arthur Tozzer, the board now included T. A. Smith, A. W. Chapman, J. C. Andrews, and E. J. Moore, all senior Turner men who had started with the company during its first few years. Smith and Moore had come up through field positions, while Chapman (Charlotte Turner's brother) was essen-tially an inside man who had become corporate secretary, and Andrews was a financial man who was corporate treasurer. More recent starters like Elbert (Ab) Abberley, who would die sixty-nine years later as Turner's oldest retiree, and Walter K. Shaw, who would himself become a senior Turner executive and the father of a future Turner chairman, were seen to be the young men to watch, along with Nelson Doe, M. A. Darville, F. H. (Dutch) Schroedel and young L. S. Homer.

The first few years after the armistice weren't good ones for the country, but by some combination of good management and good luck Turner managed to prosper. During that short postwar period, the company would prove to be almost invulnerable to the two most destructive economic forces of the day: a brief but soaring inflation and then an equally brief but harsh recession that came in its wake. The impact of the inflation that followed the war was blunted for Turner because the company still had plenty of work left to do on the big government jobs that it had started early in 1918 before the war ended. Those costs were fully reimbursable and not subject to fixed upsets, and because such work represented such a large fraction of what Turner was doing right after the armistice it served to insulate the company from the destructive impact of inflation. As to the discouraging dearth of new projects that characterized the national recession of 1920 and 1921, Turner was able to survive that without serious damage because it had already signed on to a good share of big industrial work that had been deferred during the war, and it was able to secure a meaningful share of what additional new work did surface.

Every year continued to be profitable, with substantial allocations of earnings (sometimes as much as 50 percent of what remained after dividends) distributed to implement the Additional Compensation Plan. In 1919 Turner had established for all salaried employees a Group Life Insurance Plan that provided, after one year's service, a $500 death benefit that increased at the rate of $100 per year until the benefit reached $2,000. They were benefits that wouldn't look significant in the twenty-first century, but in 1919 they represented meaningful sums and a bold departure from prevailing industry practice. In 1923 Charlotte Turner, Henry's wife, presented to the company the Turner Flag, which she had designed and sewn, to be awarded annually to the Turner office showing the greatest improvement in its performance. The flag was eagerly sought by individual Turner offices for years, but its award was suspended early in the depression and not restored until 1966.

Much of the pent-up industrial demand after the armistice came from the big textile mills in New England that had been the beneficiaries of both a very high wartime demand for their products and what had proved to be the complete inability of their European competitors to address anything but their own markets for at least four or five years. When the big profits earned by some of the American textile manufacturers during the war years threatened to bring about a congressional inquiry into the legality of such war-driven prosperity, some of the companies began ambitious expansion programs that had the effect of plowing such profits back into new construction. Turner, with a strong office in Boston by then and a reputation for being able to do big and complicated industrial jobs quickly and well, proved to be a beneficiary.

Two of the most prosperous of these big New England companies were Sanford Mills and the American Woolen Company, and they both turned to Turner to build their new mills and support buildings. During the few years between the signing of the armistice and 1922, Turner's Boston office did seventeen separate jobs for American Woolen and another six for Sanford Mills, in a whole variety of locations around New England. The company built other big textile mills too, as well as industrial plants for firms like Diamond Match, Carborundum, and Western Electric, all companies trying to make up for time lost during the war by expanding after it ended. It was profitable but difficult work, made more difficult by strikes and shortages of materials that attended the country's struggle to return to full production after the war years. In New York State, where a shortage of railroad cars was choking off the supply of cement that Turner needed for the concrete-intensive work it was doing close to home, the company chartered a fleet of barges and tugs to bring cement down from central New York State mills on the Erie Canal and then down the Hudson River into New York City.

Some foreign work entered Turner's mix during this postwar period, a new experience for the company: a large fish-freezing plant for the French government on the fogbound and thoroughly isolated island of St. Pierre, twenty miles off the coast of Newfoundland, and several jobs in the Caribbean for oil companies that were subsidiaries or affiliates of Turner's loyal friends at Standard Oil Company. They were all jobs that were done long before the advent of casual air travel, so site visits were made by steamship, often rocky and always slow. The company was averaging a striking seventy jobs a year between the time the armistice was signed and the end of 1920, completing close to $25 million worth of work in each year. These weren't the gigantic volumes of the war years, but they still set a heady pace that showed no signs of slowing until the beginning of 1921, when the bubble seemed to burst. In that single recession year the number of projects quickly fell to thirty-seven and the total value of business done in that year fell to about $8 million.

By 1922, when Turner celebrated its twentieth anniversary, the brief recession of 1920–1921 was winding down and the pace of work was returning to what it had been during the better days the company had seen earlier. Nineteen twenty-two became the watershed year that marked the beginning of a new era for Turner, and when Henry Turner addressed the ninety-eight guests who had gathered at the Engineers' Club in New York for the annual dinner that year he surprised them with what he had to say about the future. He started by endorsing a recent comment by Percy Straus, the president of Macy's, who had said that anything in business that had been done in the same way for five years or more needed to be given some very careful review. Turner Construction Company, Henry Turner reminded his audience, had been doing mostly the same industrial concrete work for twenty years, and in his view it was time for a review. He'd clearly given the matter plenty of thought, and what he proposed in 1922 was that the company reach out into an increasingly broad range of other building types, turning away from its intense concentration on the industrial buildings and concrete work that had sustained it until then, and that it take a serious look at what he and others of that period thought of as "finished" buildings. He acknowledged the special position that the company had developed and enjoyed in big concrete construction during the first couple of decades of the century, and he emphasized that he wasn't by any means advocating abandoning such a focus, but he confessed that he now thought that Turner's position as the leader in concrete work was likely to become less secure as other good firms learned how to do good concrete work too. He appears to have sensed that the volume of such work might level off or decline before long, and he proposed that even the slogan "Turner for Concrete" be retired as too limiting.

There was a curious irony in the timing of Henry Turner's epiphany about concrete work. Only two years earlier, he had been elected president of the prestigious American Concrete Institute (ACI), the industry's ranking professional organization, and in 1927 he would endow the Henry C. Turner Medal, to be presented periodically by ACI for "notable achievements in, or service to, the concrete industry." By the company's hundredth birthday, seventy-five years later, the medal had been awarded fifty-eight times, most often to distinguished consulting engineers or to engineering academics who had broken new ground in the design of reinforced concrete structures.

Whether or not Henry Turner's view of the future that evening was so prescient that it anticipated even the fundamental American cultural changes that would predominate during and after the 1920s isn't clear, but whether he anticipated them or not, such changes did occur and his new vision for the company proved to be uncannily accurate and productive.

The war, both abroad and at home, is thought by some to have exhausted the American population and perhaps to have corrupted some of the values that had shaped it during earlier years. A work ethic that had been at the heart of the industrial growth on which Turner's early prosperity had depended seemed to be giving way to a less puritanical one in which persons who had seen or heard about different living styles were becoming interested in work that was less demanding, and in recreation and leisure as well. Early in the 1920s, they were leaving rural areas and the hard lives of the farms in increasing numbers to enter what looked like the easier life of commerce in the cities. What's more, many of them were beginning to earn a good living that was only marginally reduced by modest (though widely resented) income taxes that took less than 5 percent of most incomes. There was more money to spend than there had ever been before.

Of course, Henry Turner continued to emphasize that he didn't advocate abandoning the company's solid base in industrial construction, and Turner would continue to build its share of such projects all through the 1920s, including plants for such national firms as Western Electric, Squibb, General Electric, Gillette, Humble Oil, Alexander Smith Carpet, Pratt & Whitney, and for three or four of the big cement companies, but in his view the day of the "finished" building had clearly dawned for Turner in 1922. Hotels, department stores, corporate office buildings, and a whole range of high-quality institutional buildings began to get the company's attention after that, and during the latter years of the 1920s such finished work would account for more than 40 percent of Turner's business.

Hotels led the way. In 1922, when Florida was among the first states to enjoy the emerging prosperity of the twenties, a wealthy manufacturer of chewing gum decided to enlarge a moderately successful hotel he owned in Orlando, and he hired Turner to do the construction. The office that Turner had in 1919 established in Atlanta probably couldn't have found a better transition job than renovating and building an addition to Orlando's San Juan, a well-respected old hotel in serious need of sprucing up and enlargement.

Almost half a century before Disney, Orlando was a center of the state's citrus and cattle industries, and although such commercial activities would decline in later years, the city was fairly prosperous and without much inclination to become one of Florida's glittering new resort communities. Its San Juan was essentially a businessman's hotel that catered to visiting salesmen and the like, and the plan was to keep it that way. The handsome, eight-story wing that Turner was to add to the hotel in 1922 would be attractively clad in stucco trimmed with elegant, sculpted terra-cotta, but inside the building would be a comfortably modern though fairly plain hotel with special rooms in which salesmen could display their wares. There would be few of the amenities that would characterize some of the more glamorous hotels that Turner would build later, but the hotel's owners insisted on fireproof construction for the addition, so its structural frame was done in reinforced concrete.

It didn't take long for word to get around that Turner was no longer just a builder of factories and warehouses. A little later in 1922, Henry Turner was approached by a librarian in upstate New York who wanted some construction in the rural Adirondack Mountains hamlet of Lake Placid: an ambitious request from a librarian. But this fellow wasn't just any librarian, he was Melvil Dewey, the former librarian of the State of New York who had years earlier designed and developed the Dewey Decimal System that is still in use in the cataloguing of library materials throughout the English-speaking world. Toward the end of the nineteenth century, Dewey and his librarian wife, looking for a place in which they could avoid the pollens that exacerbated their hay fever during most of the warm-weather months, had bought a farm near Lake Placid. Over the years that followed, they had invited other librarians and a good many friends to visit them there. Some built cottages on the Deweys' land and began to enjoy vacations there during winters as well as summers, ultimately joining one another to form the Lake Placid Club.

By 1922, when Dewey called Turner, the membership had grown and become dominated by wealthy city people from Philadelphia, New York, and Boston, and the club's needs had outstripped the capacity of the Dewey farmhouse and the aging wood-frame cottages that surrounded it. Now the members wanted a commodious residence building, complete with 180 comfortable, well-heated bedrooms and private baths and with central cooking and dining facilities and even a fully finished chapel. Like the San Juan in Orlando, this would be a good transition job for Turner, in every sense a finished building of high quality but without most of the elegant touches the members preferred to leave behind in the cities they came from. They wanted to feel they were in the country, but they wanted to live there in a well-constructed fireproof building, and they wanted it all as soon as they could get it. It was a good set of specifications for Turner Construction Company at that stage of its transition.

Securing and delivering materials and recruiting skilled help for a big concrete and masonry job in the rural outback of the Adirondack woods in 1922 and 1923 was no simple task, but it certainly wasn't one for which Turner's people lacked good experience. They drove the work through an upstate winter in which temperatures regularly fell well below zero, and they were able to complete it in time for the 1923–1924 winter season, an important early milestone along Lake Placid's path to its international reputation as a winter resort. A little less than a decade later, when (largely through the efforts of the Deweys) Lake Placid became the site of the first Olympic Winter Games to be held in the United States, the club's guest list would feature some of the brightest names of the day, including Adm. Richard Byrd and New York's mayor Jimmy Walker.

The first of Henry Turner's children, Henry Chandlee Turner Jr., called Chan, graduated from Swarthmore College in June 1923 with a degree in the liberal arts, and he was to cut his teeth on the company's new job at Buck Hill Falls. L. S. Homer was superintending construction of the inn's new building for Turner, a 122-room wing grander than the building that had preceded it and clad in local river-worn cobbles that would be laid up by Turner's masons. Not far away in the Poconos, another Turner job was taking shape, and it would be young Turner's second assignment: a new guest tower and kitchen for the Pocono Manor Inn, a similar vacation hotel, also founded around the turn of the century by Pennsylvania Quakers and architecturally special enough to be included, later in the century, in the National Register of Historic Places. These Pocono Mountain hotels, both influenced in design and style by traditional Quaker tastes, provided additional transitional work for the company: high-quality, attractive buildings that demanded some, but not too many, of the exotic materials and finishes that might have proved difficult for a firm still a little new to the business of elegantly finished buildings. Again, though, both these Pocono Mountain hotels relied (to different degrees) on the reinforced concrete structural frames that had been a Turner staple for so long.

The Berkeley Carteret Hotel in Asbury Park, New Jersey, built by Turner during 1924 and 1925, changed all that. It was the first of the really grand hotels that Turner would build. An elegant 420-room oceanfront resort, it overlooked the Atlantic Ocean from land that had been granted by the Duke of York 300 years earlier to a couple of favored subjects named Berkeley and Carteret. The Berkeley Carteret was designed for a wealthy clientele, and it would serve that clientele well until only a few years before the United States entered the Second World War, when the hotel was acquired by the government to house British sailors awaiting completion of ships in Jersey shipyards. After the war it would decline in condition and prestige, but what Turner's G. E. Larson built in 1924 and 1925 was a splendid, sprawling, European-style boardwalk hotel featuring a finely detailed masonry exterior and elegantly finished interiors, all built around a fireproof, state-of-the-art, reinforced concrete structural frame.

Oddly enough, the concrete design at the Berkeley Carteret didn't necessarily owe its selection to Turner, as concrete wasn't new to the fashionable seaside resort of Asbury Park in 1924. New Jersey's native son Thomas Edison had twenty years earlier applied his prodigious talent to improving the rotary kiln that Ernest Ransome had patented even before Henry Turner had come to work for him, radically improving the efficiency of the cement-manufacturing process, lowering the cost of the cement itself, and, as a result, encouraging the wider use of reinforced concrete. Edison himself had invested in a local cement-manufacturing company (Edison Cement Company) and urged the use of concrete construction wherever he could, including in Asbury Park, where at least two major structures had been built of reinforced concrete before Turner came along to build the Berkeley Carteret in 1924.

Hotels continued to be an important part of Turner's new focus throughout the 1920s, with very large projects in what was then the fashionable ocean resort of Atlantic City leading the way. The dazzling new Hotel Dennis was the first. The original hotel, started by a hospitable schoolteacher as a two-room cottage seventy-three years earlier, had grown and spread over the years until by 1925 it was ready for replacement, and its owners elected the ultimate in fireproof hotel construction: a nine-story, 500-room oceanfront building with an unobstructed view of the sea, a façade of Indiana limestone, bronze entrances, a 5,000-volume oak-lined library, lavishly appointed interiors, and construction by Turner. But it wasn't just the extraordinarily high level of finish that made the Dennis an important milestone along the new course initiated by Henry Turner's remarks in 1922. This was a building whose frame would be fashioned of structural steel and fireproofed with cinder concrete and masonry. Turner's exclusive identification with reinforced concrete structures was starting to recede.

There were one or two smaller, less extravagant Atlantic City projects during the years that followed, and a fancy one in Miami, but the style of the Dennis was recaptured in 1929 when Turner returned to Atlantic City to build the equally elegant Chalfonte-Haddon Hall to compete with the Dennis (and with many other hotels) for the abundant tourist business that continued unabated in Atlantic City through the 1920s.

There were other such hotels, too, in other locations, including the vast and luxurious twenty-six-story, steel-frame, 814-room Lexington Hotel in New York, which Turner built in 1929. But even those would pale when compared with the landmark hotel that Turner built in Palm Beach for the Flagler interests in 1926, the Breakers.

By December 1925, when the Flagler interests contracted with Turner to build the new Palm Beach Breakers hotel, Turner had acquired a base of experience and a breadth of reputation that were extraordinary for a firm that was only then approaching the twenty-fifth anniversary of its founding. The big industrial construction it had done, especially the New England mills and other large manufacturing plants, had given it solid capability in complex and demanding work, and the huge government jobs of the war years had given it experience in doing exceedingly large work under difficult conditions and on short and unforgiving schedules. The sheer scope of what they had been doing, which by 1925 had returned to an average annual value of a little over $20 million, had attracted and developed an organization that was the envy of the industry. But until the Palm Beach Breakers, Turner had never been called on to produce a building of such extraordinary quality, such elegance, that it would be regarded as one of the finest buildings in the country.

Henry Flagler had been dead for a dozen years when his Florida East Coast Hotels Company engaged Turner for the Breakers job in 1925. Flagler had first turned his attention to Florida almost forty years earlier, just after retiring as a relatively young millionaire from his profitable association with John D. Rockefeller and his Standard Oil Company. By the turn of the century he had established the basis of a new fortune in Florida land, Florida railroads, and Florida hotels. Among many other things, Flagler owned the Royal Poinciana Hotel in Palm Beach, an 1,800-foot-long wooden behemoth that would later become the largest hotel in the world, with rooms for 1,750 guests and with a dining room big enough to accommodate all of them comfortably at one time. The demand for hotel space along the Florida waterfront around 1900 was such that Flagler had added a smaller hotel on the Poinciana's beach, calling it the Palm Beach Inn, but because the guests were inclined to speak of the addition as "the one down by the breakers" it came to be called the Breakers. Before long the quieter, slightly more private Breakers, with its imposing view of the ocean, became the preferred location in Palm Beach, while the Poinciana began to fade.

But fire was still the scourge of hotels in the early part of the century, and in 1903 an uncontrollable one had erupted during construction alterations and burned the Breakers to the ground. Within a year, Flagler had replaced it with a brand new hotel even more richly finished and lavishly decorated than its predecessor and destined to accommodate an even longer and wealthier list of guests that would include various Rockefellers, Vanderbilts, Astors, Morgans, Hearsts, and assorted European nobles and U.S. presidents as well. Some of its guests would arrive by private yacht, to be moored at the hotel's private pier, some by railroad, some by motorcar. Many socialized at the hotel's private casino, some played golf (never without jackets and ties), and some swam in the surf, where hotel personnel enforced rules that ensured properly concealing bathing attire. But like its predecessor, the 1904 Breakers was built of wood, and when another devastating fire broke out in March of 1925, it swept through the building in minutes, destroying it completely but sparing the lives of all its occupants.

Flagler's heirs resolved to replace the second Breakers with "the world's finest resort hotel": an exquisite building, including, in addition to 425 elegant guest rooms, 50 well-furnished suites and servants' quarters for guests who brought along their own staffs. It was all to be ready for the 1926–1927 winter season. The architectural firm of Schultze and Weaver, who had designed New York's Waldorf-Astoria and Pierre Hotels, mandated that the new Breakers must be invulnerable to fire and hurricanes. That meant concrete to Schultze and Weaver, and even in 1925, as far as Schultze and Weaver were concerned, concrete still meant Turner.

Henry C. Turner signed an approximately $7 million contract with the Flagler group in December 1925, agreeing to completion before the end of 1926. Cliff

Wilson, who was at that time based in the new office that the company had established in Atlanta in 1919, brought Turner superintendent L. S. Homer down from the Poconos and sent him to Palm Beach to get it built. Young Chan Turner followed shortly as one of several assistant superintendents, along with Francis (Joe) Warren, a man who would become Chan's close friend and adviser in the years that followed, as another. Homer was later quoted as saying (privately) that he expected to be able to meet the schedule he was given only "if not a day was wasted, if every one of the thousands of items of different materials . . . arrived on time, if there was no shortage of labor, if there was no delay in transportation of materials, and if the weather held fairly good."

Homer's was an array of conditions unlikely to be met in 1926, and few of them were. There was a terrible shortage of skilled labor in Florida, which was experiencing an unprecedented boom in tourism and hotel construction, and Turner had to send its own foremen and other staff from New York and other offices and to undertake an extensive recruiting program throughout the South for skilled mechanics. It built a forty-bed dormitory to accommodate men until they could locate housing, which was scarce and expensive, and they built and operated a mess hall at the site. To attract and hold men, and simply to provide enough working hours for completing the work on schedule, the job was operated seven days a week, two and sometimes three shifts a day, for much of its duration.

Local sand proved acceptable for the concrete, which was mixed in two on-site plants, but coarse aggregates had to be imported from as far away as Alabama and Cuba and shipped to Palm Beach by rail or barge. Much of the other material required for the hotel originated even farther from Palm Beach, and because the work was being done long before the advent of effective long-haul highway transportation systems, most of it had to be delivered by rail. Turner built its own siding, together with a couple of long spurs that reached well into the site. But the same shortage of railcars that had plagued Turner in New York harshly limited the delivery of materials to Palm Beach, so Turner and other contractors working in the area resorted to a barter system in which materials stockpiled but not immediately needed by one contractor could be exchanged with another contractor for materials that were urgently needed. To make things worse, one of Florida's frequent hurricanes struck Palm Beach toward the end of 1926, damaging and requiring replacement of a good deal of work that had already been completed.

To deal with the unrelenting challenge of timely completion, Wilson, Homer, and their staffs devised and operated under a scheduling system that was a little like (but fifty years ahead of) the critical-path scheduling systems that would appear later in the century. Every significant event or important material delivery was tagged with a critical date that couldn't be missed, and selected Turner personnel were assigned to monitor and expedite deliveries to ensure that the dates were met. Subcontractors for the major trades were brought from all over: Howard P. Foley Electrical Company from Washington, D.C., Riggs-Distler Mechanical Company from Baltimore, and a whole contingent of subcontractors from New York, including Otis Elevator Company, Barker Painting Company, New York Roofing Company, DuParquet Kitchen Equipment Company, Hasbrouck Wood Flooring Company, and half a dozen others for the smaller subcontracts.

What was built was the ultimate in what Henry C. Turner had described as finished construction. The hotel was replete with plaster moldings and cornices, exotic wood paneling and cabinetry, elaborate stone and tile work. Turner built a temporary 15,000-square-foot shed on the site that was given over entirely to the preparation of special plaster moldings, wood trim, stone work, and other special fabrication. Many of the grandest spaces required gold-leaf ceilings and other special finishings, and a force of fifty artists was brought from Italy to paint elaborate figured ceilings in some of the large ballrooms and lobbies. The Breakers became an extraordinarily elegant hotel, designed in the style of the Italian Renaissance, beautifully finished and elaborately landscaped, and deserving of Architectural Forum's later description as "one of the country's most magnificent examples of a palatial winter resort hotel."

By December 29, 1926, it was finished, as promised, and the guests (who had to be restrained by special police during the last few days of construction) began to register on the day after New Year's 1927, Henry Turner's ambition that the company establish its credentials as a builder of "finished" structures fully realized.

While the Breakers project was underway, Henry Turner became interested in Florida as a site for a winter retreat, and when the project was winding down he joined the Highland Park Club near Lake Wales. Highland Park was a club that had been organized by a group of Quakers who had built their own cottages and a nine-hole golf course on the club's property, and Henry Turner added a cottage of his own there that would provide a winter respite for the family for years to come.

Turner Construction Company had been doing work out of town for years, managed from offices in Buffalo and, most recently, in Boston and Philadelphia, but with few exceptions its work before the 1920s had been done mostly within a few hundred miles of New York City. That began to change when the Atlanta office was established in 1919 and when an office in Cleveland was activated that same year. The adjustments that were required weren't always easy. Control in policy matters was still rigorously maintained from the head office in New York, but by the 1920s the company had become so large and its work so far-flung that some local delegation of authority in less profound matters was inevitable.

In some ways it was the field superintendents in the remote locations who felt the impact of geographic expansion most acutely. In the new modus operandi, they had to rely on unknown local unions for their skilled labor, and they had to adjust to the loss of some support from the home office. Superintendents who had managed Turner jobs in the past had become accustomed to requisitioning equipment directly from the company's own yard, almost always ensuring timely delivery and good maintenance, not to mention attractive rate schedules, and now they had to find other, closer sources.

Although the usefulness of Turner's equipment yard did shrink a little with the advent of remote offices, the preponderance of work was still in the Northeast, so it remained an important element in the system. In the very early days, Turner had maintained a small equipment yard in Jersey City, but by 1905 that had been replaced by a larger and more conveniently located one on Steuben Street in Brooklyn. Four years later, a still-larger property had been acquired on Hewes Street in Brooklyn, where stables and shops were built, but the vast amount of equipment required for the big work done during the war years soon made even the new Brooklyn yard inadequate, and in 1920 Turner acquired a large property in Maspeth, Queens, where it built an approximately 40,000 square foot complex of storage buildings and maintenance shops and its own concrete testing laboratory. Years later, as the amount and size of the equipment grew, even the Maspeth facility would be replaced by Turner's big yard in New Jersey.

Turner's trim shop, where the company produced its own doors and wood trim during the early years, had always been a well-regarded convenience, and it managed to survive the expansion mainly because shipping its products to remote locations had proportionately little impact on their cost. The trim shop had been started in 1913, when most independent trim shops were nonunion and Turner, loyal to its own unions and therefore unwilling to buy from nonunion vendors, elected to establish its own shop in Brooklyn, using union labor.

Henry Turner's 1922 decision to alter the company's course may well have been even more significant than he had anticipated. Between 1922 and 1929, the value of the company's annual volume of work increased by a factor of almost four. Its profitability remained consistently good — higher on the relatively small fraction of work that was still being done on a lump-sum basis than on the work that was being done on a fee basis — and its net worth, even after payment of dividends and generous additional compensation allowances to its employees, had increased by 130 percent. The shift to finished buildings had altered the balance between the management-intensive work the company did with its own forces and the work it subcontracted, enabling it to enlarge its volume without a linearly proportionate increase in its own staff, and the impact on its earnings was uniformly good.

Not all this broad array of new work qualified as the finished construction that Henry Turner is likely to have been picturing in the change of course he had proposed back in 1922, although by the end of the twenties almost half the company's work would in fact pass such a test. Just as the proliferation of hotels appeared to reflect the country's newly developed attention to leisure, a spate of new sports stadiums for its colleges revealed another aspect of the same cultural shift. College football was beginning to compete with baseball for the public's attention, and fans all over the country, regardless of where or whether they'd ever been to college, wanted all they could get of it. Turner had started early with a difficult stadium job for Harvard back in 1910, when it had added a concrete colonnade to the top of Harvard's seven-year-old stadium and increased its capacity by about 10,000 seats. Now the University of Pennsylvania engaged Turner to tear down the wooden stadium the college had built at Franklin Field in 1895, as a site for the first Penn Relays, and to replace it with a modern concrete stadium that would more than double spectator capacity. There was the usual catch on the Penn job: Construction couldn't start until the first of May 1922, and the stadium had to be ready in time for football season, which started late in September. Philadelphia's Pennsylvania Gazette worried in an editorial that few engineers thought such a schedule could be met, but Turner's still-young Philadelphia office took on the job. They didn't quite make it for the first game, but they didn't miss by much. With a force that almost continuously exceeded 400 men, they worked six twelve-hour days every week for almost six months, demolishing the existing stadium, forming and placing more than 10,000 cubic yards of concrete, and covering the new stadium's exterior face with almost 2 million brick. They managed to achieve substantial completion in time to seat 26,000 spectators for the second game of the season, when Penn played Navy and Pres. Warren G. Harding dedicated the new stadium between the halves. By Thanksgiving Day everything was finished, and more than 50,000 spectators streamed into the new stadium to see Penn beat its traditional rival, Cornell, by a single touchdown scored in the closing seconds of play.

Even when the season ended, Turner hadn't seen the last of Franklin Field. The stadium's complex, caisson-supported foundations had been designed to accommodate subsequent double-decking of the stands, and three years after the first job was finished Turner returned for a second one, adding another tier of seats and increasing the stadium's seating capacity to more than 77,000. Altogether, the work was done at a total (combined) cost to the University of Pennsylvania of about $1,250,000.

Other stadiums followed, at least two of them designed by Gavin Hadden, who had done the structural engineering on Franklin Field. Cornell, whose engineering alumni were well distributed in the Turner Company, came along next with its Schoelkopf Stadium in 1924, a handsome, 13,000-seat concrete crescent topped by a graceful arcade. Brown University was next with its amphitheater, a year later, and when Turner was finished Brown found it necessary to stage separate ceremonies on succeeding autumn Saturdays to accommodate the crowds that came to the dedication. In 1925 the City of Philadelphia, won over to Turner by the speed, quality, and low cost of what it had done at Franklin Field, engaged the company to build its 73,000-seat Municipal Stadium, with the understanding that C. H. Guenst, who had run the Franklin Field job for Turner, would be in charge. Guenst was a popular and admired Turner superintendent who had risen through the trades and whose brother and son would distinguish themselves as Turner foremen, so the owner's condition was an easy one for the company to meet. The stadium would be erected as part of Philadelphia's sesquicentennial celebration, and before it was finished the city would engage Turner to build a big open-air stage as well as dressing rooms for the stage on the stadium grounds, and then to build the huge Sesquicentennial Auditorium and Convention Hall and an elegant new fine arts building on the site.

Perhaps the most outstanding of the stadiums that Turner built during the 1920s was the University of Pittsburgh's, a spectacular structure for its time, designed to accommodate, in addition to football, nearly all the university's non-aquatic sports. Pitt Stadium, which cost about $2 million, provided seating for 70,000 spectators and was designed for expansion to 100,000. Turner's John Pearson was superintendent, and he brought the job to completion in about a year, just in time for Pitt's 1925 football season.

The stadium work clearly didn't fit comfortably into Henry Turner's call for more attention to "finished" buildings, but it certainly wasn't a factory or a warehouse either. And it dramatized the company's new diversity, representing an expanded interpretation of Henry Turner's 1922 view that the company needed to break out of a pattern that had been limiting it to industrial construction. There's some evidence that a similar diversification, a drift into heavy construction, might have reflected a personal preference of Cliff Wilson. Like most civil engineers who had studied at the major universities during the early part of the century, Wilson had been educated on a curriculum of bridges, dams, and tunnels, not buildings, and in fact before he came to work for Henry Turner he had worked entirely on such heavy construction.

As early as 1919, when Wilson first headed up the expansion that took Turner deep into the South, he took on a big heavy-construction contract at Standard Oil's Humble Oil Company at their Baytown, Texas, refinery. That contract included special structures for their stills, condensers, tanks, and the like, as well as a new powerhouse and staff housing. The following year, Wilson took a Turner crew to Cuba, where they joined Raymond Concrete Pile Company for another job that could be more reliably classified as heavy construction than as building construction: a new deepwater pier and headhouse for the Havana Docks Company. It was complex marine work requiring 20,000 cubic yards of concrete that had to be formed and placed in and above a deepwater harbor. F. E. Schilling, a future Turner director who had been with the company almost since his graduation from Dartmouth in 1908 and who had earlier managed the Humble Oil job for Wilson, became superintendent at Havana, and R. A. McMenimen, a future president of Raymond Concrete Pile Company, was field engineer for Raymond.

What was probably Wilson's most spectacular foray into heavy construction started in 1927, when Turner took on a contract to do the James River Bridge project, a system of roads and bridges valued at more than $5 million in 1927 and designed to shorten the coastal highway route between Norfolk and Newport News in Virginia. It was a demanding and difficult piece of heavy construction, involving almost eleven miles of approach highway and three pile-supported bridges, one of which combined almost four miles of reinforced concrete trestle construction with steel-truss construction and included a 300-foot-long lift section that rose 100 feet above high water. Unlike most similar heavy construction in later years, the James River Bridge project was a privately sponsored venture in which the financing syndicate, in anticipation of estimated toll revenues, sold enough bonds to fund the construction, and the syndicate (headed by Paine Webber) engaged Turner at the time of the first site studies to guide the selection of systems and to do the construction. The James River Bridge job, which was finished by the end of 1928, proved profitable for Turner, but subsequent markets changed and heavy construction didn't prove to be an attractive direction for the company, which had from its earliest years seen the construction of buildings as its principal work. In fact, the whole range of work in the Southern District had begun to decline toward the end of the 1920s and by the time the James River Bridge job was finished, late in 1928, the Atlanta office was closed and Wilson, by then a vice president, returned to New York.

The history of Turner's branch offices during these early years is a mixed one, suggesting a sometimes experimental approach. The company had done very little work in the Midwest before 1924, when it opened an office in Chicago, and the evidence suggests that although the Chicago office lasted into the depression years it wasn't as successful as the eastern offices during its earliest years. Turner contracts in the South were showing some growth before the company opened its Atlanta office in 1919, but even that office lasted only nine years and was closed when conditions in the rest of the country were still good. Cleveland, also established in 1919, didn't do nearly as well as Atlanta, closing after its first year, and Pittsburgh, also opened in 1919, closed after only six months. But the branches that survived their first few years — Philadelphia, Boston, and Buffalo — did well in the twenties, growing at about the same exuberant rate as New York.

New York, Philadelphia, and Atlanta had pretty much been leading the company in the construction of finished buildings during the early twenties, but Boston got its chance for some of that business in 1925 when a few of the big insurance companies decided that the time had come to build the kind of glorious home office buildings that are likely to communicate a sense of permanence and integrity to their current and potential policyholders.

The life insurance companies that were getting ready to spend big sums on construction in the mid-1920s had experienced some good years before the war, but their business had really surged after it ended, and a variety of reasons have since been suggested for the postwar popularity of life insurance. One theory holds that families who had been introduced to the concept of life insurance during the war, when they or their sons had been insured by the government, liked the idea and later bought their own policies. Another idea holds that it was the disastrous influenza epidemic of 1918, which killed more than a million Americans, that dramatized for many families the usefulness of insuring the family's means of support. And there's considerable support for an idea that the most significant factor in the increased popularity of life insurance in the early 1920s was the population shift toward the cities and away from rural areas and farms where extended families and big old houses had traditionally provided their own version of security for the survivors of a lost breadwinner.

Whatever the reasons, there was apparently plenty of money available for such construction around the middle of the 1920s, and Turner was selected to build splendid new home office buildings for three of the big insurance companies. One was in Springfield, Massachusetts, for the Massachusetts Mutual Life Insurance Company and two were in Philadelphia: one for Fidelity Mutual and the other for Provident Mutual. Turner's Boston office was selected from among eleven candidates (including New York's Fuller and Boston's Stone & Webster) to build the biggest and most glorious of the three: the one for Mass Mutual in Springfield.

Something Henry C. Turner remembered later about an early conversation with Mass Mutual's president, William McClench, went to the heart of Turner's transition to the construction of finished buildings. McClench, Turner remembered, took pains to remind him that he had not insisted that his new building be built fast. That was a disclaimer unlikely to have been heard from any of Turner's industrial customers, virtually all of whom wanted their buildings as soon as possible and some of whom probably saw speed as one of Turner's principal products. But what McClench wanted more than anything was high quality. He wanted a first-class building, elegant and sound, and he apparently wasn't ready to risk the possibility that his priorities might be misunderstood.

Henry Turner accepted McClench's specification without comment, but there's no evidence that he ever mentioned it to anyone before the job was finished. In fact, the entire 427,000-square-foot, elaborately finished corporate office

building that Turner built for Mass Mutual, together with a couple of service buildings and the landscaping of a twenty-seven-acre site, were all finished in less than
two years. Of course, it was a time before air conditioning and before most of the
sophisticated systems that make later buildings cost more and take longer to build,
so such a short construction duration for so large a project was less striking than it
would have been in a later time. But progress on the work had clearly been very
good, and McClench was agreeably surprised by it. When the work was finished, he
made no secret of his gratitude to Turner for the combination of speed and quality that had characterized it, writing to him personally to acknowledge his "deep
appreciation for the energy and diligence" with which the work had been prosecuted and of the "great satisfaction" that he and his associates felt about the work.

Like the Breakers job that the company was doing at the same time in Florida,
the Mass Mutual project left no doubt that Turner had made the change signaled
by Henry Turner in 1922. Mass Mutual was another steel-framed corporate office
building, like hundreds that Turner would build during the years that followed,
served by the latest in elevators, by heating and ventilating systems that were auto-
matically controlled, and by a modern system of underfloor electrical ducts. The
building's exterior was a combination of face brick and stone, with entrance doors
and trim made of bronze. Many of the important interior spaces were finished in
marble, and there were marble-faced fireplaces and carefully matched wood panels in the executive offices, a luxurious auditorium that seated 900 and a well-
equipped cafeteria that seated 600.

Albert Larson, who had started with Turner during the company's first year
and had come out to Springfield from Brooklyn, where he had just finished construction of the grand new James Madison High School for Turner, was superintendent for most of the work done on the Mass Mutual job. Always nattily dressed
in the suit and tie that were standard working attire for Turner superintendents in
those days, Larson had as his field engineer young Ab Abberley, himself ten years
along in a career that had included the Sanford Mills jobs and that would eventually place him on the Turner board. The work apparently went smoothly under
their direction and was perhaps most notable for a successful materials-handling

experiment described in an article published later by Abberley. Instead of building four separate material hoists to serve the large plan area, they built one oversized tower with an elevator big enough and strong enough to accommodate the small Ford dump trucks that were popular during the 1920s. Then they elevated fully loaded trucks and drove them across the completed floors to deliver materials to designated locations, a precursor to the motorized buggy system that would come along later in the century.

Like the hotels and the stadiums, the insurance company buildings seemed to come in bunches. While Turner Boston was doing a headquarters building for Mass Mutual in Springfield, Turner Philadelphia was erecting smaller but similar buildings for Fidelity Mutual and Provident Mutual. Both those buildings were designed and built in the same grand style as the Springfield building, but the Provident Mutual building, designed by Cram and Ferguson, was especially elegant. Clad entirely in limestone, some of its detailing was reminiscent of work on the Cathedral of St. John the Divine in New York, which the same architects had designed a few years earlier. And the location of the Provident building, slightly removed from the immediate center of Philadelphia commerce, reflected a humanism that characterized the style of Provident's Quaker management: They had plotted graphically the residences of all their Philadelphia employees and then, having identified their geographic center, had selected the available downtown site that was closest to it.

By 1927, when the company reached the twenty-fifth anniversary of its founding, it had become so big that a single annual dinner in New York didn't seem a practical idea any more. In its place, separate annual dinners were held in each region to celebrate the milestone. At New York's Hotel Biltmore, Navy Capt. A. L. Parsons, who had been in charge of the work Turner had done for the navy during World War I (and who would later become an admiral), told the dinner guests what a unique privilege he felt working with Turner had been for him and what an extraordinary company he thought Turner was. Similar dinners, attended by members of the company's senior staff and by Henry C. Turner, were held within a few days of the New York affair in Philadelphia, Boston, Buffalo, and Chicago.

By the time the end of the decade came into view, the broadening that had started in 1922 was a fait accompli, with Turner having extended and demonstrated its competency in substantial ways in almost every sector of construction. In 1928, it started the multiphased construction of a spectacular new department store in the heart of New York City for the Bloomingdale Brothers, for whom Turner had earlier built a 500,000-square-foot warehousing and manufacturing building in which Bloomingdale's made its own pianos and mattresses and tested in its own laboratories the products it sold in its store. A year later Turner began a similar three-phase, three-year process of renovating and expanding the Philadelphia department store of Strawbridge & Clothier, the respected Quaker merchants who had started their business there sixty years earlier. By the end of the 1920s Turner had built theaters; schools that included the Brearley School in New York and The Masters School in suburban Dobbs Ferry; and luxury cooperative housing in New York, Boston, and Chicago. The days of Turner's being thought of as simply a builder of big concrete industrial buildings were clearly over.

But this vast new volume of finished work certainly didn't eliminate or even substantially reduce the amount of industrial work the company was doing; it simply supplemented it, broadening the company's base and increasing its total volume of work. During the waning years of the decade more than half Turner's work continued to be industrial, and it included U.S. Gypsum's new plant in East Chicago, Indiana (the largest such plant in the world), Western Electric's Hawthorne Works in Illinois, and the vast manufacturing plant in Hartford where Pratt & Whitney would only a few years later be developing the aircraft engines it would produce during World War II. Turner's work volume was by this time increasing at an average annual rate of about 22 percent, and during the single year of 1929 it reached $44 million, exceeding by $8 million the largest amount of work the company had ever done in a single year.

Twenty-seven years after the company's founding, it had prospered by every measure. Its reputation was extraordinarily fine and its executive management was broad and deep, averaging twenty-three years of service with Turner. One hundred ninety-nine of its senior employees were college-educated (the largest number coming from Cornell, followed by Rensselaer Polytechnic, Swarthmore, Harvard, Dartmouth, and the Massachusetts Institute of Technology), an extraordinary number for 1929. Of a little more than 1,200 contracts on which the company had performed since its first year, almost 500 had come from firms that had previously awarded Turner at least four other contracts, and fifteen of those firms had previously awarded Turner at least twelve contracts.

The company wasn't the only beneficiary of all this prosperity. When Henry Turner reorganized its financial base in 1922, and modified it again in 1925, he did so under a plan in which the common shares would be owned (and would be available for purchase) by only those persons who were currently active in the company, leaving its 7 percent cumulative, nonparticipating preferred shares for the inactive investors. Under such a plan he had deliberately ensured that all the company's financial growth, after distribution of dividends and funds authorized under the Additional Compensation Plan, would accrue exclusively to persons who were actively engaged in the company's work. There was an understanding that such common shares would be repurchased by the company if or when their holders left the company or died, and although that provision was never formalized it was apparently always implemented as a matter of course. By the end of the 1920s, an employee who had purchased and held a share of Turner's common stock for five dollars in 1922 owned a share worth about $250.

Henry Turner's leadership had clearly been exemplary, as measured by the state of the company at the end of the decade, but his sense of what lay immediately ahead for Turner and for the country would prove to be flawed. It was probably almost impossible not to expect that all this prudent management and good work would continue to reap the same rewards, that the good times would continue and even improve. When Henry Turner sized things up not long before the end of the decade, he saw only better days ahead, giving as the basis for such optimism his own entirely reasonable perception that "there is fine leadership . . . in Washington, radicalism is on the decline, agricultural conditions have improved, . . . the railroads have recovered, world conditions have improved and money is plentiful and cheap."

Almost no one in those early days of 1929 could imagine that by the end of the year a combination of forces so complex that they are still not well understood would produce an economic collapse and a subsequent depression so profound that sixteen years would elapse and another war would be fought before meaningful recovery would be seen.

6.

Depression

T he financial collapse that left Wall Street in ruins at the end of 1929 was followed with stunning swiftness by a depression that swept across the industrialized countries of the world like a tidal wave. In the United States it didn't take long to destroy or seriously threaten the economic well-being of almost all but the wealthiest of the country's population and to wreak unprecedented havoc on its economic infrastructure, inducing enduring changes in the popular view of the responsibilities of government. By 1933, only three years after the depression had taken root, the country's gross national product had fallen by almost half, more than 10,000 of its banks had closed their doors, and a quarter of its workforce, almost 13 million people, were unemployed, compared with only a little over 1 million who had been unemployed in 1929. Construction workers, like almost all workers, had seen their wages drastically reduced, their average annual income down to $869, about half what it had been only a few years earlier.

At first, the depression didn't really have a profound effect on Turner, which by 1930 had become the sixth-largest building firm in the country, behind New York's George A. Fuller Company, Mark Eidlitz, and James A. Stewart; Philadelphia's United Engineers; and Pittsburgh's Mellon Stuart. Having just completed the biggest year in its history in 1929, Turner was by any measure a substantial and prospering firm, and when the bad days began it was in the enviable position of still having almost $15 million worth of work on its books, enough (when added to whatever new work it was still able to secure while things were grinding down) to produce some good earnings in 1930. With all that work on hand, a net worth exceeding $4.5 million, and plenty of cash in the bank, Turner was clearly better positioned than most companies to weather lean times, and the disaster that was bringing the country to its knees would take a little longer to be felt at Turner than it would take at most other places.

But as the early months of 1930 passed, the company's management needed no reminder that most of the work on hand was going to run out by the end of the year and that they would soon be competing for new work in a marketplace that was markedly different from the one in which they had been prospering. Only a few months into the year, financing for new jobs dried up, even well-advanced designs were shelved, and competition for what little new work there was fiercely intensified. New conditions militated for new strategies.

One of the best and most unexpected sources of new business for Turner during these earliest days of the depression proved to be the public sector. Turner had not many years earlier done well with negotiated contracts for public work, of course, but those had been negotiated directly with public agencies and had normally been implemented on a low-risk, cost-plus-fee basis. Competing with a large number of sometimes desperate and frequently less-qualified contractors for large, fixed-price jobs was something else again. Even during good times such work was normally so fraught with destructive competition that Turner had for the most part avoided it, and in bad times, when there was virtually no limit to what a desperate contractor struggling to survive might do to become the low bidder, it was much worse. But as it turned out, Turner was able to penetrate and compete in that perilous sector with surprising success.

The first of the big public successes was Pilgrim State Hospital on Long Island, and there were essentially two factors that made it such a good job for Turner: its timing and its great size. Although it was in every way a depression-era project, with construction starting in March of 1930 and finishing early in 1933, bids for Pilgrim State were taken when times were still good and when contractors (like almost everyone else) thought they'd stay that way forever. There had still been enough construction contracts around in late 1929 to keep the number of bidders competing for a single job down to a reasonable level, and the extremely large size of the Pilgrim State job was enough to limit the number of bidders even further. At about $11 million, Pilgrim State was at that time the biggest construction contract ever awarded by the State of New York, and its great size had the effect of limiting the number of contractors able to bid to those whose financial strength and experience compared well with Turner's. With most of the scalawags effectively screened out of the competition by the size and cost of the work, Pilgrim State was probably among the last of the good jobs of the 1920s, and Turner was skilled enough and lucky enough to land it.

What was to be built was a big, sprawling hospital that became an exercise in construction logistics, near what was then the small town of Brentwood, Long Island, far enough from any of what would later become Long Island's commercial centers that it would be necessary to build a construction camp that included a commissary and living quarters on the site. Most of the twenty-two buildings in Turner's contract were reinforced concrete and masonry structures that were big enough to consume, in the aggregate, more than 20,000 cubic yards of concrete and more than 20 million brick, and they were spread out over a site so large that management of their construction required eight separate field organizations, each with its own superintendent, foremen, engineers, and clerical staff. It was a big job, productively employing (at different times) key Turner field men like D. C Andrews, Olaf Johnson, R. V. McKee, Howard (Dutch) Schroedel, George McDonald, F. E. Conkling, and Austin Fahey, all valued superintendents or foremen whom it might otherwise have been difficult for the company to retain as the depression deepened during the three years it took to complete the work at Pilgrim State.

Turner probably owed a second large depression-era public contract as much to its financial strength and reputation as to its skills as a builder. In 1929, the newly organized Department of Sanitation of the City of New York had decided to address the increasing pollution of the East River by building a 180-million-gallon-per-day sewage treatment plant on Ward's Island, the biggest such plant in the city's history and large enough to process almost 20 percent of the sewage produced in what by then had become a city of almost 6 million people. By 1930, $30 million had been appropriated for its engineering, construction, and equipment, an amount that included almost $5 million for general construction work on the first stage of the new plant itself, and by early 1930 design work was proceeding apace. By late in 1930, when documents for construction of the first phase of the plant work were ready for bidding, new construction projects in New York had become so scarce that almost every area contractor who thought he could meet the bonding requirements for the Ward's Island job (and a few who must have known they couldn't) were ready and eager to pick up the drawings and prepare bids.

Turner was one of the horde of potential bidders that descended on the Ward's Island competition. The company had no illusions about its chances for winning such a fiercely competitive project, but there were still a great many mouths to feed at Turner in 1930 and painfully few new jobs on the horizon, so even as competitive a job as the concrete-intensive Ward's Island project seemed worth a try. By February 1931, more than half the original bidders had been sufficiently discouraged or intimidated by the job to quit, but eighteen of the toughest remained in the hunt. When bids were opened in March a Brooklyn contractor named William Gahagan, whose price was an unsettling 15 percent lower than the second bidder's price, was the low bidder at about $4 million, leaving Turner's estimators disappointed but not very surprised to learn that they weren't even close.

But all wasn't lost. Gahagan's very low bid probably worried him plenty but it worried the city, for whom timely and workmanlike completion was critical, even more. The city's commissioners gave Gahagan's submission of qualifications more than a routine review, focusing on the equipment he proposed to use for the job and on a few uncertainties in the language of the performance bond he had proposed. They dispatched a team of engineers to jobs on which he was working at the time to verify the condition and availability of his equipment, and on April 7, 1931, convinced that it was satisfactory, they voted to accept his proposal with the provision that he work out language that would allay their lingering concerns about his performance bond. It was Gahagan's reaction to the City's misgivings about his bond that opened the door for Turner.

Bill Gahagan's bonding company, itself wary of his very low bid, wanted to see him do something to reduce his level of risk on such a large and labor-intensive job before it would give any ground on the bonding terms, and together with Gahagan they searched for a way to comply. He was a well-regarded and experienced heavy-construction contractor, and a resourceful one too, and he focused on the concrete work. Gahagan's principal experience and interest had been in the heavy work, e.g., the earth moving, the big underground piping, and the rigging of heavy equipment, so he began by seeking a reduction in his direct exposure to risk by trying to subcontract the concrete work, in which he was less experienced, to some responsible and capable firm. Because the job had originally been publicly bid in the unit-price format that's customary in such work, each competing proposal had included a fully exposed tabulation of the bidder's unit prices which, when multiplied by owner-furnished quantities and added together, had produced the totals that were compared to identify the low bidder.

Gahagan therefore had full access to Turner's estimates for the concrete component of the job and after studying them, he was optimistic that he might be able to work out a subcontract for the concrete work with Turner. On May 15 he successfully petitioned the Sanitation Commission for a couple of additional weeks to allow time for working things out, and the two contractors used the time to develop a subcontract that provided for Turner's doing all Gahagan's concrete work at Turner's own price. Under the terms of the subcontract, Turner would share responsibility for managing the entire project in the field, too, and the two firms would share equally in whatever profits might be generated beyond those produced by the concrete work. The bonding company liked the plan and on May 25 the city granted Gahagan authorization to proceed, with Turner as his subcontractor.

Not unexpectedly, the Ward's Island job proved to be a challenging piece of work. In addition to the extensive preparatory dewatering and earthwork that Gahagan had to do (including the removal and disposal of 72,000 cubic yards of rock), the job required placing over 100,000 cubic yards of concrete, much of it in difficult, formwork-intensive, thin-shelled tank walls and almost all of it to be completed between the late fall of 1931 and the early fall of 1932. That meant an average daily production of almost 800 cubic yards, an exceedingly difficult task on a job in which a conservative design limited the size of concrete pours to what could be placed between expansion joints not farther apart than forty feet. It was a distribution problem that argued for an overhead cable system, but because the actual work area would cover virtually all the island's thirty acres, there was no room for the tower network that an effective cable system would have required.

Cliff Wilson, who had some good experience in such heavy construction, took over as project executive for Turner, with G. F. Floyd as his field superintendent, and they designed and installed an elaborate system of belt conveyors that distributed concrete, forms, and reinforcing steel just above ground level, often to as many as twenty concreting locations simultaneously. Materials and equipment all originated on the mainland, of course, and everything had to be delivered to the island by water, across a heavily traveled channel that was part of New York's busy harbor. Turner's concrete batch plant on the island's beach was fed from barges anchored offshore, but the rate at which concrete was demanded by the workforce was so great that a bargeload of aggregate lasted only about an hour before it had to be replaced, and a bargeload of cement was good for only a little longer. Much depended on smooth materials handling, good seamanship, and good weather, and by the end of 1932 Turner's part of the work was beginning to wind down, ahead of schedule and profitably. Continually deteriorating economic conditions during the period of construction had actually improved the job for Turner. Material costs and even union wages had shrunk while productivity had risen in a setting in which workmen saw themselves as lucky to have jobs. Turner and Gahagan worked together smoothly and effectively on the job, and for several years after its completion in 1933 they continued to bid on similar work as joint venturers, though none of their bidding panned out.

These weren't the only public projects that began to appear among the new jobs that Turner was lining up during the early days of the depression, as the backlog that had been brought forward from 1929 began to dwindle. The huge Inland

Freight Terminal that the Port of New York Authority (later the Port Authority of New York and New Jersey) wanted to build on the Lower West Side of Manhattan between Fifteenth and Sixteenth Streets was another. The port authority was responsible for virtually all the incoming and outgoing transportation systems of the port, including its bridges and tunnels and the millions of tons of freight that entered and left the city every day. It operated under rules that were a little different from those that governed most of the traditional City agencies, and it was sometimes able (within limits) to restrict its bidders on selected projects to those it considered to be properly qualified contractors. When the port authority invited bids for excavation and foundation work for its new terminal, it invited seven of the best-established foundation contractors in New York to bid, including, among others, such well-regarded firms as Raymond Concrete Pile Company and Spencer, White & Prentis, two firms that would later become frequent co-venturers with Turner on other work. One of the other bidders was Godwin Construction Company, whose bid (an unsettling 20 percent lower than the bid of its nearest competitor) would be the lowest submitted. Godwin's bid must have worried its principals, because although they were prepared to go ahead with doing the excavation and piling work with their own forces, they sought (as Gahagan had sought before them) the security of subcontracting the concrete work to Turner. That subcontract, at $185,000, was priced so low by Turner that it included neither a fee nor a contingency allowance, but it had the virtue of placing Turner on the site and was probably seen as providing a modest advantage when, a few months later, Turner would compete with nine other selected contractors for the much larger contract to build the superstructure itself.

By the middle of 1931, when selected general contractors were invited to bid for the big Inland Freight Terminal superstructure, even Turner had begun to feel the pressure of the depression. The year had started with a small backlog that was only a fraction of what 1930 had started with, and new work was as scarce and cheap as unemployed workmen were plentiful. Wages for hourly employees in the building trades had fallen by an average of 25 percent, and even skilled mechanics who were lucky enough to find jobs were working for well under two dollars an hour. The painful process of having to lay off salaried men for whom there simply wasn't enough work had begun, and the company for the first time found it necessary to establish a policy of severance pay for such employees. The policy adopted was based on years of service, with recent employees receiving half a month's pay when laid off and the longest-term employees receiving six months' pay. Arthur Tozzer had issued an internal memorandum requiring that even with the new schedule he had to be personally consulted in each case before such decisions were made final. In some cases the company was still reluctant to lay off salaried field men, even when there wasn't work for them, so a supplementary policy was established in which selected field men would be retained for up to four months, at 60 percent of their regular salary, in the hope that something might open up. Management salaries had been uniformly reduced by at least 10 percent.

In such a setting Turner, one of the contractors selected to bid on the big Inland Freight Terminal contract, was a formidable contender. It succeeded in taking the approximately $8 million job with a bid that included only the leanest of estimated costs and a spare 2 percent allowance for both its overhead and a profit. At 2.5 million square feet, the terminal was a massive building that occupied an entire city block and comprised about two parts reinforced concrete construction and about one part structural steel construction. Its sixteen very high floors generated a volume so huge that it was exceeded only by the volume of Chicago's Merchandise Mart, the country's biggest building, and its great size in the very heart of town exacerbated the usual logistical problems of materials handling and access on big urban sites. The port authority was serious about wanting its new terminal finished on time, so it wrote a paragraph into Turner's contract that provided for a penalty of $3,000 for every day by which completion was late, a great deal of money in 1931.

But no penalty was ever collected. An irony of those troubled times was that there were many more well-qualified workers available than there had ever been, and virtually every mechanic was working harder and faster than he had ever worked before. There was little wonder that jobs like this one were being finished in record time.

While these big public jobs were important to Turner during the early years of the depression, they were far from the whole story. In addition to the public contracts that the company managed to secure, it had entered the 1930s with a fair amount of big private construction still on its books, much of it work that had been planned and designed during the good days of the late 1920s and that had benefited from the momentum that large projects often accumulate, especially where money has already been raised or appropriated. Ford's new assembly plant in New Jersey was typical. A million square feet of manufacturing and support space along the waterfront at Edgewater, it was Henry Ford's defiant response to all the bad news that seemed to foretell worse times ahead. In 1930 Ford was still selling over a million cars a year and paying even the least skilled of its workers a substantial seven dollars a day when Ford selected Turner to build its big new plant at Edgewater (Turner's fifth job for Ford), together with its boiler house, a highway overpass, and a big concrete dock that extended into the river. But by the time the job approached completion, even Ford was cutting back production, laying off workers and probably regretting the big investment it had made.

Pratt & Whitney's new aircraft plant in East Hartford, Connecticut, was another of the big industrial jobs that had been planned and designed during the good days of the twenties and that Turner built during the rapidly worsening days of the early thirties. A huge, modern plant designed by Albert Kahn, who had also designed Ford's Edgewater plant and many of Detroit's other automobile plants, it included over 400,000 square feet of manufacturing space and vast research facilities that would become critical to the country's defense system less than a decade later.

There was still a certain amount of big institutional work around, too, at the beginning of the depression years, projects that had been conceived and funded during better times that became part of the backlog that would help to sustain Turner during the first year or so of the bad times. In Delaware, there was an elegant array of Tudor-style buildings for the new St. Andrew's School, an exclusive boarding school run by the Episcopal Church School Foundation and funded largely by the essentially depression-proof DuPont family of Wilmington. In upstate New York, Turner built a large and expensive new dormitory for St. Lawrence University, a traditional college building elegantly clad in local stone, but as an indication of rising uncertainties about the days to come Turner (successfully) insisted on having the personal guarantee of the university's board chairman, Owen D. Young, who was also chairman of General Electric's board, before he would sign the contract. And there were several other well-endowed college buildings in those early years of the depression, too, including a physics laboratory for Harvard, as well as a continuing but shrinking volume of industrial work that included major plants for Western Electric and U.S. Rubber Company. In the first full year of the depression Turner was able to complete a surprising seventy projects, almost $26 million worth of work, but it would be a long time before the company would build anything like that volume of work in a single year again.

The precipitous decline in work volume really began for Turner toward the very end of 1930, worsened markedly during 1931 and 1932, and by the beginning of 1933 had made it clear to everyone in the company's Madison Avenue offices that things were going to get a lot worse before they would begin to get better. Two-thirds of the country's banks had closed their doors by then, and unemployment had increased by more than a thousand percent since 1930. The gross national product that before 1930 had been rising at about 3 1/2 percent annually was now falling at an annual rate of 10 percent, and annual production of automobiles, a new and useful indicator of industrial activity, had already fallen from 5 million cars to about 1.5 million. Closer to home, new nonresidential, nonfarm construction (the kind of work that was really at the core of Turner's capability) had represented $3 billion worth of construction in 1929 but had shrunk to an almost unthinkable $350 million in 1933. In Washington, where the inauguration of the newly elected president, Franklin Roosevelt, was awaited with sometimes unrealistic hope, 20,000 men had camped out near the Capitol in an unsuccessful effort to induce Congress to grant them a bonus for their service in the war. Businessmen and institutional leaders who could normally have been expected to look to Turner for construction of new plants or other buildings were running scared, unable to find justification for building anything at all, and a good many normally

Henry Chandlee Turner,
born in 1871, founded
Turner in 1902 and was
its vigorous chief executive
until he ceded its presidency
to his youngest brother in
1941. Chairman until
1947, he died in 1954.

DeForest H. Dixon had worked closely with Henry Turner before the company was founded, became a minor shareholder and Turner's first general superintendent, retired in 1930 and died in 1956.

Walter K. Shaw started with Turner in 1913, served as vice-president, treasurer and director, retired in 1953. He was the father of Walter B. Shaw, who would later become president and chairman.

Left: Cooper shop for J. B. King & Company, Staten Island, New York, 1902. Turner's contract #1, the first of 26 with King.

Right: An elaborate load test required in 1904 to convince New York authorities that a concrete structure would be safe.

Left: Forms for an early, Turner-built staircase to serve the new subway system, New York, 1903.

*Factory for the Robert Gair
Company, Brooklyn, New
York, 1904. It was at the
time the largest concrete
building in the country.*

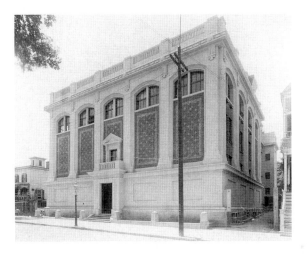

During its first ten years, Turner found itself doing construction for some of the country's most distinguished industrial firms. Shown at upper left is a plant in New Jersey for Keuffel & Esser Company, the eminent producer of slide rules and similar devices; at upper right is a plant for optical equipment manufacturer Bausch and Lomb; at left is a laboratory for pioneer film producer Biograph Company. In Connecticut it built a factory for Seth Thomas Clock Company (lower left), which had been manufacturing clocks since 1813.

Phelps Publishing Company, Springfield, Massachusetts, 1908, Turner's first out-of-town job. Top photograph shows the cleared site, middle photograph shows the work in progress, and bottom photograph shows the completed building.

Shown is the first of many projects built by Turner for General Electric Company. This one, built in 1913, was in Pittsfield, Massachusetts.

Naumkeag Steam Cotton Mills, Salem, Massachusetts, 1916. Shown are conditions when construction was about half finished (top), when it was farther along (middle) and finally when occupancy was begun, about 14 months after work had started.

*Navy and War Office
Building in Washington,
D.C., started during the
final months of WWI, was
the largest office building in
the world when it was
completed in 1919.*

Western Electric Company's New York headquarters, 1920. At 395 Hudson Street, it was virtually adjacent to the site of Turner's own later headquarters. Shown here: the site before and after demolition (top and middle) and finished building (bottom).

Three boardwalk hotels built by Turner in Atlantic City during 1924: the Dennis (top), the Berkeley-Carteret (middle) and the Haddon Hall (bottom).

The elegant Breakers Hotel, Palm Beach, Florida, built by Turner in 1926, was by many accounts the country's finest hotel. Its exterior is shown in the top photograph at the left, and two views of its exquisitely detailed interiors are shown in the two lower photographs.

Between 1922 and 1926 Turner built stadiums for Cornell University (upper left), Brown University (upper right), the City of Philadelphia (center), the University of Pittsburgh (lower left) and the University of Pennsylvania (lower right).

Top photograph shows headquarters of Massachusetts Mutual Life Insurance Company, built by Turner in Springfield and completed in 1926. Photographs below it illustrate a creative Turner approach to materials handling, many years before the advent of the motorized buggy.

In 1928 Turner began this complex, phased addition to the department store that Bloomingdale Brothers had established in the heart of New York City.

This elegantly finished building for Tiffany and Company, on New York's Fifth Avenue, was further evidence that Turner was no longer limiting itself to concrete construction during the late 1920s.

The Great Depression brought Turner into the competition for large public works projects. Shown are three, all built in the New York area during the 1930s: Creedmoor State Hospital (top), King's Park State Hospital (middle), and Pilgrim State Hospital (bottom).

reasonable people had begun to wonder whether or not things would ever get better.

Once in office, Franklin Roosevelt surrounded himself with thinkers and planners who conceived and were able to secure approval for a wide range of programs designed to remediate some of the country's problems. But in spite of good intentions, most of their efforts fell short of their objectives amid confusion between the goals of recovery and reform. The landmark National Industrial Recovery Act of 1933 managed to put large numbers of people to work in short-term projects, but when it came to the more complex and fundamental business of restoring economic activity and reversing the erosion of wages, it foundered on the shoals of competing special interests and public mistrust, and before a third of the funds it had earmarked for public works had been used, the legislation itself was invalidated as unconstitutional.

Through all this, Turner had been progressively tightening its belt: reducing staff, trimming salaries, and following (with little success) every lead that showed the slightest promise of producing a new construction contract. It was a period that took its toll at Turner, as it did everywhere. With almost no new private-sector work coming in, the company began to look again at the public sector, but by 1933 competition there had become so intense that most jobs were being awarded well below Turner's estimates of its own bare cost. And it was little wonder. The value of all contracts awarded for nonresidential construction throughout the country, about $6 billion in 1929, had by 1933 fallen to a little over $1 billion.

Turner's own staff, 400 salaried employees in 1929, was down to about 100, and the wages of the survivors were down an average of more than 10 percent. The Additional Compensation Plan, implemented through 1930, had been suspended, and branch offices in Buffalo and Chicago had been closed, leaving Boston, Philadelphia, and New York as the operating centers. Turner was hunkered down for whatever the rest of the storm had to offer.

The painful layoffs weren't the only source of personnel reduction, as there were early retirements and resignations too, including some by Turner family members who probably saw their remaining on the payroll as a potential burden to the firm. W. W., who was still in his early fifties, retired in 1931 to devote the rest of his life to public service and charity in the city of Philadelphia and among the Society of Friends, emphasizing in a letter to Henry his hope that his own resignation would facilitate the advancement of their younger brother, Archie, who upon W. W.'s retirement was given responsibility for the Philadelphia District. Henry's oldest son, Chan, who had been elected to the board only a year earlier, resigned at thirty-one to take a job in the administration of a fishery and would later resume his education briefly before rejoining Turner in 1938. Charlotte Turner's brother Wright Chapman, who had been corporate secretary, retired to Long Island, where the company's repurchase of his shares at book value facilitated his living a good and quiet life devoted largely to his duties as commodore of the Manhasset Yacht Club.

DeForest Dixon, Henry Turner's old friend from the Ransome days and one of the company's founders, appears (from his position in a late 1920s organizational chart) to have lost a little ground to the strong young leaders who had by then risen through the ranks and were calling most of the shots. He retired in 1930 at the early age of fifty-seven. Egbert J. Moore and T. Arthur Smith, two vigorous board members who had started with Turner as outside men during the first few years, retired well before either had reached his sixtieth birthday. And with the company now well into its second generation, deaths among the early executives were beginning to occur. William Lyle's was one: He had managed construction of the Navy and War Office Building in Washington and had then run the Buffalo office. His small, company-paid life insurance policy provided a modest benefit for his widow, but in the absence of any other death benefit Turner continued his salary for a year after his death, as it did for other senior executives. Within another couple of years death would claim two more senior Turner men who had been with the company almost from the beginning: J. C. Andrews, who was corporate treasurer when he died, was succeeded by Walter K. Shaw; and Henry Fox, a vice president who had started with Turner just two years after its founding, was replaced on the board by Harry Ward.

Nineteen thirty-two was the first of three losing years in what was then the company's thirty-year history, and although the net loss was modest, it was a harsh blow to a conservative and consistently successful management that had never before experienced a loss. A footnote to the losing years shows that most of the jobs that Turner did during this period were individually profitable. The annual losses derived from a combination of the failures of some of Turner's customers to pay their bills, from the failure of several Turner efforts to generate revenues from its own invested capital, from the company's commitments to maintaining its stock dividends and to redeeming its common shares at book value, and from its refusal to drive down its fixed overhead below a level it considered to be an irreducible minimum for continuing the company's effective operation.

The delinquencies by Turner's customers were almost all depression-generated, of course, but, strangely enough, few of them originated with jobs that were actually undertaken during the depression years. In most cases the problem jobs were late 1920s projects on which Turner had agreed to accept some of what it was owed in the form of what had in those good days seemed the entirely sound paper of its customers. Both the Berkeley Carteret Hotel in Asbury Park and the Lexington Hotel in New York are cases in point: When the hard times of the 1930s set in and hotel revenues plummeted, neither of those hotels was able to maintain payments due Turner. There were literally dozens of other cases like those, including a theater in the fashionable suburb of Scarsdale, New York; a Knights of Columbus building in Rochester, New York, for which payments had been personally guaranteed by a couple of wealthy members; several industrial plants and even a water company in Pennsylvania whose customers simply quit paying their bills. Every one of them had been a well-executed and profitable construction project, and each of the companies had been sound enough to convince the Turner board to accept its paper, but by the early thirties they had themselves become the victims of an unrelenting decline in economic conditions.

The impact of the downward spiral of economic conditions during the 1930s seemed to know no limits, and almost no business was spared. Turner had occasionally sought to invest its own money in ventures calculated to enhance its commercial strength, either through the control of critical materials or through an anticipated enhancement of its ability to secure new business, and almost every one of those ventures was destined to suffer from the bad times of the 1930s.

When Turner was doing a large volume of concrete work in the New York area during the 1920s, it had sought to protect its sources of aggregates while expanding its profitability by acquiring, in partnership with the George A. Fuller Construction Company, the Nassau Sand and Gravel Company on Long Island. For some years after the acquisition, Nassau earned profits from sales to New York–area contractors while ensuring good access to aggregates for both Fuller and Turner, and the plant was so successful that by 1930 it was operating on a relatively large scale and developing a small fleet of scows and barges for transporting its products by water. But as soon as the volume of new construction began to shrink, profits at Nassau changed to losses, and by the mid-thirties the business had to be sold at a price below its original purchase cost.

A luxurious cooperative apartment house in New York was another investment of Turner's that didn't work out well in spite of the soundness of the original plan. During the 1920s, the company and some of its executives saw the construction of a first-class apartment house at 53 East Sixty-sixth Street, on the already fashionable Upper East Side of Manhattan Island, as a promising venture offering a construction contract and an opportunity for deferring income as well. But the market for selling cooperatives weakened quickly before construction was finished, and Turner ended up acquiring most of the apartments for its own account, as part of a plan to market them as rentals instead. That strategy proved to be a bad one in the devastating economic environment that followed in the 1930s, when few New Yorkers could afford the high rents that were required to offset the interest and amortization on the building's mortgage, and by the late 1930s the building had been lost to the mortgagee through foreclosure. Almost seventy years later the area had lost none of the cachet that had attracted Turner's management in the first place, and three-bedroom apartments in the building were being sold to some of the cream of New York's society at prices exceeding $2 million.

Perhaps the most discouraging of the investment failures of the depression years was 1242 Lake Shore Drive in Chicago. Turner had built nearby 1250 Lake

Shore Drive on a traditional contract basis when the company was given a chance to participate as a principal in 1242 Lake Shore by investing its construction fee and limited other funds as starting capital. It was an elegant, well-designed building in what seemed to be an ideal location, and the likelihood of financial success seemed especially good because one of the other principals in the venture was Samuel Insull Jr., a brilliant, English-born millionaire who owned extensive real estate and controlled a gigantic public utilities empire that included more than 500 power plants. Insull was said to be worth more than $3 billion, but his empire became an early casualty of the depression, and when it collapsed in 1932 Insull fled the country under a legal cloud, leaving the other principals to salvage 1242 Lake Shore Drive in a hostile economic environment. It was another poor investment for Turner.

One investment that did briefly relieve the gloomy environment in 1933 was the Turner-Rostock venture. Here was an opportunity for Turner to apply its special capability in reinforced concrete construction to a new field that would be insulated from competition to a large degree and that was likely to profit substantially from the repeal of the Eighteenth Amendment, which since 1919 had made the sale of alcoholic beverages illegal. Rostock and Baerlocher was an Austrian firm whose business was the design and construction of multistory concrete tank buildings (often clad with brick) for the fermenting and storage of beer, and they had designed and installed their tanks in many of the most prominent breweries of central Europe. Their success, according to Turner's Harry Ward, who visited and reported on sixteen of these European breweries, relied on Rostock and Baerlocher's special expertise in the design of the tank systems themselves and on the unique coating they applied to the tank interiors. Between Ward's glowing report and what seemed the certainty that the repeal of Prohibition would bring with it a vast increase in the demand for beer in the United States, Turner's board was understandably convinced that representing Rostock and Baerlocher as its contractor in the United States was potentially profitable, and in 1933 the board authorized such a venture, placing Archie Turner in charge. After a slow start, a contract for one large facility secured from Schaefer Brewing Company appears to have been satisfactorily executed. But for reasons still not well understood, the consumption of beer during the period that followed the repeal of Prohibition didn't rise nearly as quickly or as much as almost everyone had expected it to, and a second contract was a few years coming. Meanwhile, Turner was spending money trying to promote the use of the system and was probably losing some of its enthusiasm for it, as a few years without additional business passed. By the time popular taste for beer had reached a level the brewers considered high enough to justify the construction of new tanks, the use of glass linings had begun to come into use and the Turner-Rostock venture passed into history.

Until 1933, a couple of years after any dividends on Turner's common shares had been discontinued, the company continued the increasingly difficult practice of paying the holders of its preferred shares the annual 7 percent they had anticipated when they bought them, but those dividends took their toll on the surplus that had accumulated during the good years. By 1934 the effect of the dividend payments and the continuing additional burden of redeeming the common shares of persons who left the company were draining the surplus, so the 7 percent payments were reduced to 4 percent and the unpaid 3 percent was accumulated as an obligation to be addressed in better times. Increasing annual operating losses, while not large, exacerbated the problem until 1935, when Turner elected to reorganize, restoring its surplus at the expense of capital and preserving its ability to implement its critical commitment to redeem common shares at book value. It would still be a few years before the accumulating deficit on the preferred shares could be paid off and full dividend payments would be resumed.

Life at Turner, like life everywhere, was very different from what it had ever been before. By 1934, with the value of work completed during the year down to about $2 million and the company's fixed costs reduced through layoffs to less than half what they had been in 1930, only the shell of the former organization was still in place. At the annual dinner at New York's Commodore Hotel, Henry Turner tried his best to assure the fifty-eight attendees that better times lay ahead, exhorting them not to allow the hardships of the times to erode their commitment to Turner's professional and commercial integrity. The practice of holding men temporarily at partial salary, in the hope that new work would surface, was reserved for "exceptional men," whom Arthur Tozzer was authorized to identify and retain at up to $1,000 per month, for periods of his own discretion.

A few executives had left the company to participate in efforts that were being made elsewhere to improve things. John P. H. Perry (who would later return to Turner) joined New York City's Emergency Works Bureau, and Robert Boyd became district director of New York State's Temporary Emergency Relief Administration.

Identifying likely prospects for new construction and becoming the low bidder were only some of the problems of the mid-thirties, as there was also the increasingly relevant matter of finding clients who were likely to be able to pay their bills. Even some that had appeared to be entirely creditworthy were by now stretching out their payments or actually defaulting, as they struggled with their own collections, and a few years into the depression at least a dozen firms that owed money to Turner were working out arrangements for discounting their obligations or paying them down over relatively long periods.

By the mid-thirties, Turner was casting an ever-widening net for new work and doing its best to secure jobs that made sense, but there weren't many to be found. In New York, it picked up a publicly bid contract to build the Bronx Terminal Markets, a surprising award in such a competitive setting, but at almost $1 million certainly a welcome one. It was an unusual, low-rise cluster of wholesale grocery terminals, owned and leased to vendors by New York City, and it was especially well regarded for the contemporary design of its entirely cast-in-place architectural concrete exterior, a feature that made it a likely job for Turner. Boston was suffering the same scarcity of work as New York and Turner was glad to get a $100,000 contract from Tufts University there, even though it required contractor-financing of half the cost of the work over a period of several years. In Philadelphia, there was a million-dollar contract to build Juniata, a privately financed low-rent housing project for which one of the new government agencies guaranteed payment and on which Turner subcontracted the masonry work to John B. Kelly, father of Grace Kelly, the future film star.

Even the normally simple task of profitably investing the company's own cash reserves that had been rendered idle by the lack of work was problematic for Turner in the mid-thirties, when most investments seemed too risky and government bonds were yielding less than 2 percent.

Of course, the despair of hard times had to be relieved, from time to time, and it was. Annual golf outings for Turner executives at Westchester's St. Andrews Club, initiated years earlier by Henry C. Turner, continued without interruption, with the Turners themselves (always Archie and often Henry or Chan or both) dominating the low scorers. And occasionally a touch of dark humor penetrated the gloom, as when a 1930s Turner man reflected on the continuing reliability of some sources of work, even in the worst of times, citing Turner contracts for a distillery and a casket-manufacturing plant as examples.

Even Cliff Wilson, long an advocate of heavy construction for Turner, was becoming discouraged as the depression deepened and the lists of bidders on the dams and bridges that were his favorite projects lengthened. He had successfully urged an association with the large Fraser-Brace Group for the purpose of bidding on construction of the diversion tunnels at Fort Peck Dam in Montana, but neither that venture nor several others like it with Fraser-Brace led to any work.

But patience and persistence did begin to produce dividends around the middle of 1935, when Wilson was approached with a proposal that Turner join with the George A. Fuller Company and with Spencer, White & Prentis to bid as a joint venture on the construction of a big dam across the Mississippi River at Alton, Illinois. Fuller was already a very well established old friend and occasional commercial partner of Turner, and the Spencer, White & Prentis firm was well known to Turner's management as a relatively young (fifteen years old) company specializing and eminently successful in the building of difficult or special foundations. Wilson, of course, was eager to pursue anything that had a reasonable chance of turning into a contract and was especially interested in the kind of heavy work exemplified by a big dam, and he was able to convince the Turner board to give the venture a try. They authorized him to head up the firm's one-third participation in Engineering Constructors, a corporation to be formed as a vehicle through which the joint venture would bid on the Alton Dam job and, if successful, would build it.

Big dams had become a vital element in the heavy construction that was being done in the 1930s, and although few of them had originally been conceived expressly to relieve the unemployment that was at the heart of the depression, they all helped. Out west, thousands of men were working on the gigantic dams that the Department of the Interior was building along the Colorado River, and thousands more would soon be added to build additional dams along the Columbia. Back east the same thing was happening in the Tennessee Valley, where the Corps of Engineers was building dams for TVA. Flood control and sometimes power generation were the principal long-term objectives for those dams, in varying proportions, but the Mississippi River dam that had caught Cliff Wilson's interest wasn't intended for either of those purposes. The dam that the joint venture was seeking to build at Alton was to be one of twenty-eight dam-and-lock combinations that were being planned along the Mississippi simply to deepen the great river's shipping channel by raising its water level all the way from Minneapolis down to the Gulf of Mexico. The dam at Alton wasn't far from St. Louis, just upstream from where the Mississippi is joined by the Missouri and just downstream from where it is joined by the Illinois. The locks that were to go along with the dam were already under construction when cost estimators from the three joint venture partners set their sights on securing a contract to build the dam.

As a surprising and encouraging indication that conditions in the economy might be improving, at least marginally, only four bidders showed up for the bid opening in May 1935, and Engineering Constructors was able to take the job with a bid of about $4.8 million, a comfortable 2 percent below the second bidder but a million dollars below the price submitted by the joint venture of western contractors who were working on the San Francisco Bay Bridge at the time of bidding. It had been expected that the Chicago contractor who was building the locks at Alton would bid on the dam too, but during the weeks just before the bids were taken, rampaging spring floods had washed out his cofferdam there and he apparently had all he could do to salvage what he was already doing, and he declined to submit a bid for the dam itself.

Alton Dam proved to be one of the smoothest and most profitable jobs Turner had done in years. When the joint venture was only a few months into the work, the unfortunate contractor for the locks project suffered still more trouble with his job and gave it up, forfeiting his contract and obliging the government to seek other bids to complete construction of the locks. That proved to be a fortuitous break for Engineering Constructors, which won the contract for completing the locks, and the Alton work became Cliff Wilson's principal interest for almost the next three years. When the work was finished in 1938 the three partners shared a welcome profit exceeding half a million dollars.

Alton Dam had been good news at Turner right from the beginning, and although some in the company's management optimistically viewed it as the unmistakable beginning of a dramatic turnaround, a more realistic perspective interpreted it simply as the waning of some of Turner's worst days and the beginning of a fairly long, slow return to prosperity. In Washington, a management committee of Acacia Mutual Life Insurance Company unanimously selected Turner from a competing group of thirty-one contractors to build its dignified granite-and-limestone corporate headquarters on a site directly across the street from the entrance to the U.S. Capitol, and another big contract came along in Washington for building an addition to the elegant headquarters of the Pan American Union. In Massachusetts, a million-dollar contract for a new high school in Fitchburg and one for almost $2 million for the Liberty Mutual Life Insurance Company headquarters building took some of the pressure off the struggling Boston office. In New York the New York Historical Society, which had been waiting since 1913 for the proceeds of a bequest from the former president of the New York Life Insurance Company, engaged Turner to add a couple of large wings to its museum and library. There was certainly no flurry of new work, but there was evidence that some of the larger, best-endowed companies and institutions that were inclined to look to Turner for construction were beginning to regain their confidence. There was some rehiring of key men, and the size of Turner's board of directors was increased to sixteen by the election of W. B. Ball, G. E. Horr, W. H. Nye, and F. E.

Schilling. Although the value of work put in place during 1935 was still only about $3.6 million, it was the last of the losing years, and by 1936, when the company actually erected almost $6 million worth of work, profitability and the Additional Compensation Plan had been restored, and Turner had moved its corporate offices to the twenty-fifth floor of the new Graybar Building, adjacent to Grand Central Station in New York.

Even in those slightly better years of the middle and later 1930s, there was little corresponding evidence of recovery in the country at large. Although government had been able to legislate reforms designed to avoid repetition of economic abuses that were thought to have caused or exacerbated the depression, and although it had managed to relieve the suffering of some of the victims, there was little evidence of recovery. Unemployment was still cruelly high and investment in new plants or equipment remained historically low. The national volume of construction during 1936 was still well below half the average volume that had been recorded for the period between 1925 and 1929, but Turner was well ahead of the curve.

Turner's own recovery continued to gather momentum into 1937, when it profitably completed almost $12 million worth of work, a volume that still included more than the usual fraction of public work secured in the competitive marketplace of a struggling economy. It was at about that time that muted but growing evidence began to develop that war might return to Europe. Almost a decade earlier, Hitler's Nazi Party had won a plurality in the German Reichstag and had been gaining power ever since, disavowing Germany's treaties, withdrawing it from the League of Nations, destroying democratic institutions, hunting down Hitler's declared enemies, and seizing adjacent territories unilaterally identified as natural extensions of the German Fatherland. By 1936 Hitler had aligned himself with Mussolini, who had annexed Ethiopia and had by then begun a regime of fascist control in Italy. The Japanese, meanwhile, sharing the totalitarian outlook of the Germans and the Italians, had become progressively more closely aligned with them. They were conducting an open but undeclared war of their own against the Chinese, bombing their cities, occupying some of their territory, threatening

American interests in the Pacific, and secretly building a powerful naval force in violation of international treaty. Despite a strong American predisposition to preserve the country's rigorous isolation from the rest of the world, a growing national interest in military preparedness began to be seen across the land.

Turner, of course, was well known to the military, especially to the navy, from its performance during the First World War, and the company was extremely well regarded by them. In 1937, when Washington's earliest, still halting moves toward military readiness began to take form, Turner became the low bidder for construction of a state-of-the-art navy facility in Carderock, Maryland, for testing scale models of naval vessels. The company built several very large administration and support buildings at the site and, as the central elements of the project, built two huge reinforced concrete testing basins, the largest such structures in the world. Each basin was about a quarter of a mile long and each was covered by a thin-shell, three-hinged concrete arch, all controlled within tolerances that the navy described later as "previously unknown . . . in the construction industry." The requirement for such preciseness was calculated to reflect the curvature of the earth along the length of the basins in order to simulate reliably the actual surface of the water at sea. The basins were capable of testing very large models of naval vessels under virtually any imaginable conditions of weather or battle and, in fact, were used in the design of many vessels that would figure prominently in the sea battles of World War II. A few years later, while the battle for the western Pacific raged, Turner would return to Carderock to enlarge the facility, adding structures and new basins and more than doubling the length of the original basins.

The impact of the Carderock work on Turner wouldn't end with the war. Admiral Ben Moreell, who had overseen the Carderock project for the navy, would interface many times with Turner during the war years and would later, for a brief period after his retirement from the navy, become Turner's president.

The war that was still a few years off would later profoundly affect Turner, of course, but during the waning years of the depression its influence was still remote and subtle. The company's annual volume of business remained between about $11 million and $12 million through 1938 and 1939, only modestly influenced (as

in the case of a Turner contract at the New London submarine base) by the growing national attention to military preparedness. What was more important to
Turner's return to prosperity during the late 1930s was the slow but sure return of
the country's confidence in itself and the future, especially among the substantial
businesses and institutions on whose willingness to risk expansion Turner relied
for work. The company's old friend, American Can Company, was among the first
to engage Turner for such work after the long, dry spell, and Children's Hospital
in Philadelphia was another. Both were doubtless glad to find Turner not much
changed from the firm they had known before the difficult times: leaner, but still
well managed and well staffed, still well organized, and still financially strong in
spite of the poor years.

Most of the country's cities were doing everything they could to encourage or
sustain whatever modest signs of economic recovery had begun to surface toward
the end of the 1930s, and New York was no exception. By 1938, plans were well
along for building the splendid New York World's Fair: a spectacular, 1,200-acre
extravaganza to be built on a landfill, where almost every country would have a
chance to reveal itself to the world and where almost every industry would be able
to display its present and future wares. The fair's developers styled it the World of
Tomorrow and scheduled April 1939 for its opening, although most of the
required drawings and specifications were still in progress during the spring of
1938. It would be a construction fight to the finish, among contractors who only a
few months earlier had barely enough work to keep a small crew busy but who were
now facing completion penalties and fighting one another for mechanics, equipment, and materials.

Turner was in the thick of things, with contracts for three of the fair's big
exhibits. The frenzied months leading up to the 1939 opening provided a stressful
but doubtless welcome contrast to the long, dry years of the depression, with the
company now assigning guards to ride material trucks from the fair's entrance to
the work sites, to ensure that other contractors wouldn't commandeer materials
that had been ordered by Turner; making estimates and completing designs at the
work sites themselves; and doing whatever was needed to bring order out of a

generally chaotic setting in which hundreds of contractors and subcontractors were working on the same site.

Probably the most dazzling of the three Turner jobs at the 1939 New York World's Fair was the General Motors Building, where a visitor got to see (and occasionally to drive) models of automobiles that were so radically different from anything anyone had ever seen before that they were thought to be outrageously unrealistic. In fact, much of what was shown would become commonplace within a decade or so. A second Turner project at the fair was a huge distillation structure built at thirty-five times the size of the laboratory apparatus it was designed to replicate, and to enclose DuPont's Court of Chemistry, where a visitor was introduced to then-new DuPont products that included nylon, neoprene, and Lucite. Still a third Turner project at the big New York World's Fair is probably more noteworthy for what it didn't show than for what it did show, an exhibit not considered important enough to rate an entire building. For this less spectacular exhibit Turner developed some interior space within what was called the Business Machines and Insurance Building, large enough to accommodate a display of contemporary paintings from each of what were then the forty-eight states and examples of the sponsor's products, including a new one identified as an all-electric writing machine. The low-profile client was the International Business Machines Company, already an important but still mid-size company with annual sales of around $35 million in 1939, but without a product deemed interesting or important enough to justify a whole building. It would be another year before IBM, later a major client of Turner's, would enter the computer business.

Like most fairs, the one in New York combined entertainment, eating, and drinking with science and art, and it was able to inform and delight a vast population that was more than ready for a good time to mark what was beginning to look like the end of a long, bad one. But by the spring of 1939, a powerfully rearmed Germany had occupied the Rhineland, Austria, and Czechoslovakia; had managed to intimidate the British and the French into a policy of appeasement for peace at almost any price; had begun the extermination of those it perceived as its internal enemies; and had formalized military relationships with fascist Italy and with the

Japanese, who were themselves well along in a brutal but undeclared war against the Chinese. The boisterous hoopla that attended the opening of the New York World's Fair in the spring of 1939 obscured, for most Americans, the sights and sounds of an extraordinarily powerful German military machine that only a few months later would move with lethal fury into Poland, plunging the world into its second major war of the century.

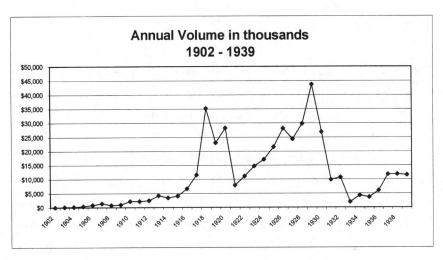

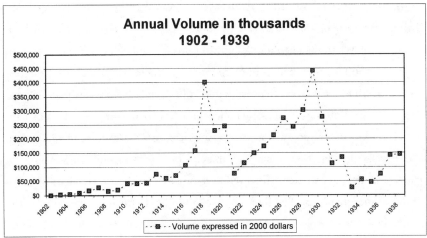

7.

Another War

War construction came thundering back into the history of Turner Construction Company in a big way a few months before the Nazi blitzkrieg into Poland and more than two years before the Japanese attack on Pearl Harbor.

For most Americans in the summer of 1939, events in Europe and Asia during the decade that was ending had been little more than casual distractions. Worrying about finding or keeping a job or about holding onto a farm were what kept people from getting to sleep at night during the Great Depression, not the behavior of tyrants abroad. The United States, honoring its international agreements, had continued through most of the 1930s to chip away at its own military capability, shrinking the size of its army and navy and scrapping productive naval vessels with a vengeance. When the likelihood of war in Europe had begun to increase around 1935, after Hitler's repudiation of Germany's international obligations, Congress had put teeth into its resolve to prevent the United States from participating in any such dangerous business by making it illegal for American companies to ship arms to belligerents in foreign wars or to arm American merchant ships. In 1936, when U.S. intelligence discovered that the Japanese were secretly building warships on Pacific islands that had been entrusted to their care after World War I, in violation of the treaties that controlled their mandate, it withheld the information from the public in order to avoid international unpleasantness. There was an understandable feeling that there was already enough to worry about at home, where in those difficult days of 1939 10 million people were still out of work and where memories of the last war, only twenty years old, were still fresh. The domestic political environment was overwhelmingly isolationist. Even the internationally minded Franklin Roosevelt, in his second inaugural address, didn't dare to mention the ominous direction of events in Europe or Asia.

But in fact Roosevelt wasn't indifferent to the likelihood that the increasingly global nature of politics and commerce would ultimately bring all these problems to American shores. He managed to divert some funds from public works appropriations to buttress the navy's faltering condition, and in 1938 Congress, increasingly worried by German and Japanese military expenditures and adventures, had authorized substantial defense allocations for the first time since World War I. Over the objections of the isolationists, the decline in American military strength was modestly slowed and, in some cases, even reversed. Congress focused much of its effort on the navy, and on naval aviation in particular, and appointed a board headed by Adm. A. J. Hepburn to ensure that funds allocated for naval expansion would be committed to building a two-ocean navy and to a dramatic increase in naval airpower. And they made clear their view that there was no time to lose.

The idea of a potential war with the Japanese was nothing new to the navy. For years, it had conducted its annual war games in the Pacific and at the Naval War College using the Japanese as the theoretical enemy, integrating whatever was then known about Japanese naval tactics and strength and simulating almost every imaginable setting for a Pacific war against them. Absolute denial by the Japanese of any foreign access to the Pacific islands it had been authorized to govern was interpreted by the navy as more evidence that something nasty was going on there, and by the time the Hepburn Board had finished its work, well-documented reports were circulating that Japanese fishermen and merchant seamen were gathering sensitive military information in American harbors up and down the Pacific.

In such a setting, the recommendations of the Hepburn Board led to the establishment of what came to be called the Pacific Naval Air Base project, a plan for building naval air stations and related facilities on remote and isolated islands located over much of the central Pacific, at distances from San Francisco that ranged from about 2,400 to 5,000 miles. The project was intended to broaden American capacity for effective air reconnaissance and to provide a vital system of air defenses for its Pacific fleet. Before it was finished, PNAB would include major naval construction in and around Pearl Harbor and on the rest of Oahu; on the islands of Midway, Wake, Johnston, Palmyra, and Samoa; and at Cavite in the Philippines. It would become one of the most ambitious construction projects ever undertaken by any government. What was built would actually cost almost $400 million in the currency of the 1940s, an amount that would be the equivalent of more than $8 billion by the time of Turner's hundredth anniversary.

It wasn't just its vast scope that made PNAB such an extraordinary project. It was a logistical nightmare, requiring large and often complex construction in some of the most primitive and inaccessible locations in the world, and it had to be done with extraordinary speed because the threat of imminent hostile action by the Japanese was part of the fundamental intelligence rationale on which the whole plan was based.

Turner Construction Company in those early months of 1939 was continuing its recovery from the worst days of the depression and not doing badly at all. Henry Turner was glad to be able to report to the stockholders that the approximately $11 million worth of construction the company had put in place during 1938 had been modestly profitable and that dividend arrears on the preferred shares, accumulated during the dark days, would be paid off by the end of 1939. What's more, he told them, almost $9 million in contract work was to be carried forward from 1938 into the new year, including work on the New England Life Insurance Company job in Boston, two hospitals in New York, a new office building for Continental American Insurance Company in Wilmington, Delaware, and a residence there for Pierre S. DuPont III. But he closed his talk with a somber warning that even with what was being carried forward, 1939 didn't promise to be a very good year for Turner. To grow, he said, the company would need a good deal more business than he was able to foresee in January of 1939, and he exhorted the shareholders to keep their eyes peeled for good prospects.

Henry Turner was certainly right about how poor the prospects were for the

Boston, New York, and Philadelphia offices during 1939, but he didn't yet know about PNAB. And neither did Cliff Wilson, who was down in Maryland tying together a few loose ends on the substantially completed and extremely successful second job the company had done for the navy at Carderock.

It was Turner's work on that Carderock project, the Admiral Taylor Model Testing Basin, that had first brought the company to the personal attention of Adm. Ben Moreell, the Utah-bred giant of a man who was running the navy's Bureau of Yards and Docks in 1939. It's possible that the admiral remembered Turner from his own Brooklyn Navy Yard days, back in 1917, when he had served there in his first post as a young ensign, but it's more likely that it was the Carderock work that was responsible for what proved to be Moreell's eagerness to bring Turner into the Pacific island work.

In 1939 Moreell was focused on the task of finding just the right combination of contractors needed to build air bases in the Pacific, and within a few weeks of the navy's publicizing its objectives, his office was flooded with applications from all over the country. In order to ensure substantial capacity and to reduce the government's risk, the Hepburn Board had stipulated that the construction organization selected for the work would have to comprise more than just a single qualified contractor, and the board had accepted Moreell's reasoning that the job should be done on an open-ended, cost-plus basis. As the scope and details of the project became more clearly defined, it became evident to Moreell that its success was going to rely to an unusual degree on the capability of the individual contractors who were selected to do the work.

He started with an elite selection panel. Once they had begun to screen out the less-well-qualified applicants, he began to encourage joint ventures among the survivors, successfully urging Turner to join forces with Raymond Concrete Pile Company. Turner and Raymond already had a long history together that included the big World War I jobs where Raymond had been Turner's piling subcontractor and the harbor work in Havana, where Bert McMenimen, younger brother of Raymond's current president, had been Raymond's field engineer. Cliff Wilson, now a vice president and a member of the Turner board, had been in charge at

Havana for Turner, and he and the Raymond people had worked together for years, more recently at the big James River Bridge job. At the very time that Moreell made his suggestion, Turner and Raymond and a couple of other contractors were bidding (unsuccessfully) as joint venturers on big dams in the American Southwest, so the proposed marriage on the Pacific job was clearly an entirely reasonable one for both. Once Turner and Raymond had organized their plan, they invited Hawaiian Dredging Company of Honolulu into the venture to strengthen it even further. Hawaiian Dredging was a marine dredging and construction company that combined a powerful local presence in Hawaii with long experience in dredging the coral that underlies every harbor in the islands.

Of course, the Hawaiian-Raymond-Turner group, whose name would soon be shortened to the sometimes embarrassingly Japanese-sounding Haratu, wasn't the only joint venture that would survive the cuts, and within another few weeks there were three such combinations for the navy to choose from. One was the big western team that had built Hoover Dam on the Colorado River, led on this project by Harry Morrison of Idaho-based Morrison Knudsen Company. Another venture was led by the distinguished old Maryland construction firm Arundel, and it included Arundel's respected Maryland competitor, Consolidated Engineering Company. All three contenders were well-qualified firms with solid experience, and during an especially hot week in June, before Washington's government buildings were air-conditioned, each of them took a turn at trying to show the Moreell panel why it should be selected for the job in the Pacific.

Harry Morrison, who appeared first, dazzled the panel with the breadth of his knowledge and experience. A big, white-haired man, Morrison looked fit and tan in his plainsman's hat and western boots, and he described with reassuring confidence the railroads that he and his partners had driven through the rugged mountains of the Pacific Northwest and the tunnels and bridges they'd built to make them work. But when it came to a detailed plan for building the Pacific bases, Morrison seemed to want the navy to leave that to him and his colleagues to figure out, more or less as they went along. He'd explored the Midway site in some detail, and he presented some good ideas for developing it, but Morrison was accustomed to being in charge and apparently didn't feel the need to consult with the navy about how he'd approach the other islands.

A dignified engineer from the Arundel group followed Morrison with a style that was substantially different, offering a carefully organized analysis of the complex administrative and management problems inherent in such a big program but largely ignoring the details of building the individual bases. It was a good presentation but less dramatic than Morrison's and apparently less convincing.

Cliff Wilson of Turner was the last to speak, and his presentation was compelling. His Hawaiian-Raymond-Turner group had come prepared with a sixty-one-page proposal listing the names and experience of most of the key personnel that each of the joint venturers was prepared to assign to the project, and it included preliminary estimates of the staggering quantities of material and the numbers of men that would be required. They presented a plan for marshaling the required resources and transporting them to the islands, and followed it with preliminary schemes and schedules for the execution of most of the individual projects. Wilson did most of the talking, but Raymond's Bill McMenimen took some time to describe his approach to recruiting manpower, and Hawaiian's Walter Dillingham added his assurance that all the personnel and considerable equipment of his firm would be committed exclusively to this project for as long as it might be required. The Turner-led presentation was, by surviving accounts, a spectacular one that left the two competing groups far behind.

By August, a decision had been made. The Hawaiian-Raymond-Turner group was selected and authorized to get the work underway on a few of the bases immediately, with the clear implication that authorization for more work would follow. An executive committee consisting of Wilson, Raymond's Bill McMenimen and Hawaiian's Walter Dillingham was established. Three days later, even before the government's contract had been received, Wilson tapped George Ferris, a promising young civil engineer who'd run the Carderock job and had worked for Wilson at Havana, to head up construction. Ferris, only thirty-seven years old, had been with Turner since the Breakers Hotel job in Palm Beach, back in the 1920s, and had made a name for himself as a man who was equally skilled in construction and in managing and getting along with people, a couple of qualifications that would stand him in good stead for the formidable task that lay ahead in the Pacific. In broad terms, Ferris would face two large and extremely complex challenges: One was acquiring and transporting to the island sites as quickly as possible the vast amounts of material, equipment, and personnel that would be needed, and the other was getting the construction itself done in a furious hurry.

Even the normally routine tasks of anticipating what and how much of anything would be required would be difficult, because in most cases the detailed drawings that were being prepared by the office of Albert Kahn in Detroit wouldn't be produced fast enough to keep ahead of construction. Quantities would often have to be estimated from conceptual studies. Worse yet, there would be little margin for error: Most of the work was to be done at virtually inaccessible sites, scattered across the Pacific Ocean, at which everything from fresh water to firewood for cooking would have to be brought in by sea, and where there would be no place within a thousand miles or more for dealing with errors.

Ferris began addressing the materials and equipment problems immediately by bringing Turner's Harrie Muchemore out from New York to design and build a warehousing and distribution center in California, where materials and equipment could be marshaled and then shipped off to the islands. Once that construction was underway, Ferris followed by establishing the core of a procurement force with Turner's Russ Fairburn and Bill Hammond in charge. Before long the California facility would be purchasing and shipping more than 50,000 tons of materials and equipment every month, much of it aboard vessels in its own fleet.

Key manpower for construction would be drawn from the staffs of the joint venturers, who had contracted to make available whatever they had, even at the expense of other, nondefense projects, for as long as required. That personnel plan pretty well provided (at least in the beginning) for the required superintendents and foremen and for a limited number of key mechanics. But it still left a need for thousands of other mechanics and unskilled laborers, so a network was established for recruiting, mainly through labor unions, all over the country. The massive stateside recruiting mechanism that resulted was able to meet the project's needs, but along with the good workers it was able to find it inevitably produced a sometimes troublesome fraction of drifters and the like, often men who were willing to accept the deprivations of life in the islands in exchange for the promise of a refuge from process servers, demanding wives, and sometimes police officers. As the work progressed, the turnover of help, not entirely unexpectedly, would be extensive and disruptive.

By winter 1940, almost 100 projects were underway, a fair number of them on the remote islands of Johnston and Palmyra and many more on and around Ford Island and in Pearl Harbor itself. The Japanese threat was increasing daily, and in the early months of 1940 it was perceived by Washington as serious enough to justify more than doubling PNAB's work scope, with new emphasis on work at Wake Island, Midway, Samoa, and Guam, where large, fully developed bases, including submarine facilities and the like, were planned. Ferris and the others, by now feeling the limits of their own capacity, convinced the navy to bring Harry Morrison and his team back into the joint venture and to add Pomeroy Steel Company of San Francisco and Byrne Construction Company of Dallas as well, in order to expand the venture's access to additional supervisory help and special equipment. Every month brought new tasks, from underground fuel storage and ammunition bunkers to hospitals, military housing, radio stations, and the like. By 1941 the immensely widening breadth of the work had used up virtually all the available manpower and much of the equipment. All work was by then being done in twelve-hour shifts, and Raymond's Bill McMenimen managed to shore up a deteriorating labor situation with an inspired arrangement in which the union leadership abandoned its traditional jurisdictional restrictions for the duration of the job, in return for good wages and one-year work contracts. But getting the work done before an expected attack by the Japanese was becoming an increasingly elusive goal. By summer 1941, with the Japanese poised for an aggressive troop movement into mineral-rich French Indochina, Washington had apparently accepted the inevitability of war and authorized a further dangerous expansion of PNAB's work to include major facilities at Cavite in the Philippines, virtually under the nose of the Japanese. That led to the addition of Bechtel Company and Utah Construction

Company, a couple of Harry Morrison's other partners from the Hoover Dam days, to the joint venture. From the beginning, the PNAB work had been driven by an urgency that demanded extraordinary effort and skills from the managing contractors, and by 1941, with the workforce approaching 25,000 men, it had become one of the largest construction projects ever undertaken, complicated by the isolated locations and physical character of the work and by the imminence of attack by a powerful enemy.

Although the original schedule had anticipated completion of everything by early 1943, much of it was ready for at least partial occupancy and operation by the end of 1941 when the Japanese attacked Pearl Harbor. There was plenty of damage to what PNAB had by that time put in place in and around Pearl Harbor, but a good deal of what had been built survived, and within hours of the attack, the forces of PNAB had assumed key roles in salvaging and rebuilding whatever was needed. At Midway, the work they had already finished escaped serious damage and has been credited with playing a major role in the later successful defense of that island and in the American naval victory over a Japanese armada that surpassed it in numbers and firepower. There was little damage to the work that PNAB had done at Samoa, which had already been an American base before the war and remained an important Allied installation throughout the conflict.

The story at Guam and in the Philippines, both perilously close to Japan, wasn't as good as it was at some of the other locations. The Japanese occupied these bases right after hostilities broke out and imprisoned everyone they could find, including the civilian construction workers. Most were not seriously mistreated and survived their captivity, but at Wake Island the story was much worse. A small contingent of marines on the island held out against the Japanese as long as they could, expecting relief that had been promised by an approaching navy force, but they finally gave up when it became evident that the navy had made a tactically advantageous but later widely criticized decision to abandon them. The marines and more than a thousand of PNAB's civilian construction workers who had been left on Wake Island were captured and imprisoned by the Japanese for the duration of the war. Most of them were cruelly mistreated, and some of them died.

The actual state of war that started with the Japanese attack on Pearl Harbor marked the beginning of the end of PNAB as a construction unit, and over a period of the next year or so its forces were withdrawn and replaced by Admiral Moreell's newly formed navy construction battalions, the colorful brigade of construction men who now added military training to their building skills and would distinguish themselves under fire as the Navy Seabees.

Although PNAB's construction activities would be phased out, their work wasn't over. Faced with the huge task of provisioning his Seabees, Moreell wasn't ready to abandon the vast procurement and distribution apparatus that PNAB had already established and that was operating smoothly from its California base. Although he accepted the need for withdrawing his civilian contractors from combat areas, he saw no reason they couldn't serve back in the States. Hardly skipping a beat, Ferris and his PNAB partners retreated to Port Hueneme, California, where they expanded and operated a gigantic, secret supply center that employed 9,000 workers and provided materials to the navy's construction forces throughout the Pacific for the rest of the war. Even that wasn't the end of it: The navy had established a similar material and equipment center in Rhode Island for supplying its Atlantic fleet, this one operated by a joint venture of the George A. Fuller Company and Merritt-Chapman & Scott, a couple of old friends and competitors of Turner. It fell to the Turner-led PNAB group to consolidate the far-flung procurement activities of both these coastal distribution centers into a single, centrally located facility to be operated by PNAB in Chicago. By the end of the war, the volume of work managed by PNAB in its stateside materials procurement and distribution activities substantially exceeded the approximately $400 million it had previously done in the Pacific islands, bringing the total value (in 1940s currency) of all the work the joint venture had done during the approximately five years of its life to a little over a billion dollars. A far cry from construction, this last phase, but every bit as critical an element as the construction itself had been in the national effort to win the war.

While the PNAB project absorbed some of Turner's most capable people over a period of almost five years, its direct impact on the operation of the company back east was itself relatively small in relation to its tremendous size and scope. PNAB operated almost entirely independently, reporting regularly in rigorous detail to the main office in New York and doubtless relying on senior management there for guidance in matters of policy but not for much else. Even the cash needs of the PNAB contractors were carefully addressed by the government, which paid the joint venture with sufficient frequency to ensure that participating companies wouldn't have to carry for more than very brief periods the huge burden of financing operations that at times reached a monthly spending rate of $40 million. The work generated substantial earnings for Turner, of course, but in the final accounting the company's share of the fee, shaped to reflect the vast size of the project and the low financial risk it imposed, was only about 1 percent of its share of the cost of work done.

Most of Turner's PNAB veterans returned to the company during or after the war, and some would go on to high-profile jobs in the company. Howard (Dutch) Schroedel, who was managing some of the Turner work at Pearl Harbor when the Japanese attacked and who later won the Navy "E" for Turner on the big airport job he supervised at nearby Barbers Point, would become a Turner vice president and later a member of its board of directors. Cliff Wilson, the stateside manager of the work and already a Turner vice president and a member of its board when the project started, would become chairman of the Turner board only a couple of years after the end of the war. George Ferris would return to New York to become a director in 1945, but the ties he had formed with the Raymond Company during the war years would prove too strong to break. A year after his election to the Turner board, Ferris would leave Turner to join Raymond as a vice president and, a few years later, would become its president. Henry Turner's own youngest son, Jim, had been working for PNAB at Pearl Harbor when the Japanese attacked, and when the war started he enlisted in the Marine Corps, returning after the war to work for the company at several locations in the United States before leaving to enter business for himself in Texas.

The Japanese enemy whose defeat had been the object of PNAB's work was, of course, only one end of an axis that originated in Nazi Germany, and when Turner first headed west in 1939 to build air bases in the Pacific, the rest of the Turner organization was at the beginning of a similar campaign that faced eastward toward Europe. Only about a month after Ben Moreell's board had selected the Turner group for the Pacific job, Hitler's forces had followed earlier moves into Austria and Czechoslovakia with a drive of unparalleled fury into Poland, linking up with their new Russian partners in eastern Poland within only a few weeks and adding to the expanding German empire 21 million Poles and vast agricultural and industrial resources. A day after the German drive into Poland started, Britain and France declared war on Germany, ending years of appeasement, and the second world war in twenty years was underway.

Until the Germans actually swept into Poland in September of 1939, the pronounced isolationist bias that had controlled American political posture throughout the thirties continued to define the nation's thinking. The neutrality legislation that had been enacted a few years earlier still made it illegal for American companies to extend credit to a belligerent nation or for American merchant vessels to arm themselves. But the events of 1939 changed many minds, and a strong sentiment began to build for doing whatever had to be done to support Britain and France. By November, Congress had enacted new legislation confirming the legality of "cash and carry" transactions in which the British and the French could pick up and pay for what they needed in American ports, and as orders for the materials of war began to show up in American plants the need for building new facilities in which to produce them began to grow too.

Business at Turner had been improving toward the end of 1939, at least as compared with the earlier depression years, although the final payment of accumulated dividend arrears had the effect of producing a net reduction in corporate worth during 1939. The company was finishing up almost $12 million worth of construction that year, about the same volume it had done during 1938, but almost every one of the nineteen contracts completed during 1939 had been secured in the still fiercely competitive market of the waning days of the depression, so there wasn't even enough profit for paying anything under the Additional Compensation Plan. The worst years were over, but times continued to be hard.

The good news in the Turner office was that almost $14 million worth of work would be carried forward into 1940, not including any allowance for what would be generated under the new navy contract, so guarded optimism was mixed with uncertainty as battle lines in Europe were staked out.

Even when fighting actually began in Europe, it would still be a few months before American industry would feel its impact. The British started with a blockade of limited effectiveness against the Germans, avoiding any serious ground fighting while efforts at reconciliation with the Germans continued, and the Russians, newly linked in a brief alliance with the Germans, intimidated the Baltic countries and then the Finns into coming over to their camp.

The French, meanwhile, scurried to make up for lost time. Although they had dominated the limited amount of aerial combat of the First World War, they had virtually ignored their defense systems during the interwar years and had allowed their air force to deteriorate badly. Early in 1939, aware that airpower would probably be the decisive factor in any future conflict, they resolved to build an effective air force of their own as quickly as they could, and they turned to a couple of American manufacturers to help them do it.

They started with the Glenn L. Martin Company, for the airframes, and Martin, whose Maryland plant was already stressed to capacity by American orders, brought in Turner to build a big new factory as quickly as possible. The Albert Kahn office prepared drawings in Detroit, and in thirty-four working days during February and March of 1939 Turner was able to convert Kahn's drawings to foundations and a superstructure for Martin's new 400,000-square-foot aircraft plant at Middle River, Maryland. By spring of 1940, the first new airframes of the Second World War were starting to emerge from the new plant.

To power its new planes, the French turned to another Turner customer, Pratt & Whitney of Hartford, Connecticut. The original Pratt & Whitney Company had been producing fine tools in Hartford for three generations when, fifteen years earlier, young Frederick Rentschler had convinced the company that they should be turning their attention to producing aircraft engines in an unused section of their big plant. Once Pratt & Whitney accepted the idea, they put Rentschler in charge of implementing it, and within a few years he had built and expanded a thriving, horizontally integrated engine-manufacturing conglomerate that by then included Boeing, Chance Vought, and Hamilton Standard; would later include Sikorsky; and would soon be called United Aircraft. In 1929 Pratt & Whitney brought Turner Construction Company to Hartford to build the first of what would become a complex of huge manufacturing buildings in which Pratt & Whitney and Hamilton Standard would produce most of the aircraft engines and propellers used by the Allied side during the Second World War. But by 1939, the big Hartford plant was using every available square foot of its space, and when the French came along with an order for engines to power the planes that Glenn Martin was producing for them in Maryland, there simply wasn't enough available space for the job. That was when Pratt & Whitney brought Turner back to Hartford to build the first new structure of what would become one of the largest and most productive aircraft engine plants in the world.

Meanwhile, the war in Europe was heating up and moving badly for the French and the British. In the spring of 1940, the Germans had driven north to swallow up Denmark and Norway, and then west to absorb Luxembourg, Belgium, and Holland, revealing in savage ways the strength of a military force that had been almost a decade in the making. By May, they had slashed through French defenses and the French army itself had effectively collapsed, leaving a British expeditionary force of almost 400,000 men to be driven back to the north coast of France to await the heroic rescue that would return them from Dunkirk to safety. By summer the French government had fallen, and the Germans, exulting in victory and declaring the conquest of England their only remaining task, were preparing the siege of London. Winston Churchill, having taken over as prime minister, mounted the ramparts to rouse the soul of the British people.

American reaction to events in Europe was swift and decisive. In September 1940, Congress enacted the first peacetime military draft in the country's history, and Roosevelt sent fifty overage destroyers to the British in exchange for long-term leases at strategically attractive bases in the North and South Atlantic. As soon as the 1940 election confirmed public support for Roosevelt's interventionist perspective, new legislation authorized him to "sell, transfer, exchange, lease or lend" materials of any description to any country whose defense he felt was vital to the defense of the United States and to make available to such nations the ship-yards of the United States as well. Whatever remained of American neutrality was abandoned, and the country's role as the "arsenal of democracy" was formalized, effectively defining the course of Turner Construction Company's work for the next few years.

Once the French fell, the British took over delivery of the aircraft they had pre-viously ordered from Martin and then assumed the engine contract they had made with Pratt & Whitney, adding an even larger order for engines of their own. Now, even the building that had been added for the French at Hartford wasn't enough, so Turner was engaged again, this time to build another 400,000 square feet. And that was only the beginning: The aircraft industry's response to Roosevelt's call for 50,000 airplanes per year had the effect of requiring still another approximately 600,000 square feet of manufacturing and support space at Hartford, and Turner's Boston office moved substantial forces there for what was clearly going to be an ongoing construction operation of extraordinarily large proportions.

Jim Allaire, who would retire as a Turner vice president forty-two years later, spent his first years with the company as a young engineer on the Pratt & Whitney job. Only a year out of Cooper Union when he was hired in 1939, he began his Turner career as a timekeeper there, doubling as a line and grade engineer on weekends. It was a time when Turner was still doing virtually all its general con-struction work with forces in its own direct employ, without subcontractors, and management's idea was that the critical task of recording the workers' time and producing a database for cost estimating would be best undertaken by the bright young engineers who were learning the business. Allaire and his Turner comrades worked seven days a week at Hartford to ensure completion of two gigantic new manufacturing buildings and a couple of support structures within the ninety days that had been scheduled, and sixty years later he still remembered seeing Pratt & Whitney mechanics setting up their tools in one end of a Turner project while structural steel was still being erected at the other end. They were heady days, with the winds of war blowing with increasing force and Turner people finding themselves at the center of a monumental national effort to prepare for what lay ahead.

The government, beginning to fear that further concentration of manufacturing at Hartford would exhaust the available labor supply of the region, and apprehensive about the security of a critical defense plant built so close to the coast, tried to induce Pratt & Whitney's management to build its next plant nearer the center of the country, but Hartford didn't like the idea. They saw the abundance of highly skilled craftsmen in the Connecticut Valley as one of their principal resources, and they didn't want to abandon it. As it turned out other, less obvious Connecticut sources that Pratt & Whitney's management hadn't counted on would surface as well, before it was all over. In a telling interview, years later, a retired foreman remembered that although the skilled Yankee machinists (of which he was one) were indeed an absolutely vital resource at Hartford, he had been surprised to learn on the plant floor itself that they weren't the whole story. He remembered with sometimes grudging admiration the Connecticut Valley women and the totally inexperienced family men who had come into the plant to work alongside the old-timers, and how they had become highly skilled at one or two isolated processes that contributed in major ways to the output of the plant.

The catastrophe at Pearl Harbor increased and dramatized the urgency of the need for more production, and when the manufacturing areas of the new buildings at Hartford reached almost 3 million square feet in 1942, Pratt & Whitney sent Turner out to build three big satellite plants for them in the neighboring Connecticut towns of Willimantic and Southington and in the nearby Massachusetts town of East Longmeadow. Steel was the natural structural material for the satellite plants, with their large, open spaces and long spans, but by 1942 virtually everything the steel mills were producing was needed for making weapons, ships, and other materials of battle, so the Kahn office in Detroit designed the new satellite buildings in concrete, taking Turner back to its roots in big concrete. The satellite plants were built on a crash basis, three shifts a day, seven days a week, and by late 1943, when their enormous roofs were being painted the greens and browns that had been designed to make them appear from the air to be farms, Pratt & Whitney mechanics were already down below installing tools for making engine parts.

News from the war fronts was uniformly bad through most of 1942, relieved only briefly by a glorious American victory at Midway that restored sagging morale. The Japanese were adding to their forces all over the South Pacific, moving them increasingly close to the coast of Australia, and Rommel was driving across North Africa, pummeling the British and, toward the end of the year, the first of the newly arrived Americans as well. The struggle that still lay ahead for the Allies demanded a vast amount of additional aircraft, and even with their new satellite plants in New England, Pratt & Whitney needed more space for building more engines. By then they (and the licensees they had authorized to manufacture some of the engines) were producing half of all the horsepower being used in American combat aircraft and a good deal of additional British aircraft as well. But it wasn't enough. With pressure from Washington mounting, Pratt & Whitney's management accepted the government's insistence that they build a new plant in Kansas City, Missouri, where it was felt there would be an abundance of skilled manufacturing labor and enough housing and other services to support them. Long Construction Company of Kansas City was proposed as the contractor, but by that time Pratt & Whitney's management was loath to undertake major construction without Turner, so it induced the two firms to join forces to do the job. The 3.5-million-square foot plant they would build would be the largest manufacturing building in the world.

Ground was broken for the big new plant on the Fourth of July, 1942, on a sprawling site just outside Kansas City that had formerly been an automobile speedway. Missouri's Sen. Harry Truman, still relatively little known outside the state in 1942, took the platform to tell a crowd that had assembled for the ceremonies how desperately the plant was needed, appealing to them to recruit as many workers as they could to help with the construction. Dramatizing the urgency of conditions, a hundred recruits were sworn into the army on the spot.

Albert Kahn had died a month earlier, but while the groundbreaking was in progress in Kansas City, his office in Detroit was scurrying to convert what had originally been a structural steel design for the plant into a concrete design, like the one used back east. And at the same time the Turner-Long joint venture began its effort to recruit construction workers in an area where virtually every able-bodied man had already taken a job in a defense plant or entered one of the military services. Elmer Ford was placed in charge for Turner at the home office, and M. H. (Deke) Parsons was given responsibility for running the job in the field, with Bill Brown assisting as local purchasing agent and L. P. Farnham as job accountant.

In some ways the Kansas City job was reminiscent of the concrete giants that Turner had built for the government during the First World War, but it was more complex and even more reliant on massive traveling forms and elaborate material-handling systems. A whole generation had been replaced on the Turner payroll since those World War I days, and except for a few old-timers there were few men still around who had worked on the earlier jobs. But the technology was still there, well documented in Turner's archives and available to its engineers and foremen. What was adapted and redesigned proved to be spectacularly successful at Kansas City. Thin-shell, barrel-shaped concrete roofs (almost 400 of them) were built in sections 80 feet long by 1,000 feet wide using prefabricated wood forms that were placed and lowered by pneumatic jacking systems and moved every seven days along rails that had been cast in the slab below. It was all protected from the cold Missouri winter and then from drenching spring rains by a heated canvas enclosure that was moved along on its own set of rails. By the end of 1943, Pratt & Whitney engines that would drive some of the war's most effective aircraft began to emerge from the big Kansas City plant.

Aircraft was so central to the country's war effort that Turner's work was virtually dominated, during the early years of the 1940s, by what was needed to produce it. Very early on, even before the United States entered the war, Republic Aviation had brought Turner out to Farmingdale, Long Island, to build a 500,000-square-foot plant for manufacturing its dazzling new P-47 Thunderbolt, the first airplane to challenge successfully the high-speed German fighters that had controlled the air during the first months of the war. With no time to lose, Nelson Doe, a veteran of Turner's New England– and New York–area work and now general superintendent for the New York territory, established a seven-day work schedule that included a night shift that would work on a five-acre site lighted by a battery of giant carbon arcs. Doe tapped Larry Gilmore to run the job. With construction labor in increasingly short supply as the draft and other defense projects absorbed most of what there was of it, Turner abandoned its tradition of doing virtually all the work itself and subcontracted both the masonry work (to Natco, which also manufactured the brick and tile that were used) and the finishing of the concrete slabs (to Brennan and Sloan), exploiting the labor reserves of those subcontractors to ease the problem of developing an adequate workforce quickly. The round-the-clock schedule paid off, and Republic began tooling work inside the big new plant less than six months after ground had been broken. Five months after that, the first P-47, powered by a Pratt & Whitney engine, was rolled out onto the runway and spirited off on a journey that would place it at the heart of the North African campaign.

Of course, even these gigantic new manufacturing plants weren't all there was to the business of providing the United States and Great Britain with the airpower that would be needed to win a war against the Germans and, between 1941 and 1943, against the Italians. The planes that were produced had to be adapted for use in different battle zones, and Turner was brought into that process too. In July 1941, the Army Corps of Engineers selected Rome, New York, a city of 34,000 in the center of the state, as one of two places through which all new aircraft would pass before going on to the battle zones of Africa and Europe. At the new Rome base, later called Griffiss, military aircraft would be prepared for combat, adapted for specific destinations, fitted out with armament and special equipment, tested and modified as needed, and finally turned over to crews that would fly them to the war zones by way of bases that had been established in Canada, Newfoundland, and Greenland. Rome, New York, would be the last stop before heading off for Europe for thousands of airplanes desperately needed and eagerly awaited by British and American forces, and it would be larger and more advanced than any U.S. airfield existing at that time.

It would be a furious struggle to get the Rome facility finished in time for receiving and processing the large number of airplanes that would start coming out of new plants all over the country by the middle of 1942, and the army picked a joint venture of Turner and the Louis Mayersohn Company of Albany to build it. Mayersohn was a well-established upstate New York highway contractor, and with a 2,600-acre site to clear and grade and almost five miles of runway to build at Rome, Mayersohn was a good choice. Turner's job was to build hangars with 300-foot clear spans, engine test buildings, engine repair buildings, supply depots, administration and medical buildings, housing, and other infrastructure appropriate to what would become, for all practical purposes, a self-sufficient town. And it all had to be done fast, regardless of increasingly critical shortages of skilled labor and vital materials, and regardless of the relentless power of winter in central New York State.

It took a big Turner staff to manage the sprawling job that was to be done at Rome, and some of the men who were in charge would later go on to important posts in the company after the war. George Horr, the Turner executive in charge, was already a seasoned veteran. A 1911 graduate of Lafayette College, he'd been a member of the Turner board since 1935 and would become a vice president when the Rome work got started. Nicholas B. O'Connell, a younger Turner veteran who was made field superintendent at Rome, would become a Turner vice president a couple of years after the job was finished and would join the board a few years after that. M. K. Walsh, who had already been working for Turner for twenty-five years when he came over to the Rome job, became its job accountant. The list of other men who worked at Rome is punctuated with names that would become part of the company's management during the years that followed. It included, among many, Hank Gally, Harry Welty, Ray Cusick, and Walter B. Shaw.

When work at Rome got underway in the fall of 1941, the job was thought to be an approximately $10 million project, certainly a big job in 1941 dollars but nowhere near as big as it would actually become. As soon as the United States entered the war in December, Washington more than doubled the scope of work at the Rome base, adding a hospital, significantly expanding the housing and the infrastructure needed to support it, and increasing the cost of the work to almost $23 million. It would take a workforce that often exceeded 3,000 men to meet the schedule, but the new base became operational in the fall of 1942, just a year after it had been started, and it became a critical link in a system that, by 1943, was beginning to alter the probable outcome of the war that was raging abroad.

Airpower was and continued to be the dominant factor in the great struggle to defeat the enemy, but it certainly wasn't the only factor. From the end of 1942 and later, American foot soldiers would be moving from one bloody battlefield to another across North Africa and then across the Mediterranean into southern Europe, while their counterparts in the Pacific would be fighting an ugly jungle war in New Guinea and on Guadalcanal, in the first phases of the American drive toward Japan. These were armies that needed the traditional weapons and equipment of the foot soldier, and such matériel, as well as the troops themselves, had to be transported to the battle zones in merchant ships protected by the navy. All this equipment had all been in perilously short supply when the war started, and manufacturing plants had to be hurriedly expanded or built from scratch all over the country to produce what was needed before the enemy could convert his early military superiority into a catastrophic American defeat.

Building or expanding existing plants for producing what was needed began for Turner as early as the spring of 1940. The Birdsboro Foundry in Pennsylvania had been doing marine casting work for years before damaged British naval vessels that had been patrolling the North Atlantic began lining up at its docks along the Schuylkill instead of limping back for repairs in England. Birdsboro was soon swamped with orders, so they brought in Turner to expand their foundry. But the demands of British and then American shipping continued to grow, and three years and many projects later Turner was still there, having expanded the original Birdsboro Foundry and built another ten acres of new plant as well, including testing and inspection shops and assembly and administration buildings.

The Bullard Company in Bridgeport, Connecticut, was another manufacturing firm caught up in the demand for expanded industrial production more than a year before American entry into the war. By spring 1940, Bullard was already one of the country's largest and most prestigious manufacturers of machine tools when the demand from new defense plants in Europe and the United States began to exceed the company's capacity. Bullard equipment could be found in almost every kind of plant in those days, but in 1940 it was its special application to aircraft manufacturing that was responsible for a backlog that had grown from a few months to a few years. It was a backlog that couldn't be tolerated by firms tooling up to produce airplanes for national defense. Bullard's space needs were large, and they weren't ordinary by any measure: They needed heavy power, high-quality lighting and ventilating, and a good deal of big, ruggedly built industrial space with long roof spans and floors that could handle loading up to 800 pounds per square foot. And they needed all of it in a terrible hurry. Turner had built Bullard's only other major addition twenty-four years earlier, on the eve of American entry into the First World War, and in 1940 the company returned to Bridgeport to expand the plant again. Like the plant at Birdsboro, the Bullard facility kept growing as orders for the company's products proliferated. Starting with a foundry expansion, it soon included a big new assembly plant, a warehouse, an office building, and even the reconstruction of its ovens. The work was relatively difficult too, with some of it designed in structural steel and some in reinforced concrete, a section of it bridging a tidal stream and most of it supported by piled foundations. E. L. Courter ran the job for Turner, and his staff included E. H. Andresen as assistant superintendent and Spencer Robinson as job accountant. George Morrison, an especially distinguished Turner man who would later go on to senior management in its Chicago office, was not long out of MIT when he became timekeeper on the Bullard job during that summer of 1940.

As the European war intensified toward the end of 1940, and the country shifted onto a complete war footing, defense work continued to crowd out Turner's remaining civilian work a few jobs at a time. In Brooklyn, the navy came back to Turner to build another of its big concrete storehouses, this one sixteen stories over a foundation that Spencer, White & Prentis's chief engineer later described as the most difficult he had seen in thirty years of foundation work. Its 6-foot-diameter, 150-foot-deep caissons took almost a year to install, but once they were in place Turner built the big superstructure in six months, with Walter Conlin in charge and Carl Fritch as project engineer.

By 1941, with the French defeated and the British embattled, the need for intensifying and expanding American production was dramatic, and although the United States had not yet actually entered the war, the country was fully mobilized for it. Military conscription was in full effect, of course, and a priority system for obtaining construction materials had been instituted that made it almost impossible to build anything except what would be required for the defense of the country or its allies. Virtually everything being built was war-related in one way or another. For anything that did qualify for construction, the urgency of the times militated against waiting for completed drawings, so experienced contractors who could marshal the required forces quickly, who could address complex projects vigorously without benefit of detailed documents, and who could be trusted with cost-plus construction contracts found themselves in great demand. Turner, of course, met all those criteria, so it was natural that it was sought after almost anywhere a new defense plant was to be built or an existing one was to be expanded or modified.

In Massachusetts, General Electric's plants were working around the clock to keep up with British and American orders, and when even that wasn't enough, they called in Turner to build more manufacturing space. In Everett, the result was a vast, windowless manufacturing complex with a bomb-resistant basement under most of it, all supported by 770 caissons drilled through a former swamp. At nearby Lynn, where GE was producing reduction gears for the navy's turbine-driven ships, it was a similar but even larger plant.

Most of what was built was intended for manufacturing heavy equipment or parts needed in the manufacture of weapons or ships, but not everything was. In Brooklyn, Turner built its fifth addition to the Squibb pharmaceutical plant, and a year later Turner would build a similar plant in Pearl River, New York, for Lederle Laboratories, which manufactured critically needed penicillin. For Federal Radio, which manufactured radios and telephones, Turner built a big new plant in Clinton, New Jersey, that was designed around a manufacturing process that was suddenly and radically changed when the building was almost complete. The redesigned building had to be fully underpinned from within and it required construction of a full, deep basement under what Turner had already built as a single-story, basementless plant on grade. Walter Jackson was the harried superintendent who ran that ill-fated job for Turner, and M. J. Roach was his engineer. Perhaps the least conventional of Turner's war plants was built in New Milford, Connecticut, for a sixty-year-old Swiss Company named Maggi. A complex plant comprising two buildings, it would produce bouillon cubes as field rations for battle troops. Harold Seward ran the job for Turner, with Walter Rumble as his assistant.

By 1943, this prodigious expansion of the country's productive capacity had begun to pay dividends, and there was evidence that the tide of war was finally turning in favor of the United States and its allies. In the Pacific, reinforced American land and sea forces had successfully initiated the bloody campaign that would take them back to the Philippines, island by island. Rommel's army in North Africa had been defeated, and an American armada of more than 3,000 vessels was steaming north across the Mediterranean for an invasion that would start on the island of Sicily and fight its way up through the underbelly of Europe toward Germany. The Russians were only a few months from annihilating some of the same German troops that, two years earlier, had brought the French to their knees and driven the British from the continent, and secret plans for landings on the north coast of Europe were already being developed by the Americans and the British. It had taken a couple of years for the mobilization of American industrial potential to reach its full stride, but by the middle of 1943 forces ranged against the Axis powers were building to a level that would exceed anything the enemy would be able to match.

The significant fraction of this success that was due to the prodigious achievement of American industry certainly owed something to the contractors who had built the infrastructure so well and quickly, and Turner's work by any measure exemplified that extraordinary feat. But by the middle of 1943 most of the new and modified plants had been pretty much completed, and although the implements of war would continue to be produced at unprecedented rates, once the factories themselves had been built or expanded the need for further construction began to decline sharply. To make matters worse for contractors like Turner, there was virtually no alternative market for construction in the civilian sector because the materials needed were for the most part the very materials that were required for the production of aircraft, military vehicles, weapons, and other war-related equipment. Ensuring the availability of such critical materials for military use was the goal of a rigid system of government-mandated priorities that effectively precluded any activity in the civilian sector.

Turner had by 1943 completed a couple of consecutive years of work that exceeded in volume anything it had ever done before, even during the most prosperous years of the late twenties. In 1941 the company had completed almost $48 million worth of construction, and in 1942 that figure had increased to $88 million. Even after it had paid its preferred shareholders all of what remained in accumulated dividends and had added dividends on its common stock as well, and after it had restored bonus distributions to employees under the Additional Compensation Plan, its net worth had increased from about $2.2 million in 1940 to a little over $2.6 million in 1943. The increase, although substantial, wasn't linearly proportionate to the increase in volume, of course, because the fee rates applied to the work Turner was doing during the war were significantly lower than those it had been able to earn in commercial work in the private sector, but the company's growth was nonetheless substantial. Its salaried staff of supervisory and administrative personnel, 213 persons in 1940, had by 1942 risen to 1,033. But by the middle of 1943 it had fallen back to around 500, largely because of the inroads of the military draft and because so much of the major work was beginning to wind down. By late 1943 the company's management was once again scanning the horizon for signs of new work, this time focusing more on ways of maintaining staff for the expected demands of the postwar economy than on seeking areas of new growth.

The early 1940s had brought important changes in the company's operating staff and a few within its board of directors as well. In 1941, at the age of sixty-eight, Henry C. Turner had resigned as president, relinquishing the position to his younger brother Archie, but continuing on as chairman of the board. Archie, who had been working closely with his older brother for almost ten years as a vice pres-

ident and as a member of the board, had turned over his own previous responsibilities as head of the Philadelphia territory to Henry Turner's oldest son, Chan,
who had returned to work in the company in 1938 after a six-year voluntary
absence that had coincided with the worst years of the depression. Board member
Arthur Tozzer, a Turner elder statesman, had died in 1942 after thirty-seven years
of service. A former general superintendent, he had run some of Turner's biggest
jobs during the First World War, had later managed the Boston territory, and had
served a term as president of the Associated General Contractors of America
(AGC). Tozzer was replaced on the board by Elmer Ford, a Harvard-educated
Turner veteran who had six years earlier succeeded Tozzer as operations manager
in Boston. Ford's election to the board preserved its membership at sixteen, the
level to which it had been increased a few years earlier, and it comprised, in addition to Ford and the three Turners (Henry C., Chan, and Archie), Robert (Cliff)
Wilson, Walter K. Shaw, Harry Ward, John P. H. Perry, William H. Nye, Fred
Schilling, George Horr, William Ball, DeForest Dixon, Egbert J. Moore, A. Wright
Chapman (Charlotte Chapman Turner's brother), and T. Arthur Smith (the old-
timer who had run the original subway stair job in the first days of the company).
Moore would die later in 1942 and be replaced on the board by Ab Abberley, and
both Chapman and Smith would retire three years after that and be replaced by
Chan Turner's close friend and his colleague Francis B. (Joe) Warren and George
Ferris. It would still be a while before Turner shares or seats on its board of directors would be held by outsiders, and every director in the early 1940s was either an
active or retired Turner man.

For a while the search for new work was probably more difficult than it had
been during the depression, when there was work to be done but when fierce competition drove prices down to unacceptable levels. By the end of 1943, with most
of the construction needs of the military fairly well met and with most of the basic
materials of construction being directed into production of the implements of war,
there just wasn't much new construction of any kind in the pipeline at any price.
The gross volume of building work that was put in place in the United States during 1944 (the volume that Turner would have seen in 1943 as the source of its next

year's business) was just under half of what it had averaged during the preceding three years.

It was future work, of course, that concerned the planners at Turner in 1943, not current work. There was more than enough of that. At the end of 1942, the company had about $44 million worth of work remaining to be carried forward into 1943, and even at the end of 1943 there was almost $8 million worth of such work to be carried forward into 1944, all of it critical to the war effort.

One of the more spectacular jobs of this later war period was the 2-million-square-foot manufacturing plant that a Turner-Raymond joint venture built outside New Orleans for Andrew Jackson Higgins, a flamboyant and often brilliant industrialist who had made a name and a considerable fortune for himself building small boats, mostly of wood, before the war. By 1943, according to a usually reliable source, the navy was operating a little over 14,000 vessels, of which almost a thousand were big fighting ships and the remainder were all small craft, including more than 12,000 that had been built and/or designed by Higgins Boat Company. Higgins boats included the vaunted PT boat and a wide variety of landing craft and similar vessels. In 1943 the government was searching for a solution to the growing shortage of cargo aircraft, and it contracted with Higgins to produce a large number of giant wooden cargo airplanes, a task for which it felt his broad experience in wood construction would qualify him. The order, for 1,200 airplanes, was at that time the largest single aircraft contract the government had ever written. It wasn't the first time the government had brought Higgins into manufacturing something other than small boats: Almost a year earlier the Maritime Commission had awarded him a big contract to build a fleet of Liberty-type cargo ships. But after he had done some work on the difficult, 1,100-acre site and actually started construction of a building, the government, asserting that the steel required for the ships had to be diverted for another use, cancelled the ship contract and began dismantling the building. Higgins had made no secret of his anger, charging that the cancellation was a surrender to the influence of other shipbuilders, and it was thought by some that perhaps the later cargo airplane contract, which required construction of a plant on the same site, was an effort to pacify him and the large

New Orleans constituency that shared his views. A joint venture of Turner and Raymond Pile was engaged to build the big plant, and behind the leadership of George Horr and Nicholas O'Connell (both fresh from the Rome air base job) a crew of almost 5,000 men working eight-hour shifts around the clock six days a week, completed construction of the gigantic manufacturing space, together with a large engineering building, test buildings, kilns, lumber storage buildings, paved roads, and three miles of railroad tracking, all in less than seven months.

An extraordinary achievement for the builders, but nowhere near the contribution to the war effort that so much of Turner's other work had represented. Before production of the cargo planes had really been started, the government changed its mind again and suspended the order for the wooden planes in favor of a smaller order for aluminum cargo planes, this time because it was felt that the wood, by now in short supply itself, could be more effectively deployed elsewhere. Higgins grudgingly went forward with the smaller contract and with other work in the building, but the plant was never really fully utilized.

As Turner's search for new work intensified, it moved in some surprising new directions. One produced an ill-fated mining venture in West Virginia with its friends from the Rome venture, the Mayersohn Company of Albany. Coal was much needed and in short supply, and Mayersohn had a good deal of equipment that was well suited for strip mining, but subsurface complications and the exigencies of the marketplace conspired against success, and the venture was abandoned with a modest loss in 1945.

But not all the new directions proved disappointing. A more productive one was found in service contracts where not much if any actual construction was required but where the company's enlightened and effective approach to management was admired and sought. Turner was already deeply involved in the navy's procurement program, in which company personnel were managing a big purchasing and delivery system for the government, and Turner's senior management was apparently satisfied that while the demand for actual construction continued to lag, such contracts might indeed provide a way of ensuring the continued employment of key personnel. And although the fees were modest, they paid their share of the overhead.

One big service contract the company acquired provided for Turner's joining with the Alabama Dry Dock and Shipping Company in running its expanded shipyard at Mobile, Alabama, to produce oil tankers. ADDSCO had been building ships at Mobile since 1916 and was evidently very good at it, but the demand for building more and bigger tankers quickly under the urgent conditions of the Second World War by 1943 had begun to swamp the company. Between 1941 and 1943 it had built about twenty of the required 523-foot-long, 5,400-ton ships, each capable of transporting about 141,000 barrels of desperately needed oil, but there were many more to be built after the middle of 1943 and ADDSCO needed help. A force of about 22,000 persons was required to operate the yard effectively, and the available local labor pool was down to mostly unskilled workers who had never worked in a shipyard before. Training schools had to be established, as well as an approach to production that would integrate the newly trained workers effectively.

In fact, though, it wasn't ADDSCO's labor situation that was causing most of its trouble, it was the firm's inability to marshal the management personnel needed to run a vastly expanded, increasingly complex shipbuilding operation. Such people were a good deal more difficult to find than unskilled workers who could be trained on the job. In the middle of 1943, ADDSCO turned for help to a joint venture of Turner and Turner's old friends (and occasional joint venture partners) at Spencer, White & Prentis. A partnership was formed and the two New York construction firms assigned about twenty of their own best managers (among them Turner's Dutch Schroedel, George Floyd, and Harrie Muchemore, recently returned from the Pacific) to various departments of the shipyard that included personnel services, accounting, production, plant maintenance, engineering, and legal. Spencer, White & Prentis's F. B. Spencer took over as general manager of the yard, and Cliff Wilson became executive in charge in New York. The production rate was markedly improved: By the end of the war seventy-eight additional ships had been successfully produced, with the joint venture sharing in the yard's earnings as well as in the savings generated below upset costs that had been previously negotiated with the government.

Of the variety of ventures into which the war years carried Turner Construction Company, there probably wasn't one that would take it as far from its roots as the Roane-Anderson project in Oak Ridge, Tennessee. Oak Ridge was a 59,000-acre wilderness that had been acquired by the U.S. Army in 1942 as the site for laboratories and factories it would build for extracting from special, imported soils enough uranium to produce a nuclear bomb. It was work that had been intensely studied and planned but that had never before been done, and it was fraught with uncertainties and shrouded in secrecy. It was at the core of a high-stakes race against powerful and skilled enemies in Germany and, it has since been learned, in Japan.

The Army Corps of Engineers had its hands full in 1942. While it was building the industrial facilities and all the infrastructure required to house and provide for the needs of what was estimated would be as many as 75,000 staff and service persons at Oak Ridge, it was also at work in Los Alamos, New Mexico. There the corps was building the facility at which the products of the Oak Ridge plant would be integrated into the deadly weapon itself and where it would ultimately be tested.

One thing the Corps of Engineers had neither experience in nor taste for was actually managing the complete new town it was building at Oak Ridge. The task of managing Oak Ridge would be virtually the same as the task of managing any modern city of 75,000 persons, except that this one would be created all at once, rather than over the years it would normally take for a city of such size to grow from a tiny hamlet, accumulating infrastructure and institutions along the way. Oak Ridge would have to start right off with a complete system of housing, streets, transportation, schools, shops, hospitals, recreation, sanitation, fire protection, electric power, traffic control, police, and the like. No small task for anyone, least of all for a military organization committed to overseeing the production of the most powerful weapon in history. What the army wondered, in 1943, was who in the world was capable of doing such a job and could be trusted with it.

The search for an existing organization to manage Oak Ridge was undertaken a few years before the intense specialization that would characterize industry later in the century had begun to develop, so it wasn't easy for the army to identify suitable candidates for the job. What it wanted was an organization that was accustomed to solving a broad range of frequently unanticipated problems, that was capable of marshaling resources, and that was experienced in the management and administration of large and sometimes diverse vendors. Some of the army's senior officers had recently seen Turner in action on the Rome air base project and they brought the company's name to the attention of Gen. Leslie Groves, who was running the nuclear bomb program. Groves took a long look at Turner and liked what he saw.

The army followed with a contract requiring Turner to manage everything at Oak Ridge, except the actual, totally restricted production plant itself, for a fixed annual fee. Turner formed a management subsidiary for the work, naming it Roane-Anderson after the two Tennessee counties that met on the Oak Ridge reservation, and the subsidiary acted as town manager at Oak Ridge under the army's direction until 1946 and then under the U.S. Atomic Energy Commission's direction until 1951. In that year, with the pace of postwar construction accelerating almost everywhere in the country, Turner elected to refocus on construction itself, requesting and securing a release from the Roane-Anderson contract.

George Horr, who had been the top man for Turner at Rome, became the executive in charge at Oak Ridge, and Clinton Hernandez, who had entered Turner's employ when he closed his own construction firm in Yonkers, New York, at the beginning of the war, became Horr's on-site project manager. About thirty-three other Turner men went down to Oak Ridge to run various departments of the town government, employing as many as 10,000 workers at different stages in the life of the contract and gradually refining the process to include subcontractors and independent concessionaires for operating shops, eating establishments, rental housing, and other elements that lent themselves to such arrangements. It would be an eight-year project for Turner, about as different from construction work as anything the company had done, but one in which it distinguished itself, earned a fee, and kept some key staff well engaged during a period in which, at least until the end of the war, contracts for new construction remained scarce.

Nineteen forty-four finally marked the beginning of the end of the war. In

June, the largest armada in history returned troops of the Allied nations to the French beaches from which they had been hurled four years earlier, and by spring 1945, they were advancing through Germany's Ruhr Valley on their way to the Elbe, where they would meet their freshly arrived Russian allies. American and British aircraft were bombing the cities of Germany with a relentlessness never before seen in warfare, while out in the Pacific, Halsey's Third Fleet had defeated the Japanese at Leyte Gulf and U.S. Marines were poised for taking Iwo Jima and Okinawa. American airplanes were intensifying the bombing of Japanese cities, and Douglas MacArthur, back in the Philippines as he had promised, was organizing a land invasion of the Japanese mainland. By May of 1945, the Germans had surrendered, and after the atomic bombing of Hiroshima and Nagasaki in August, the Japanese followed suit. The United States, after almost a million casualties, including 300,000 deaths, was at peace again.

Turner emerged from the long struggle even stronger that it had been when the war started. About half the 186 Turner men who served in the military returned to the company's employ, and of those who didn't, some remained in the service, some found employment elsewhere, two had been killed in action, and one had died while in service. Salaried employees when the war ended numbered 375, up from 213 when the war had started. The company had done about $252 million worth of construction during the six years that had elapsed between 1940 and 1945, more than it had ever done in any comparable period before and even a little over 50 percent more than it had done between 1924 and 1929, its previously busiest six-year period. It had maintained profitability too, although its earnings during the war years, limited by the very low fees it had accepted for the government work and by an "excess profits" tax on profits that exceeded what had been earned during a government-selected period of the depression, were only about half what they had been during the 1924–1929 period. Nonetheless, the company's net worth, after all costs and taxes and after dividends and added compensation to employees, had increased by more than 25 percent, from about $2.2 million in 1940 to about $2.8 million in 1945.

Some of what happened quietly after the final armistice said a little about the company itself. Archie Turner wrote to each former Turner employee who had served, inviting his return to the company's employ and enclosing a check for what was estimated to be income that had been lost during the war years. Not much later, the results of audits of firms that had done work for the government during the war years generated rebates from some that were found to have profiteered, but no rebate was ever asked of Turner. Navy Secretary James Forrestal, in a letter to company president Archie Turner, wrote of Turner's "pre-eminent role in building a great arsenal at home and a bridge of vital bases across the Pacific," adding that Turner "deserved to carry forward into the peace the pride of a great achievement."

There was doubtless some uncertainty among the company's managers as to just what the postwar years would bring, but they knew that they were well prepared for just about anything. Through the combined impact of the depression and then the Second World War, they had been tempered and strengthened, and the possibilities seemed vast.

8.

Transition

Once peace came, the world pretty much had to start over. The bloodiest and most destructive war in history had left more than 50 million people dead, almost two-thirds of them civilians, had reduced much of Europe and some of Asia to ruins, and had prostrated a significant fraction of their populations. The task of effectively rebuilding the communities that had been ravaged by war seemed almost hopelessly daunting to some of those in responsible authority and simply impossible to others.

In the United States, which had lost almost a third of a million of its own in the fighting, fewer than a dozen of them civilians, things were a good deal better. The country itself had been spared the terrible impact of an attack on its own soil, and for the second time in a quarter of a century had emerged from a war as creditor to most of the world. But concerns about the future abounded. Memories of the depression were fresh, and a good many informed thinkers wondered whether the expected postwar decline of world markets would mean a return to hard times at home. With almost 15 million Americans expected to return from military service, apprehension about unemployment was widespread, and there was fear that a concurrent explosive inflation would exacerbate conditions as soon as wartime controls of prices and wages were relaxed. Everyone welcomed the end of war, but many worried about it too.

Almost two full years before the fighting ended, the capable but sometimes unpredictable American industrialist Henry J. Kaiser had generated his share of public criticism by encouraging American businessmen to begin thinking about and planning for the expanding economy that he was convinced would accompany the eventual end of the war. It was an impolitic thing for him to discuss, at a time when American forces were beleaguered in much of the world and battle casualties were rising, but Kaiser, who at the time of his injudicious comments was furiously engaged in the production of steel, cement, and magnesium for the military and in building the largest merchant fleet in history, was an unconventional man inclined to speak his mind.

Not everyone thought Kaiser's comments inappropriate. Archie Turner, who had been running Turner Construction Company since his brother Henry had relinquished its presidency in favor of its chairmanship in 1941, thought Kaiser was absolutely right, and as early as May 1943, he had initiated a program of consultation with past and potential Turner clients that focused on postwar planning. In 1944, with the war raging, he had assigned six Turner men the task of interviewing more than 600 major industrial and commercial executives around the country about what they planned to do after the war. Almost a third of them revealed that they had definite plans for building, and that was information that wasn't lost on Archie Turner or his board.

Of course, expansion of facilities would be more easily said than done. Even after the signing of peace agreements, it would be a while before the War Production Board authorized resumption of large-scale civilian construction. Even when the board did begin to relax its restrictions, material shortages abounded. Price controls that were allowed to remain had the effect of dissuading some manufacturers from producing what was needed, intensifying some problems while solving others. It was a complex transition that required the careful dismantling of systems that had been put in place to ensure the availability of critical materials during the war years, and it was going to take a while to work out.

But whenever this suggested postwar construction boom did materialize, Archie Turner had made sure Turner Construction Company was ready for it. During the last year of the war, the company had completed a relatively modest $15 million worth of new building construction in spite of restrictions, and it had done what was estimated to be an additional approximately $100 million worth of service work as well, e.g., the management work at Oak Ridge and at the Alabama shipyards and the huge navy procurement contract. After all its costs, including its 1945 contribution to the company's Additional Compensation Plan, and after paying dividends to its shareholders, Turner was showing a net worth that was approaching $3 million, almost all of it sufficiently liquid to be characterized as working capital. And largely through Archie Turner's diligent implementation of the findings of the 1944 study of postwar, private-sector planning, the company was able to bring forward into the uncertain period that began in January of 1946 a backlog of almost $43 million worth of new business. Few construction companies could show such strength at the end of the war, and it was clear that Turner's recovery from the dark days of the depression was just about complete. Archie Turner himself was at pains to ensure that the recovery wasn't seen by anyone as an exploitation of war conditions, reminding the big crowd of men and women who attended the first postwar annual Turner dinner late in 1945 that although net earnings during the war years (including 1940) were a good deal better than anything the company had seen during the terrible years of the Great Depression, they were still less than half what Turner had seen during a comparable span of years between 1924 and 1929. Turner's postwar strength wasn't just economic, by any measure. At the end of 1945, the company had a salaried staff that included 335 officers, executives, and engineers as well as 40 superintendents who averaged a little over seventeen years with the firm. Forty-eight of the 186 employees who had gone off to war had already returned to its employ, and more were returning every month as the release of military personnel went forward. Especially critical to the company's transition into the expansion that was expected to follow the war were the seasoned managers whom Turner had been able to retain right through the war years, even during the most recent, increasingly lean days in which civilian construction volume had fallen off sharply. Their having remained in the company's employ was for the most part the result of Turner's success in securing the important management contracts that had provided employment for senior people when there just wasn't enough new building construction work to go around.

Just below these senior managers in the company's postwar hierarchy was a crop of younger men who were coming out of the military and either returning to resume Turner careers interrupted by the war or joining to start new ones. A fair number of them, including Walter K. Shaw's son (and future Turner chairman) Walter B. Shaw, Bob Hettema, and Gib Allen, had done their wartime duty with the navy's Seabees and had never been far from construction work, albeit under conditions that were radically different from anything they'd seen before the war. Bob Marshall and Lou Hall had both returned after especially distinguished and hazardous duty in the South Pacific as Navy Frogmen, the underwater demolition men who would be succeeded by the Navy Seals. Sixty years later Kevin Dockery's Navy Seals would document the extraordinarily heroic work done by these underwater demolition teams and would feature extensive interviews with Bob Marshall. George Morrison, Henry Gally, and Tom Broidrick were back from service in the Army Corps of Engineers; Herb Conant, another future chairman, came a few years later after duty with the Marine Corps; and Ed Clarke joined after service in the Army Air Corps. It would be only a few years before these returning veterans would be followed by younger men like Herb Church, Bob Kupfer, Al McNeill, Hal Parmelee, Les Shute, Ralph Johnson, Dick Corry, Bob Meyer, and Gene von Wening to round out the new crop of rising stars.

With plenty of work to do, with a good and growing staff of people to do it, and with plenty of cash in the bank, Turner was well positioned when the war ended. But nothing is perfect, and there were occasional problems. One was the sporadic and often ineffectual nature of the government's effort to phase out its wartime system of price and wage controls. It was an effort that ran into its share of snags before it would begin to succeed toward the end of 1946. There were alternating periods of relaxation and restoration of controls that confused and irritated contractors bidding on new work, all during a period when costs were beginning their postwar rise. By the end of 1946, Turner's own cost index was 75 percent higher than it had been before the war began and 23 percent higher than it had been as recently as 1945, when the war ended. It would rise by another 20 percent during 1947. Few in Turner's estimating department had ever had to deal with escalation on such a scale, and costs were running much higher than anything that had been anticipated. It was a circumstance that would lead to Turner's first steps toward a formalized program of risk management: the suspension of price guarantees until things stabilized.

The Turner board itself, sixteen present or former company executives, had before the end of the war noted that about half Turner's preferred shares and almost 20 percent of its common shares were held by persons who were no longer active in the affairs of the company, and they didn't like it. Fearing that voting control might pass to such an inactive group, they secured shareholder approval for splitting the common stock, which could be acquired only by active employees, ten shares for one, facilitating the further distribution of shares to active employees and solving the problem of control.

But not all of what was happening in the boardroom could be so easily managed. At the very end of the war the directors were surprised to learn from Archie Turner, who had been running things since 1941, that he wanted a significant reduction in his responsibilities. A vigorous and athletic man all his life (as an undergraduate he had led his Swarthmore lacrosse team to a national championship and had in recent years regularly dominated Turner golf outings), he was only sixty years old in 1945, but the pressures of the war years had apparently taken their toll. The board, in consultation with chairman Henry Turner, began deliberating ways of accommodating his request.

Meanwhile, a postwar boom in Turner's fortunes was gathering momentum. Big and important jobs were underway almost everywhere. Probably the most important of the first postwar projects was the grand new headquarters building for the John Hancock Mutual Life Insurance Company in Boston. It was the eighth such headquarters building that Turner had built for a major insurance company, and it wouldn't be the last. Twenty-six stories tall, sheathed in granite and sandstone, and topped by a graceful tower designed to double as a television antenna as soon as broadcast television became commercially viable, the building would be the tallest in Boston, and the selection of Turner to build it was widely regarded as an acknowledgment that Turner had become the premier builder in town. The

Cram and Ferguson design celebrated the end of the private building famine with just about everything the state of the building art could provide: sixteen high-speed elevators and eight floors of generously sized passenger escalators, an auditorium that was described by one reviewer as a scaled-down Radio City Music Hall, and miles of the new, movable steel office partitions that would appear in just about every office building that followed. The building's 700,000 square feet of interior space was richly finished, and their climate and lighting were controlled by the latest technology in high-quality air-conditioning and electric systems. Electric heating coils kept snow off the sidewalks that surrounded the building. And although the building's steel frame would render Turner's construction schedule dangerously vulnerable to the steel strike that was to come a few months later, it would forever lay to rest the notion that Turner was essentially a concrete contractor.

The project executive on the Hancock job was M. H. (Deke) Parsons, a Turner veteran who was married to Henry C. Turner's daughter Katherine. Parsons reported to Bill Nye, who was in charge of the Boston office after the war. Bob Hazard was the project superintendent.

Not everything that was built on the Hancock site had been planned by Cram and Ferguson. One added starter was the "Critic's Corner," a small, canopied grandstand that Turner built at the sidewalk level to accommodate about twenty "sidewalk superintendents" at a time. Most such visitors came to peer into the 45-foot-deep excavation to watch the driving of at least a few of the 1,600 steel piles that went down an average of 155 feet through Back Bay fill and clay to reach bedrock. The piles were designed to support a 10-foot-thick reinforced concrete mat that would carry the building's massive columns. Before the work was finished, more than 20,000 of the curious had taken a turn in the sidewalk grandstand.

While the Hancock Building was rising to dominate the Boston skyline, an entirely different but equally significant early postwar Turner job was taking shape on the campus of Princeton University in New Jersey. There, Turner was building the splendid Harvey Firestone Library that had been pretty much designed (by O'Connor and Kilham) since 1944, but that had ever since been awaiting the signal that the government would permit such construction to proceed. It was in every sense as splendid a library building as John Hancock was a corporate office building, but its scale was smaller and finer and it was an even richer building, set in the middle of the campus of a functioning university. Dutch Schroedel, who had made a name for himself on the Pacific Naval Air Base work, was in charge. His assistants were Walter B. Shaw, son of Turner veteran and director Walter K. Shaw, and himself a future chairman of the company, and Robert Marshall Jr., young Shaw's good friend and a future vice chairman of the company himself. Part reinforced concrete frame and part structural steel frame, the Firestone Library would rely on almost all Turner's building capabilities. The historically important 117-year-old residence of scientist Joseph Henry had to be moved to another part of the campus before excavation could proceed, and then extraordinary techniques would be required to ensure that extensive rock blasting wouldn't damage valuable stained-glass windows in adjacent university buildings. To complicate things further, the fossilized remains of ancient crustaceans were found in the excavation, and all construction had to be suspended for a few days while they were carefully examined and removed by paleontologists. The physical remoteness of the campus required that all the library's concrete, about 20,000 cubic yards of it, be batched on-site. The building's interiors were of museum quality and included oak paneling fabricated in England and installed by Turner carpenters, as well as marble and other cut stone work that comprised materials selected abroad by the architects and fabricated in the United States. An air-conditioning system designed to address the special needs of rare and old books had to be installed with extraordinary preciseness. But it was really the exterior domestic stonework that was at the center of Turner's tasks on the Firestone Library: Fifty-two hundred tons of Foxcroft stone, as rough as it had been when it came out of a nearby Pennsylvania quarry, were trucked to the site to be split, dressed, and set by thirty-nine masons employed directly by Turner, many of them brought from Italy to do the work. It was said to be the largest such stone job in the country. By spring 1948, two years after the five sons of donor Harvey Firestone (all Princeton alumni) had joined in the cornerstone laying, the building was turned over to the university.

All three of Turner's offices were busier than they had been since the early days of the war. On the Upper East Side of New York, the new Sloan-Kettering addition to Memorial Hospital, a fourteen-story steel frame and masonry cancer research laboratory, began to emerge from a deep and difficult excavation. Turner's A. C. Gallagher (who would die of a heart attack while construction was in progress) was in charge of the job, a precursor to the extensive hospital and laboratory work that the company would be doing in the years that followed. Only a few blocks away, Turner was renovating and adding to the Bloomingdale's store it had built before the war. In Maryland, the navy had brought Turner back to double the size of the Admiral Taylor Model Testing Basin that the company had built at Carderock before and during the war. Near Parkersburg, West Virginia, Turner was building a big chemical plant for the Calco Division of American Cyanamid: five manufacturing buildings and sprawling infrastructure that included a railroad spur, a power plant, and a whole system of mechanical and electrical distribution. There were two big brewery jobs in the New York area, both incorporating the Rostock tanks that were still a part of the Turner capability, albeit a shrinking one. One of the breweries was Turner's seventh contract for Ballantine's, and the other, in Brooklyn, was Turner's seventeenth contract for Schaeffer. The war years were well behind Turner by 1946, a year in which the company worked on twenty-two separate private-sector projects.

There was construction to be done everywhere, and getting its share of the new jobs was the least of the company's concerns, once this postwar rush to build began to gain momentum. Almost everything Turner was doing was for firms for which it had built previously, and there was a special, understandable pride about building for such manufacturers as Johns Manville, CertainTeed, Congoleum-Nairn, and U.S. Gypsum, all manufacturers of building products themselves who could be expected to be especially selective about picking a firm to build their plants. Turner put in place almost $30 million worth of construction in 1946, twice what it had done in 1945, adding another $100,000 to its net worth after distributing half its earnings (under the Additional Compensation Plan) and even after paying its taxes and generous dividends. It would carry forward a striking backlog of almost $58 million worth of work into 1947, and would have to turn away work from such potentially important clients as Burdine's, the Florida retailer, and the Ford Motor Company because, although the staff was by then up to 458 salaried persons, the company's conservative management was loath to take on more work than it felt it could effectively supervise and control with the staff it had.

Nineteen forty-six was an important year in the boardroom too. To accommodate Archie Turner's request for a reduction in his responsibilities, Henry C. Turner, now seventy-five, had resigned the chairmanship and successfully urged the board to assign that post, less demanding than the presidency, to Archie. That meant that a new president would have to be selected, and some in the firm thought that young Chan Turner, now forty-four years old, should get the job. He'd received much of the traditional Turner training, starting as a timekeeper and rising through the ranks, and he'd been successfully running the Philadelphia office since 1938 and serving on the board of directors for half a dozen years as well. But it now seems clear that Henry C. Turner didn't feel that his young son was quite ready for the top job in 1946, and a decision was made by the board to go outside the firm for a president, for the first time.

Its choice was the man who had been in charge for the navy at Carderock and then, as chief of the navy's Civil Engineer Corps, the senior officer and guiding spirit of the Pacific Naval Air Base project and later founder of the navy's Seabees. Admiral Ben Moreell had known a good deal about Turner for many years, and he'd seen the company at especially close range from the time the Carderock work had been started in 1937 through all the years of the PNAB work. Now he was retiring from the navy after thirty-three years of service, the only man to wear the four stars of a full admiral without having graduated from the Naval Academy at Annapolis. Still vigorous at fifty-four, Moreell was looking for a second career that would make good use of his skills and talents, and Turner looked like an ideal setting. The relationship between the company and Moreell had been an extremely good one right from its beginning, and the personal friendship that had developed between Moreell and Turner's Cliff Wilson is credited with being a major factor in the board's decision to offer the position to Moreell and in Moreell's decision to accept it. There were high hopes for what the retired admiral would achieve with Archie Turner providing the needed private-sector guidance from the chairman's perspective. The decision was made that Archie Turner would resign the presidency and assume the chairmanship in October 1946, when Adm. Ben Moreell would assume the presidency.

But it wasn't to be. On a trip from his home in Swarthmore to an apartment he maintained in White Plains, New York, Archie Turner was stricken by a heart attack and hospitalized. He would die a week later, never having served as chairman.

The whole carefully fashioned plan for new management had faltered, and before long it would unravel completely. Within a few months, Admiral Moreell himself would receive from the powerful Jones & Laughlin Steel Company an invitation to assume its presidency, under a contract that would not only provide for an extraordinarily high salary but would include a provision that would ensure the financial security of the admiral's family long after his retirement or death. Moreell graciously offered to reject the Jones & Laughlin offer and to stay on the job at Turner, but the seasoned and cautious Cliff Wilson counseled for accepting the resignation. He reasoned that Moreell would eventually regret declining such an attractive offer and that Turner would suffer the consequences. Mindful that Turner's good friends and frequent clients among the Mellon family held large positions in the ownership of Jones & Laughlin, the board ratified Wilson's advice by accepting Moreell's resignation. A few years later Turner would be doing major construction for the Mellons in Pittsburgh.

The untoward turn of events that had suddenly deprived Turner of its chairman and its president only a little more than a year into the company's difficult transition from a wartime mode into a radically different peacetime mode would have been a trial for any board, and it was difficult for Turner's. A plan of succession that had been painstakingly deliberated and carefully implemented had collapsed before it ever really had a chance. But it's an ill wind that blows no good, and the turmoil generated by the extraordinary events of late 1946 and early 1947 wasn't without some benefit for Turner. The board's reaction was to select Chan Turner as president and Cliff Wilson as chairman "to stay the younger man's hand."

9.

Chan and Wilson

Not surprisingly, more than enough uncertainty lingered in the Turner boardroom in the early months of 1947. During a winter that hadn't yet ended, the founder had resigned the chairmanship, the president had resigned and died before beginning his work as the new chairman, and the new president had resigned to accept a better offer from Jones & Laughlin. The board had selected as its new chairman a capable and admired engineer who had been with the firm for almost forty years and who continued to favor heavy construction over building construction as the company's central business, and it had selected as its new president the forty-four-year-old son of the founder, the first person to fill that post who hadn't been trained as an engineer. Such was the management setting as the company prepared to deal with an accumulated backlog of almost $60 million in construction contracts that it brought forward into 1947, the largest such backlog in any peacetime year in its history.

Cliff Wilson, educated in civil engineering at Columbia and weaned on bridge and tunnel work with the Pennsylvania Railroad before he joined Turner in 1907, was remembered by a colleague as a "construction man's construction man." He had pretty much been the firm's elder statesman since Henry C. Turner had turned the presidency over to his own younger brother in 1941, and he'd been managing work for the company almost since its earliest days, starting with the Gair buildings. Wilson had built some of the big navy projects in Brooklyn during the First World War and had gone on to build Standard Oil's Baytown refinery and to upgrade the Havana waterfront. During the 1920s, Henry Turner had sent the trusted Wilson to Atlanta to establish a whole new territory, and he'd been the company's top man on the Breakers Hotel and other southern work Turner did after that. It was Wilson who'd brought the company into the big James River Bridge job in Virginia and into the extraordinarily successful Alton Dam job, and most recently he'd been Turner's top executive on the PNAB work and on the big contracts that sprang from it. At sixty-four, he was the consummate Turner loyalist, devoted to the Turner family and to the company, and he'd been working toward the top job for a long time. From all accounts he relished it when it came.

Chan Turner was only five years old when Cliff Wilson started working for his father. He was the oldest Turner of his generation, and like the company itself he would turn forty-five in 1947. He had been a junior at Swarthmore College when Cliff Wilson was elected to the Turner board in 1922, and the next year he had joined the company himself to learn the business in the same way that every other beginner learned it in those days: first as a timekeeper, then as a field engineer, later as an assistant superintendent, and then as a superintendent, with an occasional detour into estimating and sales along the way. He certainly had a name that wouldn't do him a bit of harm in Turner Construction Company, but the word had been passed that no favoritism was to be shown the young Turner, and by 1932 he'd effectively established a reputation of his own as a serious and diligent manager. But the depression had eroded the company's workload by then and substantially reduced its salaried staff as well, and Henry C. Turner, determined to avoid even the appearance of favoritism, had asked young Chan to take a leave of absence. It was six years before he would return to the company to run the Philadelphia office, seasoned by a few years in finance and other areas of general commerce and broadened by some extended education at Columbia. Since his return to the company, he'd led the Philadelphia territory through some difficult but improving years and he'd been elected to the company's board and to its important executive committee. He was no engineer, probably not even much interested in or well suited for the technical side of Turner's business, but he knew the company from top to bottom, knew a good deal about corporate management and finance, and had been raised and trained in an environment that ensured a serious commitment to continuing and building on what his father had started. Contemporaneous descriptions of Chan Turner characterize him as a gentle, entirely civilized man of uncommon charm, admired and extremely well liked by colleagues and subordinates, and as a man whose behavior was to a great extent shaped by a strongly focused loyalty to the company and a determination to serve it effectively. Written correspondence between young Chan and his father at the time of Chan's selection as president reveal a close and warm relationship between the two men, one in which the Quaker tradition of addressing one another with the formal "thee" and "thy" of another age lasted well into the 1940s.

Cliff Wilson and Chan Turner would make an interesting and effective team: an older, more experienced, and technically superior chairman, accustomed to direct involvement with his staff, and a younger man sophisticated in general commerce and eager to justify his elevation to the presidency in a firm that had been founded and dominated by his family for half a century. Chan had earlier confided to his father some uncertainty about the board's selection of Wilson as chairman, anticipating that such a choice might suggest a lack of confidence in him as president, but he was assured of the board's confidence. According to contemporaneous accounts, the two men worked very well together. Wilson, reluctant to abandon completely the earlier operations role that had kept him in direct touch with the construction work itself, was committed to providing support to the founder's son, and Chan was resolved to accept all the help he could get.

One of the first big contracts for the new administration was one that bore the clear stamp of the new chairman, who rarely missed a chance to bring Turner into a heavy-construction project whenever an attractive one came along. Almost as soon as Wilson became chairman, Turner joined five of the country's most powerful heavy-construction firms in a joint venture formed to seek a big job on the Mississippi River, just a few miles downstream from the Alton Dam job that Turner and a couple of partners had successfully finished a few years earlier. The six co-venturers called themselves River Construction Company, a new corporation that included, in addition to Turner, Morrison Knudsen (twelve years after it had finished at Hoover Dam), Spencer, White & Prentis, and Raymond Concrete Pile of New York, as well as Winston Brothers and Al Johnson of Minneapolis. Four of the co-venturers, including Turner, each subscribed to 20 percent of the new corporation's shares, and the other two each subscribed to 10 percent.

For years a natural loop in the route of the lower Mississippi River had presented a daunting hazard to navigation. What was called the "Chain of Rocks" along the bed of the river's loop made navigation of deep-draft shipping so risky that it simply wasn't commercially viable for the large vessels that plied the river in the 1940s. The plan of the Corps of Engineers was to build an eight-mile canal across the loop that would allow shipping to bypass the Chain of Rocks altogether, and River Construction Company's goal was to secure a contract to build the two big locks that would be required for the canal. It was a big job: One of the locks was to be bigger than the famous Gatun Lock on the Panama Canal and the other was to be almost as big. River Construction's bid of about $16.5 million took the job handily, a slightly disconcerting 7 percent less than what the second of three bidders wanted for the work and less by as much again than what the third bidder wanted. With Cliff Wilson's memories of success on the Alton Dam still fresh, Lock No. 27 at the Chain of Rocks site looked like it had the potential for becoming a good job in June of 1947, but it clearly would be no pushover.

The vagaries that have placed heavy construction among the most hazardous of contracting specialties were destined to make the Chain of Rocks job one that Turner would have been better off without. Lou Hall, a 1935 RPI graduate who had started with Turner before the war and had recently returned from distinguished navy service in the Pacific, went out to take charge of the big concrete job that was to be done, and his memories of the experience were still vivid fifty-two years later. The bureaucracy that some of Turner's partners had built into the joint venture was frustrating to Hall, who was accustomed to a leaner approach, and from the outset it irritated him as inefficient and expensive. The job was run from the Illinois side of the river and fell within the jurisdiction of trade unions based in Granite City and East St. Louis, Illinois, where some of the country's toughest postwar union bosses were in power, so the venture soon found itself exclusively dependent on the union for every mechanic on the job and virtually powerless to control the quality of its workforce.

It was no surprise that the best mechanics weren't assigned to work for a joint venture out of New York, Boise, and Minneapolis while there were southern Illinois contractors looking for men, especially when the joint venture wasn't prepared to buy its way into the union's favor. Productivity lagged, the schedule slipped, and costs rose. Even the geology of southern Illinois opposed profitability. The contract had provided that the government would furnish all the fine and coarse aggregates for the 400,000 cubic yards of concrete that were to be placed, but the fine aggregate, instead of being a natural sand, was in fact a finely crushed limestone. It was a material that tended to form into clumps when it got wet and/or frozen, producing concrete that was difficult to handle and imposing still further burdens on the job's costs. By the time it all wound down, almost three years after its start, the joint venture would be $2.5 million in the red, and 20 percent of that loss was Turner's.

Fortunately, the outcome of the big job on the Mississippi wasn't typical for what would characterize the early years of Chan Turner's presidency. Those years started with a job of exceptionally high profile that was being designed and prepared for construction even as he began his term as president: It was the permanent headquarters in New York for the United Nations. With generous help from the Rockefellers, later supplemented by an interest-free loan from the U.S. government, the UN had acquired about seventeen acres of land on New York's East Side and was in the process of demolishing the slaughterhouses and run-down tenements that covered it. An international team of architects headed by Wallace K. Harrison and Max Abramovitz was well along on design work for the striking collection of buildings that would provide operational and administrative headquarters for the world body, and efforts to find a contractor or a group of contractors to whom the construction work itself could safely be entrusted were underway. Early in 1948, the UN's planning group found what it was looking for, and it negotiated an approximately $24 million contract with a joint venture that included Turner, George A. Fuller Company, Walsh Construction Company, and

Slattery Construction Company to build the first phase of the work: a thirty-nine-story building that would house the United Nations Secretariat and foundations for a variety of other adjacent structures. Over a period of about the next year, the General Assembly Building and other work would be added to the job, increasing the contract to more than $40 million.

Although the United Nations project had an extremely high profile, and although Turner was indeed one of its four builders, the company hasn't been inclined to emphasize the project in publicity about its own history. Turner and Walsh each held only 28 1/2 percent of the shares of the joint venture, and Slattery Company, which did the foundation work, held another 10 percent. The remaining 33 percent of the shares was held by George A. Fuller Company, which performed as the lead contractor, filled the top field positions with men from its own staff, and effectively managed the project. Turner had full responsibility for what was classified as engineering, a function that included mainly the processing (and some preparation) of shop drawings, the negotiation of subcontracts, some of the cost estimating, and the analysis and processing of the abundance of change orders that were bound to attend such work. And although each of the four joint venturers shared the financial risks of the work and was equally represented by its chief executive on the committee that controlled policy, Turner's management has traditionally been inclined to favor in its publicity those projects that the company did alone or on which it was the lead contractor.

But there was plenty to do at Turner's offices on the twenty-fifth floor of the Graybar Building during those early years of Chan Turner's presidency. By the time he and Cliff Wilson assumed the leadership in 1947, the boom in postwar construction had been gathering steam for a couple of years and was ready to hit its full stride. Turner put in place more than $60 million worth of construction during 1948 alone, an increase of 25 percent over an entirely satisfactory 1947 and more than twice what it had done during 1946. By 1951 the company's annual volume would exceed $100 million for the first time, an amount that would make it the equivalent of almost a billion dollars' worth of work at the time of Turner's hundredth birthday.

Statistics for the period confirm that Turner was well ahead of the industry in its postwar growth during the early years of Chan Turner's presidency. Its annual volume actually increased by a little over 250 percent between 1946 and 1951, about twice the rate at which nonresidential construction was increasing in the country as a whole, and even an adjustment of 25 percent to account for inflation doesn't significantly alter the evidence that the company had entered an extremely good period in its history.

Some of the new jobs were the very big ones that are bound to attract the broadest attention and that become important features in the company's history, but certainly not all of them were. In 1948, only two of Turner's thirty-five new contracts were for more than $2 million, and although the fraction represented by the larger jobs would increase gradually after that, even in 1951, the first $100 million year, only eight of Turner's twenty-nine new jobs were for more than $2 million. Of course, a $2 million job in 1951 was the equivalent, after allowing for inflation, of an approximately $20 million job in the currency of the beginning of this century, so contracts for $2 million or less in 1951 weren't necessarily small ones, but they weren't the major projects that would attract the widest attention in the 1940s and 1950s.

In many ways the smaller projects provide useful insights into what the company was doing during the period, and a few of them proved to be important in determining Turner's subsequent directions. Early in 1948, the Alexander Smith Carpet Company, for whom Turner had done a great deal of work at its vast Yonkers, New York, plant, came along with a proposal for the company to build a warehouse in Chicago that would normally have been considered too small to justify building so far from home. But there had been increasing indications that Chicago, where the company had previously launched an unsuccessful branch that it later closed, might now be on the brink of the kind of growth that would support an office. George Frost, who had worked for Turner on the Glenn Martin plant and at Carderock before the war and on various GE plants in New England during the war, was finishing up work for Turner on the big Calco chemical plant in West Virginia when he was tapped to go out to Chicago to build the concrete warehouse that Alexander Smith wanted there. Forty years later, well into his eighties and still vigorous, Frost remembers that the company broke with tradition by subcontracting both concrete and masonry work on the Alexander Smith job as a way of easing its way into the unknown labor market of Chicago. It was a new experience for a superintendent accustomed to the control inherent in having most of the workmen employed directly by Turner, but it provided an early introduction to an approach that would become standard when the company later began its shift into what would be called "construction management."

And it was a good beginning for a Turner office in Chicago, which started modestly enough with only a few employees in small quarters, with Rudy Cullum in charge and Ed Courter, who would himself become manager when Cullum died in 1949, as general superintendent. The Alexander Smith job that had justified the move there was starting up, and a second Alexander Smith job was waiting for Turner in Minneapolis. But getting new business in those early days of the new Chicago office was mainly a matter of getting the Turner name onto some invitation-only bid lists and establishing conclusively that Turner was in Chicago to stay. At that stage there was no bona fide cost estimator in the Chicago office, but within a year George Morrison showed up to take on the job of purchasing manager and to do what could be done locally to put together bids. In the beginning Morrison, who would later move up to a Turner vice presidency, would carry the preparation of a bid as far as he could in Chicago and then board the New York Central's Commodore Vanderbilt for the overnight trip to New York, calculations and subcontractor bids in hand, for completing the proposal in New York. There, he'd be joined by Rosie Rosenburgh, Turner's critically important chief estimator who — with Chan Turner, Joe Warren, and George Horr — was one of the four-person inner circle that was making most of the company's critical decisions in those days. By the following evening the required adjustments would be completed, appropriate subcontractor figures inserted or adjusted, and Morrison would be on his way back to Chicago to submit the bid. An inefficient process at best, one unlikely to succeed often, where last-minute adjustments in subcontractor and vendor figures were so difficult to make, and certainly a process likely to exhaust Morrison.

But it was what had to be done in those early days in Chicago and would soon be replaced by an approach in which Rosenburgh would go out to Chicago himself for long enough to put the final bid together.

In fact, it all worked out well, and Turner's well-established eastern reputation began to become known in Chicago. Soon the company was being invited to bid good work in the area, and it began to win its share in competition with local contractors. One important job the Chicago office was able to secure in that early period was a research laboratory in Skokie for the Portland Cement Association, a job that brought with it a special prestige: The principal U.S. authority on concrete construction had included Turner among the Chicago contractors it would consider for its own state-of-the-art laboratory. It was a building designed to demonstrate as much as possible about building in concrete, and when PCA accepted Turner's bid, it was a feather in the cap of the young Chicago office. The laboratory, still functioning at the beginning of the twenty-first century, went on to become a center of study and development in concrete construction, providing a setting for much of the early work in ultimate strength design, air-entrained concrete, precast and prestressed concrete, ultra-high-strength concrete, and the like.

As Turner's presence in Chicago grew, negotiated jobs increasingly entered the mix. Within a few years only about half the work was being secured through lump-sum competitive bidding, normally on an invited basis, while the other half was being negotiated on a basis that didn't include price competition. George Morrison likes to describe conditions in 1948 and 1949, when the local competition was reported to be speculating aloud about whether or not Turner would last in Chicago, and then to mention big, important Chicago jobs like the Inland Steel Building, the Lake Meadows Housing Project, and the Lutheran Aid Building, all built by Turner during the 1950s under lump-sum contracts secured through competitive bidding. By the mid-fifties, Morrison remembers, Turner was turning away invitations on important jobs because it had become too busy on the work it already had in hand.

Back east there had been plenty going on while Turner's foothold in the Midwest was becoming stronger. Not long after the end of the war, board member

Walter K. Shaw reported hearing about a promising real estate developer in the Midwest named John W. Galbreath. Shaw's attempts to secure work from Galbreath didn't succeed at first, but things began to change when Galbreath showed up in 1947 with a couple of small warehouse–office buildings for Turner to build in New York and Philadelphia. Turner, with the company's old friend William Higginson along to do the design for one of them, did the jobs with enough skill and speed to make a believer of Galbreath, a sophisticated and perceptive farm-bred man from Ohio. By the end of the 1940s Galbreath had become an extremely successful broker and investor, well on his way to national prominence as a powerful developer of urban real estate, and he apparently found just the kind of contractor he'd been looking for when he discovered Turner. Over the next few decades Galbreath would bring Turner into a far-flung program of urban high-rise construction that would include more than seventy-five projects and that would change the skylines of more than a dozen of the country's largest cities.

There were other important things going on back east during those postwar years too, and with more than 500 salaried employees on the payroll there was no relaxing the company's effort to obtain its share of whatever was coming along. Lou Hall came east from the ill-fated Chain of Rocks job to take on the field supervision of the bus terminal Turner was building for the Port of New York Authority, after the port authority had made its controversial decision to award the job to Turner in spite of its having been the second bidder. D. C. Andrews would be Turner's project executive, and Walter Conlin its general superintendent. This was to be no repetition of the Chain of Rocks job. Here the work would be effectively prosecuted, would be finished ahead of a tight schedule, and would be seen as an important factor in sustaining Turner's reputation as a contractor who could get things done well, on time, and at a competitive price. And there were jobs for many of the company's old customers too, most of them big expansions that had been deferred because of the war. Chan Turner, still adapting to his corporate responsibilities, worried aloud that the 500-person Turner staff would be difficult to sustain unless what had become an average of two to three new jobs a month could be increased, and he brought the company into half a dozen competitions on big, publicly bid civil works projects around the country, usually in joint ventures with other contractors, to boost the volume. But the Chain of Rocks experience had slaked the company's appetite for such risky ventures and what the estimating department generated to get such competitive projects didn't produce any new work. Chan Turner's concerns about volume weren't really justified by the company's performance: The annual volume of work put in place continued to rise at a rate faster than the rate of the still-modest currency inflation, and profitability was maintained with a fully engaged staff.

In New York modest jobs like a new hospital in Poughkeepsie and a new printing plant for the *New York Daily News* were typical of many good jobs that kept plenty of people gainfully employed but that didn't always get the notice that the larger jobs got. In like fashion there was a continuing stream of such work in New Jersey, where Turner's industrial work dominated. There were dozens of small plants, each requiring its own special attention, and one was for the Neogravure Company, the company that printed *Time* and *Life*. Bob Hettema, a 1940 Purdue graduate not long out of the Seabees, was in charge there, and his recollection of how ingenuity carried the day there says something about what a Turner superintendent's job was all about. The contract documents had called for 7,500 friction piles to be driven into a shallow layer of clay, where they were expected to fetch up. But the layer they penetrated proved to be too thin and the eight-inch tips of the wood piles were punching through to a layer of unsatisfactory material below. It would have been a long way down 'through the substrata before the piles could be expected to hold, so it was decided to try driving the piles upside down instead, transmitting some of the load through the butt ends of the timber piles and saving an estimated half a million dollars in the process. It worked. Hettema, who would later manage some of Turner's largest jobs, is long retired from the company but is still playing golf almost every day and is quick to remember and describe the piling coup at Neogravure. After his Turner career he went on to join the engineering faculty at Penn State, from which he retired during the 1990s.

The country's transition from a wartime economy was well behind it as the 1940s came to an end. As in New York, more than half the new business of Turner's

Boston office was by those years being secured by negotiation, often without competition and usually from owners for whom the company had built many times
before. William Nye and Elmer Ford, both newly elevated to the Turner board, ran
the Boston office, where Nye was charged primarily with securing new work and
Ford was the man who saw to its construction. Their negotiated work was keeping
them busy in the late 1940s but an occasional bidding competition for an especially
attractive job was still there to test their mettle from time to time. In 1948 and 1949
they acquitted themselves well on several of these. One was for an especially glorious new stone-clad chapel that Cram and Ferguson had designed for Boston
University, and a couple of others were additions designed by the distinguished
Boston architectural firm of Shepley Bulfinch for Deaconess and Massachusetts
General Hospitals.

Ernest Bear, another man recently elevated to a position on the board of directors (and the father of Turner general superintendent Bill Bear, who would retire
from the Philadelphia office in the 1970s), had by the end of the 1940s taken over
the job vacated by Chan Turner in Philadelphia. When the senior Bear left in 1950,
Dutch Schroedel, who had distinguished himself on Turner's Pacific islands work,
succeeded him, and although the volume of work in Philadelphia didn't grow as
rapidly as it did elsewhere during these years, it was a busy place. There was the
usual array of small industrial work that had been the bread and butter of the
office for years, but during the period following the end of the war a large volume
of multifamily-housing construction in the Philadelphia area came Turner's way,
and by the early 1950s housing had become the largest single building type in that
office.

It was the big urban skyscrapers that got most of the attention during these last
years of the 1940s and on into the 1950s and beyond, as Turner's direction for the
second half of its first century began to take form. The country had emerged from
the Second World War as its most prosperous survivor, and its cities were becoming the thriving commercial centers of the expanding industries and of the emerging new ones that came with peace. Some of the great manufacturing companies
and many of the prospering service companies, increasingly reliant on support

from other firms for specialties they had neither capacity nor taste for providing themselves, and dependent on big pools of white-collar workers, were establishing or expanding corporate headquarters in the major cities. Along with corporate headquarters came an exponential increase in the demand for additional office space to accommodate the smaller companies that would be providing services to them. It was a good time to be in the construction business, especially for a fifty-year-old, well-staffed, well-financed construction company with a reputation for competence and integrity.

Of course, Turner wasn't the only firm so well positioned. George A. Fuller Company, Turner's frequent competitor and occasional joint venture partner, was actually a little larger and a little older than Turner. Originally from Illinois, Fuller had built New York's Flatiron Building and its Penn Station and more than a small share of the city's high-rise buildings as well. Starrett Brothers & Eken was another construction firm that was well positioned for taking on some of the big urban work that was coming along. It had little need to mention anything except that it had built the Empire State Building when it was seeking new business. There were a few others, too, who would be competing with Turner for the prizes that lay ahead: Thompson-Starrett, which was loosely connected by a family relationship to Starrett Brothers & Eken, and Vermilya-Brown, the firm that had succeeded Marc Eidlitz in New York, were a couple of them. William L. Crow, Hageman-Harris, and John Lowry were others that had done a good deal of urban high-rise work during the first half of the century. And there were similar, equally solid construction companies in cities like Houston, San Francisco, and Los Angeles, all poised for roles in the postwar growth that was coming to those cities.

More than a few of the new postwar corporate office buildings that would show up on New York's skyline would be owned by insurance companies. They were firms that needed and wanted a lot of space, and with plenty of money in their treasuries they favored building and owning over paying the high (and rising) rents that were being asked for the shrinking supply of available existing space in New York and other big cities. Mutual of New York (later MONY) was among the first to build, and it commissioned Shreve, Lamb and Harmon to design a corporate headquarters to replace the one on Nassau Street that they'd occupied for 107 years. After checking with the long list of major insurance companies for which Turner had by then built corporate headquarters, they engaged the company to build theirs. There was new work starting almost everywhere when field-work for the MONY job started in the fall of 1948, with Turner's Ab Abberley as project executive and Walter Jackson in charge in the field. Despite mounting competition for materials and labor and the heaviest snowfall the city had seen in sixty years, Turner was able to get the foundations ready for steel by spring. Pressure to meet a July 1950 completion date was real, because MONY planned to rent out about a third of the building and wanted to be sure it would all be ready for tenants before competing new space became available. Bethlehem Steel erected its twenty-five levels of steel in only thirteen weeks, thought to be a record, and by Christmas Turner had the building fully enclosed and sheathed in lime-stone and granite. In April 1950, Gen. George C. Marshall and Capt. Eddie Rickenbacker were among speakers at a dedication ceremony that included the sealing of documents within the cornerstone, to be opened in what was viewed in 1950 as the unthinkably distant year 2000. By the first of May MONY and some of its tenants had begun to move into the new building.

More than a year before the MONY building was dedicated, Turner had begun construction of a similar high-rise office building across town on the east side of New York's Manhattan Island for MONY's competitor, the Massachusetts Mutual Life Insurance Company. Mass Mutual, for whom Turner had years earlier built a corporate headquarters building in Springfield and for whom Turner was in 1949 building an addition to the Springfield building, wasn't seeking any new space for itself. What Mass Mutual wanted was a good safe place for investing its capital, and it had decided that an office building of extremely high quality, well designed and well constructed, on New York's Fifth Avenue should do the trick. It acquired a site adjacent to Rockefeller Center, at 600 Fifth Avenue, and engaged the distinguished architectural firm of Carson & Lundin, some of whose principals and staff had worked under Wallace Harrison on the original design of Rockefeller Center itself during the 1930s, to design a suitably elegant building. And they hired

Turner to do the construction. Before Turner's Nils Nilsson could start the new building, the church that had occupied the site for eighty years had to be demolished, and that meant opening the sealed lead box that the builders of the church had inserted in its cornerstone back in 1869. Like General Marshall and Captain Rickenbacker at the MONY dedication, the church fathers had left in the sealed box what they hoped would provide future builders a glimpse into life in the middle of the preceding century: ten- and twenty-five-cent currency bills issued by the government during the Civil War, newspapers of that period, and the like. For a few minutes, when the box was opened, the furious race to modernize the big city slowed.

But there was very little in the twenty-six-story building that Turner built at 600 Fifth Avenue that would remind anyone of the nineteenth century. What Carson & Lundin designed was intended in every possible way to reveal the state of the building art in 1949. It was one of the first buildings to use the Robertson cellular decking that provided centering for the concrete floors and underfloor raceways for the new electrical and communication systems that were emerging in 1949 and expected to proliferate. And 600 Fifth was among the first buildings to use the new lightweight plaster materials that made it possible to fireproof steel without imposing the massive and expensive dead loads that were inherent in concrete fireproofing. Like all the high-quality postwar office buildings, this one was fully air-conditioned, but there was a novel twist in its design: 600 Fifth Avenue was among the few new buildings in New York to rely for its refrigeration on the steam absorption process, in which the only moving part is a pump. The finished building, a limestone tower that resembled and was connected by tunnel to the dignified Rockefeller Center complex, was about as modern as such a building could be in 1949.

There was another aspect of the work at 600 Fifth Avenue that would prove to be as important to Turner as its architecture or its technology. After construction was underway, Sinclair Oil Company signed a long-term lease for about half the space in the building, and the man who had brought Sinclair and Mass Mutual together proved to be Turner's new friend John W. Galbreath. It was another chance for Galbreath to see Turner in action, this time on a major urban building, and it would be only a few months before he would be looking for a contractor to build his own first urban high-rise complex, the U.S. Steel–Mellon Bank building in Pittsburgh.

Galbreath, a physically slight man of great wealth and vast charm, had been putting together successful real estate ventures since his graduation from Ohio State in 1920. During the depression he had earned large brokerage commissions by convincing a number of wealthy families in Ohio to mortgage their properties and to invest the proceeds in heavily discounted distressed properties that he correctly anticipated would later be restored to their rightful values. Combining the abundant cash proceeds of his brokerage activities with a quick wit and an ingratiating style, he had gone on to buy up whole company towns that had been built for industrial workers and to lease the properties back to the companies that had built them or occasionally to the workers themselves. By the 1940s Galbreath had accumulated a substantial fortune and was beginning to live a baronial style that included racehorses, private aircraft, and elegant homes, all the while profitably buying and selling more properties. By the late 1940s Galbreath had (with singer Bing Crosby) purchased a controlling interest in the Pittsburgh Pirates baseball team, had substantially expanded his interests in breeding and owning racehorses, and had concentrated what remained of his abundant energies and resources on what he had come to regard as the considerable economic potential of large, high-quality urban real estate. He liked and owned some fine old buildings, but his real focus by 1948 was on building and owning the dazzling new urban skyscrapers to which he wisely predicted a whole new generation of corporate managers would soon be flocking. His strategy was to identify the most promising cities, acquire properties in their best locations, commission the country's best architects to design buildings for them, and then to engage its best contractors to build them. By the end of 1948 he had pretty well decided that Turner would be his builder.

The first big Galbreath job was the million-square-foot, forty-one-story office building that would anchor the Golden Triangle that had been conceived as the centerpiece of Pittsburgh's postwar urban renewal plan. The venerable Mellon

Bank would occupy the first eight floors (and provide the interim financing for the project), and 3,200 executives and other employees of the U.S. Steel Corporation would occupy the rest. Galbreath brought Harrison and Abramovitz directly from their work on the United Nations headquarters in New York to design the building, and he named it 525 William Penn Plaza.

Turner brought former army colonel George Reaves down from Boston, where he was finishing up the company's twenty-story New England Telephone Building, to run the job. Reaves, a West Pointer who had worked for Turner during the 1920s and early 1930s, had returned to Turner after wartime military service that had included his capture by the enemy and his escape from a prison camp. He was an imposing man whose intelligence and understated style were effective in bringing calm to sometimes tense situations. Reaves had done almost every kind of construction, from railroads and bridges to high-rise buildings, and he was ready for 525 William Penn Plaza. The foundation was just as nasty a job as deep foundations under high-rise buildings in congested urban centers usually are: three basements well below street level and then piling driven eighty-five feet through clay to twenty-ton rock, all adjacent to busy roads, utilities, and structures that had to be thoroughly isolated from the impact of the new construction. Turner subcontracted the foundation work to a local contractor with a provision that the work had to be done on a three-shift basis, seven days a week to ensure completion by spring 1950. By April, the first of about 15,000 tons of structural steel was being erected and the pressure for occupancy in 1951 was turned up. Every steel product that could be used at 525 William Penn was integrated into the design, from the structural steel frame itself, with its cellular steel floor systems, to stainless-steel doors for each of the twenty-five high-speed elevators, stainless-steel panels for the lobbies, and floor-to-floor stainless-steel spandrel panels with integral stainless-steel windows applied to the building's exterior between its stone panels. Even most of the interior partitions were made of steel. In addition to providing an entirely modern environment for its corporate headquarters, U.S. Steel was going to have a building that would effectively provide a full-scale display of its products. Fully air-conditioned, of course, and with every power and communication system known to the designers in 1949, it was finished in time for occupancy to begin around the middle of 1951.

The Pittsburgh building for U.S. Steel and Mellon added another spectacular high-rise to the ones that Turner had already done in Boston and New York, clearly strengthening its growing position among the elite group of builders who were doing the top-quality high-rise work. Less than a year before the Pittsburgh building was finished, the Chrysler interests contracted with Turner to build a thirty-two-story tower just east of its Chrysler Building on New York's Forty-second Street, to increase the capacity of its rental holdings there by about half. By the end of 1951 tenants were beginning to move into what came to be called Chrysler East.

Almost across the street from Chrysler East, along the south side of Forty-second Street, John Galbreath was back to Turner a few months later for what would become New York's Mobil Building, at forty-five floors and 1.6 million square feet the largest and most spectacular of all the city's postwar skyscrapers. The Mobil Building was another Harrison and Abramovitz job, but taller and broader than 525 William Penn Plaza and even more continuously swathed in stainless-steel panels, a curtain wall so vast that it took five companies to produce the panels. Turner's position as a high-rise builder had been well secured by the 1950s and would be sustained throughout the rest of the century.

Whether the company's simultaneous continued performance as a serious builder of low-rise institutional and industrial buildings during this period of high-rise activity was a result of good planning or simply an accident of the marketplace isn't clear, but in fact most of what Turner was doing during the 1950s continued to be such low-rise work. Despite the growth and profile of its urban high-rise commercial construction, the company's business continued to be dominated by more and more of the institutional and industrial work it had been doing for years.

The Ford work in Kansas City was a case in point: It dramatized the company's role as a builder of big industrial plants. Around the middle of 1950, Jim MacAlarney of Ford's executive staff at Dearborn had approached Turner's D. C. Andrews in New York about building the million-square-foot assembly plant in Kansas City that the big carmaker was planning as a replacement for the aging facility it had there already. Turner had done plenty of work for Ford before, including its plant at Edgewater, New Jersey, but Ford's decision to call on it for the work at Kansas City was most likely the result of Turner's performance on the big plant that it had built there only a few years earlier for Pratt & Whitney in a joint venture with Long Construction Company. Mindful of the importance of local participation, MacAlarney wanted another Turner-Long joint venture, one that would again link Turner's special capability with Long's well-established following in the Kansas City area to ensure getting the new plant on line as soon as possible.

As it turned out, there would be no Turner-Long Company on this Ford job. That corporate name had apparently been rankling in the minds of Long's people ever since the Pratt & Whitney job, and Bob Long made it clear in 1950 that this time it would have to be Long-Turner. That's what it was when Lou Hall was brought back from New York to run the job early in 1951.

Ford was in a furious race with its Detroit competitors in 1951, and the Kansas City assembly plant, which was designed to employ 3,000 workers and to produce 700 vehicles per day, was part of a $500 million effort to come in first. The pressure on Long-Turner to get the plant ready for production was intense from the first day, and Long-Turner was ready for it. But terrible weather was a formidable adversary that even their best efforts were unable to overcome. Rain plagued the job almost daily throughout the rest of the winter and into the spring, turning the Missouri clay to mud and effectively preventing significant progress on grading the 150-acre site or on installing foundations for the new plant. By the middle of spring the situation was no better. The patience of Ford and Turner executives in Detroit and New York was beginning to wear thin when the terrible floods of 1951 inundated much of the Midwest, and their devastating effects were described and illustrated in newspapers and on movie screens all over the country. In fact, the floods that were given all the attention didn't actually affect the Ford construction site at Kansas City at all, but the publicity about the flood damage had the effect of softening attitudes in Detroit and New York, giving Hall and his Turner people some relief. By summer things had begun to dry out and construction moved into high gear.

Progress after that was good, with reliable subcontractors and a skilled workforce giving Long-Turner a chance to show what it could do. Hall reported to D. C. Andrews in New York for a while, but after the unanticipated death of Andrews it was Ed Courter in Turner's still-young Chicago office who took over as project executive. Except for a local teamster boss who initiated conversations in his office by laying a pistol on his desk, local union relationships that had been established over the years by Long were helpful and effective. Within a few months the site had been graded, five miles of railroad track was being installed, and structural steel was beginning to rise, bringing the sprawling new plant closer to its goal of completion in 1952.

But events unrelated to construction or to automobile production would alter the availability of materials and, in minor ways, the form the plant would finally take. In 1950, a communist army had streamed southward across the thirty-eighth parallel in Korea in an effort to topple the South Korean government and to drive what remained of American occupation forces from the Korean peninsula, and not long after that an American-led United Nations army had driven the North Koreans back into their own territory. Harry Truman had mobilized the country for a limited war, and the Ford Motor Company had agreed to suspend its plan to assemble cars and trucks in Kansas City in favor of a plan to build wings for B-47 bombers instead. As it turned out, the geometry of the plant, as designed, was well suited for wing production, and Long-Turner was given an extra order to build the big steel jigs that would be needed to produce wings for six-engine B-47 Stratojets. It was all in a day's work for the Long-Turner crew and for Lou Hall, who would by March of 1952 begin turning over parts of the plant to the government and to the Ford people who would be running it for them. The first wings were turned out by Ford in February 1953, and their production would be continued at Kansas City until 1956, when Ford would reclaim the plant for automobile and truck assembly.

The Midwest had begun to rival the East as another locus of big Turner work. The Kansas City job, although it was actually run as if it were part of the Chicago office, was really too big for the staff there and ended up being operated first as a New York job and then pretty much as an independent unit. But another big Midwestern job came along in 1952 that would be operated independently of the

Chicago office right from the outset: the White Pine Copper project for the Copper Range Company.

Copper Range, whose home office was in Boston, had acquired vast land areas in the copper country of northern Michigan, along the shore of Lake Superior, where it intended to build facilities that would employ 3,000 workers and where it planned to mine and process enough ore to yield 75 million pounds of copper every year for a long time. The company had established a Michigan subsidiary called White Pine Copper Company and had staffed it with copper industry specialists it had recruited from all over the world: geologists, mining engineers, smelting specialists, metallurgists, and the like. And White Pine Copper had contracted with the government to deliver more than 60 million pounds of copper every year for seven years. All it had to do now was produce it.

Copper Range knew just about everything there was to know about copper and copper mining, but it didn't know enough about all the other things that would be required at White Pine to take them onto its own shoulders. Its boss, Morris LaCroix, turned to his old friend Cliff Wilson for help, and he ended up awarding Turner a tremendously broad contract that stipulated that Turner would have full responsibility for the design and construction of the whole project. The work to be done included engineering and construction of the mine shaft itself, the refining plant, the big on-site power plant, the railroad spur, and housing for the workers, as well as all the complex infrastructure that would be required to sustain a whole new population, including a school, a hospital, and shops.

Cliff Wilson himself assumed the role of principal in charge on the White Pine job, and Clint Hernandez in New York became the project executive. Turner's top man at the site itself was George Reaves, the former army officer who had just finished up the U.S. Steel Tower at 525 William Penn Plaza in Pittsburgh and who would later go on to become general manager of the Boston office and a company director. Reaves developed his own staff to run the job, and it was rich in young men like Bob Kupfer, Andy Miller, and Reino Kinnunen, all of whom would later rise to prominence in the firm. One of his senior engineers was Myron (Mike) Hinckley, a native Californian who had been working in South America for

Raymond Concrete Pile when Raymond had joined Turner in 1939 for the PNAB work in the Pacific, and Raymond had sent Hinckley out there to run some of the work. In Hawaii, he had found himself in a group that was dominated by Turner men, and after the Pacific work he was one of those who had stayed on with Turner. From the Pacific project he had gone on to become chief engineer for Turner's Roane-Anderson Company at Oak Ridge before going out to White Pine, and when the Michigan work was finished Hinckley would put in another twenty-five years with Turner before retiring in 1977. Jerry Mandel was another young engineer on Reaves's staff and all his memories of White Pine are good ones, starting with the day he was told he was going to be assigned to duty there. He had started in the field for Turner just after the end of the war, still fairly fresh from Pacific duty as an infantry paratrooper, and had later gravitated to the New York office. When Cliff Wilson called him into his office in 1950 to offer him a position on the White Pine job, Mandel remembers his own dilemma: He had been studying law at night for three or four years and was a month from getting his degree and not much inclined to give it all up to head off to the Upper Peninsula of Michigan. But that day in Wilson's office turned out to be a lucky one for him. Wilson's own son had just finished law school, and the boss was entirely sympathetic to Mandel's situation, granting him a delay until graduation. By the time he got to White Pine he had a law degree, a credential that Reaves found especially useful when the unusually broad swath of responsibilities that had been given to Turner proved to include an occasional legal matter. Mandel remembers the work at White Pine for its extraordinary breadth, but he has a special place in his memory for the bearskin that was given to him as a memento of the day a black bear was shot on the still-primitive and isolated work site.

At that point in its history Turner had no interest in (and not much capacity for doing) design work, and before much time went by the company subcontracted all the engineering for the power plant at White Pine to Stone & Webster, all the planning and design for the residential work to Pace Associates, and all the specialized design work for the mining and milling facilities themselves to the Western-Knapp Engineering Company. But the company retained for itself the management of all the construction work, even including building the mineshaft itself. By 1954 White Pine Copper, with more than $70 million worth of engineering and construction in place, was up and running.

The joint leadership of Chan Turner and Cliff Wilson was clearly working extremely smoothly and effectively, and by the time the company's annual work volume had passed the hundred-million-dollar level in 1951 any doubts that might have lingered about the younger man's ability to take command had been well resolved. Wilson, now approaching retirement age, was able for the most part to settle into the traditional advisory role of chairman, while Chan focused on managing the company's operations.

There were exceptions to that conventional division of responsibilities, of course, and one of those surfaced in the work the company took on for the Safeway grocery chain in the early 1950s. Almost a quarter of a century earlier a man named Lingan Warren, in those years a lumber broker in Florida, had sold material to Turner and had apparently been so impressed by the way the company did its business, and by Cliff Wilson himself, that he never forgot them. Warren had gone on to become president of Safeway in 1934, and by the 1950s he was pretty much running the big grocery chain by himself, getting into every detail of its management, from checking what was on the shelves at the stores to determining who would do the company's construction. No one who knew Warren at Safeway was surprised when he announced in 1950 that all the new construction the company was going to be needing, as it tooled up for the proliferation of stores that would attend the population's move to the suburbs, was going to be done by Turner Construction Company. Cliff Wilson himself was probably more surprised than pleased to learn that Warren was planning to rely entirely on Wilson's personal supervision of the process.

Turner started the Safeway work with a couple of huge plants at which Safeway would store and refrigerate virtually all its products and through which the extensive trucking that was at the heart of its distribution system would be routed. One building was to be erected in Maryland and the other in New Jersey. Bob Hettema ran the New Jersey job and remembers the extraordinary pressure he felt at having the chairman of Turner's board of directors personally supervising his work and regularly stopping by to check its progress. But his recollection is that Wilson was eminently pleasant and helpful, and he remembers especially clearly that Wilson was always considerate enough to give adequate notice of an upcoming visit with an announcement left over from his navy dealings at Carderock and in the Pacific: "Permission to come aboard, sir."

The work at Safeway's big distribution centers wasn't the end of Turner's work for Lingan Warren, and what came later says something about Turner's breadth and flexibility. Warren awarded the company a contract to build sixteen small grocery stores for Safeway in and around the New York area, including a few in Connecticut and New Jersey, with a request that they be done quickly, in two batches of eight apiece. They were small jobs, by Turner standards, but they offered a good chance for some of the younger engineers in the organization to run their own jobs. Each job got its own engineer with a tight budget of time and dollars; Lou Hall, just back from the mammoth Ford job in Kansas City, was given the task of making sure they did what they promised.

These relatively small Safeway jobs weren't uniformly popular in the company, where there was some prejudice against doing such work. But many years later, when such small jobs became a separate and earnings-rich marketing target for Turner, this kind of resistance virtually disappeared.

But the little Safeway stores were a far cry from most of the work that Turner was doing elsewhere as the midpoint of the 1950s approached. Back in Connecticut, where Turner had built the huge factories and laboratories in which Pratt & Whitney had built the aircraft engines that dominated American aviation during the war, the age of jet aviation was dawning. It started with the Andrew Wilgoos Turbine Laboratory, a gigantic, windowless research and development barn on the shores of the Connecticut River, where power for the experiments would be produced by boilers salvaged from four huge warships intercepted on their way to the scrap heap. The big Wilgoos Labs were only the beginning. The lion's share of what Turner would build for Pratt & Whitney during the early fifties comprised two entirely new Connecticut manufacturing plants, one at Bradley

Field in Windsor Locks and the other in North Haven, each with a floor area exceeding 500,000 square feet.

Meeting an especially demanding schedule on the Pratt & Whitney work would put Turner to some harsh tests. The plants were part of a national program to increase aircraft production during the Korean War, and the pressure to maintain timely delivery of construction materials was intense. Tom Gerlach Sr., a young Turner expeditor who would later rise to a senior vice presidency, was dispatched to Indiana to follow a critical rail shipment all the way to Connecticut to ensure that it wouldn't be shunted aside along the way. More than fifty years later, Gerlach remembered driving alongside the train's route for four days, stopping at each checkpoint to convince local trainmasters (when necessary) to allow the critical car to continue. The schedule held, and even for many years after the end of hostilities in Korea a workforce of more than 10,000 workers would continue to be employed by Pratt & Whitney in the plants that Turner had built for them in Connecticut.

In Kentucky, there was more of the same. Five huge, 100-foot-high manufacturing buildings were built for General Electric Company on a 700-acre site GE called Appliance Park, near Louisville. There GE would produce the washing machines, dryers, ranges, refrigerators, room air conditioners, and other appliances that would change the lives of a postwar population that had finished their educations under the GI Bill, had married, and were now beginning to raise families and to purchase houses. Turner and Struck Construction Company of Louisville, a partner selected as a concession to GE's commitment to local participation in all its work, did the job as a joint venture. They subcontracted to local firms all the drilled caisson work and the moving of almost 2 million cubic yards of dirt, and they subcontracted the mechanical and electrical work to joint ventures of relatively small local firms linked to larger firms from New York and Chicago, but they did all the rest of the construction work with their own forces.

By 1953, the prospects suggested in the 1950 corporate statement had certainly been confirmed. Between 1950 and 1953, a period in which the total value of awards for new nonresidential construction in the country as a whole was growing at about 5 percent per year, the average annual rate at which Turner's work was growing was almost 20 percent, a remarkable and entirely valid measure of real growth in a period when the annual inflation rate was still only about 5 percent. Even after taxes and dividends and after its annual contributions to the Additional Compensation Plan, the company was able to increase its net worth to about $3.7 million by the end of 1953.

There had been changes, of course, in how and by whom the company was being run, and there were more to come. John P. H. Perry, Walter K. Shaw, and Harry Ward were all gone from the board by the end of 1953, to be followed soon by Elmer Ford. In that same year founder Henry C. Turner, whose health had begun to decline, resigned from the board and went into full retirement. Turner executives Ab Abberley and Dutch Schroedel had already been added to the board during the few years leading to the surge of retirements, and Nicholas O'Connell was about to be added. It was still a time in which all members of the board were men who were either active in the operations of Turner Construction Company or recently retired from them.

But during 1952 that tradition of inside directorship was to be violated for the first time when the board accepted Chan Turner's radical proposal to invite an outsider to become a director. The man who accepted the board's invitation may have been an outsider to construction, but he was no outsider to Turner: He was Howard S. Turner, nephew of the founder, son of the company's wartime president, Archie Turner, and the forty-one-year-old first cousin of Chan Turner. Educated in the liberal arts at Swarthmore College and later in chemistry and chemical engineering at MIT, where he had been awarded the Ph.D., he would come to the board with eleven years of varied research and product development experience at DuPont. In addition, he'd been employed at a senior level by Pittsburgh Consolidation, the country's largest commercial coal company, where he had organized and managed a multimillion-dollar research program that included the construction of its facilities. He made no claim to being a muddy-boots builder, but he was seen to be smart, well educated, and thoroughly experienced in ways that could be very helpful to the Turner board. And he was a Turner.

The board made some other important decisions during 1953, and some of them would have more than casual impact. One of them increased company salaries across the board and modified the Additional Compensation Plan in such a way as to ensure that a return of at least 6 percent of the company's net worth be demonstrated before further contributions to the Additional Compensation Plan would be authorized. A second important action of the board during 1953 was its decision to acquire the assets and the corporate name and business of an old, friendly rival in Cincinnati, effectively establishing a Turner branch office there. Ferro Concrete Construction Company of Cincinnati had, like Turner, been a child of the Ransome organization and had, like Turner, been born in 1902. When Turner was setting records for building the largest reinforced concrete buildings in the country during the early years of the century, Ferro was setting records for building the tallest ones. In 1903, Ferro had built the sixteen-story Ingalls Building in Cincinnati, then the country's tallest reinforced concrete building, and since then Ferro had distinguished itself throughout Ohio as a builder of big and tall reinforced concrete structures. But in 1953, when family members there had begun to retire, there was no one left to continue Ferro's management, and a Turner offer to acquire the firm was accepted.

A third decision of the board, made during the closing days of 1953, was to accept the resignation of Cliff Wilson, after forty-six years of service, leaving the chairmanship as well as the presidency to Chan Turner.

10.

Chan

T he significance of Cliff Wilson's retirement at the end of 1953 was largely symbolic. He'd joined the company during its earliest days, made an enormous contribution to its growth and development, managed many of its most important jobs, and very late in his long career had finally settled into a role that was more senior adviser than manager. Of course, his chairmanship had been extremely valuable in reassuring old customers that there was continuity at the top during a period of radical change at Turner, and his judgment as the board's elder statesman had certainly been valued, but any misgivings that young Chan had expressed to his father about the potential impact of Wilson's chairmanship during his own presidency had long since proved to be unfounded.

As it turned out, Chan had by the end of Wilson's term come to rely increasingly on the support of two other board members whose insights and skills he regarded especially well. One was Francis (Joe) Warren, who had started with Turner at about the same time as Chan and who had worked very closely with him for years as the two of them made their way up the company's corporate ladder. The other was Carleton (Rosie) Rosenburgh, who had shaped and more or less dominated the firm's vital cost-estimating department. Warren was a native Canadian who was just Chan's age. He had graduated from McGill University in Montreal in 1924 and gone right to work for Turner, first intersecting with Chan on the Breakers Hotel job in Florida after only a few years with the firm. At that time the two of them were a couple of earnest young men trying, for what were probably entirely different reasons, to learn everything they could about the business and to acquit themselves well, and they hit it off professionally and socially. After some years in the field, Warren began to gravitate toward the administrative and financial side of the business and became Chan's most trusted adviser, later becoming corporate treasurer, then executive vice president and a member of the board of directors, and finally vice chairman of the board. Rosie Rosenburgh was a couple of years younger than Joe Warren and had graduated in engineering from Yale in 1926. Like most of these fellows, he had gone right to work for Turner, moving around in a variety of positions in the field for a few years, but by the 1940s he was beginning to focus on the cost-estimating component of the firm's work. Cost estimating was thought by many in the firm to be an absolutely critical element in Turner's success, and, especially during the years when a significant fraction of the firm's work was still being secured in lump-sum, competitive bidding, there was evidence to support such a view. By 1945, Rosenburgh had become chief estimating engineer and a couple of years after that he was elected to the board of directors, where an already close relationship with Chan became even closer.

Warren and Rosenburgh were fairly typical of Turner's senior management, which averaged more than thirty years' service in 1954. By then the company had completed more than 2,500 jobs for a range of customers that included some of the country's most successful firms, twenty of them companies for which Turner had previously done more than ten other jobs. When Peter French of the great British construction firm Bovis returned to England after visits with the leading American construction firms in 1954, he wrote to Chan to tell him that his visit to Turner had been the highlight of his American tour and that he aspired to modeling his own firm, already one of Britain's largest and most successful, along Turner's lines.

Turner's recent history and its future prospects had rarely been more favorable than they were in the mid-fifties when Chan Turner combined the chairmanship with his presidency. A sometimes fragile armistice had ended the war in Korea after American casualties had reached nearly half their World War I level, and although the almost simultaneous collapse of the French in Indochina suggested an ominous potential for further conflict along the Pacific Rim, the United States was glad to return to the peace that had followed the end of World War II. American industrialists and venture capitalists moved quickly to revive an expansion that had been inhibited by the demands of the Korean War, and commercial activity abounded. Within twenty-four months, General Motors became the first American corporation to earn more than a billion dollars in a single year.

Some of the older board members had retired, including Elmer Ford, who had started with Turner on an addition to the Harvard Stadium, and Bill Nye, an elegant, Back Bay Bostonian whom a former subordinate would remember years later as a "distinguished man who carried a cane." They'd been replaced by younger men. Of course, this was still a time in which all the board members were either active or retired Turner employees or members of the Turner family, and it would be some years before the idea of mixing some outside experience with their own would induce the board to invite membership from outside that small group.

In June 1954, Henry C. Turner Sr. died after a year in a Pennsylvania nursing home, and his death would be followed within just a few years by the deaths of several of his colleagues from the company's earliest days. DeForest Dixon, who had been his associate at the time of the company's founding, died in 1956, and his passing was followed by the deaths of F. E. Schilling and Walter K. Shaw, whose son would a couple of decades later become president and chairman. John P. H. Perry, the aristocratic colleague of Henry Turner who had late in his life married (and divorced) the best-selling mystery writer Mignon Eberhart, would die soon after that and Ed Courter, only a few years after serving as general superintendent and then manager in the Chicago office, would die at only fifty-two just a year or so later. When Chan Turner took over the chairmanship in 1953 all but two of the board's members were active Turner employees and deeply involved in the company's regular operations. The exceptions were Cliff Wilson, who had stayed on the board for a few years after retiring from both its chairmanship and his vice presidency and who would himself live only another few years, and Howard

Turner, Chan's young cousin and the only board member who had never worked for the company.

Turner's new acquisition in the Midwest, Ferro Concrete Construction Company, proved an immediate success, contributing substantially to Turner's 1954 earnings and justifying Chan's decision to make the first of what would later become a whole series of moves toward establishing a Turner presence in the Midwest and then in the West. Herb Mode, a Swarthmore-educated engineer who had been functioning as director of personnel in New York, was made vice president in charge of the new Cincinnati holding, with Don Burbrink, who had come along from the old Ferro Company, at his right hand. The new acquisition had brought along a host of important Midwestern industrial customers, including Cincinnati-based Procter & Gamble, Cincinnati Gas & Electric, Cincinnati Bell, and Cincinnati Shaper, and jobs for several such firms were in progress at the time of the acquisition or were developed right after it. Even more important, Turner's new base in Cincinnati placed it close to the center of John Galbreath's headquarters in Columbus. The big Galbreath jobs in New York and Pittsburgh were well along or had been completed by then, and Turner's establishing a base in the center of John Galbreath's home territory brought the two firms closer together. Within a few years it would lead to a substantial new Turner office in Columbus itself and to an even closer and more effective association between the two firms.

The Cincinnati move wasn't Turner's only move beyond its traditional boundaries in the mid-fifties. At almost the same time as the Ferro acquisition, the company signed a contract with the Bethlehem Mines subsidiary of Bethlehem Steel Company to build a big iron-ore mining and pelletizing plant in the remote village of Marmora in the Canadian province of Ontario. It was another job like White Pine Copper, in an almost equally remote location that's remembered by a veteran of the job as having about 1,200 citizens and very little inside plumbing, but as a place (in the Canadian tradition) that had a modern ice skating rink and seven uniformed hockey teams. It was a big job, even for Turner, and it led to the company's establishing an office it maintained in Toronto for a few years, in what proved to be a failed hope that there might be enough business in Canada to justify a permanent presence there.

The still-young Chicago office had by the mid-fifties come very much into its own. Rudy Cullum, its first manager, had died only a couple of years after the office opened and had been replaced by his general superintendent, Ed Courter. But by the mid-fifties Courter had been brought back to New York, and Clint Hernandez, who had been project executive at Oak Ridge and at White Pine, had taken over the growing Chicago office. Nils Nilsson, who had built the prestigious 600 Fifth Avenue building in New York, was general superintendent, a title that would later become project executive. Turner was finishing construction of four twelve-story apartment houses in Chicago, contemporary buildings designed by Skidmore Owings & Merrill for New York Life Insurance Company's new Lake Meadows housing project, and it was gearing up for construction of the first two of four additional twenty-one-story apartment buildings that would follow as part of the same complex. By then Turner had built or was building big manufacturing plants in the Chicago area for a variety of firms that included Minnesota Mining and Manufacturing Company, and it had started work there on what would become a campus of traditional buildings for the Catholic Foreign Mission Society of the Maryknoll Fathers. When Lou Hall was brought out to build the Sinclair Oil Company Building, a ten-story office building for the Galbreath interests that would be the first new structure in the Chicago Loop in twenty years and probably the Loop's first ever to be fully air-conditioned, Turner's position as a presence in the Chicago construction market began to be taken seriously.

Much of the work that had preceded the Sinclair Building, including all the Lake Meadows and the Maryknoll work, had been secured in the sometimes difficult setting of competitive bidding, but the Sinclair job was built under a negotiated, guaranteed-maximum-price arrangement that included all the tenant work, and after it had been built there was a general shift toward negotiated contracts in Turner's Chicago office.

Herbert Conant, who had started with the company on the UN job in New York, was fresh from a few years as project engineer on Turner's big Mobil headquarters building there when he was brought out to Chicago in 1956 to work on the new Harris Trust building. Harris Trust was a prestigious downtown bank and office building for a venerable Chicago institution and a good illustration of the kind of work that was now beginning to come into Turner's Chicago office. Another contemporary Skidmore Owings & Merrill design, the job would demand almost all the builder's skills: demolition of existing structures in a dense urban setting, conversion of an existing garage for office use, construction of a complex foundation, and construction of an elegant office tower wrapped in stainless steel. Al Sanchez and Doug Meyer, a couple of young Turner men who would later rise to senior positions in the company, worked under Conant on the project, which would prove to be the first of a long series of Turner contracts with Harris Trust. Conant himself, still only about thirty years old, would a little more than twenty-five years later become CEO of Turner.

The earlier fifties had been good ones back east, too. The Boston office, in addition to its continuing industrial work in Connecticut for Pratt & Whitney and Hamilton Standard (by then both part of United Aircraft) and for submarine builder Electric Boat in Groton, had been busy with an array of distinguished Boston-area buildings that included Aldrich and Kresge Halls at the Harvard Graduate School of Business Administration, a glorious new chapel and other buildings at Smith College, and a growing portfolio of hospital and other institutional work. In Philadelphia, there was a similar picture: industrial buildings for the principal manufacturing firms of the region, including Wyeth Labs, American Can, RCA, and Formica, mixed with an approximately equal amount of refined finished work at such places as St. Andrew's School in Delaware. In 1955 Turner Philadelphia completed the difficult construction of a gigantic new printing plant and office building in the urban center of Philadelphia for the *Philadelphia Bulletin,* the first of a series of newspaper projects that would be undertaken during this period by different Turner offices, including one for the *Boston Globe* and another for the *New York Daily News.*

Although all the offices were thriving, it was work in the New York region that produced the lion's share of an annual construction volume that by the mid-fifties was approaching $150 million. New York's dominance wasn't surprising. It was the country's biggest city, generating many of its biggest projects, and of course it was the location of the company's headquarters, a place where it had been known and well regarded for years. Turner's work there was big and varied, including at one time in the 1950s a new terminal building at Newark International Airport, a substantial but "temporary" building that would years later be converted to hangar space when an even bigger and grander terminal replaced it, and a host of other big jobs. Just north of the city in suburban White Plains, Turner would build a fortresslike structure with a heavily reinforced cast-in-place concrete frame enclosed by limestone-clad cast-in-place reinforced concrete walls, all designed to provide a disaster-resistant nerve center for AT&T's emerging microwave-based, security-sensitive national communications system. The building was characterized by its owner as being able to survive the explosion of 20,000 tons of TNT within half a mile of its center.

At the same time, in nearby Connecticut, Turner was getting ready to start construction of one of the earliest of the splendid, postwar corporate headquarters buildings that were just starting to follow the early signs of the population shift to the suburbs: a sprawling state-of-the-art building designed by Skidmore Owings & Merrill for the Connecticut General Insurance Company (later, after it merged with the Insurance Company of North America, CIGNA) in Bloomfield. It was a splendid place, complete with every imaginable provision for making more pleasant and effective the work of administering a great insurance company, including bowling alleys and beauty shops, and set among 268 acres of luxuriously landscaped Connecticut countryside. The Connecticut General job came along early enough in the new trend toward locating headquarters buildings in the suburbs that it attracted a great deal of favorable notice for its architect and its owner, and equally favorable attention for its builder as well.

Through all this, while the big new commercial and institutional projects were getting most of the attention, there was no slackening in the traditional diet of industrial work that had been a Turner staple for many years. In addition to the Bethlehem Mines work in Canada, there was still an abundance of plant and factory construction for such regular Turner clients as Scoville Manufacturing, for whom the company had previously done twenty-five other jobs by 1955, and for Westinghouse, General Electric, RCA, and many other clients of long-standing. In an especially large and demanding industrial venture that started late in 1952, Turner's Roane-Anderson subsidiary, by then winding down its work at Oak Ridge, had become the "local" (Tennessee-based) member of a joint venture partnership with Fraser-Brace Engineering Company of New York for building a paper mill about forty-five miles from Chattanooga for Bowaters Southern Paper Company. It was a big job that included not only a rambling manufacturing complex but also a power plant, three miles of railroad construction, and the broad infrastructure that would be needed for processing and converting to paper almost 200,000 tons of pulp every year.

In 1956, when the company was finishing work on the Galbreath-sponsored Mobil Building on New York's Forty-second Street, Turner moved its own corporate offices from the nearby Graybar Building, where they had been since 1927, to the thirty-sixth floor of Galbreath's sleek new stainless-steel skyscraper.

Meanwhile, a new historical force had been gathering momentum, and like the wars, depressions, and sweeping cultural changes of earlier years, it would profoundly influence Turner's course. This time it was the computer. Increasingly familiar to the scientific community during the late 1940s, in the early 1950s it began to move from the laboratory to the factory, attracting the attention and interest of industry, business, and government, and in only a few more years it would become a powerful force in the culture and commerce of the world.

In the beginning, for Turner the impact of the computer was limited essentially to the business of doing construction for the companies that would produce it, but it would soon spread to almost everything Turner touched, from the expanding aviation industry that was among the first to sense the potential impact of computer-based systems, to the broad variety of laboratories, hospitals, schools, and factories that were the core of the company's business. Board members like Howard Turner, who had brought new perspectives from outside the company, were beginning to see computer-based applications for Turner, mostly for accounting processes and the like, but it would still be a few years before the company would itself begin to rely on computer-based systems for scheduling and administering its own work.

In the early 1950s Remington Rand, already an entrepreneurial conglomerate with interests in many product lines, was farther along in the business of designing and building computers than anyone else. It had even demonstrated to millions of early TV watchers that its giant UNIVAC could accurately predict details of the 1952 presidential election that had been incorrectly predicted or missed entirely by traditional forecasters, and Remington Rand was spending half again as much money as IBM for further research that was expected to produce a commercially viable line of computers. And companies like RCA, Raytheon, General Electric, Sylvania, and others weren't far behind Remington Rand. IBM had made a less dramatic start with something it called its Defense Calculator, which it was producing in Poughkeepsie, New York, but Thomas Watson Sr., almost eighty years old by then, wasn't very optimistic that the electronic computer would ever be able to replace the punch-card system of calculation that had been at the core of IBM's success for years. He recognized the importance of electronics but was inclined to see it only as a way of improving existing technologies like punch-card systems and typewriters, and in 1950 IBM was profitably renting and sometimes selling a vast amount of such traditional equipment to industry and government.

Watson's son, Thomas Watson Jr., saw the future differently. He was enthusiastic about the potential of the electronic computer, encouraging increased attention to its production, and by 1952 he had successfully advocated construction of a big engineering laboratory a couple of miles from IBM's plant in Poughkeepsie, mainly for the development of electronic computing. For all practical purposes it would be the beginning of a campaign that would ultimately elevate IBM to a position of unmistakable dominance in the design and manufacture of electronic computers.

Chan Turner saw the future in like terms, and largely on the strength of the half-dozen jobs that Turner had already done for IBM at its central New York State plants, he made it his business to secure a contract to build the new laboratory at Poughkeepsie. Voorhees, Walker, Smith, Smith and Haines, a prominent New

York–based architectural firm, was engaged by IBM to design the new Poughkeepsie lab and by early 1953 Turner had started construction, with Bob Hazard running the work in the field and the now senior Nick O'Connell managing as project executive from the home office in New York. The building would be a good, practical facility for what IBM expected its needs to be in 1954, a vast improvement over the big old riverfront house in which its small Poughkeepsie engineering staff had been working and certainly vital for accommodating the hundreds (later thousands) of new engineers who would be brought in by IBM to speed the company's progress into the computer age. But it was a far cry from some of the architecturally glorious laboratories that would follow later under the younger Watson's leadership.

Before and while the new laboratory was being designed and built at Poughkeepsie, young Watson was spending a good deal of his time in Cambridge, Massachusetts, and in Washington, D.C., focused on one of the most important sales IBM would ever make. With the cold war threatening to heat up, the U.S. government had decided that the country needed a comprehensive aircraft-warning system, and it had commissioned MIT in Cambridge, Massachusetts, to design it. MIT, as soon as its design showed signs of promise, needed a reliable manufacturer to build computers for the system, which it called SAGE (Semi Automatic Ground Environment). By 1952 its scientists were looking over the small number of companies they thought might be set up to do it. IBM, which by then had its Defense Calculator up and running, looked best to MIT and was engaged to build a prototype.

That was good news for IBM but it was only a first step, as the real prize would be a later contract to build the forty-eight giant computers that would be required to put SAGE to work. Young Watson wasn't about to risk waiting for all the required government approvals and authorizations, so he simply proceeded to tool up for the big job with nothing more than a handshake from the government official in charge. With that informal agreement, he had secured for IBM an inside view of the state of the art and an invaluable chance to refine its own approach to the manufacturing that would be required.

IBM quickly made a decision to build the required new plant in Kingston, New York, just twenty miles up the Hudson from the Poughkeepsie plant and on the opposite side of the river. The plan was to build the SAGE computers there and, when they were finished, to transfer some of Poughkeepsie's electric-typewriter production to the new Kingston plant, freeing up space in Poughkeepsie for what young Watson correctly anticipated would be a permanent and increasing demand for the production of computers.

By late 1953 Giffels & Vallet of Detroit had begun to design a 460,000-square-foot manufacturing plant for a raw site in Kingston and, with it, designs for all the support facilities that such a huge new plant would require. Within a few months they were ready for a contractor to build the place, and IBM's Military Products Division, a survivor of its wartime munitions production at Poughkeepsie, brought in Turner. But like General Electric on Turner's Louisville job and like Ford on Turner's Kansas City job, IBM was sensitive to the importance of local involvement in major construction and, in this case especially, eager to ensure the best possible access to local labor, materials, and subcontractors. The solution was a joint venture between Turner and Campbell Building Company of Poughkeepsie, a substantial local contracting firm that had been doing work in the area for years. Turner retained firm control with 80 percent of the joint venture's shares.

In the early spring of 1954 Turner brought Bob Hettema back from Chicago to run the job. Turner's IBM work in the Hudson Valley had already begun to spill over into other jobs, and Nick O'Connell was managing it as project executive from a New York base with Mike Roach operating as general superintendent at the sites. Once the urgent military demands of SAGE were overlaid on the customary industrial imperative for speed, pressures to complete the job as soon as possible accumulated quickly. Ground was broken in April, with a goal of being ready for the start of IBM's special interior fitting-out work early in 1955. Progress was good, and by spring of 1955 Turner was building raised floors in one end of the plant to accommodate underfloor cooling systems for the equipment while concrete floor slabs were being poured at the other end.

In hindsight, the problems of keeping ahead of the customer's needs seem almost predictable. About halfway through construction, the computer revolution overtook IBM's own strategic planning. Poughkeepsie's appetite for more space for producing its own computers had increased even faster than expected, and IBM elected to satisfy it by moving all its typewriter production up to Kingston even before the SAGE project was finished. That would require vastly expanding the new construction at Kingston with still another 320,000 square feet of manufacturing and related space. For Turner, that meant radical changes that included not just adding to the originally planned building but expanding the support facilities that were already well along too. Later in 1955, steel for the added areas was being set and by the end of the year IBM was able to produce its first trial run of 100 typewriters in its new plant at Kingston. One task after another was added to Turner's Kingston contract, and whole new contracts were added as well. By 1956, with the SAGE project well advanced, a hugely expanded plant that would ultimately employ 10,000 persons was producing electric typewriters there. Years later (but before the electric typewriter joined a growing list of products rendered obsolete by the computer), the whole electric-typewriter group would be shipped off to Kentucky to allow Kingston to convert entirely to computer production, like its already computer-committed big brother in Poughkeepsie.

The furious pace of work at Kingston had kept Turner's upstate forces plenty busy, but not too busy to do more work at the Poughkeepsie plant itself. Even before the new engineering laboratory there was finished, young Watson had begun to feel that such a laboratory wasn't going to satisfy the company's newly expanded research needs after all and that there needed to be a new facility for doing more basic scientific research. Toward that end he engaged the distinguished architect and industrial designer Eliot Noyes, who was already designing some of IBM's industrial products, to design a splendid research laboratory to be built at a cost of about $2 million near the engineering laboratory in Poughkeepsie, and early in 1955 IBM brought the Turner-Campbell joint venture back to Poughkeepsie to build it. Until the great Watson Laboratory was built years later in Yorktown Heights, New York, this Poughkeepsie laboratory and a few others like it would be the centers of scientific research for the company.

The initial impact of the computer age had been felt by Turner through its work at Poughkeepsie and Kingston, but that was only the beginning. It would still be some time before the computer would find its way into Turner's offices, but the country's big hospitals, its universities, and most of its other institutions would soon begin to adapt to the new technology, with industry and commerce following quickly, and Turner would find itself in the business of building for almost all of them.

The airlines, which early on had seen the computer on the horizon, were in the vanguard. The computer would not only speed the design of their big new aircraft, it would transform the technology of the reservations systems that were essential to their business. Before the 1950s ended, New York's Idlewild Airport (later called JFK) would begin an ambitious upgrading and expansion of its facilities, and before long Turner would have contracts to build some of its most striking new terminals.

One of the first of Turner's new jobs was a terminal at Idlewild for Pan American Airways, a great circular structure in which an approximately 125,000-square-foot roof cantilevered out over the edges of about 100,000 square feet of enclosed space below, looking to one admiring critic like a glorious umbrella. And at almost the same time Turner built a spectacular new terminal at Idlewild for American Airlines, one of the first of a long series of projects the company would do for American. When the American Airlines project was finished, the airline was so pleased with Turner's performance that it loaded all the men who had managed it onto one of its big new jets and took them for a memorable spin down the coast and back. There were other jobs at Idlewild too: a building for Seaboard Western Airlines and a small, elegant bank that Skidmore Owings & Merrill had designed for National City Bank (later Citibank) that was probably seen and admired by more people than saw and admired the terminal buildings themselves since it was located along the main entrance road into the airport and noticed by almost every arriving or departing passenger.

The early airport work wasn't limited to what was done at Idlewild. A few miles away, at New York's LaGuardia Airport, Turner would a few years later replace with an elegant new building the tiny structure that had served as LaGuardia's main arrival building since the 1940s. Designed by Harrison and Abramovitz, it was a crisp, fully air-conditioned structure that never lost its contemporary luster. The new building, almost forty years old at the time of Turner's one hundredth anniversary, was among the first to position all its passenger entrances along the arc of a giant circle, with a series of passenger corridors radiating toward the tarmac like the spokes of a giant wheel.

As the company moved closer to the start of the 1960s, its momentum was powerful and growing, sustained by the increasing volume and variety of its work. A general level of national prosperity, only occasionally interrupted, had encouraged the growth of retail commerce, and Turner was building or expanding some of the East's largest and most fashionable department stores: John Wanamaker's, Lord & Taylor, Strawbridge & Clothier, and Snellenburg's in the Philadelphia area; the 113-year-old G. Fox and Company's store in Connecticut; Bonwit Teller in New York City; and on Long Island a new Macy's store advertised by its owner as the largest store in the world.

Even for an experienced contractor like Turner, new jobs brought new and different challenges. When B. Altman's management engaged Turner to build a couple of upscale branches in the suburbs, it requested that Turner maintain the same old-world creakiness in the new wood floors that Altman's customers had come to like in its old wood floors.

Hospitals were beginning to react to the increasing public demand for better health care, and Turner was already building new ones or expanding existing ones in Embreeville, Pennsylvania, and in Baltimore, Wilmington, and Cincinnati as well. In Pittsburgh, it would soon start construction of a new 824-room, 22-story hotel for Hilton: a sleek, contemporary high-rise concrete paean to the new age in architecture and a far cry from the traditional hotels that Turner had built years earlier in Atlantic City and elsewhere.

The work was clearly dominated by big, modern buildings, most of them designed for owners who were for the most part seeking the latest and best and who were almost uniformly impatient to get it. But not every job that was done during that expansive period would fit that pattern, and the great Baltimore cathedral was one notable exception.

The Roman Catholic Archdiocese of Baltimore, the country's oldest, had by 1952 waited a little over 150 years for its own grand cathedral. In that year it commissioned the Boston architectural firm of Maginnis Walsh & Kennedy to design it for them, with Frederick Law Olmsted, who had made his name as the designer of New York's Central Park, providing the landscape design. Two years later the archdiocese selected Turner to do the construction. It would be a glorious building, designed in a style that overlaid a slightly contemporary veil on an essentially Gothic form. Longer than St. Patrick's in New York and with spires that soared the equivalent of sixteen stories above Baltimore's Charles Street, it would be called the Cathedral of Mary Our Queen. The cores of its great walls and towers would be built of solid brick sheathed on all their exposed faces with almost 20,000 tons of Indiana limestone. The building's exteriors would be punctuated by bronze and stained glass windows from the shops of the country's most distinguished designers and artisans, and its floors would be granite, marble, and terrazzo. Turner's Dutch Schroedel, by then vice-president in charge of the Philadelphia office, would be the project executive. The discovery that Schroedel and the archbishop of the Baltimore archdiocese had played football against each other as high school boys was said to have leavened the negotiations for the contract. Turner's H. W. "Barney" Oldfield, a 1934 graduate of RPI, would be the field superintendent. It would take Turner a full five years to complete the job, a triumph of speed, some said, when compared with the centuries it took to build the great cathedrals of Europe.

By 1958, when *Engineering News-Record* published the first of what would later become its annual survey of the country's largest contractors, ranking them by volume of work completed, it identified Turner as second only to George A. Fuller among contractors specializing in building construction, and the firm's annual volume of work would soon pass $200 million. New York was still regularly accounting for well over half the company's annual volume, with Boston, Philadelphia, and Chicago following with an average of somewhere around equal fractions of the remainder and with the still-young Cincinnati office doing a little less. Corporate earnings had continued strong enough to increase the company's net worth to almost $5 million, even after regular annual payment of a 7 percent dividend on the preferred stock and annual payments on the common stock that averaged more than 6 percent of its book value.

But construction contracting is rarely without risk, and from time to time even the normally conservative management at Turner was bound to stumble, as it did in 1959 when it took on what looked like a generously profitable $15 million contract to build a 205-acre commercial theme park called Freedomland on a filled-in site in the Bronx section of New York City. The park was to be a sprawling, interactive array of imaginatively designed exhibits, amusement rides, and restaurants, all built on a map of the United States that would be laid out to scale on the ground. Each exhibit was to express a part of the history and culture of the region on which it had been overlaid, and it was expected that visitors from all over the world would wander through the displays and experience the sights and sounds of the country's wide-ranging cultures. The architects and designers were, for the most part, talented veterans of the acclaimed Disneyland theme park in California and well suited for the task. Turner was selected as the principal construction contractor, sharing some engineering responsibilities with the Aberthaw Company of Boston, a 40 percent joint venture partner brought in by consultants Cabot, Cabot & Forbes. The land was owned by the project's organizers, Webb & Knapp, a big, well-established New York real estate firm for whom Turner had done work before (on Chrysler East) and whose history included multimillion-dollar urban development projects in Denver, Washington, Chicago, New York, and Pittsburgh. Its president, William Zeckendorf, a brilliant if unpredictable practitioner of the sometimes arcane art of urban real estate development, had once managed the Vincent Astor properties and had years earlier spotted and hired a young I. M. Pei directly from MIT's College of Architecture to design Webb & Knapp's own buildings. Zeckendorf was a well-known figure in New York real estate, living and doing business in very high style, traveling the country in a private DC-3 airplane. He had been, in fact, the key figure in assembling the land on which the Turner Walsh

Fuller Slattery joint venture had a decade earlier built the United Nations head-quarters in New York.

The task of doing $15 million worth of light construction might have seemed trivial when compared with the monumental character of most of Turner's other work, but Freedomland was to be no trivial job. The work, much of it the uncon-ventional product of theatrical concepts and almost all of it unique, was started in 1959, with an unforgiving opening date scheduled for the summer of 1960, leav-ing less than a year for construction. Turner's Bob Kupfer, who would become a Turner "co-president" years later, remembers the company's on-site mill as being one of the largest in the country and an average workforce that rarely included fewer than 250 carpenters. Everything was complex, even the lath-and-plaster work that was required for producing all the special shapes and effects imagined by the designers. The electrical work was special enough that Turner found it necessary to bring in the national electrical contracting firm Fischbach & Moore to do it, and meeting New York City's demanding fire protection codes with what was mostly wood-frame construction was a formidable task as well. Exacerbating the demands of an oppressively short schedule, Ed Sullivan came along near the end of con-struction with a request that part of the project be completed in advance to allow for a June broadcast on his Sunday evening television show, requiring difficult and expensive rescheduling by Turner during the finishing weeks of the project. By the time the work was finished, Turner was operating the job three shifts a day, seven days a week, in order to finish on time. Opening day came as scheduled, and although its 35,000 visitors overwhelmed most of the park's services, it was deemed a success, and Turner submitted its final bill.

But six months later, Webb & Knapp still owed Turner almost $3 million, and prospects for its collection had started to look bad. The number of daily visitors to Freedomland had by then declined to a level that was insufficient to generate an operating profit and, worse yet, William Zeckendorf, vastly overextended in other projects, had accumulated a short-term debt that exceeded $10 million. He became evasive, treating Turner's appeals with indifference and often refusing to see Kupfer or Joe Warren at all and dealing abruptly with them when he did. By the end of the year it had become evident that Turner's bill wasn't going to be paid.

Turner's own employees had, of course, been paid, so most of the unpaid balance was money owed by Turner to its subcontractors and material suppliers. But the company refused to pass its setback on to them. The smaller ones, and others who seemed unlikely to be able to absorb a loss, were paid in full. Individual arrangements were made with the rest, varying with the amounts and circumstances, but in all cases requiring that much of the unpaid balance be paid right away and by Turner itself. The company ended up taking a loss on the job of about $2.2 million at the end of 1961.

The impact of the Freedomland disaster was softened a bit during the following year. Turner and Zeckendorf were able to work out a settlement that reduced Turner's loss by half, and a few years later Zeckendorf, apparently feeling a belated twinge of conscience, brought Turner into a lucrative construction-management contract for what was then called the Delegates Building for United Nations personnel, a big, aluminum-clad luxury apartment project (with office floors below) almost adjacent to United Nations headquarters in New York. Zeckendorf's Webb & Knapp had joined with Alcoa to sponsor the project, and Turner became the lead partner (under Lou Hall) in a joint venture with New York's HRH Construction Company, to manage its construction.

While occasional losing jobs were thought by most contractors to be more or less inevitable, they had been rare for Turner. By 1960 less than 20 percent of the value of the company's work was being secured through risk-sensitive competitive bidding, and even when it was secured in such a process, the invited bidders had usually been screened by the owner in advance and tended to be of Turner's own stripe. That didn't eliminate risk, of course, but it reduced it. The company was at some risk on some of its negotiated jobs too, where it often guaranteed the upper limit of cost to the owner, but in general these risks were easier to manage. Although such guarantees were common for Turner, they normally weren't formalized until design work was well advanced and costs had been firmly established. And besides, such projects didn't reflect the intense pressure of competition that was inherent in traditional lump-sum bidding. As to the kind of risk that brought down the Freedomland job, the risk of default by an owner, Turner's clientele was for the most part extremely solid, and there had been no such problems since depression days. At the time of the Freedomland job, before *Fortune* began publishing its annual list of the country's top 500 corporations, the magazine published an annual list of what it considered to be the top fifty firms. By the time of the Freedomland work, Turner had completed a total of almost 250 separate projects for thirty-five of the firms listed.

There wasn't much time for stewing about Freedomland in the rush of jobs that kept Turner busy as it entered the 1960s. In spite of Chan Turner's regularly conservative and sometimes pessimistic annual forecasts, annual volume was continuing to increase and had passed $200 million, with earnings (except during the Freedomland year) by now regularly exceeding 10 percent of net worth. Optimism in the marketplace, the essential fuel of new construction, was widespread, and signs of the political and social turbulence that lay ahead in the 1960s were almost nowhere to be seen.

By the time the new decade began, Turner was increasingly seen as a builder specializing in high-rise urban structures. Such buildings had attracted wide publicity and did, in fact, represent a substantial and increasing fraction of the value of the company's work. High-rise buildings by Turner were by then prominent along the skylines of Boston, New York, Philadelphia, Pittsburgh, and Chicago, and more and taller ones were coming along every year.

At only nineteen stories, the headquarters building in Chicago that Turner had finished in 1958 for Inland Steel certainly wasn't among the tallest of the new towers, but it was among the most distinguished. Inland wanted to ensure that the building would be a special, highly visible showroom for its products, so it had engaged Skidmore Owings & Merrill to design it. Chan Turner wanted the job badly for Turner's Chicago office, and because this was a case where securing the contract still meant being the low bidder, Turner's estimators had pulled out all the stops and taken the job at what proved to be a very tight price. Lou Hall, by then comfortably reestablished in the East after a run of Midwestern jobs that had included the nearby Sinclair Building, was induced by Chan Turner to return to Chicago to build it.

The work got off to a slow start. It required a forty-foot deep sheeted hole with steel piles driven to refusal in place of the usual Chicago caissons, all in the heart of the busiest section of one of the country's busiest cities. A recent sheet-piling failure on a nearby job had made the locals skittish, so Turner brought in its old friends at Spencer, White & Prentis to do the foundations, and they'd have their work cut out for them. Site conditions made access and storage exceptionally difficult, and the sheeting had to be braced in a pattern designed to allow later bearing piles to be threaded between the cross braces. And just to make an already beleaguered job more difficult, an adjacent theater that had been shuttered during the bidding period had reopened and was showing the hit play *My Fair Lady* to big crowds, a circumstance that would normally have been of little interest to a contractor. But the show's Wednesday matinee performers couldn't easily accommodate the noise and vibrations of pile driving, so good neighbor Turner was obliged to suspend work on those afternoons, a difficult and expensive concession. The superstructure, on which Turner was doing its own concrete work, had its own idiosyncrasies. Field connections for the steel frame were among the first to be made with high-strength bolts, a new technique that would eventually replace virtually all field riveting. Even finishing the job was made more complicated than usual when a portable arc light being used by the architect to illuminate the exhibition hall during an evening inspection ignited some draperies and caused enough damage for concern. A difficult job, certainly not a very profitable one, but one that would later be identified by Paul Goldberger, the architecture critic of the New York Times, as one of the outstanding buildings of the period. And the Inland Steel job would be another confirmation that Turner was in Chicago to stay.

Although Chicago was the birthplace of the skyscraper, New York had by this time become its home. There, Turner had built or was building a substantial fraction of the new high-rise office buildings that by the 1960s were once again changing the skyline of the city. There were many of them, including the thirty-eight story, 1.8 million-square-foot home office building that Skidmore Owings & Merrill had designed for the 102-year-old Equitable Life Assurance Society, described at the time as the largest privately owned building in the world.

But among the new generation of New York's towers the Chase Manhattan Building may have been the most important for Turner. Another Skidmore building, at sixty floors above the street it was the tallest building to be erected in New York since the Empire State Building, and Turner's contract to build it was a valued prize. For Turner, the Chase job had an added significance: Although the company had really been doing construction management in one form or another almost since its beginning, the Chase contract was certainly the largest and perhaps the purest of its construction-management contracts. Here Turner would provide no guarantee as to cost, would be virtually free of traditional contracting risks, and would write all its subcontracts as agent for the owner. The Chase tower is thought by veterans of that period to be the job that really established Turner's leadership in the rarefied environment of extremely high-rise, extremely high-quality urban construction.

Chase had contracted separately (with another firm) for the foundation work, which burrowed five levels below the street and would eventually include the bomb shelter mandated by the Rockefellers, but Turner was brought onto the site in 1957, as soon as the subgrade work got underway, to give the company the better part of a year to become acquainted with the job. It was a period that provided an ideal opportunity to consult on design, costs, and methods and to prepare for the superstructure tasks that lay ahead. The technology of skyscraper construction had by then moved ahead fairly sharply: Structural materials and the computer-assisted capability of engineers to use them effectively had been substantially enhanced, passenger elevators had become much faster and more sensitive to the special needs of high-rise buildings, new curtainwall materials and designs had been developed (and on this project would be tested in a mock-up building that Turner would build on Long Island), new materials for fireproofing the structural frame were proliferating (including asbestos systems that were later found to be carcinogenic and would have to be removed), and, of course, new concepts for controlling the physical environment of the building's interiors were surfacing all the time. The Chase tower, built when a generation of postwar high-rise office buildings was starting to mature, had the luxury of an especially discriminating owner, and the elegance of earlier buildings found its way into some of the building's public spaces. Turner's contract included all the tenant work, and even extended to the installation of some of the Rockefeller family's art collection.

Some of Turner's most senior people managed the Chase work, including Deke Parsons as project manager at the site and the dignified Ab Abberley, whose judgment as senior project executive is uniformly recalled by veterans of the job as being a controlling force in its success. Some of the younger men who would later rise to senior positions cut their teeth on the Chase job. Les Shute, who headed up cost-estimating work for the job, would only a few years later become the company's youngest vice president at thirty-seven, and he'd go on to become general manager of the New York territory before becoming a senior vice president of the firm. Paul DeMange, another member of the promising young group on the Chase job, would later manage the San Francisco territory.

At the time the Chase project was getting underway, the City of New York was well along in a process it had started a few years earlier that would affect much of what Turner would be doing in the city during the eight years that would begin in 1958 and continue into some of 1966. Through its Committee on Slum Clearance, of which the powerful Robert Moses was chairman, the city had acquired an approximately seventeen-block blighted area on the west side of Manhattan and planned to relocate its population and demolish its run-down buildings. The idea was to resell the land at discounted prices to qualifying organizations that could demonstrate the commitment and ability needed to replace what had been removed with worthwhile projects of their own. Once Moses had swung into action, some of New York's most powerful and prestigious community leaders had joined forces to advocate successfully that part of the acquired area be committed as a location for building a center for the performing arts. Before long they had organized a constituency that started with the Metropolitan Opera Company (which had already decided to abandon its obsolete opera house) and the New York Philharmonic Orchestra (which had been notified by its landlord that its lease at Carnegie Hall was to be terminated in 1961). It was a group that would soon expand to include the Juilliard School, the American Ballet Theater, and at least a dozen other prestigious New York organizations with a focus on one or another of the performing arts. By 1956 an organization called Lincoln Center for the Performing Arts had been established, and with Wallace Harrison as its coordinating architect, it had begun the work of planning for construction of a complex that would become the cultural center of New York and a model for similar programs in cities all over the country. They would eventually build a 2,800-seat concert hall, a 3,800-seat opera house, a 1,200-seat drama theater, a 2,000-seat dance theater, a library, a museum, and the Juilliard School. Altogether, they'd spend almost $150 million for construction.

Selecting a contractor to build such a center wasn't nearly as difficult as expected. The four firms who were widely viewed as the best contractors in town, Turner, Walsh, Fuller, and Slattery, had only a few years earlier finished work as a joint venture on the United Nations headquarters, and they were especially well known to Wallace Harrison (the lead architect on the UN job) and to Robert Moses (the key figure in just about any construction in which the City of New York had a hand). In addition, all four (especially Turner) were well known to the industry and community leaders who would be making or influencing decisions at Lincoln Center. In December 1958, a new joint venture of these four firms was authorized by Lincoln Center to begin work as construction managers for the new complex, just as they had done at the United Nations headquarters, but with one change: This time Turner would be the lead contractor, with 30 percent of the shares.

Building Lincoln Center probably came as close as any twentieth-century project could to building a grand palace. What was designed was a complex of monumental structures swathed in Italian travertine: big, beautiful, complex, and expensive. Little would be spared to ensure that its theaters and concert halls would be the best in the world, sited in what would become the most glorious setting in New York. But palace-building in ancient times may have been slightly easier by virtue of the absolute authority of a single infallible royal figure, vis-à-vis Lincoln Center, where each building would have its own world-renowned architect and each would provide facilities and services for one or more different, independent members of the Lincoln Center family of performing artists — a formidable task.

Even the demolition would be difficult, albeit a two-edged sword for Turner. One existing reinforced concrete structure, which had been built by Turner as a multistory Cadillac showroom and maintenance garage forty years earlier, had been so solidly built that its frame was able to resist the power of the wrecking ball for more than six months before giving up.

The first new building would be Philharmonic Hall (later called Avery Fisher Hall) and Max Abramovitz, Harrison's partner, had been designated its architect. Although drawings were nowhere near complete early in 1959, a groundbreaking date in May was considered essential for the 1961 occupancy that had been promised the soon-to-be-dispossessed Philharmonic Orchestra, so the joint venture was authorized to proceed with foundations. After a few months, with foundation work proceeding on schedule, a bigger, larger slice of superstructure work was added on the basis of still-preliminary cost estimates that were fairly close to budgets. But as the design began to mature, the building grew bigger and even more splendid, and by spring 1960 the joint venture's cost estimates were 30 percent over budget. The Philharmonic managed a year's reprieve from its landlord at Carnegie Hall, taking some pressure off the schedule, and the joint venture did what it could to find savings to offset the growth in costs, while it moved ahead through strikes and labor shortages toward an opening in the middle of 1962.

Meanwhile, three other nationally prominent and appropriately creative architects were proceeding with ambitious designs for other buildings on the site. Philip Johnson was designing a theater for dance, Eero Saarinen a drama theater, and Skidmore Owings & Merrill's Gordon Bunschaft a library-museum complex. Like earlier designs for the main concert hall, all these were growing bigger, richer, and more expensive every month, and when the joint venture presented its estimates of cost in the spring of 1962, the figures struck one of the center's shocked board members as a "cold shower." Redesigns and some recriminations followed, together with a decision to dismantle the joint venture and assign construction of the projects individually to the joint venture partners, a decision encouraged by the partners themselves.

Turner was awarded the lion's share of the work: completion of the dance theater, which had already been started and would later be named the New York State Theater because of a substantial contribution the state had made to its cost; and total construction of both the drama theater and the library-museum complex, which had by then been consolidated into a single project to be named after its donor, Vivian Beaumont. The opera house contract was awarded to Fuller, the Juilliard School contract was awarded to Walsh, and the city worked out a contract with Slattery to build an underground parking garage.

After the complexity and awkwardness of having multiple contractors working on multiple projects with different architects, having Turner as an individual contractor was a breath of fresh air for Lincoln Center. Of course, with designs in flux there would still be plenty of problems, but they were addressed systematically and resolved. When it surfaced that George Balanchine, whose New York City Ballet Company would perform in the New York State Theater, had never really understood the drawings he had approved before construction, Turner demolished the completed orchestra pit that Balanchine now found too small and replaced it with a larger one. Later, when the director of another performance company found the pit too big, an arrangement for filling the extra space with removable seating was worked out. With it all, the New York State Theater was finished on time and within 1 percent of budget. Over at the Beaumont, which now included the library, Eero Saarinen's death just before the start of construction had been a demoralizing event that added to the difficulties. A final estimate by the joint venture, made just before its dissolution, showed another frightening 30 percent overrun, but Turner, working with Maurice Allen, Saarinen's colleague and successor, and with Gordon Bunschaft, was able to complete the work within the original estimate.

Philharmonic Hall was opened late in 1962 with a festive concert presented exclusively for an audience of the project's construction workers and their families. Almost two years later the New York State Theater was opened, just in time for it to meet Lincoln Center's commitment to provide high-quality space for performances and public events associated with the 1964 New York World's Fair. By the end of 1965 the Beaumont had opened too, and by the following spring Turner had finished up at Lincoln Center.

The Lincoln Center period had been an exuberant one for New York, and for Turner as well. While Turner's work there was winding down, the city had been gearing up for its world's fair, and once again Turner would find itself the contractor of choice for major corporations and institutions planning the kind of futuristic exhibits that not every contractor was qualified to build. General Electric was one of them. Its auditorium revolved around a fixed stage, a glimpse into technology that was still to come, designed by Welton Becket and built by Turner. The General Motors exhibit was another, a glimpse of the future not unlike what Turner had built for GM at the 1939 fair. The Johnson's Wax exhibit was among the fair's most spectacular, featuring an ellipsoid theater perched thirty feet above the ground. And there were others: one for the brewers of Rheingold Beer, one for a state-of-the-medical-arts organization called Atomedics, and several for state and national exhibitors like the State of Oklahoma and the Republic of Indonesia, all built by Turner. The company built a complicated, pile-supported foundation for the IBM exhibit, but another firm won IBM's superstructure contract in a bidding competition.

By the 1960s Turner was busy almost everywhere in New York, with high-rise work getting the lion's share of public attention through buildings for the Irving Trust Company and an extraordinary expansion from mid-rise to high-rise for the Morgan Guaranty Trust building on Fifth Avenue. On that unique job Turner added fifteen stories above what McKim, Mead & White had designed in 1898 as the twelve-story Sherry's Restaurant and Hotel. The elegant Sherry 's building had been acquired by Morgan in 1919 and renovated then for its own use, but now Turner had the task of enlarging the original foundations; gutting, reinforcing, and renovating the entire structure; and then adding fifteen stories to it. Bob Hettema, who would retire from Turner a dozen years later and go on to a second career on the faculty of Penn State, was in charge at the Morgan Guaranty job.

At the Rockefeller Institute, where some of the most important medical research of the period would be done, Turner was building a campus designed by Harrison and Abramovitz that included an auditorium with a ninety-two-foot-diameter concrete dome that would prove difficult enough to require its being built twice. When the forms were stripped after the first try, Turner's Nelson Doe wasn't satisfied with the quality of the concrete he saw. The unusually intense concentration of reinforcing steel that had been required for the thin-shell dome had inhibited adequate distribution of the wet concrete and Doe didn't like the look of the hardened concrete. He ordered it jackhammered out and rebuilt.

New York's United Engineering Center, where nineteen of the country's principal engineering societies would maintain their offices and a library, made some engineering history of its own. It was among the first of the buildings in which all field connections for structural steel would be welded, a technique that had much to be said for it but that never really offered an effective alternative to the increasingly popular high-strength-bolting approach that was faster, more easily controlled, and cheaper.

In 1963 Turner started work on what Lou Hall describes as one of the most difficult projects of his career, an extraordinarily complex hybrid of architectural concrete and structural steel that challenged even the best of Turner's subcontractors and sent at least one of them to bankruptcy court. It was Roche-Dinkeloo's nationally acclaimed architectural triumph, the headquarters building in New York for the Ford Foundation.

Few jobs were as demanding as the one Turner's forces started about 1963 at New York's Penn Station. There Turner had the task of demolishing much of the stately old station and thoroughly renovating the rest of it, all while ensuring that there would be no interruption in the operation of the railroad. To make that already challenging project even more difficult, Turner's contract required threading a system of massive new foundations between the tracks themselves, to support later buildings that would include the new Madison Square Garden, another Turner job. Paul DeMange, a young, New York–bred engineer fresh from the big Chase job, remembers the Penn Station work as living testimony to the single-mindedness of New York commuters. What he remembers best is their following,

without protest, convoluted and regularly changing pedestrian routes laid out by
Turner to lead them to and from their trains, oblivious to the hazards of new plaster and paint or objects falling from above, in relentless pursuit of transportation
to or from their jobs.

Turner did hundreds of jobs during this period of the early 1960s, averaging
around fifty per year. Its average annual volume of work was by now approaching
$200 million, and its annual net earnings after all expenses and dividends regularly
exceeded half a million dollars, a consistent and acceptable return of about 10
percent on a net corporate worth that by 1960 exceeded $5 million.

By 1963 Chan Turner had led the company for sixteen years, and any uncertainties that might have attended his selection in 1947 had long since disappeared.
An intelligent and capable man of quiet charm, he had been immensely successful in his management of the firm, extremely popular within and beyond it. Even
at the time of the company's hundredth anniversary, thirty-nine years later, he'd
be described by Turner people old enough to remember him as a man of uncommon decency. Chan was sixty-one years old in 1963, and although he appeared to
be in generally good health, he had never been a robust man (his father's letters
to him during his early days in the presidency were dominated by suggestions for
reducing his workload and conserving his energies), and he began to consider the
important matter of his successor.

In a time when many of the firm's senior managers served on the board of
directors, the natural source of candidates for a successor to Chan was the Turner
board itself. But distinguished old-timers like George Horr, Walter K. Shaw, Bill
Ball, Bill Nye, and F. E. Schilling had all retired or died during the 1950s, and even
Clint Hernandez, who had been elected in 1957, had retired in 1960. Ab Abberley
was just a year from his retirement. Neither Bob Frost nor Charles H. Wilson, a son
of Cliff Wilson who had joined the board after his father's death, appeared to be
a candidate. Chan's old and very close friend Joe Warren would have been a natural successor, but he was Chan's contemporary in age and would himself be retiring from Turner within a few years. The same age constraint applied to directors
Rosie Rosenburgh, Dutch Schroedel, Nick O'Connell, George Reaves, and Herb

Mode.

Walter K. Shaw's son, Walter B. Shaw, and Robert P. Marshall Jr., a couple of rising stars who shared distinguished war records and outstanding (almost identical) work histories at Turner, seemed almost perfectly suited for the top job, but they both were very new to the board, both were still in their forties, and both were probably thought by Chan to be not quite ready for the presidency.

There was one board member who was especially well regarded by Chan for his intelligence, his integrity, and his broad experience in business. He was Chan's younger cousin Howard S. Turner, Archie's son, and he was Chan's choice for the presidency. Since 1952, when Chan had recruited him to serve as Turner's first "outside" director, Howard had become steadily more intensely involved in the board's work, bringing his own analytical perspective and broad experience in business to the board and expanding the directors' perspectives beyond the limits of their own experience. Chan and the board had learned soon after Howard Turner's election that although he held a doctorate in chemical engineering and had spent much of the earlier part of his life in scientific research, he had long since shed his laboratory coat. At Pittsburgh Consolidation Coal Company and later at Jones & Laughlin Steel Company, to which Adm. Ben Moreell had recruited him, he had been managing big corporate divisions. Budgets, personnel, sales, cash flows, and the like were no strangers to him, and although the construction of buildings was something in which he had no direct experience, Chan and the other directors felt that such operating matters could be left to the company's already well-trained and seasoned operations managers. What they saw in Howard Turner was a man who had brought his own considerable intelligence to bear on the problems of managing the kind of far-flung organization that Turner was becoming, and there was general agreement that he was well suited for the presidency.

In 1964 the board chose Howard Turner to become the company's fifth president, to start in the spring of 1965, with the provision that Chan Turner would remain as chairman. It was understood that Chan would gradually cede executive power, and that within a few years he would relinquish the chairmanship itself.

11.

Chan and Howard

W hen Chan Turner turned over the presidency of the company to his fifty-four-year-old cousin in the spring of 1965, he was still a long way from abandoning his role as its chief executive officer. Still only sixty-three years old himself, he'd lived at the center of the company's authority all his life, had worked directly for Turner since 1923 except for a few years' hiatus during the depression and had been its president since 1947 and its chairman since 1953. To many who knew Turner, and to organizations like the Associated General Contractors of America and the New York Building Congress, in both of which Chan had held high offices, Chan *was* Turner. Relaxing such deeply embedded connections was something that was going to take a while. And besides, Chan was a part of so many important issues that had originated or that had been developing during the early and middle 1960s that a precipitous break would have been disruptive.

Probably the most important of these developing issues was the opening of Turner's new West Coast office in Los Angeles in 1964. A western presence is something that had been discussed in the boardroom, off and on, since early 1963, but what appears to have precipitated the decision to make a definite move was the success of the Galbreath interests in organizing a venture to build a high-rise tower in Los Angeles, coupled with John Galbreath's own resolve to engage Turner to do the construction.

By 1964, Turner had already done more than twenty jobs for Galbreath or for

Galbreath-Ruffin, a company Galbreath had formed with his New York–based colleague, Peter Ruffin. Galbreath's work was almost all big and spectacular, and it was becoming profoundly important as a factor in Turner's success and direction. In addition to the earlier towers in Pittsburgh and New York, it now included the new forty-one-story building at 633 Third Avenue in New York that would a few years later become the site of Turner's own corporate offices, and it was growing at a fast clip. Galbreath had by this time become a national figure, one of the most successful and powerful of the new urban developers, and his commitment to having Turner do all his work was unswerving.

Galbreath's Los Angeles project would be an office tower whose principal tenant, at least at first, would be the Connecticut General Insurance Company, for whom Turner had recently completed a corporate headquarters complex in Connecticut. As designed by Harrison and Abramovitz, the new building would be forty-two stories tall, the first high-rise tower in Los Angeles, and the tallest building in the western United States. Breaking such new ground was an attractive challenge for Turner, but doing it alone, 3,000 miles from home, struck Chan Turner as a little too risky. He initiated a search for a local joint venture partner or, better still, for a potential West Coast acquisition. The search turned up a few prospects, including at least one design-build firm, but Chan and his board opted for Twaits-Wittenberg, a well-regarded local general contractor, founded in Los Angeles forty years earlier by a civil engineer named Ford J. Twaits. Twaits had died and been succeeded by a partner named Carl Wittenberg, who was himself ready to retire, and the company was for sale.

Twaits-Wittenberg was a little like a small Turner, doing almost $10 million a year, much of it with its own forces. They had built the famous Los Angeles Biltmore Hotel and had continued to do their share of the important work in Los Angeles, most of it by becoming low bidder in competitions among groups of preselected contractors. They'd never done any high-rise work, but they had a respectable list of local clients in the area who were expected to continue to look to them (or their successors) to do their construction. Most important, they had an experienced and capable staff of office and field personnel and a good following among local subcontractors, which was just what Chan was seeking.

Turner's experience with the Ferro acquisition in Cincinnati had been an entirely favorable one, and the Twaits-Wittenberg acquisition looked like it held the same promise. In March the two companies held a joint dinner at the Los Angeles Biltmore to announce the acquisition, and on April 2, 1964, it became formalized. Carl Wittenberg joined the Turner board for what would prove to be only a year or so. The new firm would operate (for a while) as Turner Construction Company, Twaits-Wittenberg Division, with a plan for dropping the Twaits-Wittenberg name later.

The West Coast acquisition made Turner's California start easier than it would have been without it, of course, and during the early months of the new venture's life the principal business at hand was winding up jobs that were already on the smaller firm's books, including an upscale condominium project in Hollywood and foundations for a May Company store in San Bernardino. Twenty-eight men from Twaits-Wittenberg's staff had come over into Turner's employ, including some skilled foremen and superintendents, but with the big Connecticut General job about to get underway Turner sent veteran O. H. (Herb) Pintard out from New York to run the new Los Angeles office. Pintard, who was already a vice president and who would become a director within the year, was a mechanical engineer who had started with Turner in 1942 and had been part of its senior management for years. In addition, New York sent a couple of younger but well-tested Turner people out to support Pintard: Jim Allaire, who had started his Turner career on one of the early Pratt & Whitney jobs just a few years after his graduation from Cooper Union in New York and who had most recently been project manager on the big Lincoln Center job, was sent out to be the senior project executive (later operations manager) in Los Angeles; and Eugene von Wening, the capable, thoroughly experienced Cornell-educated engineer who had married one of Chan Turner's daughters, was assigned the critical job of developing new business for the young office.

Merging a couple of construction companies from opposite sides of the continent wasn't expected to be easy, especially on a project that was bigger and taller than anything that had ever before been done in the area, but by all accounts it went surprisingly smoothly. Charlie Enscoe, who had been Twaits-Wittenberg's lead superintendent for years, was selected to run what was still being called the Connecticut General job but would soon be renamed the Union Bank Building after its principal tenant. Harrison and Abramovitz's design provided for integrating a system of exposed cast-in-place concrete spandrel beams and concrete columns into a traditional high-rise steel frame, and Enscoe surprised his new bosses by fabricating all the formwork for spandrels and columns off-site, while the steel was being erected. That made it possible for him to carry the concrete work up simultaneously with the steel with almost no time lost for form construction, and it allowed for pouring concrete in four locations at a time, stiffening the frame as it rose and accelerating the work.

A few doubts about the westerners lingered, and one day Peter Ruffin wondered aloud whether Enscoe, whose tallest previous job had been only ten stories, would be up to dealing with Union Bank's forty-plus. "When we finish the tenth floor," Enscoe told Ruffin, "I'm going to build three more ten-story buildings, each one above the one below it."

Turner relied mainly on western subcontractors for Union Bank, but for specialties like structural steel, where there was still insufficient local capability, the company brought in vendors and subcontractors from wherever it could find them. The new western Turner men proved to be skilled and experienced, but they are still uniformly quick to acknowledge a special debt to Turner, to which they soon became fiercely loyal, for training them in work they hadn't done before. Charlie Enscoe, now well into his eighties, still speaks of the company with the passion of a true believer. When he sees the Los Angeles skyline he thinks of it as a full scale Turner City. Chuck Harger, who had been a Twaits-Wittenberg labor foreman in his twenties when Turner acquired the company, became an assistant superintendent under Charlie Enscoe on the Union Bank job and later went on to become operations manager for Turner's Western Region. He speaks of his own Turner training under Pintard, Allaire, and von Wening, including time spent in each of the company's major disciplines, as defining experiences in his career.

Of course, it wasn't all one way. When Turner brought out its eastern-generated, union-mandated system for paying the men in cash, instead of by check, complete with brass identification tags for each employee and complex interdepartmental cross-checking procedures, delays and long waiting lines abounded until the westerners made it clear that it wasn't necessary to pay in cash in their part of the world. Under less deeply entrenched union regulations in the West, the trades out there had long since accepted the concept of paying by check. And Jim Allaire learned early on that the last thing in the world the Turner people should do is to try to force all their eastern methods on their new western colleagues, who regarded Denver and everything on the far side of it as "the East" and were inclined to mistrust much of what originated there.

Just a little more than a year after the first columns had been set on the Union Bank building, Connecticut General Insurance Company began moving its staff into the building, and it was soon followed by Union Bank's own people and by the rest of the tenants in Galbreath's not yet fully leased building. Such fast work would have been impressive even back east, where high-rise buildings were springing up all the time, but in Los Angeles it was spectacular, and it established a course for Turner's western group that would lead it to some of the area's most important construction contracts.

Turner had picked a good time to enter the western marketplace, just about when computer technology was starting to enhance the commercial, professional, and educational attractiveness of life on the West Coast and when transportation and other technologies were encouraging and facilitating a westward shift in the population. But at the same time dark historical forces were finding a center in California. By 1963 the United States had about 11,000 troops in South Vietnam as "military advisers," and in the summer of 1964 the tragedy of Vietnam would begin to gather its awful momentum. More than half a million military personnel and millions of tons of supplies would pass through California's ports before the whole thing would end, about eight years later, with almost 50,000 American dead and another 300,000 wounded. And only a few miles from where protests against the Pacific war would find a platform, race riots would erupt in the summer of

1965 that would burn down most of the Watts section of Los Angeles, killing thirty-four and injuring another thousand. Turner's men could see the flames from the upper levels of the Union Bank's steel framing, and when shootings on the free-way were reported and absenteeism on the job became serious, the Union Bank work site was shut down. But within a week, as soon as things began to settle down, both black and white workers began returning to the job and work was resumed.

Ironically, the defining impact that the Galbreath work would have on Turner's mid-century business would in fact be intensified by the kind of inner-city disaster that had been so destructive in Los Angeles. Planners in many cities that had already experienced urban violence — or who had recognized and resolved to remediate conditions they expected to produce it — were by the mid-60s begin-ning to translate their ideas into construction, and John Galbreath was in the van-guard of the developers who would get the work done. In most cases, the cities acquired blighted inner-city properties, relocated their occupants, and then invited proposals from responsible developers like Galbreath to replace the run-down buildings with new, socially and economically desirable infrastructure on land the cities (usually with state and federal help) would provide at low cost to the developers. It was an approach that required developers who had Galbreath's imagination and nerve and who had the economic strength to get the work done.

And it was Turner to whom Galbreath would look for implementing his urban development proposals. Earlier in the 1960s, Galbreath had brought Turner into one of the first of such programs in Newark, New Jersey, but after several years' planning and efforts to seek tenants for new buildings there, the project had foundered in what was later shown to be a welter of political corruption that ended with the prosecution of several of the city's highest officials. But Newark was far from typical, and in most cases the projects proved to be good for the communi-ties, good for Galbreath, and good for Turner. In Cleveland, for example, Galbreath took on a major urban renewal assignment in 1964, and Turner's Chicago office sent Herb Conant over to head up construction. The project was a good one for Galbreath and eminently successful as urban renewal, and within a little over a year Conant, who had made a name for himself on the Harris Trust work in Chicago, had developed so large a volume of new work for the budding Cleveland branch that the board made it a fully fledged Turner office. A year later Cleveland was producing more than 10 percent of the company's total volume of construction and an even higher fraction of its earnings.

By 1965 Galbreath, sensing the potential breadth of urban renewal and other large-scale development work that lay ahead, was able to induce Howard Turner to open a Turner office in Columbus itself, to facilitate even further the good working arrangement between the two firms. Turner's Chicago group was already building Galbreath's twenty-five-story Columbus Center office building there, and the two companies would be among the new building's first occupants. Galbreath's approximately fifty-person staff occupied one floor and Turner's modest staff took space on another floor, within easy hailing distance of one another.

But even that didn't entirely do the trick for Galbreath, whose projects, all built by Turner, were proliferating. Turner had brought Don Burbrink up from Cincinnati to run the new Columbus office, and once John Galbreath saw the nature of Turner's operations at close range he decided that having Burbrink on his own staff might be even better. He successfully importuned Howard Turner to authorize Burbrink's transfer to the Galbreath staff, and by 1966 Jerry Turner, Howard's brother, had moved from the firm's Philadelphia office, where he had been for twenty years and was then purchasing manager, to succeed Burbrink in the management of the Turner office in Columbus, while Burbrink moved into the Galbreath headquarters.

By about that time John Galbreath was getting close to seventy, and he'd accumulated a fortune that was large enough to allow him the vigorous indulgence of his own broad interests. Their variety and potential impact on Turner were nowhere more evident than in New York. Galbreath, who had married the Firestone widow after his own first wife had died, was by then living in grand style, mostly on his 5,000-acre horse farm in Ohio, and traveling the world by private airplane. Commerce apparently remained his central interest, and he continued to address it with spirit, taking big risks and dealing only in very large projects, but he was as aggressive in his charities and in his sports interests as he was in his business.

He loved baseball and owned (with others) the Pittsburgh Pirates baseball team.

But John Galbreath's overriding passion was for racehorses. During his lifetime he'd bred hundreds of them at his farm, including two Kentucky Derby winners and countless other nationally known thoroughbreds, and he had served several terms as chairman of Churchill Downs in Kentucky. In 1963, he had taken on the chairmanship of a committee that the privately owned New York Racing Association had formed to remediate architectural and structural problems that had virtually shut down the clubhouse and grandstands at Belmont Park. The whole place was falling apart. It had been condemned as structurally inadequate, and the task of Galbreath's committee was to rebuild the place as well and as quickly as possible. He called in his friends at Turner, and Chan Turner assigned responsibility for the project to Bob Kupfer, who had just finished up Turner's analysis of New York City's proposal to build the World Trade Center near the Battery. With Turner's advice, architects for the racetrack were selected, a design was prepared, a construction sequence was established, and cost estimates were made. Around the middle of 1964 Turner was awarded a contract to manage the construction.

The formal award to Turner was made at a meeting of the New York Racing Association at its elegant headquarters in Saratoga Springs, where Turner would manage additional construction. But the racing association's work wasn't what turned out to be the high point of the day for Bob Kupfer. What made the day an especially important one for him and for Turner was a conversation he had with John Galbreath about a job that Turner would soon be doing in Hong Kong.

Galbreath, as Socony Mobil's real estate consultant, had been asked by the big oil company to determine the highest and best use for an obsolete fifty-acre tank farm it had owned in Hong Kong since the late nineteenth century but which had long since outlived its original purpose. What Galbreath had by then been discussing with Chan Turner and Joe Warren, and what he had proposed to Mobil, was construction of about 13,000 apartments on the property, at a rate of about 1,000 per year, to be sold as condominium units. His concept suggested high-rise buildings, and what Galbreath had recommended to Mobil was that Turner be brought in to study the idea and, if it became a real project, for Mobil to engage Turner to manage the process of development from start to finish. It was a concept of monumental proportions, and it certainly got the serious attention of Bob Kupfer.

The Hong Kong idea began to move into its next phase a few days later at Mobil's headquarters on Forty-second Street (the company was only then beginning to be called simply Mobil) and at Turner's headquarters just a few floors below. Turner's Jim Allaire was still working in New York at that time, and he joined Joe Warren and Rosie Rosenburgh on a twenty-one-day whirlwind trip to Hong Kong to size up the scheme in more detail. They looked over the site, reviewed preliminary sketches that had been prepared by a local architect, interviewed vendors and contractors, and made some preliminary cost estimates. What they reported back to New York apparently convinced Mobil's management and Turner's that the scheme made sense, and a decision to go forward was made, with Turner in full charge.

There was a vast amount of preliminary work to be done before any dirt was going to fly in Hong Kong. Laws had to be written to legalize the sale of condominiums, studies had to be made to establish the sizes and types of units and the prices and rates at which Hong Kong was prepared to absorb such new housing, consultants had to be identified and engaged to establish a vocabulary of systems and materials for the job and then to implement their findings with working designs.

In the plan that emerged, Turner, John Galbreath, and Peter Ruffin would share equally a total of 10 percent of the equity in the project, and Mobil would hold the remaining 90 percent. It would be called Mei Foo Sun Chuen (literally "Beautiful Company"), the name by which the Chinese fondly remembered the old Standard Oil Company, which had first brought them evening light in the form of kerosene lamps. It would come to be called simply Mei Foo. It would comprise ninety-nine twenty-one-story, cast-in-place reinforced concrete buildings and all the required infrastructure, a project that would rival in scope some of the biggest projects that Turner had ever done. It would house more than 75,000 persons and become the largest privately financed housing project in the world.

Bob Kupfer was given senior on-site responsibility for Turner, and by spring 1966, when the huge task of planning the venture had been brought to a point at which construction could be started, he moved to Hong Kong. Designs and cost estimates reflected exhaustive local consultation, studies of local customs and preferences, and analysis of costs of comparable housing in the region. And all of it had been filtered through Turner's own experience and production capability.

Turner was awarded a cost-plus annual fee contract, and Bob Kupfer began to assemble a management force that would eventually number about sixty, including a core of about a dozen key Turner men who would come over from the United States. The group briefly included a young Bob Fee, a future Turner president, together with a few other future company executives like Shelby Reaves (son of former executive vice president George Reaves), Roger Turnier, and several others. Local and regional contractors, for the most part, were engaged to perform the work and by the end of 1966 the first thousand units were under construction.

The biggest task was the concrete work. The concrete itself was batched by an Australian contractor engaged exclusively for that purpose, and it was formed and put in place by several local contractors engaged by Turner. The pace of the job, for which materials and equipment were obtained from every continent except Antarctica, quickly ramped up to the thousand-units-per-year goal, but there were bound to be problems.

In 1966 the cultural revolution erupted on mainland China, and for a period of several months in 1967 it surfaced as rioting in Hong Kong. There was some sabotage at the Mei Foo site and ample reason to fear for the safety of Americans working there. There was also enough uncertainty in the Hong Kong community to bring the sale of apartments to a temporary halt, but eventually the trouble passed and both the work and the sales resumed. Later, some structural failures unrelated to sabotage occurred, creating much anxiety at the site and threatening condemnation of one entire building. But extensive further investigation by outside consultants determined that the failures had been the result of isolated deficiencies that weren't widespread, and after remedial work had been completed, construction was resumed.

More than 13,000 units had been built and sold by the time the job was completed in 1978. Sales of the apartments made the project an entirely satisfactory one for Mobil, and the capital gain they generated for Turner on its 3 1/3 percent interest in the project, when added to the management fees the company had earned during the job's approximately twelve-year duration, made Mei Foo a good job for Turner as well. Apparently the families who bought the units did well too. Bob Kupfer estimates that units that were originally sold for a little more than $12 per square foot during the 1960s could be sold during the 1990s for about $750 per square foot.

Turner's domestic Galbreath work, and the company's considerable volume of Galbreath-inspired work, would continue well into the 1980s. By that time Turner had built major urban projects for Galbreath in Akron, Cincinnati, Columbus, Cleveland, Denver, Lexington, Louisville, Milwaukee, Toledo, and elsewhere, a volume that represented hundreds of millions of dollars in construction cost. Even later, when Galbreath's interest in doing urban development work as a principal had waned, he provided consulting services to other developers who were eager to get the benefit of his experience and perspective, and he regularly (and successfully) urged that Turner be engaged for the construction, generating another substantial source of business for Turner.

As vast and profoundly important as the Galbreath work was, Turner's average annual volume of work had by the end of the 1960s reached $300 million, and by the early 1970s it was approaching $600 million. By that time even the Galbreath (and Galbreath-inspired) construction put in place in any single year by Turner rarely represented more than about 10 percent of the company's annual volume. With effective business units in eight cities distributed across the country, and with each of these units expanding and prospering, Turner had grown well beyond even the considerable base represented by the Galbreath work.

As the 1970s approached, Turner had ample reason to be pleased with its decision to establish itself on the West Coast. The Twaits-Wittenberg legacy of personnel had proved to be every bit as good as expected, according to Jim Allaire, and although its legacy of jobs and clients was disappointing, producing a brief lean period for the young Los Angeles office, the outlook quickly brightened. Turner's still-modest Los Angeles staff was briefly sustained by tenant work on Union Bank and other relatively small jobs until late 1967, when the company's friends at the Equitable Life Assurance Society decided to build for Equitable's own investment in Los Angeles. Turner had only a few years earlier finished Equitable's big New York headquarters, and the big insurer had resolved to engage Turner for its western project as well. The Equitable building in Los Angeles, a thirty-two-story tower within a mile or so of the Union Bank Building, was a natural one for Turner, and the firm's performance attracted a good deal of favorable notice in the heart of what was becoming one of the country's most important growth areas.

One direct result of the spate of successful Los Angeles high-rise towers was a decision by the Atlantic Richfield Company (later ARCO) to engage Turner to build its 3.5 million-square-foot headquarters building in Los Angeles. Even bigger than its L.A. predecessors, it would be one of the largest privately owned office buildings in the world, almost twice the size of the huge building that Turner had completed for Equitable in New York, the previous record holder. Turner had done its share of work over the years for Atlantic Oil Company in Philadelphia, and when Atlantic merged with California's Richfield to form Atlantic Richfield, the big new company that emerged included Turner among the contractors being considered for building its corporate headquarters in Los Angeles. Not surprisingly, the candidates included the largest and most prestigious contractors in the country, but an ironic twist had the effect of advancing the case for engaging Turner: ARCO was determined to use a Los Angeles contractor for the work, and although by that time Turner had been established in Los Angeles for only a few years, it was already regarded as a local firm.

Associated with ARCO in the ownership of the project was the Bank of America, its powerful and quiet, if not entirely silent partner, and the big California bank (which would establish its regional headquarters in the building) had its own favored contractor: the Robert E. McKee Company, a well-established Texas-based firm with a substantial Los Angeles presence. To satisfy the bank, it was agreed that Turner and McKee would take on the work as a 60 percent–40 percent joint venture, with Turner having the larger share and each firm contributing staff and support. From all accounts it was an entirely successful partnership.

ARCO's project was a high-quality corporate headquarters, the kind that Turner was accustomed to building. It was about four times the size of the recently completed Los Angeles Equitable Building and almost five times its cost, and it would take three years to build. The architect, Albert C. Martin Company of Los Angeles, had performed as a local associate for Harrison and Abramovitz on the Union Bank Building, but this time it took on the primary architectural and structural engineering commissions itself. Martin's design comprised two fifty-two-story towers and a low-rise section, and it provided for burrowing 105 feet into the underlying clay to provide for what was intended as a parking garage and a couple of levels of shops and restaurants.

ARCO was a successful job, but it wasn't an easy one. Excavation for the deep foundations was problematic from the first, at one time threatening to undermine the adjacent road system. But Turner brought in the California office of its good friends Spencer, White & Prentis to do the sheeting, and Jim Allaire is quick to acknowledge Turner's debt to this resourceful subcontractor for avoiding serious trouble.

The ARCO job broke some new ground too. The black Canadian granite used for the building's skin, quarried in Canada and shipped to Italy for fabrication before being shipped back to North America, was among the earliest on which thinly sliced stone panels would be integrated with concrete backing and erected as granite-faced precast panels, stiffening the stone a bit while reducing the dead load imposed by traditional heavy masonry backup construction. Even ARCO's elevators were state of the art, rising the full height of the building in only thirty seconds.

By the time things at ARCO began to wind down, the Los Angeles skyline was becoming a Turner skyline, and it was easy to understand Charlie Enscoe's idea that looking at a photograph of the changing city was like looking at one of the annual Turner City images. A good many Turner-built California towers would follow ARCO, starting with the big Security Pacific Bank building, on which super-intendent Enscoe would later be described by a Security Pacific executive as Turner's best salesman.

What had started in Los Angeles in 1964 was destined to become the center of a far-flung locus of work for Turner in the West. Later in the 1960s, Turner and sixteen other firms that included architects, engineers, lawyers, planners, and sociologists involved in the planning, design, and construction of buildings were brought together up north in Oakland, across the bay from San Francisco, to do an extensive, government-sponsored study of urban housing. The whole thing was being managed for the Department of Housing and Urban Development (who called it their "In-City" project) by Henry J. Kaiser's Kaiser Industries, many of whose interests were centered on construction and construction products, and it was designed to elicit the best and latest thinking in the field. Turner was represented on the panel by Jerry Mandel, who was later joined by Paul DeMange. Their principal task was to evaluate and make recommendations as to the constructibility of what was proposed. Almost two years after the study was begun, the panel produced an exhaustive report but not much that would lead directly to any actual construction, although the essence of the report was later integrated into the urban renewal component of Lyndon Johnson's Great Society program.

Whether or not Turner's involvement in the Kaiser study was a factor of any significance in the company's expansion from Los Angeles into northern California isn't really clear, but not long after the study was started, Chan Turner sent Jack Quinn out to San Francisco from New York to set up a small sales office there and to see what he could do about establishing a Turner presence in northern California. Quinn, a Cornell-educated civil engineer, had most recently been part of the small New York marketing group that was headed by another Cornell alumnus, Ed Clarke. Shortly after Quinn had settled into modest quarters in San Francisco, where he shared a receptionist and a conference room with neighboring tenants, Turner entered into a contract with Kaiser Industries to build its Ordway Building in Oakland, a spectacular high-rise office building that Skidmore Owings & Merrill had designed, and Chet Vaughan was given the task of manag-

J. Archer Turner, the youngest of Henry Turner's brothers. He started with the company in 1919, led it as president through the WWII years and was elected chairman in 1946 He died before starting his term as chairman.

Henry Chandlee (Chan) Turner Jr., Henry Turner's oldest son. He joined the company when he graduated from Swarthmore College in 1923, served as president from 1947 to 1965 and as chairman from 1954 to 1970.

Howard S. Turner, a son of J. A. Turner, had served as a Turner director for 13 years before leaving the senior management of Jones & Laughlin Steel Company to become president of Turner in 1965. In 1968 he became CEO, and in 1970 he succeeded his cousin Chan as chairman, retiring in 1978.

Adm. Ben Moreell, founder of the Navy Seabees, retired from the U. S. Navy in 1946 to become president of Turner, but after a little more than a year in that position he resigned to become CEO of Jones & Laughlin Steel Corporation.

Robert (Cliff) Wilson, who joined Turner in 1907, served as chairman from 1947 to 1954, when he retired.

Robert P. Marshall Jr. started with Turner in 1939 and took enough time off during the war years to distinguish himself as an officer in the special warfare unit that would later become the Navy Seals. He retired from Turner in 1983, as senior vice-president and vice-chairman.

Eugene von Wening Jr. started his Turner career in the East, just after WWII, but spent most of it in the West, where he headed the Western Division. An executive vice-president who was seen by many as a potential CEO, he died in 1987.

The Pacific Naval Air Base
project was said to be the
largest construction
contract in the country's
history. Shown at upper left
is an aircraft hangar
Turner was building on
Midway in 1940. At
upper right are
underground fuel storage
facilities under construction
in Pearl Harbor Below
the underground storage
photograph is a
camouflaged above-ground
tank at Pearl Harbor.
Shown at lower right are
fires at Midway after a
Japanese attack.

War construction dominated Turner's work between 1940 and 1945. Shown at upper left is the Turner-built Republic Aviation plant on Long Island, and shown at upper right and center are Pratt and Whitney plants in Connecticut and Missouri, respectively. Shown at lower left and lower right are interiors of a Pratt and Whitney plant and a Bullard Company plant, both in Connecticut.

Home office building for the
John Hancock Mutual
Insurance Company. It was
the first major office
building to be built in
Boston after the war.

At 1.6 million square feet, Socony Mobil Oil Company's building (now called Exxon Mobil's building) on New York's 42nd Street was in 1956 among the city's most spectacular post-war skyscrapers.

*The Ford Foundation's
architecturally acclaimed
headquarters building in
New York was built by
Turner during the mid-
1960s, and was said to be
as difficult to build as it
was beautiful to behold.*

The graceful Fidelity-Girard building in Philadelphia was among the most distinguished projects done by Turner's Philadelphia office during the 1960s.

Turner completed the New York State Theater at Lincoln Center for the Performing Arts in 1963, in time for it to be integrated in programs of the New York World's Fair, which opened in 1965.

Center photograph shows Philharmonic Hall at Lincoln Center, completed in 1962 by a joint venture headed by Turner. Shown at the lower right is the Vivian Beaumont Theater at Lincoln Center, completed by Turner in 1965.

In 1959, when Turner finished work in Baltimore on the magnificent new Cathedral of Mary Our Queen, it had been almost five years since ground had been broken. Nonetheless, progress was well regarded when compared with the hundreds of years required for building similar cathedrals elsewhere.

U.S. Steel's 64-story, triangular plan headquarters, completed by Turner during the late 1960s, was Pittsburgh's tallest building. Photographs of the intense urban site are shown at left, and the finished building is shown below.

In 1970, Merrill Lynch was the main tenant of this 54-story, Turner-built office building at One Liberty Plaza in New York, close enough to the World Trade Center to be damaged in the attack of September 11, 2001.

In 1972 Turner's still young Los Angeles business unit, in a joint venture with the Robert E. McKee Company, completed work on these two 52-story, granite-sheathed towers for Arco. The upper photograph shows construction in progress, and the lower one shows the finished project.

When Turner completed
construction in 1973 of this
office tower for Standard
Oil of Indiana (later
Amoco), it was (at 1,137
feet) the tallest building in
Chicago, only 100 feet
shorter than the Empire
State Building.

*The John Fitzgerald
Kennedy Library in
Dorchester, Massachusetts,
was completed by Turner in
October, 1979.*

*The Fourth of July, 1976,
was an auspicious date in
Colorado for more reasons
than one. On that date
Johns-Manville's new
Turner-built headquarters,
shown here, was dedicated.*

ing its construction. It would all be done under the aegis of the Los Angeles office, of course, under Gene von Wening, who shuttled between Los Angeles and San Francisco, with DeMange operating from a base in Oakland and occasionally sharing Jack Quinn's small office in San Francisco. It was a start, and within the next couple of years the small San Francisco group would take on construction of a big Internal Revenue Service building in Fresno and a Marriott Hotel in Berkeley, along with a few smaller jobs. In 1968 the San Francisco office would appear in the company's annual report as the ninth of Turner's fully fledged business units, and by 1970 the new office would be doing a little over 20 percent as much work as its very active big brother down in Los Angeles. Together, the two California offices accounted for a little over 11% of the approximately $550 million worth of construction that Turner put in place during 1970.

These were good times for Turner, whose annual volume of construction had increased by a factor of five since 1960, while the volume of private-sector nonresidential construction in the country had only doubled during the same period. In the Midwest, which had until the early 1960s rarely accounted for more than about 15 percent of the gross business of the company, Turner's four offices (Chicago, Cleveland, Cincinnati, and Columbus) produced more than 43 percent of the company's 1968 volume, including a striking $56 million worth of work in Cleveland alone. Between Herbert Conant's showing in Cleveland and similar successes the company was enjoying in Cincinnati, where another future president and chairman named Al McNeill was beginning to attract notice, those two offices had reached a stride that by the end of the 1960s would be regularly producing close to $100 million in volume each year. Columbus, of course, was still getting to its feet, but even there it would be only a few years before major work would begin to come its way. The Galbreath-inspired offices, while still much involved in the big developer's work, had gone well beyond the reliance on Galbreath contracts that had characterized their earlier years.

Chicago, of course, where Herb Church had taken over for Walter B. Shaw as general manager in 1968, was still the core of Turner's Midwestern business, and it continued second only to New York in terms of volume and earnings and, to a

large extent, in terms of the consistently distinguished quality of its clientele. By
the time the 1960s began to play out, Turner had become the preeminent builder
in town, having pretty much passed major competitors like A. L. Jackson, Gust K.
Newberg, Pepper Construction Company, and even the venerable George A.
Fuller Company, which had been started in Illinois before the turn of the century
and had been regarded as the most formidable of all Turner's competition.

By the end of the 1960s Turner in Chicago had a history of major completed
projects and a backlog of equally large and prestigious jobs ready to start. In 1968
it began work on the Chicago administrative headquarters that Harry Weese had
designed for Time-Life, a thirty-story building that would be especially noteworthy
for its enclosure, a contemporary skin that was Bethlehem Steel's version of U.S.
Steel's Cor-Ten and whose surface was designed to reveal a controlled, uniform
rusting, neatly punctuated by gold anodized window frames. It was among the first
of the high-rise structures to use double-deck elevators that could board and discharge passengers on two floors at once. For Turner the Time-Life Building had
an additional historical significance: It would be among the last big structural concrete jobs that Turner would do with its own forces in Chicago, as the momentum
increasingly shifted away from performing such construction work and toward
managing it.

After Time-Life came one of Chicago's most prestigious construction contracts,
the eighty-two-story, $120 million headquarters building for Standard Oil
Company of Indiana (later Amoco). At 1,137 feet, it was the tallest building in
Chicago and among the tallest in the world, only about 100 feet shorter than New
York's Empire State Building. Designed by a joint venture of Chicago's Perkins &
Will and New York's Edward Durell Stone, it resembled Stone's General Motors
Building in New York but was more than half again as tall. Almost everything about
the building was special, starting with the oversized caissons that had to be drilled
to rock through eighty feet of Chicago's clay and the massive reinforced concrete
members that were required to deal with shear forces in the structure. Even with
55,000 tons of steel going into the building's structural frame, there still remained
95,000 cubic yards of concrete for Turner to place. And Standard Oil's vertical

transportation system was just as extraordinary, with double-decked, high-speed elevators even more advanced than the ones that had just been installed in the Time-Life Building.

On the Standard Oil job Turner's Bernard (Bernie) Newton started out as project engineer and finished as project manager, and he still thinks of it as the supreme experience of his working career. A former Marine Corps officer, he had started with Turner on the Lincoln Center job in New York and had transferred to Chicago when it was completed. An intensely loyal Turner partisan, he'd retire in 1998. Newton remembers the early subgrade struggles that slowed foundation work on the Standard Oil job, delaying the start of structural steel until spring 1971, and then the pressure to maintain a cycle of seven floors per month that would pace the rise of steel, concrete, elevators, and curtain walls for the tower, once the massive steel frame had been brought laboriously up through five subgrade levels and a thirty-five-foot-high lobby floor.

But as fond as Newton's memories of the work are, they're mixed when it comes to the elegant white-marble curtain wall that enclosed the soaring tower. After painstaking early studies, the owners and their architects had rejected Vermont marble and Georgia marble in favor of a beautiful white marble that's quarried in the Carrara Mountains of Tuscany, the very stone that Michelangelo had used for his sixteenth-century masterpiece, David. The pure white stone that was selected was purchased directly by Standard Oil from an Italian supplier, sliced into panels about an inch and a quarter thick and a little more than three feet wide, and then shipped from Italy to the job site. There it was raised piece by piece and connected to the building's intricately prepared structure through a system of stainless-steel angle supports, while the great steel frame inched its way up, producing a brilliant white enclosure neatly framed by vertical ribbons of glass more than a thousand feet long. By late 1972 Standard Oil's people were beginning to move into their new headquarters, and by the end of 1973 things at the site were starting to wind down, with everyone pleased with the splendid new building.

But Newton's recollection of how that began to change a few years later is equally vivid. Five or six years after initial occupancy, people began to notice what they called a "pillowing" effect in the marble panels: They were bowing out, and for a few years after that the face of the marble was monitored for further deformation. In 1985, Standard Oil/Amoco commissioned two Chicago engineering firms to inspect the cladding at closer range, and although they documented the bowing, it wasn't until about 1987 that it was recommended that stainless-steel strapping be applied to some of the panels, mainly to ensure the public safety. The deformations, most pronounced on the sides of the building that were exposed to more direct sunlight, were attributed to temperature differences between the exposed faces of the panels and the shaded faces of the panels, and the unanticipated inability of the thinly sliced marble to absorb such differences without permanent deformation. By 1988 Amoco had gone to more exhaustive testing that revealed strength reductions that exceeded acceptable limits, and a decision was made to remove all the marble and to replace it with two-inch-thick granite panels brought in from North Carolina, less white than the marble and heavier by enough to require reinforcement of some of the building's steel columns.

Much of the goodwill that had characterized the effort to find a solution had (understandably) begun to disappear when the tremendous cost of the remedial work began to be understood, and Amoco did its best to recover some or all of its costs from the architects, the marble supplier, the marble erector, and Turner. The matter went to court, and after more than a year's deliberation a verdict was returned against Amoco, effectively absolving the designers, the suppliers, the erectors, and, of course, Turner. By about 1992, the splendid white tower Turner had built on Randolph Street in Chicago had become a light-gray one, and the marble that had been removed had been sold off by Amoco for use in small sculptures and, in a crushed form, for decorative landfills.

Even Amoco's distinction as having Chicago's tallest building didn't last. Not long after the building was completed, Chicago's Sears Tower passed it by a few hundred feet, reducing Amoco to second place. An ironic footnote to being topped by the Sears Tower is that Turner had originally been asked to consider taking on construction of the Sears contract itself but had declined because it felt that working on two such jobs in Chicago simultaneously, in addition to extremely large jobs for IDS (in Minneapolis) and for Illinois Bell, might dilute Turner's efforts and deprive Standard Oil of the attention that its extraordinary job was due. At that time, George Morrison had the unpleasant task of explaining Turner's difficult decision to Skidmore Owings & Merrill's Bruce Graham, who was designing the Sears building, and having to hear Graham call Howard Turner in New York to protest what he interpreted as a slight to his prestigious firm. Morrison's recollection is that there was a subsequent cooling in relations with Skidmore, but over the years that followed the breach appears to have healed.

Back east, these had been busy years for Turner too. In 1970 the Philadelphia office put in place more than $60 million worth of work, a little over 11 percent of the company's gross product that year, and its earnings were equally strong. For years, the Philadelphia office had continued to take on significant (though declining) amounts of fixed-price work, some of it competitively bid and much of it performed by forces in its own direct employ. But by the end of the 1960s that had begun to change, as it was changing almost everywhere. Of Philadelphia's 1970s work, less than 3 percent was done under fixed-price contracts, and only a tiny fraction of that was secured competitively. The performance of work by forces employed directly by Turner's Philadelphia branch, vis-à-vis work performed by subcontractors, would for all practical purposes end during the 1970s on an ironically appropriate project, an approximately $40 million office building for the Philadelphia Electric Company. On that job, where Turner did the structural concrete work itself, the contract included renovation of the client's original six-story office building, which had been built fifty-four years earlier by Turner Concrete Steel Company, Turner Construction Company's predecessor in Philadelphia.

Turner was doing plenty of important work from its Philadelphia base during the late 1960s, including the World Bank in Washington and big jobs for DuPont and Evans-Pitcairn, among others. But Bob Marshall, the future Turner vice chairman who was managing the Philadelphia office during that period, thinks of the Fidelity Mutual–Girard Trust Building as being among the most important. Fidelity Girard would be a dignified, granite-clad, high-rise office building, designed by the office of Vincent Kling. Its height would be limited to thirty-eight stories to conform to the century-old tradition (since violated) that no building in downtown Philadelphia should be higher than "the top of Billy Penn's hat," an elevation established by the statue of William Penn above Philadelphia's city hall. The approximately $40 million contract to build Fidelity Girard was an eagerly sought and elusive one. Because Turner had done so much industrial work in the Philadelphia area for many years, there was still a lingering inclination to regard the firm as essentially a builder of industrial structures, not as an expert in the construction of finished buildings like Fidelity Girard. That was by this time an entirely outdated viewpoint, but it was one that may have been encouraged by some of the well-established Philadelphia competitors who were being considered for the job, and Marshall realized he would need an edge. He found what he wanted in the new automated-scheduling technique that was gaining favor in the industry, the Critical Path Method (CPM). Marshall and Vincent Bush, a thirty-two-year Turner veteran who had been operations manager in Philadelphia since 1953, studied the preliminary drawings for the Fidelity Girard Building and developed a critical-path schedule for building it. In a time when critical-path schedules tended to be extremely large and complex, this one was more than twenty feet long and black with notations of the thousands of activities that were being integrated into the system. As Marshall remembers it, when he and Bush rolled it out and pinned it to the wall of the boardroom in which they were being interviewed, it dazzled the interviewers. Whether it was the CPM schedule or the recommendation of New York's Carl Morse, the Morse Diesel Construction Company principal who had been engaged by Fidelity Girard to advise them, isn't clear, but Turner was awarded the contract and the results were good.

Turner's Boston branch in the late 1960s was a little ahead of Philadelphia in terms of the volume of work it was doing and the earnings it was generating, having increased its annual production during the decade by a factor of more than six. Now it was fairly regularly producing almost 15 percent of the company's total annual volume. George Reaves had been running the Boston office until his retirement in 1964, when Wallace Creelman, a solid Turner veteran who was related by marriage to Howard Turner, took over the job.

During the 1960s Turner in Boston stayed a little closer to the company's traditional style than some of the other offices did. Its work spanned a wide variety of job types and sizes, it asserted its continuing competitive strength by picking up a few new jobs each year in competitive bidding, and it was still successfully resisting the trend toward subcontracting all its concrete and masonry work to others. One competitively secured job was the Mather Residence Hall at Harvard, and it was followed by a good deal of negotiated work on the campus over the years that followed. Another was the high-rise Earth Sciences Building that I. M. Pei had designed for his alma mater, MIT. Ted Rhoades, who would become chief estimator in Boston and later contract manager there, was an estimator in the Boston office when the company submitted its winning bid for Pei's MIT project. He'd been with Turner since graduating from Princeton in 1949 (with both bachelor's and master's degrees in civil engineering) and had gone on to Boston in 1958 after working for the company in Philadelphia, New York, and elsewhere. Rhoades remembers thinking of the MIT job as a good chance to get started at MIT, an opportunity to show the people there what Turner could do. His estimate of the impact of Turner's getting the Earth Sciences job was right on target, and the company would indeed do much more of MIT's work after that job was finished. But Turner's estimate of what it would cost to build the Earth Sciences building, which was dominated by exposed, architectural concrete, wasn't as good. Pei was among the first of the young architects who had decided that carefully formed and placed concrete could be made architecturally attractive. But there hadn't been enough of it done before 1962 to give Turner a good basis for estimating its cost, and what was estimated just wasn't enough.

Landing the Earth Sciences job certainly wasn't all bad. In addition to establishing itself with MIT, Turner was able to learn a good deal about producing and estimating the cost of architectural concrete, and it would profit from its hard-won lesson on other jobs. Later in the decade, when Dr. Edwin Land added the use of color to his already revolutionary Polaroid camera technology, his young company was awash in orders and desperate for new plant and support facilities. He turned to I. M. Pei to design space that would provide an appropriate architectural setting, and Pei, eager to have his concrete work properly executed, was pleased to learn that Turner had been selected to do the construction. But with Polaroid's tight schedule and with a New England winter coming on, Tom Gerlach and his colleagues at Turner were wary of architectural concrete and counseled against it. Pei remained committed to a cast-in-place solution until the initial design conference with Polaroid and Turner, but the combined resistance of the owner and the contractor won the day. An unhappy but essentially practical I. M. Pei accepted the decision graciously and designed what proved to be an elegant and widely acclaimed building in structural steel and precast concrete, and Turner built it. There would be many more buildings for Polaroid on various sites around Boston, and Ted Rhoades remembers the pressure to do the work well and quickly, with preliminary drawings "sometimes coming in on Friday for construction that was to start on Monday."

A few years after the Earth Sciences job was done, Ted Rhoades moved up to become contract manager in Boston, a Turner title that translates roughly into manager of business development. But before he abandoned his role as chief estimator in the Boston office, Rhoades had the job of spotting and bringing along a successor, and the recommendation he made is one that thirty years later he's frank to say he thinks was one of his best. He suggested Harold Parmelee, a younger man he had described in an earlier personnel evaluation as a man who had what it would take to become president of the company. Some years later, Parmelee did become president.

During the later1960s the Boston office was almost always doing hospital construction at one local institution or another: sometimes for Deaconess Hospital, sometimes for Peter Brent Brigham Hospital, sometimes for Cardinal Cushing Hospital, sometimes for New England Baptist Hospital, and almost every year one building or another for the continually expanding Children's Hospital of Boston. A decade later the company would reap additional rewards of the early hospital work it had done in the area when it entered a period in which it became the country's leading builder of health care facilities.

Increasingly large and varied as the Boston work became, it would be the city's towering office buildings that would firmly establish and sustain Turner's dominance in the Boston construction marketplace during the 1960s. In the city's urban center it was one giant high-rise building after another for Turner, each somewhere around forty stories tall, each designed by a nationally prominent architect, and most costing more than $60 million. By 1970 the Boston skyline, like the skylines of other cities across the country, would become newer and higher, and Turner of Boston, whose annual volume was by then approaching $100 million, would be the principal agent of change. The buildings included one for what was then called the Employers' Group of Insurance Companies (later called Commercial Union) at 1 Beacon Street, as well as a couple of big office buildings for a few of the region's leading banks: one for First National Bank, a controversial design by Campbell and Aldrich of Boston, and another for the Shawmut Bank, both on Federal Street, two institutions that would eventually be absorbed into the Fleet banking conglomerate.

There was a small but important element of Turner's success in Boston that derived from work it didn't do. During this intense period of high-rise building in Boston, Turner was seen as the likely candidate for building the spectacular sixty-story headquarters building that I. M. Pei had designed for the John Hancock Insurance Company, and Chan Turner went up to Boston for the critical interview. Favorably disposed as everyone was toward Turner, Hancock's people were surprised and disappointed to learn at the interview that Chan Turner opposed and would resist the inclusion of a liquidated-damages clause in the construction-management contract. Turner explained that he regarded the relationship between the construction manager and the owner as a partnership with almost identical objectives, and that in such a setting a provision for imposing a penalty on the construction manager for delayed completion would be divisive and counterproductive. It was a compelling philosophic argument, one that went directly to the heart of how Chan Turner perceived Turner's relationships with its clients, and he did his best to convince the Hancock people that such a provision was neither in their interest nor in Turner's. But they would have none of it, and the contract was awarded to the Gilbane Building Company of Providence. Subsequently, the job ran into an array of extremely nasty problems, the most spectacular of which was the glaringly public failure of its window-glazing system. When big panes of glass began falling from some of the building's windows, endangering the public safety, the surrounding streets had to be roped off, disrupting pedestrian and vehicular traffic in one of the city's busiest areas, generating widespread bad feeling and a spate of big and costly lawsuits. Whatever disappointment might have lingered in the Turner camp about the loss of the Hancock job was probably materially softened when details of the glass problem became a regular feature of the evening news on national television.

Even with the broadening of the company's base to nine cities, and even with the robust growth that all its offices were experiencing, more than one-third of Turner's gross business throughout the 1960s was still being done by the New York territory. Annual volume there passed the $150 million level during the late 1960s and by 1970 it would pass $200 million, with a variety of work that ranged from a cloistered monastery along the bank of the Hudson River to some of the city's tallest and grandest high-rise office buildings. The late 1960s was the period in which Turner's New York office finished up its complex renovation of Penn Station, and then followed (in a Turner-dominated joint venture with the Del Webb Company) with a spectacular new Madison Square Garden over the Penn Central's tracks, covered with a cable-supported roof that left the interior virtually column-free.

There was probably no job during this period that strayed farther from the already multiple pathways of Turner's experience than the big Federal Office Building and Courthouse the company would build for General Services Administration on New York's Foley Square. Controversial from its very start, it had long been opposed by an outspoken group of architects who didn't like its design and would at one point mount an unsuccessful lawsuit to force a change in its location. It was a job that was about as different from what Turner could be expected to seek at that stage of its history as any job could have been: a very large public project in the heart of one of New York's most congested areas that would be awarded to the lowest bidder in an aggressively fought open competition likely to be joined by every contractor who could marshal enough money to post a bond, regardless of his capability.

But the job had one saving grace that probably caught the attention of Turner's management. At an estimated $60 million, it was to be the largest project ever awarded as a single lump sum by GSA, and its sheer size might very well screen out some of the scalawags. When bidding day came and went, late in 1962, there was disappointment but not much surprise in the Turner office. The low bid, at about $57 million, was more than $2 million lower than Turner's bid, and there was another price between the lowest bid and Turner's.

But the story wasn't over. A few months later, Chan Turner was called by GSA's contracting officer and told that the government, after a thorough investigation of the three lowest bidders, had rejected the first two in favor of Turner. By early March Turner had a contract in hand and was mobilizing for the job, and a few weeks later demolition of the few buildings still on the site was underway.

Even for Turner, and even for New York, the Federal Office Building and Courthouse was a big job: thirty-eight stories of fully finished office space, plus some penthouses and basements, together with a fully developed traditional courthouse connected to the office building by pedestrian links at each floor. The venerable Lou Hall, veteran of many of the company's biggest and toughest jobs, took executive responsibility for the big job, with an on-site staff that included a project manager, several field superintendents, and several project engineers. Jack Woolf, a civil engineer who had started working for Turner the day after he graduated from Union College in 1955, was one of the project engineers, and his recollections are clear, especially the ones about the foundation work.

The building was to be carried on a massive reinforced concrete mat as deep as fifteen feet in some places, and the mat was to be supported by a grid of long steel piles driven to refusal. Spencer, White & Prentis made short work of underpinning a couple of adjacent buildings, one nineteen stories and one six stories, and once that was done it didn't take Turner long to dig deep and to protect the adjacent streets with a system of soldier beams and lagging. By the time the summer heat began to moderate in 1963 a joint venture of piling contractors headed by Horn Construction Company was setting up to drive the 90- to 100-foot-long steel H-piles that would support the big mat. It was only a few days after the driving began, as Jack Woolf remembers it, that a circular area of earth around each driven pile began to sink, leaving an ominous pattern of craters averaging about six feet in diameter and becoming, in some cases, as much as three feet deep. Clearly the driving was consolidating some of the underlying materials, perhaps threatening the stability of adjacent structures, and it was something that had to be watched. The work was permitted to go forward carefully, and regular observations of adjacent structures, all of which Turner had surveyed before the start of work, were intensified. A few weeks later there was a failure of a section of sheeting, threatening the stability of the adjacent city street it had supported, and within another few weeks the earth support under the newly installed underpinning of an adjacent structure showed signs of failure as well. Spencer, White & Prentis returned to the site and did what it could to stabilize things with supplemental underpinning, but the situation was clearly deteriorating. GSA brought in William Meuser, the distinguished engineer and soils expert whose firm had designed the foundations. Meuser was at first inclined to support GSA's contention that all of what was happening should be considered the sole responsibility of the contractor. But when a Turner field party reported that the top floor of an adjacent building had shifted about seven inches toward the new work, both Meuser and GSA changed their minds, deciding quickly that the conditions being encountered were dangerously different from those anticipated in the design. Woolf remembers that it was just a day or two after the assassination of Jack Kennedy, late in 1963, that the order came down from GSA to stop all work at the site.

What the stop order meant was that all fieldwork was suspended until the government got its act together. The adjacent buildings had to be acquired, all their tenants (mostly lawyers) had to be relocated, and the buildings themselves had to be demolished and carted away. Changes in thinking about subsurface conditions had to be reflected in a new foundation design, and, in addition, the latest thinking of Lyndon Johnson's newly installed administration (including some new GSA officials) had to be factored into the basic redesign of the building itself. It would be early 1965 before an order to resume fieldwork would be issued by GSA.

Meanwhile, Turner hadn't been idle. Most of the staff that had been on the job had been assigned to other duties, but Jack Woolf and a few others had been retained in New York and assigned the task of analyzing the costs of the suspension and remobilization, the cost implications of the delay itself (including the impact of a still-modest cost inflation), and of course those of the revised design. The results of their work were passed up to Chan Turner, a consummate negotiator by most accounts, and to Joe Warren, his exceptionally capable and technically skilled executive vice president. By the time it was all sorted out, Turner's contract had been increased by almost $7 million.

Once work was resumed, it proceeded effectively but, of course, it wasn't without problems such as are to be expected on any big and complex urban project. An early problem showed up when the anchor bolts for the big steel columns proved to have been improperly set, and it demanded resolution before steel construction could proceed. A young Bob Fee had been attracting some attention for his skills as a field engineer on the Bethlehem Steel Company's Research Center project, his first Turner job, and he was thought to be well suited for sorting things out at Foley Square. He made short work of the anchor-bolt problem, probably attracting the favorable notice of some of the company's senior people in the process. His progress in the company after that was substantial and consistent, leading to the presidency thirty-two years later. There were other problems too, of course, including a few labor disputes and some disruptive on-site clashes between conflicting community groups seeking (in the early days of civil rights protests) to advocate for minority employment, but by the end of 1969 the job had been well and profitably completed.

Foley Square may have been a profitable bump in the road for Turner, but it wasn't a precursor to a new direction, and competitively bid public projects like Foley Square never became a staple of Turner's diet. During the later 1960s, it would be the high-rise buildings of the private sector that would dominate the work of the New York office.

Almost a decade earlier, the Chase Manhattan building had laid the groundwork for such a direction in unmistakable terms, and by the late 1960s, when the pace of commerce was accelerating rapidly in New York and land costs were making high-rise construction the only practical mechanism for expansion, Turner was in the thick of it.

Three huge buildings, all started in 1968, exemplified the company's work, and they were almost within earshot of one another in Manhattan. The Galbreath-Ruffin group had joined forces with U.S. Steel and Merrill Lynch (who would be the building's principal tenants) to build a fifty-four-story, Skidmore Owings & Merrill–designed tower they would call Trinity Place, on Liberty Street. Turner had to start its work there with the unpleasant task of arranging for demolition of one of the most treasured buildings in New York, the Singer Building, upsetting many architecture buffs and historical purists. The old building didn't give up easily, and foundations to support the new 10,000-ton column loads had to be threaded between and around the massive caissons that had supported the original cast-iron frame. The soaring new building was as crisp and contemporary as Skidmore Owings & Merrill could make it, with deep, exterior spandrel beams completely exposed to the weather on every floor to show off the structural innards of the frame itself. It was on this Trinity Place job, later called One Liberty Plaza, that future Turner president Bob Fee would have his first significant command, with responsibility for finishing the interiors of the forty floors that Merrill Lynch would occupy. And the building, which faced the World Trade Center complex, would be one of the damaged but structurally sound survivors of the terrible disaster of September 11, 2001.

A few blocks north of the Trinity Place job Turner would almost simultaneously build another urban giant, this one as rugged and burly as the Trinity Place job was sleek and delicate. Here Turner would erect what the building's own architect called a twentieth-century, windowless fortress in which the New York Telephone Company would install its equipment. Although the granite-clad building would show only twenty-nine floors above grade, it would be almost 500 feet high, because the average floor-to-floor height needed for the big gear it contained was seventeen feet six inches.

Lou Hall was top man for Turner on these big jobs, and he remembers the third one, the McGraw-Hill Building in Rockefeller Center, as being the least pleasant experience of the lot. Designed by Harrison and Abramovitz, it was a huge, single-tenant headquarters building, bigger and more expensive than any of the other high-rise skyscrapers that Turner was doing at the time, and, of course, it had its share of problems. George A. Fuller had done a good deal of Rockefeller Center's work before Turner was brought in to do McGraw-Hill, and Hall thinks some lingering resentment against Turner made things difficult at the site. In fact, there were two other big projects underway at Rockefeller Center when Turner was doing the McGraw-Hill job, one for Exxon and one for Celanese. Morse Diesel Construction Company was building the Celanese tower and George A. Fuller was doing the Exxon building, so Rockefeller Center was in some ways an even busier place to work in during the late 1960s than the rest of New York, which was experiencing an unprecedented boom in downtown office construction. Hall's recollections of the McGraw-Hill job are softened a little when he remembers the elegant interiors that were designed by Alfred Easton Poor, a New York architect well known to Turner from earlier work together. Unlike most other high-rise office buildings, McGraw-Hill had been designed as a headquarters for a single company, with no outside tenants, and many of its interiors were appropriately luxurious, requiring a higher quality of materials and workmanship than would normally be seen in commercial work.

Hall, now in his eighties and still fit and trim, hasn't lost much of the good-humored crustiness that served him well as one of the most effective of Turner's senior people. His reputation as a tough taskmaster was well deserved and he got all three jobs done, including extensive and demanding tenant work, by 1974. The three high-rise office buildings alone represented well over $300 million worth of construction at the time, almost a billion dollars' worth when expressed in the currency of the company's hundredth birthday.

The biggest and perhaps the grandest of the towering office giants built by the New York office of Turner during the late 1960s and early 1970s wasn't built in New York at all; it was built in Pittsburgh, Pennsylvania. It was the grand new headquarters building for U.S. Steel, which had outgrown the building that Turner had twenty years earlier built for it in the same city. Almost everything about the new U.S. Steel building was extraordinary. At sixty-four floors above grade, it was Pittsburgh's tallest building, 841 feet high, and at almost $125 million, it was the most expensive of the big domestic jobs that Turner would do in the late 1960s. Its 44,000-ton steel frame had to straddle both the old Pennsylvania Canal and the active Penn Central Railroad tunnel that Turner would relocate and rebuild, threading it through the building's lower reaches in a new reinforced concrete tunnel and supporting it on a vibration-isolating concrete and steel trestle. The sixty-four unique triangular floors that Harrison, Abramovitz & Abbe had designed to be virtually column-free would be supported at their perimeters by eighteen big box-shaped steel columns, each fabricated of heavy steel plate, set three feet outboard of the building's exterior wall and welded tight to hold a total of 400,000 gallons of water (with antifreeze added) designed to convey heat away from any possible building fire. And both the big box-shaped columns and the curtain wall would be fabricated of U.S. Steel's Cor-Ten, giving Pittsburghers a chance to see the building take on the ultimately uniform coloring produced by the oxidation of the steel, an effect that was briefly made less attractive when the rusty residue was inadvertently blown by high winds onto a neighboring building.

Ray Cusick, who had been with Turner since his graduation from Notre Dame in 1944, was designated project manager for the U.S. Steel job. Educated as an architect, Cusick had by the late 1960s come to be regarded in the firm as one of its master builders, and U.S. Steel was to be his masterpiece. During his earliest years with Turner he'd been recognized as one of the rising stars, and he was one of those given a small Safeway store to build, to provide early experience in running work. Not long after that Cusick was managing big jobs that ranged from large industrial buildings for the Stanley Works in Connecticut to the elegantly finished high-rise Interchurch Center in New York. Most recently he'd been managing Turner's reconstruction of the grandstands at Belmont and Saratoga racetracks, a couple of jobs that John Galbreath had steered to Turner when he was heading up the New York Racing Association's efforts to restore those venerable old landmarks.

Dick Corry, who would later go on to build more of Turner's tallest skyscrapers, came over to Pittsburgh from the Erieview Tower job in Cleveland to be superintendent on the big U.S. Steel job, his first major command in what would become almost thirty years of high-rise building. A stepson of Turner engineer Bill Cunningham, Corry had become a civil engineer at Purdue in 1950 and had been working for Turner ever since, and this would be his trial by fire. It would require a deep and complex foundation considered so difficult by local foundation contractors that Turner couldn't subcontract it at an acceptable price and had to build it with its own forces. Little of what would follow during the three years of the project's life would be easy, and much of it would be made more difficult by an especially militant group of labor unions that had focused on the high-profile U.S. Steel job as a good place for staking their claims.

Even Turner's management system on the big U.S. Steel job didn't follow an entirely traditional course. Howard Turner, who had taken on Turner's presidency only a little more than a year before the job started, and who exemplified a new trend toward separating the company's most senior management from its working operations, surprised some by accepting the role of project executive on the job himself. In fact, after his years in Pittsburgh, he wanted to be able to deal effectively with U.S. Steel people who'd be likely to look to him for answers about the job, and the role of project executive provided a mechanism for staying close to it. It worked out well, with most of the conventional, operating responsibilities of the project executive being managed by Ray Cusick.

By 1970, Howard Turner had been president for a little more than five years and he'd been chief executive officer for two years. Since he'd started, the annual cost of all construction in the country had increased by about 26 percent, while Turner's own annual volume had increased by more than 300 percent and its earnings had regularly exceeded 15 percent of its net worth, even after substantial contributions to its Employees' Retirement Plan. The company was even more robust than it had been when he had come aboard.

Almost since the company's inception, it had been repurchasing its shares approximately at book value, normally when tendered by an employee who was retiring, but in 1969 it was decided to abandon that practice in favor of allowing the development of a free market for buying and selling the shares. By acquiring stock from shareholders who wanted to sell and by adding some of its own treasury stock, the company was able to place about 20 percent of Turner's shares in the over-the-counter stock market, providing for the first time a free market for trading them and a valid mechanism for valuing them. It was a desirable change for shareholders who wanted to redeem their shares at a time of their own choosing and especially for aging shareholders who wanted to be sure that their survivors would have a market for their inherited shares.

Persons close to Virginia Melick Turner, Chan's vivacious and perceptive wife, quote her as saying that by 1970, as the date of Chan's retirement approached, he was having serious second thoughts and wanted to remain in the job for another year or so. But by then it was clearly too late. His old friend Joe Warren had preceded him into retirement, and Chan had long since passed along to Howard Turner what amounted to full control. His retirement was merely confirmation of his cousin's succession to the leadership of the company.

There had already been a few signs of differences between the approaches of the two Turners, most notably in the makeup of the board itself. Howard Turner was a man who felt strongly that the board should be staffed to address as effectively as possible such broad issues as company focus and direction and that it should leave operating issues largely to an operating committee. Although the board still included the vice presidents who managed the territories, plus a few other senior executives, there were now a few new faces from outside the company, and its profile looked a little more like the profiles of boards of some of the corporations that Howard Turner knew well. The addition of William Greenough, chairman of Teachers Insurance and Annuity Association and of John L. Burns, former president of RCA, reflected his enthusiasm for broadening the perspective of the board and thinning out the influence of persons actively involved in the company's operations.

There had been some management changes within the company too. Les

Shute had become general manager for New York and Bob Marshall, who had just finished a stint as contract manager in New York, had gone down to Philadelphia to run that office. Marshall's good friend Walter B. Shaw, who had started with him at the Princeton Library a little over twenty years earlier and whose history at Turner had been almost identical with Marshall's, was designated to succeed Howard Turner as president. A son of former executive vice president Walter K. Shaw, he had been considered the heir apparent for some time.

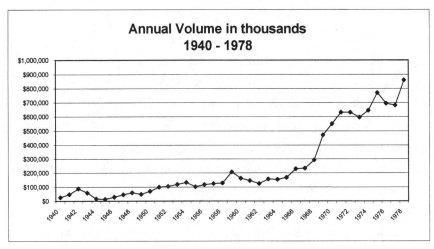

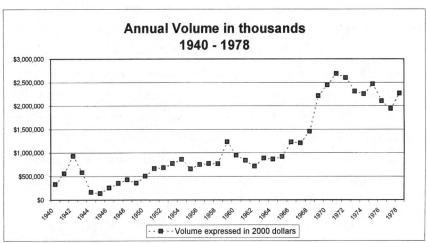

12.

Howard and
Walter B. Shaw

No one who knew Turner Construction Company should have been surprised when the board elected Walter B. Shaw to become president and chief operating officer of the company starting on January 1, 1971. He'd been on an increasingly certain course for the job since 1940, when he'd spent the summer between his junior and senior years at Cornell running line and grade for Turner, where his father, Walter K. Shaw, was a vice president. Two years later, after his first full year as a civil engineering graduate at Turner, the navy had shipped him off to the Pacific, where he'd see early and serious action as a Seabee officer at Guadalcanal, at New Guinea, and in the Admiralties. Three years later, immediately after the war, he and Bob Marshall traded their navy uniforms for civilian clothes and Turner hard hats and came together as assistant superintendents under Dutch Schroedel on the Firestone Library job at Princeton.

Not long after work on the Princeton Library was finished, Shaw was brought into Turner's New York contract department, where over the next few years he (and others) would seek and secure some of the company's most important jobs and where he would become manager in 1954. Handsome, well-educated and bright, by many accounts as charming as Chan Turner himself, the tall, pipe-smoking Shaw represented Turner exactly as Turner wanted itself to be seen during the 1950s, and he's been described as a superbly effective salesman. There were two or three other bright stars on the Turner horizon during the 1950s, but if there was anyone more likely than young Shaw to make it to the top job, he hadn't shown up by 1960, when Shaw was made a vice president and sent out to the Midwest to head up the growing Chicago office. By 1966 he had responsibility for all the company's Midwestern operations, and in 1968 he was brought back to New York to become executive vice president under Howard Turner. His elevation to the presidency at the end of 1970 was unlikely to have been a surprise to anyone who'd been paying attention.

But Walter Shaw's subtitle when he took on the presidency was chief operating officer, and Howard Turner, who had succeeded Chan in the chairmanship, retained the title of chief executive officer. Howard, a strong and vigorous executive, had pretty much been given free rein by his cousin Chan, especially during the last years of Chan's tenure, and by 1971 the control that had been passed along to him by Chan was still half a dozen years away from being passed on to Walter Shaw.

The scope and nature of the work the company was doing had changed measurably during the quarter of a century that had elapsed since the end of World War II, when Turner had been averaging about $25 million worth of work a year, much of it done by forces in the company's own direct employ, and when its salaried staff of about 400 was operating from three offices and doing fewer than thirty-five jobs a year. By 1971 ENR's annual list of the country's top 400 contractors showed Turner as the country's leading building contractor, i.e., as the firm whose annual volume of construction exceeded the like volume of any other firm whose principal work was limited to the construction of buildings. Turner was now putting in place almost $600 million worth of buildings a year, operating nine offices, and completing almost 100 jobs a year with a salaried staff of about 1,300. Its style was well along in a shift away from one that had not much earlier been dominated by the actual performance of work and toward one in which it its principal business was the procurement and management of work performed by subcontractors.

Howard Turner had been watching those changes unfold since 1952, when he became a board member, and he'd been an active participant in bringing some of them about since 1965, when he became president. None of it bothered him a bit. Trained in science and weaned on the management styles of a couple of big and aggressive industrial corporations, he knew the hazards of the status quo, and because he was unfettered by the mythology of construction tradition, departure from the well-worn path traveled by his predecessors wasn't difficult. He saw Turner as a big, strong, and well-financed business that could be managed in ways that would make it bigger and stronger and would enable it to do more of what it had already been doing and to do other profitable things as well, not all of them necessarily limited to the construction of buildings. He brought to the company a sometimes controversial ethos that sought new directions for Turner, and, of course, new directions are rarely without risk.

One direction in which the company had occasionally moved in the past, with mixed results, had from time to time brought it into the business of developing investment properties for its own account. Its prewar ventures in such development had been almost uniformly unsuccessful, but during the 1950s and 1960s there had been modest profits from buildings it developed for itself in St. Louis and elsewhere. As recently as 1957, when the Harvard Graduate School of Business Administration analyzed Turner in one of its case studies, Turner executive Joe Warren had told the Harvard interviewer that although the company might occasionally consider real estate investment again, it was doubtful that anything substantial would be developed.

But Walter Shaw liked the idea of development work, and when he was running things in Chicago during the 1960s he had discussed some of his ideas with a man named Jim Griffis, an engineer who was representing the developer on a project Turner was building. Griffis was a man with a good deal of real estate experience in Chicago and he thought that what Walter Shaw was talking about would make good sense for Turner.

By about 1970 the idea of getting into some work for the company's own investment had become a good deal more serious for Walter Shaw, who was by then based in New York, and he called Griffis to talk to him about coming to work for Turner and heading up a development subsidiary to implement his ideas. Griffis balked at the idea of a New York base. He was a Chicago native with a good job there and he didn't want to move. But only a year later, when things had changed for Griffis, he called Shaw to see if the offer was still good. He was surprised to learn that Turner had by then not only acquired an attractive parcel of undeveloped land on Chicago's fashionable Lake Shore Drive but that it had actually started construction of high-end condominium apartments on the site. It was a good call for both Griffis and for Shaw, and Griffis was hired to run the newly organized Turner Development Corporation (TDC), which had been formed to identify and develop work for the company's own investment. The plan was for Turner to apply its skills and resources to the business of merchant building, in which the company would develop and build for its own account, then sell what had been built and move on to the development of other such properties. It was a good opportunity for Griffis, and he appeared to be just the right man for the job: a fellow who understood a lot about real estate and a little about construction. With the job just getting underway, the timing seemed to Walter Shaw to be just about right.

Unfortunately, it wasn't. What had been a very strong real estate market in the Chicago area during the 1960s had by the early 1970s begun to weaken, and sales that every developer would like to make before his building has been completed were slow to materialize. Exacerbating the problem, the severity of Chicago's winter weather slowed the cast-in-place concrete work, delaying construction and the availability of completed units. George Morrison remembers that the TDC people who were trying to sell the apartments complained to the brass in New York that construction delays were costing them sales, and the relationship between the real estate people and the construction people (never a very warm one) cooled. It was not a happy situation.

Ever optimistic, those most seriously committed to the real estate program induced the board to move ahead with another such venture even before the first one showed signs of better health, and in 1973 TDC acquired a second Lake Shore Drive property near the first one. Within a year or so the distinguished architect Harry Weese had completed a design for a second upscale residential condominium project on the newly acquired land, and by 1976 Turner was building additional expensive condominium units (including duplex apartments facing the lake) in a seventy-six-unit high-rise tower on the second parcel. But conditions became even worse. The last units remaining in the first building were finally sold only after prices were reduced, and sales in the second project moved at a snail's pace. When more time had passed and only a few of those had been sold, a Canadian developer came along with an offer to buy all the remaining units, and Turner sold out to him at what was thought to be a bargain price. But the Canadian's results were even worse than Turner's, and before all his units could be sold he had lost what remained to the mortgagee.

For a while after that, Turner Development Corporation drifted in and out of other, mostly less ambitious development work, more commercial than residential, doing a little work in Texas and Illinois and some in New Jersey and at a few other locations as well, and spending a fair amount of money looking for new propositions. By the end of 1977 Turner Development was still an unpopular cousin to most of Turner's people, with little to show for all its work except a deficit of almost $2 million. It would be the 1980s before serious development activity would be resumed by TDC, this time with an exclusively commercial (rather than residential) focus, and with what seemed to some to be a more promising approach. What nobody knew in the closing years of the 1970s was that TDC's fortunes in the volatile 1980s real estate market would prove to be a good deal worse and more damaging than they had been in the 1970s.

Of course, such poor results hadn't seemed even remotely likely back in the Turner boardroom of the early 1970s, when things were going well and optimism was widespread. A few of the old guard had been skeptical, especially some diehards who never entirely accepted the idea that the company could be run by a man who had never had any mud on his boots. They were inclined to feel that Turner should stay clear of ventures that weren't wholly or mostly reliant on its proven construction skills, but by and large their opposition to the move into development hadn't been very vocal and the program had been allowed to develop.

During those first years of Howard Turner's chairmanship, Chan Turner had quietly continued his association with the board by heading its executive committee, but his role after retirement became relatively passive and was brief. He moved his office to a smaller space in the company's headquarters and gave up his devoted secretary of many years, Helen Wood, who went on to work for Bob Marshall, recently returned to New York from Philadelphia as vice chairman under his old friend Walter Shaw.

One day in April 1973, Chan succumbed to a massive stroke that ended his life at seventy-one. He was mourned by an extraordinary number of people who, through professional or social association with him, had come to admire his intelligence and integrity and in many cases genuinely loved him for his gentle, quiet charm. Almost thirty years later, Howard Turner would remember clearly his cousin's Quaker funeral and his own emerging awareness of being without Chan's valued support for the first time.

A good share of what Howard Turner brought to the company would influence its course as much through changes it would bring to the perspectives of its managers as it would through his own direct initiatives. By the early 1970s, the Mei Foo work was well along and proving to be an extremely profitable venture, and Bob Kupfer had begun to seek additional work for Turner in the Hong Kong and Singapore areas. In 1971, when he brought in a contract to provide construction-management services to First National City Bank (later Citibank) for the work the bank was doing in Hong Kong, the board affirmed its enthusiasm for an expanded international presence by establishing Turner East Asia Limited, the predecessor to Turner International Industries, with Kupfer in charge.

Like Walter Shaw, Bob Kupfer enjoyed the luxury of working for a chairman who prized imagination and the courage to steer new courses, and like Shaw he would have the support of a board that was likely to follow the chairman's lead. Kupfer had already shifted his base to New York by then, leaving Roger Turnier in charge in Hong Kong. Turnier, an engineer who had been with the company since 1950 and who had been at Kupfer's right hand in Hong Kong almost since the beginning of the Mei Foo work, took over responsibility for managing things in Hong Kong after Kupfer's return to the States. There was plenty of construction going on and even more in the planning stage in Hong Kong, and Turnier addressed the task of securing some of it for Turner.

But Hong Kong didn't develop as well for Turner as the company had hoped it would. There was substantial local resistance to the construction-management approach advocated by Turner, and except for situations in which there was an American connection of one sort or another, little profitable construction work developed after the First National City Bank job except for a few consulting contracts for projects that ended up being built by local contractors and an occasional, small construction-management job for Turner.

But Turnier, buttressed by regular visits from Kupfer and a few from Howard Turner, continued his quest for new business in Hong Kong and increasingly along the rest of the Pacific Rim, and by 1972 there were signs that the picture might be brightening. Several attractive consulting jobs surfaced in Singapore, about 1,500 miles from Hong Kong, some involving the work of I. M. Pei, whose architectural firm in New York knew and regarded Turner well. Little of it was exactly the kind of construction-management work Turner was seeking, but it was productive work and it introduced Turner to Singapore. And, of course, it made Singapore aware of Turner.

In 1975 Singapore Airlines was ready to go ahead with construction on one of the most important projects in the Far East: an approximately $200 million complex at Singapore's new Changi Airport. It was a very large and complex job that was well suited to a construction-management approach, and the airline narrowed its choices to Bechtel, the powerful California-based engineering and construction firm, and Turner. Both firms were well qualified for the job, but Kupfer and his people brought to the negotiation a promise that the employment of local firms to do the work would be an essential element in Turner's plan, and Singapore Airlines decided in Turner's favor.

Five separate projects would be built by Turner and its subcontractors at the Changi Airport, more or less simultaneously, over an approximately five-year period that started in 1976. The dominant structure was a huge aircraft hangar with the longest clear span then extant. Its interior was so vast that it allowed three 747s to be serviced side by side, with room to spare. Wrapped around the hangar's sides was a nine-story administration building, and nearby were a flight kitchen capable of preparing 50,000 meals every day and a huge engine-overhaul complex, as well as a big cargo center. It was the state of the art in airport construction in the late 1970s.

Turner's responsibilities at Changi went beyond construction management. Its agreement with Singapore Airlines committed it to turning over as much of the process as possible to Singaporeans, and from the beginning it awarded major contracts to local firms and hired local staff personnel wherever possible. By the time the company began to reduce its own on-site staff in 1981, almost all its approximately sixty positions were held by Singaporeans.

Meanwhile, Hong Kong's failure to develop much beyond Mei Foo hadn't by any means meant the end of Turner's efforts to broaden its international presence. By 1975 the company had organized Turner International Industries (TII) to tie together its interests in work outside the United States, and Bob Kupfer had joined with Bob Nilsson, who'd been with Turner since 1963 (except for a four-year stint as a Marine Corps officer that included a year's voluntary service in Vietnam), to push out into Pakistan and across the Middle East in search of such work.

Securing new work in those areas proved to be a little easier than securing it in Hong Kong. For one thing, much of it was being designed by American architectural and engineering firms who knew and regarded Turner well and who understood and were sympathetic to its construction-management approach. For another, some of the American firms involved were still new enough to the Middle East to appreciate being able to do business with a company that spoke their language and understood their objectives. Mobil Oil, Turner's staunch friend since Standard Oil days, was among the company's earliest and biggest customers in the Persian Gulf area in the mid-1970s, when Turner built Mobil's employee-housing complex in Jedda, on the Red Sea, and would go on to provide consulting services on a wide range of other work as well. A thousand miles east of Jedda, a new $30 million Sheraton Hotel would be another construction-management job for the company in the later 1970s, this one on the gulf itself at Dubai. It was a time when oil revenues were still generating vast new government projects in the Middle East, and Turner International was becoming an increasingly important player, providing construction management and a broad array of consulting services on such jobs as the King Khalid Military City and King Abdulaziz University. By 1977 Turner International had a staff of more than 100 and was billing about $25 million a year for the work it was doing in the Middle East. Prospects looked very good.

Turner International didn't end its activities on the shores of the gulf. A little over a thousand miles farther east, one of the most important projects of the 1970s was taking shape in Karachi, Pakistan, where the Aga Khan was developing a plan for building a 673-bed hospital and university complex near the Arabian Sea. He had inherited his position as head of Islam's Ismaili sect from his grandfather in 1957, when he was a twenty-year-old student at Harvard, and he had since then been investing most of his energies and resources in strategies designed to enrich the spiritual and secular lives of his almost 20 million devoted followers.

The Karachi project was to be a vast teaching hospital that would bring good medicine to the Aga Khan's people, and he had engaged the distinguished American firm of Payette Associates to design it. But the first project had run into structural problems, and Turner International was brought in to implement a plan for solving them. The success of the remedial work brought Turner to the attention of the Aga Khan himself, who began to see the company as a key figure in implementing his master plan for the hospital.

It would be a successful but difficult project for Turner, continuing into the 1980s. Turner became a key figure in the complex process of getting the facility underway, providing the whole range of preconstruction services that were essential to optimizing and completing a state-of-the-art working design: establishing budgets and schedules, identifying and analyzing alternative schemes and materials, estimating costs, forecasting cash flows, and the like. But an organization in which the authority of the leader is absolute and in which the unquestioning resolve of the working staff is to implement his wishes didn't make for a good working environment for an American-style construction manager. The inclination of the Aga Khan's staff to press its sometimes unreasonable demands at all hours of the day and night often made things difficult, exacerbating the already difficult problem of maintaining a stable workforce in a relatively remote location that hadn't been very attractive to most of Turner's people from the start. When the time came to take on the management of the construction work itself, Turner respectfully declined but consented to stay around long enough to manage much of the bidding and related matters.

Turner International was doing some traditional construction in Pakistan at the same time. When the American Embassy in Islamabad was sacked and burned in 1979, the Foreign Buildings Office of the U.S. State Department brought Turner in to rebuild it, paying its bills with a combination of U.S. dollars and Pakistani rupees. The rupees, not useful to Turner anywhere but in Pakistan, would have been problematic except for a later State Department job on which the company was able to do its local purchasing with them.

But in spite of all Turner International's individual successes, its goal of profitability remained elusive through most of the 1970s. Discrete projects regularly showed reasonable earnings at their sites, but the economic burdens of having to identify and secure contracts for work on these often remotely located and widely spaced projects and then to provide executive oversight for their construction were difficult to amortize without an extremely large construction volume, something Turner International had not yet been able to achieve. When travel and housing subsidies for some of Turner's people were considered, the overhead burden made profitability almost impossible. By 1978, when Howard Turner relinquished the corporate chairmanship to Walter Shaw, results that had been produced by Turner's projects in the Middle East and in East Asia seemed to some in Turner's management to be insufficient to justify continuing to seek work abroad. But there was still enough optimism about the future of international work to carry the day, and Turner International survived to push on into the 1980s and beyond.

Meanwhile, some streamlining had been going on in the boardroom back in New York. In 1973, when Turner was operating ten widely separated and busy domestic offices as well as Turner East Asia and Turner Development Corporation,

Howard Turner resolved to free the board of the increasing problem of maintaining meaningful direct linkage between all those offices and the board itself. His strategy was to identify the domestic offices as independent territories (later as independent business units) and to organize them into three large regions, each to be managed by a senior vice president whose authority would be considerable and who would report to (and serve on) the board. It was a plan that was designed to allow routine problems to be solved at the regional level, leaving only those issues considered appropriate for the board's attention to be passed on to New York, and it worked. It was an important step in the accelerating growth and development of the network of separate and widely spaced business units that would lie at the core of Turner's strength later in the century and into the next one.

The new Western Region included everything from (and including) the Chicago territory westward (to and including) the offices in Los Angeles and San Francisco and, before long, Houston and Denver. It would be headed by Herbert S. Church Jr., who'd been with Turner since 1943 and had been managing its Chicago office since 1968. The Central Region, under Herbert D. Conant, the former Marine Corps sergeant (and future Turner CEO) who had made such a spectacular success of the Cleveland office, would include Cleveland, Cincinnati, Columbus, and later Detroit. The third region, the Eastern Region, which included New York, Boston, and Philadelphia, would be headed by Bob Kupfer, who would continue as manager of Turner's international work as well for a few years.

Under the new regional plan, and with Turner Development Corporation and Turner International in place (and no real indication that either of them would eventually become anything less than substantial contributors to the company's earnings), Turner had something of a new look by the mid-1970s. In February of 1972, its shares, until then traded over the counter, had become listed on the American Stock Exchange, providing a much broader and more effective market for them. It was a time when the computer was beginning to find its way into Turner's offices, with a new UNIVAC on-line at corporate headquarters, but with the complete automating of its systems awaiting the later arrival of the personal computer, when almost every workstation would have access to the data it needed. And some of the turmoil that had characterized national affairs during the 1960s and early 1970s had begun to subside, with the Vietnam War over and the post-Watergate transition substantially completed. The oil embargo had triggered an unsettling inflation of costs, but Turner had to a large extent (though not in all cases) begun to protect itself against the perils of unforgiving cost guarantees by requiring that appropriate flexibility be written into its contracts.

The new regional plan was given an early boost by an approximately $100 million contract that touched two of the three regions. The Public Buildings Service, which had responsibility for managing most of the federal government's construction, had taken a new approach to building three giant centers that the General Services Administration wanted for processing Social Security payments. In the new approach, a single firm would be engaged by the government to manage a process in which an array of contractors, selected through competitive bidding, would do the construction mostly on the basis of performance specifications. One of the three centers was to be built in San Francisco, although it actually ended up being built on a site in nearby Richmond, California; one was to be built in Chicago; and a third was to be built in Philadelphia.

The very idea that the government would be negotiating a construction-management contract for its work was attractive to Turner, and indeed it effectively started a trend that would continue to produce valued business for the company for years. But the additional idea of the government's contracting for the actual construction of the work on a performance basis, an arrangement in which the design of components would be left to the construction contractors and in which the acceptability of products and systems would be based on their performance characteristics, was radical and for the most part untested. Turner had a month earlier competed unsuccessfully to manage PBS's first such contract on a job in Beltsville, Maryland, and had resolved to make another try on the Social Security payment centers project.

Late in 1971 the government selected Turner as its construction manager for the entire three-site project from a group of six of the country's most substantial firms, giving equal weight to the management fee quoted by each and to the score by which the technical capability of each firm was rated. The decision was easy: Turner's fee was the lowest of the lot, and its score for technical capability was the highest.

Overall design responsibility for all three centers rested with the architecture and engineering firm of Leo A. Daly in Omaha and with the architecture firm of Nolen Swinburne & Associates of Philadelphia, who were designated the executive architects. Once Turner had been selected as construction manager, the process of completing design documents with its help came next. Local architects in the three cities were added to the team within a few months, and by late 1972 the government had accepted a bid from a joint venture headed by Owens-Corning Fiberglass to put in place at all three sites the basic systems of the buildings, which had been defined by the design team to include the structural framing; the floor and ceiling sandwich, including mechanical and electrical work; and all the interior partitioning. But the Owens-Corning group needed a construction manager of its own, so it engaged Tishman Construction Company, one of the five managers who had lost out to Turner in the original competition, producing the ironic result that Tishman ended up reporting to its competitor, Turner. Over the months that followed, dozens of additional, "out of system" contracts were awarded by the government to complete the big, often unlikely, and sometimes unwieldy combination of manufacturers, vendors, and contractors that would be managed by Turner.

Turner placed its own John Hanft in charge. A 1940 graduate of Cooper Union with four and a half years' wartime service with the army engineers and a little more than twenty-five years with Turner behind him, Hanft had started in New York on Turner's port authority bus terminal job but had been working in Philadelphia ever since, first under Dutch Schroedel and then under Bob Marshall. By Hanft's later recollection, the Social Security centers would require his spending at least half his waking hours for about the next five years in airplanes that would take him between New York, Washington, Philadelphia, Chicago, Omaha, and San Francisco.

Although all three designs were based on the same performance criteria, what emerged from the drawing boards of the three independent architects were solutions as different from one another in form and appearance as day is from night, so the contract became in every respect three independent construction projects. The work progressed well in Richmond, California, and in Philadelphia, where Turner superintendents Louis Uhl and Harvey Hirst, respectively, were in charge of fieldwork. But in Chicago, where Turner's Dick Hoyt was in charge, nature conspired against progress. After the job had been excavated down to the level of a lower basement, and piles had been driven from that level, an intense rainstorm soaked a thin, subsurface layer of clay and turned it plastic. The weight of the overburden above the plastic clay forced it out like squeezed toothpaste into an adjacent, deeper excavation that had been prepared for elevator pits and the like, and the massive lateral movement of these subsurface soils radically altered the position and condition of the piles, rendering them useless. By the time a new design had been prepared and some of the piles had been removed and replaced by new ones, more than a year had been lost and a great deal of money had been spent by the government, all while Turner stood by.

But with it all, even the troubled Chicago job took only a little over three years to finish, the others having by then been occupied, and a few years later GSA would engage Turner to manage construction of another of its big jobs. But by then, although the construction-management concept had been fully accepted by the federal government, the "performance" basis for individual construction contracts had been abandoned and the traditional method of contracting for individual elements of the work through competitive bidding (under the construction manager's supervision) had been restored.

Turner's growing inclination to expand into new locations had by the 1970s become part of its modus operandi, and much that was going on during the mid-1970s seemed to militate for even more of such expansion. The company's capacity and appetite for the big jobs that had by now come to dominate its work had grown substantially, but there was clearly a limit to the amount of such work likely to surface in any single location at any single time, even in the largest of the urban

centers. As a result, Turner's management was continually watchful for new locations where signs of approaching urban development opportunities might be coming into view.

The Central Region, headed by Herb Conant, may have been the most vigorously expansive of the new regions. The annual volume of work it had been doing
and the earnings it had been generating, already substantial, would almost double
during the 1970s. Cleveland itself, the principal office in the region, had been
started only a few years earlier as a satellite of the Chicago office, and Conant had
been quick to sense its potential as an independent territory of its own. Turner had
started there with Galbreath's "Jolly Green Giant" (Erieview Tower was clad in a
green glass skin), bigger than any other building in town except for one prewar
structure that spanned the railroad tracks, and special enough to bring plenty of
attention to Turner. What's more, Conant, who had been moving around the
country for a while, liked Cleveland and saw it as a place in which he might like to
settle. Doug Meyer, Dick Corry, and Al Sanchez, a few other Turner regulars who
had done their share of traveling, felt the same way. Although Corry and Meyer,
who would later distinguish themselves as the company's premiere high-rise
builders, would be moving on to other Turner territories in the not-distant future,
Al Sanchez, a talented engineer who had also been educated in law, would settle
in Cleveland.

It was a period in which many of the jobs would be developing men who would
years later appear among the company's leadership, but Erieview has come in for
some special attention for producing a bumper crop: One chairman and a host of
other senior executives eventually surfaced from among a management group that
included, in addition to Conant, Dick Corry, Ralph Johnson, Al Sanchez, Dick
Duffy, and Doug Meyer.

With signs of potential business abounding, Conant wanted to begin seeking
new business in Cleveland right away, but because Turner's young office there was
being funded entirely by Galbreath (Erieview was still Turner's only job in town)
he couldn't do it. Undeterred, he negotiated an arrangement with Galbreath's
people that permitted him to devote some of his time to other business in return

for Turner's absorbing some of Galbreath's overhead costs in Cleveland. Before the punch list on Erieview Tower had been cleaned up, Turner was starting to penetrate the Cleveland market.

Conant was proved right about Cleveland. The new Turner office flourished, doing major and continuing work for some of the big Cleveland firms and institutions, especially for the expanding hospitals of the region, including the Cleveland Clinic, the University Hospitals of Cleveland, Cleveland Children's Hospital, St. Vincent's Hospital, the Podiatric Hospital of Cleveland, and others. Before long, the Cleveland office had its own satellites in Columbus and Detroit.

Years before the Cleveland work began, a Turner critic had characterized Turner's management executives as "contractors in striped pants," a slightly barbed but widely heard and not entirely baseless suggestion that the company's style tended to be very conservative and perhaps slightly elitist. Herb Conant brought a new, less conservative style to the job. When a Cleveland developer client complained to him that his own partner was collecting brokerage fees for arranging financing on their own projects, Conant made the complaining fellow Turner's own joint venture partner in a new construction company he formed to do the building, entitling him to a share of the construction fee that was about equal to his partner's financing fees. Of course, Conant first made sure the total construction fee was increased sufficiently to ensure that Turner's own fee wouldn't suffer. Not exactly Henry or Chan's style, but these were new times, and it worked.

By about 1974, when Conant and Al Sanchez were starting to look at Detroit with more than casual interest, the Detroit General Hospital was organizing a partnership with Wayne State University to build an approximately $400-million hospital. Turner became one of the candidates for the contract to manage its construction. It was a big and prestigious job, certainly a potential starting place for a new Turner office in Detroit, and the Cleveland staff pulled out all the stops to get the contract. The presentation they developed seemed to be going well, as Conant remembered it almost thirty years later, until halfway through it when the president of Detroit General Hospital and the chancellor of Wayne State, a couple of fellows whose votes would surely be critical in the selection process, got up and left. It wasn't seen as a good sign by Conant or Sanchez, but it proved to be meaningless: By evening Turner had been selected, and a condition of selection was that Turner would establish an office in Detroit to run the job. Ralph Johnson, who was Cleveland's operations manager and who had earlier worked under Conant in Chicago (and who would years later become president of the Associated General Contractors, the industry's principal trade group), was tapped to establish and manage the new office and to run the new project. When Johnson went on to San Francisco a few years later, he was replaced in Detroit by Vic Cestar, and not long after that Cestar was replaced by Len Perna, who had been assistant project manager on Turner's big Lincoln Hospital job in New York during the earlier 1970s. Soon there was more work in the Detroit office, including renovation of the Detroit Stadium, and a new Turner base had begun to gather momentum.

Back in Cleveland, Turner was growing accustomed to getting its share of the big jobs it went after, but not all of them, and certainly not always right away. About 1973 the county commissioners of Cuyahoga County had talked with Turner (and others) about working with them and their architects on the design of a big new Justice Center in Cleveland and about managing its construction. Conant was especially eager to be selected for jobs like this one, which promised to open up an important new sector for Turner. After being interviewed, he had gone off to Florida for a vacation, confident that good news would follow. But he was to be disappointed. The George A. Fuller Company was selected, and Conant had the task of consoling his staff and encouraging it to move on to the next big job. But that wasn't the end of it. A little over a year later the commissioners were back, entirely dissatisfied with Fuller's performance in the design and planning phase and already well into the process of terminating their contract with Fuller and ready to negotiate a new one with Turner. It was an especially valued contract, under the circumstances, and not only because the fee was much higher than the one Conant had originally proposed. It established relationships in Ohio that would be extremely helpful to Turner later, especially when the company was being considered for a contract to provide construction-management services on the new State

Office Building in Columbus. On that job, which would be the first at the state level to depart from Ohio's custom of engaging four separate prime contractors through a public bidding process, the governor himself campaigned for the selection of a construction manager instead, and Turner was awarded the job.

Some territories began to produce their own satellites. Around 1976, an engineer in the Cincinnati office named Jim Stievater was able to convince Vic Smith, who was running the territory, that if Turner wanted to garner business in the South it was going to have to reestablish an office in Atlanta, where the company had years earlier closed the office it had first established in 1919. Stievater, who'd been working for Turner since his graduation from RPI in 1961, wasn't fazed by the fact that Turner had no work at all in Atlanta, because it was the whole South he was addressing as a marketplace, and within a few months he had indeed landed a contract for building Mercy Hospital in Miami. A few jobs in the Atlanta area followed, mostly hospitals, and there was increasing evidence that a new territory might be in the making.

During that same period, the new Western Region, under Herb Church, was able to hold its own. Chicago was the region's headquarters, but it wasn't Chicago's work that was responsible for its good volume. It was a combination of the growth the Western Region was experiencing out on the West Coast and the addition of a couple of new offices.

Not that Chicago was sitting on its haunches during the 1970s, when it was averaging almost $100 million worth of construction annually and was doing some large and important work, but it wasn't a period of growth for the office. In fact, the annual volume of work done in Chicago, still about $120 million in 1972, declined every year between then and 1977. But even with its declining volume, Turner remained the company to reckon with in Chicago, and during this period it built Philip Johnson's big IDS complex in Minneapolis, more Harris Trust work in Chicago, the Illinois Bell building, Montgomery Ward's world headquarters, and the big Lutheran Aid building, all of them larger than $25 million, some of them larger than $40 million, and the IDS complex larger than $80 million.

A sense of Turner's impact on the Chicago skyline was captured years later in a letter written by Turner loyalist Bernie Newton to one of his eight sons on the occasion of the son's return to Turner after having left the company for a while. The excerpt that follows reveals a pride in Turner that Newton had earlier reserved exclusively for the Marine Corps.

Perhaps you don't know it, but Turner "owns" several streets in and just outside the loop. Take West Monroe: The Inland Steel and Xerox buildings at Monroe and Dearborn; two Harris Trust Buildings each adjacent to their big old masonry head-quarters, three of four corners at Monroe and Franklin; on LaSalle Street: the presti-gious award winner at Adams and LaSalle, 180 and 200 North LaSalle Street and the Builders Building at LaSalle and Wacker. On North Michigan Boulevard: 3 buildings adjacent to each other, Apollo, 500 North Michigan and an education office building, across the street at 625 North Michigan and the Elizabeth Arden building just up the street. Then just off Michigan was the ADA (American Dental Association) and the Time-Life Building. Did you know that Time-Life was the first successful use of double deck elevators in the United States? That led to using double deck elevators in the Amoco Building which allowed the designers to use only 40 pas-senger elevators. Standard elevatoring would have required 56 elevator shafts, what's worse, 56 elevators shafts, eating up rentable space — another major achievement of Turner, Chicago.

[In the excerpt, the author has underlined Turner projects of the late '70s.]

Turner's dominance in Chicago notwithstanding, there were a good many mouths to feed there and the development of new markets in the region under its management was increasingly seen as a way to shore up a declining volume of work. A few years earlier, one of those clients who regularly return to Turner with new jobs had appeared on the scene: Metropolitan Life Insurance Company. The big insurer had entered into a joint venture with Trammel Crow, a successful Texas-based real estate company, to build a high-rise office complex in the heart of the bustling and prosperous oil center of Houston, and it saw a special need on the job for Turner. Trammel Crow had brought along the well-established Texas firm of Linbeck Construction Company as its own contractor, but Met Life wasn't prepared to enter into such a major construction project, then estimated at about

$20 million, without having its friends at Turner by its side. The partners worked out a plan for a Turner-Linbeck joint venture to do the construction, with Turner the majority partner. Turner sent Bill Altom, who had been with the company since 1954, down from Cincinnati to run it. Altom, educated in electrical engineering at the University of Tennessee, had done a little of almost everything at Turner, and when things in Houston were being organized he was doing marketing for the company in Cincinnati. When Howard Turner learned during a visit to Cincinnati that Altom would like to get back into construction, he tapped him for the Houston assignment.

What Turner-Linbeck would build in Houston was a million-square-foot, high-rise office building called the Allen Center, named for the two brothers who had owned the land on which Houston had been established 135 years earlier. The Allen Center was about as different as it could have been from most of the commercial high-rise work Turner had been doing. In an effort to avoid the premium costs and delays that had been wreaking havoc in the oil-country building boom, the building had been designed around a hybrid structural system that relied mostly on structural precast concrete, some of it to be integrated at the site with reinforced concrete, together with some conventional cast-in-place concrete framing, some structural steel framing with cast-in-place fill and finish on metal deck. With subcontractors in Houston taxed to capacity, the joint venture did its own concrete work, threading a delicately balanced path through the whole varied array of systems and materials to maintain schedule. Even the conventional systems weren't ordinary. To avoid overstressing Houston's marginal soils, multiple basements were excavated to remove a mass of earth sufficient to balance some of the new loads that were going to be imposed by the building, and then a deep, reinforced concrete mat was built to carry the columns. About thirteen months after the start of work, the first tenants began moving into the building. At a little over twenty dollars a square foot and just a little over a year to build, the strategies had apparently worked.

But by the time the tenants had begun moving in, the fierce pace of real estate activity that had characterized Houston during the late 1960s and early 1970s had slowed, at least temporarily, and the bloom had faded from the relationship between Met Life and Trammel Crow. Further plans for Allen Center II that had been in the works were shelved, and the joint venture between Trammel Crow and Met Life was dissolved. Altom and his prospering Houston office, which now included Carr Gerringer (who'd come down from Chicago) as operations manager and high-rise specialist Dick Corry (from Cleveland via Pittsburgh) as the office's only project executive, had managed to secure enough other good work in town to justify Houston's being made a fully fledged territory.

By about 1975 what proved to be only a temporary lull in Houston's growth had passed, and Met Life had found a new partner in Century Development Company, a big local development firm that, like Trammel Crow, brought along its own contractor. But once again Met Life successfully insisted that Turner control whatever construction was to be done, and a new joint venture between Turner and Century's friends at Miner Dietrich Construction Company was established.

As it turned out, there was a good deal more to be done at the Allen Center than had been already been done by Turner-Linbeck: two more office buildings, each bigger than the first one; a Le Meridien (later DoubleTree) Hotel; and the development of an extensive urban site. By 1976 Allen Center II was underway, this time with somewhat simplified structural systems, and by 1977 Allen Center III was coming into view. Turner's other Houston work was growing apace as well, approaching an annual value of $20 million, including extensive work for Shell Oil Company and a computer center for Texaco. By 1978 Houston had returned to its earlier pace and would soon be exceeding it.

It was out on the West Coast that some of the ground being lost elsewhere in the Western Region was being recovered. During the period in the 1970s when Chicago's volume was declining, annual volume in the Far West held fairly steady. The L.A. office was just beginning to come off a series of high-rise skyscrapers during the early 1970s when Security Pacific, a big western bank that later became part of the Bank of America, decided to build an approximately $100 million tower of its own on a difficult site in downtown Los Angeles called Bunker Hill. The office of Albert Martin, which had earlier associated with Harrison and Abramovitz on the design of the Union Bank job and had been the principal architect on the ARCO job, was designing the building for Security Pacific, and Chuck Griggs was in charge for them.

There really wasn't anyone in town who could match Turner's credentials for the job. The bank wanted an L.A. builder, and except for C. L. Peck, who had taken on a consulting contract for the project, Turner was now the only qualified contractor who could pass that test. But Herb Pintard, who was running the L.A. office, and Jim Allaire, who was a project manager there, wanted to make sure. At lunch with Griggs a while before the decision was to be made, Allaire asked him what he thought Turner should do. "Just tell them that the people who ran the ARCO job will run this one", Griggs told him. That was good news for Jim Allaire, who had himself been the project manager on ARCO, and it must have been good news for Charlie Enscoe, who had been project superintendent. It was good advice too. Turner's proposal stipulated that the ARCO crew would run the Security Pacific job, and it won the award.

Big jobs like Security Pacific notwithstanding, Turner's L.A. people were regularly watchful for signs of major work everywhere in the West, and they didn't have to wait long. The Johns Manville Company, for whom Turner had been doing work since the earliest years of the century, decided in the early 1970s to abandon its eastern roots in favor of building a splendid world headquarters on a spectacular site in the Rocky Mountains, and they had used an architectural competition as a basis for selecting Turner's old friends at The Architects Collaborative (TAC) in Cambridge, Massachusetts, to design it. Herb Pintard and his staff in Los Angeles were inclined from the beginning to see the JM job as one that had Turner's name on it, and there was apparently some merit to their view. Nine construction managers were considered for the job, and Turner proved to be the first choice of both the owner and the architect.

An architectural scheme had already been developed when Turner was selected, but its details remained to be worked out, and JM's management was in a hurry. With a plan for about 712,000 square feet of well-finished space to be distributed in a couple of seven-story structures so long (almost a quarter mile each) that the curvature of the earth had to be taken into account when they were laid out, Turner had a big job to build on a site that was three miles from the nearest highway, with neither power, water, nor other services. Cost estimates and schedules needed to be worked out while details were being developed, and orders needed to be placed and fieldwork initiated for some elements of the work, while design calculations were still being made for others.

Security Pacific was still getting the lion's share of Jim Allaire's time back in Los Angeles, so Herb Pintard took on the role of project executive himself until Allaire could give JM his attention. Howard Clunn, an engineer who'd been with Turner since 1947, was brought out from New York to do some of the early conceptual estimating required until further-developed drawings would become available. By spring 1973 Turner had established a small office in nearby Denver, reporting to Los Angeles, and not much later Doug Meyer, the MIT-educated Minnesota native who had been one of the Erieview Tower stars and had since managed some of Turner's most important projects, came west from the IDS job in Minneapolis to run the Johns Manville job and some of the other work that Turner had begun to pick up in the Denver area. Fieldwork on JM began late in 1973 when Dave Scrivner, a Lehigh graduate who had been working on a Turner job in Cincinnati, came out to Denver as project manager.

The site itself was nothing less than spectacular, a sprawling ranch nestled into the foothills of the Rockies. A family of eagles that had been living only a hundred yards from the edge of the excavation abandoned its nest as soon as dirt began to fly but was back as soon as steel had been set in 1974; they remained in residence throughout the job.

As soon as the JM job became sufficiently advanced, Turner's administrative personnel moved out to the site, leaving its downtown space to serve as an early office for what was becoming an active satellite of Los Angeles. Denver was still something of a boomtown early in the 1970s, profiting from times that were still good in the oil business and to some extent from the promise that oil from local shale deposits would bring additional prosperity. Within its first year in Denver, Turner had started work on an almost 800,000-square-foot, twenty-three-story metal-and-glass headquarters building for Mountain Bell and had contracted to build a spectacular new concert hall that New York architects Hardy, Holzmann and Pfeiffer had designed for the Denver Symphony Orchestra. Almost thirty years later, architect Malcolm Holzmann would describe how pleased he had been when he learned that Turner had been selected to build the concert hall, remembering with more than a little gratitude the special attention that Turner and Turner's Al McNeill had given a much smaller project the company had built for Hardy, Holzmann and Pfeiffer in Cincinnati many years before the Denver job.

Not long after the Johns Manville job was started, its management had decided that the Fourth of July, 1976, would be about as auspicious a date as could be found for dedicating the new building, and when that date came, Turner was ready. The building was substantially complete, and Johns Manville sent personal invitations to everyone who had participated in its design and construction to attend the gala festivities that celebrated its dedication and the two hundredth birthday of the Republic on the same glorious day.

Out in the Bay Area of California the 1970s were good years for Turner's fledgling San Francisco office too. Gene von Wening, with Jack Quinn and Paul DeMange, had carved out a secure niche in the closing years of the 1960s, and by the early 1970s the San Francisco office was well established and becoming a serious contender in local construction, with annual volumes averaging about $15 million and peaking to over $30 million during 1974 and 1975. A development venture in Oakland that comprised the Grubb & Ellis real estate firm and San Francisco–based Dillingham Construction Company was probably about as important as any job in the Bay Area for giving Turner's still-young San Francisco office some real momentum in the early 1970s. The development team had contracted with the City of Oakland to build its City Center, a big project intended to spark the renewal of downtown Oakland, and it was, of course, anticipated that Dillingham would do the construction for the venture. But when Dillingham realized that the city required that 50 percent of the construction workers themselves and a significant fraction of the subcontractors would have to qualify as members of minority groups (and that those stipulations were supported by the city's right to exact very large penalties for failure to comply), the firm, loath to take on the substantial task of finding enough minority workers and firms to meet the city's requirements, backed away from doing the construction.

But Turner saw the job as a chance to assert its own commitment to minority hiring and to become part of the city's revival, and the company stepped in with an effective plan of its own, taking on Dillingham's contract with the Grubb-Dillingham joint venture. Jack Quinn was able to work out a more flexible set of rules with the city, essentially by setting the original requirements as goals and adding a serious commitment that Turner would make every effort to reach them. As it turned out, there were times during the construction that followed when the 50 percent goal was exceeded, but there were times when it wasn't, too. Finding minority-owned businesses proved more difficult than maintaining the targeted percentages among the workers, but Turner took a big step toward solving that problem by bringing in a local, minority-owned construction firm as its own joint venture partner in the construction management. The job went well and the City was pleased enough to award additional work to Turner later, using the same guidelines.

At about the same time as the Oakland work was being done, Jack Quinn heard that the grand barons of the Southern Pacific Railroad wanted to generate some income from one of their valuable San Francisco properties by placing a commercial office building on it. To do that effectively, Quinn realized, they would need as a partner a developer like Turner's good friend John Galbreath, who although well known in southern California, was relatively unknown in the Bay Area. And Galbreath could certainly be expected to ensure a role for Turner. The Galbreath–Southern Pacific venture materialized, and its product was an approximately 1,700,000-square-foot high-rise office building, designed as a pair of towers by Welton Becket and called One Market Plaza. As it turned out, Southern Pacific's roots were so deep in San Francisco's ground that Turner had to settle for a joint venture with the long-established and distinguished local contractor, Dinwiddie Construction Company, which had built some of the city's most important buildings. Dinwiddie proved to be an entirely competent and agreeable partner, and while the two contractors participated about equally in staffing the project, it was one of the few joint ventures in which Turner accepted a minority position, in this case 45 percent.

By the mid-1970s Turner's momentum in San Francisco was considerable, with a large number of jobs that included more high-rise office buildings, work at Stanford University, and, of course, the West Coast component of the big Social Security Payment Center project in Richmond. There was some early talk about a big convention center too, but there really wasn't anything definite yet.

Growth was the watchword in the American West of the 1970s, when the westward movement of commerce and population continued to encourage the kind of large-scale building construction that was Turner's stock in trade. In 1976 the federal government awarded the company a contract to manage construction of what ultimately became a $76 million headquarters building for its National Oceanic and Atmospheric Administration in Seattle. Gene von Wening had been watching Seattle for a while, mindful of its growing role as the major springboard for people and goods heading for the Far East or for Alaska, another region that struck him as a candidate for a Turner office. The Alaska idea never materialized, but when the government turned to Turner again a few months later with a contract to build its big airmail facility at the Seattle-Tacoma Airport, von Wening sent John McCarthy up to run the job and to explore in more detail the idea of establishing a Seattle office. By the end of 1976 McCarthy, a young engineer who'd spent most of his five years with Turner working on the Oakland projects, had helped to establish San Francisco's first satellite office in Seattle, and only a few years later he'd be part of establishing another satellite in Portland, Oregon.

Back east, where most of Turner's work had traditionally been centered, things were less good and there were signs that they might get worse before they got better. Even in the early 1970s, construction in what was now called the Eastern Region had never accounted for less than half the firm's annual volume, but that fraction was declining and would eventually shrink to about one-third. Much of the shrinkage reflected the exuberant growth of the other regions, of course, but some of it reflected a slowing in some of the older, well-developed eastern territories like

New York. It wasn't without significance that the annual meeting of the company's shareholders was held in Columbus, Ohio, in 1975 instead of in New York. With things declining back east it was a good chance for Howard Turner to dramatize for some of his new outside directors the company's substantial presence in another region.

Not that there wasn't growth in the East, too, but it just wasn't as exuberant as what was going on in the Midwest and in the West. When Tom Gerlach had been brought down from Boston in 1970 to replace Bob Marshall as territory general manager (TGM) in Philadelphia, allowing Marshall to move up to New York as senior vice president under Walter Shaw, the Philadelphia office had been doing about $60 million a year in business. But by the time Gerlach left Philadelphia five years later to take over the Eastern Region from Bob Kupfer, whose responsibilities at Turner International were expanding, Philadelphia's annual volume had almost doubled. Gerlach had managed to maintain the enviable roster of institutional and industrial clients he had inherited from Marshall, including the likes of Penn Mutual Insurance Company and DuPont, and they provided some of the big work that sustained the office. But he and contract manager Donald Turner, a brother of the company's chairman and the father of the future director of national marketing, Tom Turner, had also successfully courted developers like Evans-Pitcairn, which had as a financial base some of the resources of Pittsburgh Plate Glass Company, and Oliver Tyrone, a substantial Pittsburgh-based developer who was a smaller version of John Galbreath. Probably even more significant was Gerlach's success in making committed Turner clients of Radnor Corporation and Chilton Publishing Company, a couple of Sun Oil Company subsidiaries for which the Philadelphia office would do many millions of dollars' worth of construction during the 1970s. Ironically, Gerlach attributes the critical Sun Oil connection to a recommendation made for Turner by a senior person at Evans-Pitcairn, and he attributes the later Oliver Tyrone connection to a recommendation made by a senior person at Sun Oil. But he's quick to emphasize that each of those recommendations was based on someone's good experience with Turner, i.e., they weren't political.

The big Federal Reserve Bank was another big and important Philadelphia job that Gerlach remembers well, but not just for its approximately $50 million cost. What he remembers best is that Chan Turner, no longer chairman but a former general manager of the Philadelphia office, had come down to Philadelphia to head up the interview himself.

Gerlach's most important and enduring success in Philadelphia may have been his role in reaching out into other locations to establish new Turner offices or at least to prepare the ground for establishing them. He studied an array of possible expansion sites and identified two of them as potential Turner offices: one in Pittsburgh and the other in Washington, D.C.

Pittsburgh, where Turner had been doing work for years but where the company hadn't maintained a full-fledged office since it had opened and closed one there in 1919, came first. Even when Turner built the big University of Pittsburgh stadium there in 1925, management had felt it could most effectively handle the work from a Philadelphia base. Except for the two big high-rise Pittsburgh office buildings for U.S. Steel, both of which had been managed by Turner's New York office, everything the company had done there had been built by its Philadelphia territory, and corporate management had never seen a need for reestablishing the office it had discontinued so quickly in 1919. But in 1974 Turner was awarded an approximately $12 million contract to build an especially exquisite museum in Pittsburgh for Richard Mellon Scaife in memory of his mother, Sarah Mellon Scaife, the daughter of Andrew Mellon. Scaife engaged architect Edward Larrabee Barnes to design it, and he engaged Turner to build it. Gerlach assigned responsibility for managing the work to a Turner veteran named Andy Miller, a native Pittsburgher himself who had started with the company on the U.S. Steel job at 525 William Penn Place during the 1950s and had since then managed some of the Philadelphia office's most important work. Only a few months after the Scaife job was started, Mercy Hospital in Pittsburgh contracted with Turner for an approximately $20 million project, and once Miller added that job to his responsibilities the Turner operation in Pittsburgh, still under Philadelphia's management, became substantial. When the administrator for Pittsburgh's Montefiore Hospital called Miller a year or so later to tell him he'd lost confidence in the contractor he'd been using for his hospital's big capital improvement program, the time for a permanent Turner presence in Pittsburgh seemed to have arrived at last. Gerlach moved quickly to secure the necessary approvals from New York, and by 1977 he had put Miller in charge of a new Pittsburgh office.

Washington was next. Turner had been doing some work in and near the District of Columbia for years, going back to the First World War, but it had been sporadic. By the mid-1970s there was an increasing volume of new construction being done in and near the District, the lion's share of it by a few big locally based contractors that included the George Hyman Company (later renamed Clark) and Blake Construction Company, but it wasn't until the government began to accept the idea of negotiating contracts for managing its construction that the picture began to change. In 1975 Turner was awarded a management contract for building the approximately $30 million Federal Home Loan Bank Building in Washington, intensifying the company's interest in the area. When such new work was added to work the company already had in progress at Johns Hopkins University in Baltimore and to the major projects that were expected to come along soon at the National Institutes of Health in Bethesda, momentum for establishing a permanent Turner base in Washington increased. By 1975 Al McNeill, by then a rising vice president who had spent the early 1970s in New York as corporate manager of operations, had arrived in Philadelphia to replace Tom Gerlach as TGM, freeing Gerlach to take over from Bob Kupfer as regional senior vice president for the Eastern Region. McNeill would bring his own considerable energy to the Philadelphia operation, especially to the fledgling Pittsburgh office and to a new office that would start coming to life in Washington early in 1978.

To give Washington a strong start, McNeill tapped J. A. (Jeb) Turner III, who'd by then been with Turner in one way or another for all of his thirty-six years, to manage it. A third-generation Turner, he was born on the very day of the Japanese attack on Pearl Harbor, while his father, J. A. (Jerry) Turner II, himself the son of J. Archer Turner, was working on one of Turner's Pacific Naval Air Base jobs. McNeill completed the core staff in Washington about a year later when he brought Ralph Johnson in as operations manager, and in 1980 Washington became a fully fledged Turner office.

The 1970s were less kind to the Boston territory than they were to some of the others, especially during the early years of the decade. The huge office buildings that had been started there at the end of the very busy 1960s were finishing up, and although there continued to be new work for some of the area colleges and the usual diet of relatively small hospital renovations and additions, the Boston office of the early 1970s found itself relying to a larger extent than it had expected on tenant work in its completed office buildings as an important source of new business. But by 1978, when the growing national resolve to build a new health care infrastructure had begun to translate into construction, things began to turn around in Boston. Several of the hospitals for which the company had been doing the ongoing, small jobs characteristic of such institutions decided to join forces to build an approximately $80 million new hospital they'd call Brigham and Women's, and they hired Turner to manage the work. It was the beginning of a return to prosperity in Boston that would flourish in the 1980s.

Like Boston, New York would see the heady days of the 1960s enter a surprisingly abrupt decline during the early 1970s, with most of the huge office tower jobs winding down and little evidence that there would soon be another wave of such projects in the city to replace them. Health care had begun to gain acceptance as a major public responsibility, and Turner was doing an increasingly large share of the building that would be required to provide it in New York, but such occasional bright spots were tempered by serious problems that were overtaking New York City itself, and Turner wouldn't escape their impact.

Ever since the end of World War II, when the manufacturing firms that had traditionally employed persons of low skills in New York had begun to move their plants to parts of the country where wages and other costs were lower, immigration of the very persons who would normally have looked to such firms for employment had increased dramatically. One result was the city's radically increasing cost to provide the newly arrived, unemployed, and often destitute families with the services and economic help they needed to survive. At the same time, large numbers of middle-class New Yorkers began a sustained flight to the suburbs, harshly undermining the tax base from which the revenues the city needed would have to come. It was a bad situation that was becoming worse every year. Eventually that combination of forces made it virtually impossible for New York City to raise enough money from taxes to pay for the services it was being called on to provide, and by the early 1970s it had become evident that the city had been borrowing heavily to fund its programs, increasing its annual cost of operation and critically undermining its credit. Corporations and urban investors who might have built new facilities in New York began to abandon it in droves, opting for suburban sites or abandoning their construction plans entirely and exacerbating the city's plight. By March 1975, the banks that had been underwriting New York's notes and bonds refused to continue to do so, and it took a coalition of state officials, local pension and union fund managers, and others vitally interested in the city's survival to rescue it from bankruptcy.

A bad situation certainly, especially in an industry in which the two essential fuels of the marketplace are the availability of capital and a high level of confidence that the future is bright enough to justify investing in new construction. In New York, both of those had sunk to perilously low levels by the middle of the 1970s, and the bottom pretty much dropped out of new construction. Turner's New York staff was disheartened, of course, but it was a long way from being immobilized by the situation. Les Shute, who was running the New York territory, was quick to see that some of what was happening in the wake of the City's financial collapse might actually favor Turner over most of its competitors, and he capitalized on an ironic feature of the bad times. Although the rush of big, high-rise buildings had abruptly ended with the financial collapse, some of the city's big corporations had already begun to plan their new headquarters buildings in the suburbs, and the style of what they wanted to build tended to favor Turner over the investment builders with whom Turner sometimes had to compete for high-rise projects in the city itself.

Connecticut General Insurance Company had led the way during the earlier 1960s with the splendid suburban headquarters that Turner had built for it in

Bloomfield, Connecticut, and Turner's longtime client, American Can, followed suit in 1968 with a corporate headquarters building designed by Gordon Bunschaft of Skidmore Owings & Merrill to be built by Turner in Greenwich, Connecticut. At almost 600,000 square feet, the American Can project was a sprawling, low-rise glass-and-concrete structure artfully nestled into the low hills of southern Connecticut to blunt the impact of its intrusion into the suburban landscape. It was the kind of elegant and innovative building that had come to characterize Skidmore's work, with concrete walls sandblasted to reveal a coarse white aggregate imported from Georgia, more single glazing than would have been acceptable a few years later, and with a structural frame of long-span concrete tees precast in New Haven and left exposed without ceilings in most of the building's spaces. The extensive single glazing wasn't the only feature that would have been unlikely in a later design: All the top executives were quartered in an elegant little building of their own, on the same site but separated from the locus of the workers. Bill Arnold, an engineer who would retire from Turner after thirty-eight years in 1990, was project manager on the job, and Bob McBride, a Swarthmore graduate who would retire in 1991, after forty-one years, was project engineer. Bob Nilsson, who would spend much of his later career in Turner International, was in charge of the extensive site-development work that's been described by some as being as dramatically effective as the building itself.

The suburban corporate headquarters building became almost as important a building type for Turner in New York during the 1970s as the high-rise office building had been during the 1960s. Before the end of the decade, the New York territory would build almost $300 million worth of such buildings for some of the largest of the country's corporations, while New York City struggled to regain its balance.

Hospital construction was another specialty that buttressed the New York market in a major way during the 1970s. It had begun to gather momentum during the 1960s, when federal and state funding programs were being designed and implemented, but it wasn't until a little later that it became a major focus for the company in the New York territory. Lincoln Hospital, one of four gigantic new hospitals the city had been planning for years, was, at about $121 million, the first of the very large ones for Turner, which was awarded a contract to manage its construction in 1971. By the end of 1973 Turner in New York had contracts for another half-dozen new hospitals, and by 1977 the New York office was managing construction for, or had recently completed work on, seventeen big hospitals in the region, at a total cost of about $500 million. These were the early years in the growth of a specialty that Turner would not much later come to dominate.

There were many other jobs, of course, including an especially elegant new office building that Roche-Dinkleoo had designed for UNDC, a public-benefit corporation charged with improving the area around the headquarters complex that Turner and its joint venture partners had years earlier built for the United Nations in Manhattan. It would provide high-quality space for visiting dignitaries and offices for some of the embassies and missions in the area, and it was another job on which Turner's competitor, Carl Morse of Morse Diesel Construction Company, had been Turner's advocate on the selection committee.

But with it all, it was becoming an increasingly difficult struggle to secure the high volume of work to which the big New York office had become accustomed and which its staff and facilities had been developed to manage. The robust marketplace that had characterized New York during the 1950s and 1960s had for all practical purposes collapsed, with little evidence that there would be a revival in the near term, and as the later 1970s approached, Turner's management in New York was seeking new work even more aggressively than it had been seeking it before. Bob Marshall and a group of distinguished architects and others in the industry joined forces in a program of seminars that took them around the country to explain and promote the idea of construction management among potential purchasers of new construction, with considerable good effect that was felt mostly in territories other than New York. But no lead that had any promise of producing new business for New York was ignored.

It's been said that there's no worse time for a contractor to be bidding for new work than when it's badly needed. In the late 1970s Turner's New York office joined with two other firms in a joint venture to seek contracts for building what eventually became almost $100 million worth of sewage-treatment structures in the Passaic Valley of New Jersey, and their low bids brought them the job. The company had by then long since drifted away from the hurly-burly of competitive bidding on public works, and it was to regret its return to it. Between a difficult labor setting in New Jersey, a complex and in some respects untested design, and a type of work that departed from most of the company's own recent experience, the Passaic Valley job proved to be a very bad one for Turner. Its joint venture partners performed poorly and eventually approached financial insolvency, creating a setting in which Turner was obliged to carry the burden of completing the work virtually alone. By the time the job was wound up in 1982, the company had lost almost $10 million, exacerbating an already bad situation that would worsen as the New York territory yielded to the temptation to secure additional work in the riskintensive setting of aggressive competitive bidding.

In April 1978, Howard S. Turner, a vigorous sixty-six years old, passed the chairmanship of the company along to its president, Walter B. Shaw, to whom he had a year earlier handed over his responsibilities as chief executive officer. Howard Turner had retained the chairmanship for an extra year at the board's request and would remain on its executive committee for a few years after that, until his retirement. His continuing to serve on the board after his retirement as chairman, as Chan Turner had done before him, didn't require any special action by the board, because an earlier provision originated by Howard Turner himself had exempted retired chairmen from that restriction.

The board he left to Walter B. Shaw was, of course, different from the one he had inherited seven years earlier. Turner executives Wally Creelman, Bob Frost, Herb Pintard, Rosie Rosenburgh, Les Shute, and Chan Turner were all gone. Bob Hollister, who had finished up as manager in Cincinnati, and Charlie Powell, who had been brought to New York some years earlier as an adviser to Walter Shaw, were gone too. Howard Turner remained on the board to serve under Shaw, and the company's management was represented by Herb Church and Tom Gerlach, who had served since 1972; by Herb Conant, who had served since 1973; and by Bob Kupfer, who had served since 1974. Five of the board's twelve directors came from outside the firm: William Greenough, who had retired from Teachers Insurance and Annuity Fund; Charles Wilson, by then retired from Philip Morris; Herbert Johnson, retired from Jones & Laughlin Steel; and John Burns, a private investor. James T. Hill Jr., a director of Alcan Aluminum and of Itek, served on the 1978 board but died within the year and was replaced by Robert W. Lear, an industrialist who was a visiting professor at the Columbia University Graduate School of Business. With 42 percent of the directors now coming from outside the company, Shaw's board was a far cry from the boards of Chan Turner's day.

Howard Turner could certainly reflect on his stewardship with comfort. During his term, stockholders' equity in the company had approximately doubled, to almost $26 million, and earnings were regularly producing (and often exceeding) a return of about 12 percent on net worth. In 1977 alone the company had done work on 150 separate projects that were being managed by its sixteen independent business units, up from the nine units he had inherited in 1971. The increase in the number of independent business units, most of which were as large as (or larger than) any of Turner's local competitors, would become a powerful factor in the company's own growing strength in the national marketplace. By the end of the century, the extension of that growth would place the company in the extraordinary position of being able to do work of almost any size in almost any part of the country, with forces that would effectively combine strong local capability with national management.

When Turner celebrated its seventy-fifth anniversary in 1977, there was a good deal of well-justified pride. A year earlier the company's newly formed Quarter Century Club had inducted into its membership ninety-three employees who been with Turner for twenty-five years or more, and with a backlog of almost $2 billion in contracts to be executed over the next few years there was optimism almost everywhere.

13.

Shaw

Walter Shaw was a soft-spoken, pipe-smoking man whose style as chairman was entirely different from his predecessor's. His old friend Bob Marshall, who'd been close to Shaw since the two had worked together on the Princeton Library job just after they had returned from navy service and who became his vice chairman in 1978, has described Shaw as less assertive than Howard Turner but substantially more sensitive to the thinking of his board. Shaw was the popular son of a former vice president and treasurer of Turner, and although he had already loyally served many years on the board under Howard Turner, whose vigor had never waned, he brought his own approach to the job.

He was an optimistic man, and in 1978 there appeared to be plenty of justification for optimism. The annual volume of work in place and corporate earnings were both at record levels and increasing every year, and even young subsidiaries like Turner Development Corporation and Turner International, a couple of Shaw's special interests, had survived some difficult years and were showing signs of turning around. The company's $2 billion backlog of future work was bigger than it had ever been, and it was hard to imagine that the future was anything but bright.

Almost as soon as Shaw took over the chairmanship, an extraordinary job came along that would certainly have offended the Quaker sensibilities of the founding Turner and might even have given some pause to his less conservative son Chan.

It was a huge gambling casino that Bally Manufacturing Company was planning for Atlantic City, New Jersey, the emerging East Coast Babylon that was being developed to challenge the well-established one in Las Vegas. By 1978 Bally, the country's leading manufacturer of equipment for the gaming industry, had been envying the profitability of some of its vastly successful customers for a long time. Bally had started almost fifty years earlier as Lion Manufacturing Company, specializing in the manufacture of pinball machines, and later, as Bally Manufacturing Company, it had moved into the business of making slot machines. It had grown quickly into a large company whose shares in 1969 began trading on the major stock exchanges, and it wasn't long before internal pressures to become even bigger began to intensify. By 1978 a plan to enter the casino business itself had been ratified by its board, and the company had engaged the prestigious architectural firm of Skidmore Owings & Merrill to design what it hoped would be the most spectacular of a new crop of gambling casinos, complete with full-service hotels and parking structures, that were beginning to emerge in Atlantic City.

Of course, a big gambling casino in Atlantic City didn't look like a job that Turner was likely to get, although Bally was in the process of assembling a waterfront property that was occupied by a couple of grand old hotels, of which one already had a place in Turner's history. Its plan was to renovate the Dennis Hotel, which Turner had built back in the 1920s (when Turner dominated the construction of seaside hotels in Atlantic City) and to demolish the Marlborough-Blenheim. Bally was already working with another contractor, and until the fellow made an ethical blunder, it didn't look like there was any likelihood that there would be a place for Turner on the new job. The errant contractor had acquired a financial interest in the ownership of one of the hotels that Bally needed, apparently expecting that the acquisition would force his selection for the construction contract, but Bally was so resentful of the tactic that it dismissed the contractor and brought in Turner, whose integrity was well known. The project that emerged would come about as close to being a war campaign as anything Turner had done since the days of the Pacific Naval Air Base contract.

The job would include demolition (by implosion) of one hotel, an addition and renovations to about half a million square feet of space in another new construction of almost a million square feet of casino and related space (including fifteen restaurants) as well as construction of a structure for about 2,000 cars. It was all to be designed and built within a little less than one year. Unlike war work, there weren't any lives at stake, but there was plenty of money at stake, and the incentives to spend everything it would take to build such an enormous complex in such an extraordinarily short time were compelling. One such incentive was a multi-million-dollar tax credit that would no longer be Bally's if the casino failed to open during 1979. Another was what was being estimated as a daily gambling revenue exceeding half a million dollars, starting on opening day.

Bill Arnold, by that time a twenty-four-year Turner veteran who been with the company since his days at Harvard and Cooper Union, was selected as project executive with Tom Gerlach as officer-in-charge. While Skidmore Owings & Merrill moved ahead with the design, and while permission was being sought from the Landmarks Commission to demolish the Marlborough-Blenheim, Turner began excavation and pouring of foundations within the very footprint of one of the existing hotels. Orders for structural steel were placed without benefit of details, on the basis that everything would be worked out at the shop drawing stage, and orders for large quantities of granite were placed on a similar basis to ensure timely fabrication and delivery. A Turner staff of fifty-four was developed to supervise a workforce that would reach 2,700, and by some accounts the area began to look more like the Normandy beaches on the day of the Allied landings than like a construction site.

The pace never slackened. As the deadline drew closer, Bally authorized Turner to go to a seven-day workweek, but at that point Turner drew the line: Conditions had already reduced productivity to dangerously low levels and it was felt that any further acceleration would produce nothing but higher costs. By October, Bally's people were beginning to install their own elaborate equipment in preparation for a December opening, and just before Christmas 1979, the job was finished. Gamblers thronged the place, eager to spend as much of their money as they could, the restaurants were filled, the hotel was fully booked, the State of

New Jersey was delighted to have added another big revenue generator in Atlantic City, and Bally, which had by then paid (or committed to) Turner almost $210 million, was happy. Years later, Bally would be acquired by Hilton Hotels for about $2 billion, and some time after that the firm would become independent again and join with a number of other major casino operators to become the biggest gaming firm in the country.

Turner was, of course, pleased that it had been able to do the nearly impossible job it had been assigned, and it was certainly not unhappy about collecting its fee. But there were some in Turner whose views about the job were mixed. The company had built a reputation for being able to do even its biggest and most challenging work efficiently and economically, and the idea of throwing economy to the winds, even when directed by the client to do so, wasn't universally popular at Turner.

Not all of what was going on during those late years of the 1970s was as colorful or as profitable as the Bally job, but there was enough of it to increase the total volume of construction that Turner put in place in 1979 to $1.5 billion. That was almost twice what the company had done during the previous year and it was profitable enough to increase net earnings proportionately. Nineteen seventy-nine was the first year in the company's history in which its annual volume exceeded a billion dollars, and although there were variations from region to region it was a success that owed something to each of its territories.

Although this significantly increased volume of business that Turner was doing included its usual wide variety of work, it was probably the acceleration of health care construction in the East and in the Midwest that was driving the latest surge, punctuated by an occasional job for one or another of the pharmaceutical manufacturers who were gearing up for the related profusion of activity their industry was still to experience. In 1979, forty-nine separate hospital jobs were active in Turner's Eastern Region alone, including twelve that had been started that year and including some that would lead to more and even bigger work at the medical centers of Yale University and the University of Pennsylvania and at the new teaching hospital complex that the State of New York was building in Stony Brook, Long

Island. The building of new health care facilities had spread to the Washington, D.C., area, where Turner was almost a third of the way along on about $100 million worth of work at the National Institutes of Health in Maryland, a job that would be at the heart of a later decision to give Turner's Washington office full credentials as a stand-alone territory.

The big new health care market was at its most intense in the easternmost population centers, where facilities built early in the century had long since begun to wear out and needed to be replaced. But a similar picture was developing inland too. By the end of the '70s more than one-third of the value of all projects being done by the combined territories of Cincinnati, Cleveland, Columbus, and Detroit were classified as health care or hospital work.

As the 1980s came into view, something else was happening that would affect the company's workload every bit as profoundly as the health care work and that would drive Turner's volume to even higher levels during the years to follow. The urban centers of the country, where overbuilding, social turmoil, and in some cases economic collapse had until about the middle of the 1970s tended to discourage new commercial construction, were now beginning to rebuild. And where Turner's share of such major commercial work in the past had been dominated by contracts with big insurance companies and other major corporations, now an increasing share of it would come from large, well-financed private-sector developers who saw Turner as the builder of choice.

Part of such work continued to be big construction for Turner's old and intensely loyal friends in the Galbreath Company, which was still a major developer of high-end commercial properties throughout the country. But by the end of the 1970s some effective Galbreath competitors had begun to surface, and within the decade that followed, especially strong ones like Gerald Hines, Boston Properties, Oliver Tyrone, Tishman Speyer, and Maguire Thomas would become major factors in Turner's work.

Of course, not all the new developers were as big as Galbreath, or even as big as Hines and the others. In Chicago a pair of smaller developers named Marvin Romanek and Eugene Golub had already proved to be every bit as committed to

Turner as their larger competitors. Romanek and Golub had started out by developing some properties in Chicago without Turner, but as soon as they entered the business of higher-quality, high-rise buildings they began a long association with the company, which assigned Anton (Tony) Bajuk to manage their work in the field. By that time it had been almost twenty years since Bajuk had come to the United States from his native Slovenia to study at Harvard, where a student group was underwriting the expenses of displaced European students. He'd gone to work for Turner as soon as he graduated and had been with the company almost continuously ever since. Once he started running Turner's Romanek-Golub work he never quit, moving from one such Turner-built project to another until his retirement in 1982. Bajuk remembers the Turner relationship with Romanek-Golub as one of mutual confidence and trust, never burdened by a dispute that couldn't be easily resolved between the two parties and never once disturbed by the word "lawyer." The jobs went smoothly and successfully, the hard work occasionally leavened by humor. Their Xerox Center project, a twenty-seven-story Chicago office building designed by C. F. Murphy's Helmut Jahn (and named for the copier maker even though it had leased only two floors), was distinguished by its insistent whiteness. Its exterior panels had been painted a brilliant white in the factory, and its big entrance lobby was finished in white marble. On the day the building was dedicated, Bajuk remembers hearing one visitor ask when the patient was going to be wheeled in.

In Pittsburgh, where the company's work had been pretty much dominated by hospitals since the finishing touches had been put on the big U.S. Steel building in 1971, a profusion of very large commercial office buildings began about 1978. Turner was by then working on preconstruction studies for a glorious metal-and-glass skyscraper that PPG was planning in the heart of Pittsburgh's Golden Triangle, right in the shadow of buildings that Turner had already built and within a few blocks of the half dozen or so other office towers that it would build there within the next few years. PPG's plan was to occupy its new building as a corporate headquarters but to provide enough extra space to accommodate a few other high-quality tenants, including Duquesne Light Company, the local public utility. But competition for such attractive tenants was keen in 1978, and while PPG was negotiating with Duquesne, a local developer named Eddie Lewis with plans for his own grand new office building made Duquesne an offer it was not inclined to refuse: Lewis's Oxford Development Company offered to buy the aging downtown building in which Duquesne had been operating for years as a quid pro quo for taking space in the spectacular high-rise that Oxford was planning to build only a few blocks away. Duquesne accepted. Lewis had commissioned Turner's good friends at Hellmuth, Obata + Kassabaum (HOK) to design an approximately 1-million-square-foot high-rise tower he'd call Oxford Center, and once he had the signature of his prime tenant all that remained was to find the money to pay for the place and the right contractor to build it. He was able to find both when he met with the top brass at Mellon Bank, in the building Turner had built for Mellon and its cousins at U.S. Steel a couple of decades earlier. Mellon's management liked everything about the building Lewis was proposing, but they wanted to know more about who would be doing the construction. It wasn't until Lewis assured them that it would be built by Turner, who had successfully done an especially nasty, smaller job for him in nearby Monroeville a few years earlier, that Mellon agreed to finance the project.

Those were heady days for Turner's Andy Miller and his Pittsburgh staff. Even as they were gearing up for the work on Oxford Center and continuing with their preconstruction work for PPG, they were called in by U.S. Steel to discuss a project that would be even bigger than Oxford Center and only a few hundred yards away from it. As part of its investment in Pittsburgh's renaissance, U.S. Steel was going to develop a big commercial office building for its own investment on a nearby site then occupied by the Carelton House Hotel, which it planned to demolish by implosion. The new building's main tenant was to be the Dravo Company, the venerable engineering and construction giant that had been in Pittsburgh for generations, and U.S. Steel had commissioned Welton Becket, the California-based architect, to design an approximately 1.7-million-square-foot skyscraper around Dravo's sometimes special needs. After all the work Turner had done for Big Steel there wasn't much need for them to get to know each other, and by spring 1980 Turner had a contract to build what by then was being called the Dravo Building. Now the relatively young Turner office that Andy Miller was running had its share of big new work, and it was ready for it.

Eddie Lewis at Oxford wanted to be the first to offer high-quality new space to Pittsburgh firms, and he worried a little that Turner's big contract with U.S. Steel might slow things down on his job, but he accepted Andy Miller's assurance that Turner wouldn't allow that to happen. Later, when Miller proposed buying the structural steel for Lewis's building from U.S. Steel (a matter addressed on Lewis's yacht off Nantucket Island), Miller's assurances that Turner's order for the Lewis job would be well treated (even though U.S. Steel and Lewis were in a race to finish in time to capture tenants) carried the day.

Into this increasingly intense environment another rising development group came along in 1980, with plans for staking its own claim in Pittsburgh, its hometown. The Oliver Tyrone group was planning a twenty-five-story, cast-in-place headquarters building for National Steel Company there and it awarded Turner a contract to build it as well as two similar (but not identical) office buildings, one in Philadelphia and one in Cleveland.

By that time Turner in Pittsburgh was about as busy at it could justify being, and Miller and his colleagues in the Grant Street office decided that for a while, at least, what they were doing was going to have to be enough. Between these jobs and the rest of their work, they clearly weren't going to be able to do the big PPG job for which drawings were approaching completion. When PPG asked Turner to bid against two other firms for its construction contract, Miller declined, leaving the job to be won by a joint venture of Pittsburgh-based Mellon Stuart and Washington's Hyman (later Clark) Construction Company.

The cast of characters who figure in Turner's early 1980s Pittsburgh history didn't end there. By the time the steel frame for the Dravo Building was topped out in 1982, the fortunes of the Dravo Company itself had declined, and Dravo realized that it wouldn't be able to use the space it had contracted for after all. But the market for such space in thriving Pittsburgh was good, and the Mellon Bank itself, bursting at the seams in its Pittsburgh quarters, was seeking new space in which to consolidate its far-flung staff. Mellon acquired the lease rights from Dravo, became U.S. Steel's tenant, and the building became One Mellon Bank Center. By the time construction of the building began to draw to a close, the prosperous Mellon Bank decided it didn't want to be anyone's tenant after all and purchased the whole building, lock, stock, and barrel. For Turner, it was all in a day's work.

Elsewhere, although the important niche that Turner had carved out for itself in the West during the mid-1960s had grown broader and deeper, the momentum of high-rise construction had begun to diminish in southern California and some of Turner's attention had shifted to the strong start it had made in the Bay Area up north around San Francisco. By 1977 the City of San Francisco had selected Turner from a competing array of some of the country's most prominent contractors to manage construction of what would be called the Moscone Convention Center, a contract that is thought by some to have been critical to Turner's eventual dominance of the market for major building work in northern California and the Northwest.

Moscone was the wave of the future. For the Bay Area itself, it would prove to be an immensely successful convention center and a valued community resource, built almost entirely underground and designed to support landscaped recreation areas and low-rise community-sponsored structures on its ground-level roof in a style that would satisfy even the harshest critics of urban development. For HOK and T. Y. Lin, its gifted architects and structural engineers, Moscone was the locus of some of their most demanding and brilliant work: seven acres of column-free underground space built below the water table, designed to accommodate severe seismic forces and covered by long-span, cast-in-place reinforced concrete arches built to support extraordinary loads. For Turner, which had the job of putting it all together, Moscone was the ultimate in construction management and a model for a great deal of future work that Turner would undertake as a construction manager. Doug Meyer was brought out from the big Johns Manville job in Denver to build the Moscone Center, and everything from such nonconstruction issues as bonds and legal conflicts to the planning and scheduling of concrete pours was considered to be within the scope of Turner's management responsibilities. Starting before the architect was selected, Turner had been scheduling and consulting on major elements of the process for almost two years before field construction actually began. Ultimately the company would award and manage the work of more than thirty individual trade contracts. Dick Dorais, then a young Turner engineer who more than twenty years later would become general manager of the company's entire Western Region, remembers being the first Turner person to work at Moscone and the last to leave when the job was finished in 1982.

By 1982 Turner in San Francisco had put the Moscone job pretty much behind it, a highly visible and effective tribute to the construction-management approach, and the company was starting to look northward for further development of satellite offices it had opened in Seattle and Portland. Down south in L.A. — soon to come under Barry Sibson's management — Turner was poised at the edge of a new period of growth that would make it the West's dominant builder.

The rush of urban high-rises that had been built by Turner in southern California during the late 1960s and early 1970s had set a pace that would be hard to maintain, and those years were followed in the region by a period in which the company would content itself with a palette of often large but less spectacular urban and suburban work and would seek to diversify its markets. It was during that period that the construction-management approach that had gained favor back east and that would work so well in San Francisco had first been explored by a few private owners and public agencies who were planning major construction programs in the southern California. Moscone was a useful and convincing model, of course, but anything that departed from the traditional process of completing all the construction documents and then finding a low bidder was still seen by many in the region as untested.

In fact, the line between traditional construction contracting and what was being called construction management was less clear than some thought. Within Turner, construction management was being defined as an arrangement in which the firm performed no actual construction with forces in its own employ (except for "general conditions" work) and in which contracts for construction were established directly between the performing contractors and the owner, preserving the public bidding methodology normally required by law and ensuring that the managing contractor would not be placed at risk. There was occasionally some irony in the interpretation of just what was really meant by construction management, as in the case in which Johns Manville Company had only a few years earlier attributed some of its preference for engaging Turner on its Denver project to Turner's advocacy of the construction-management approach and had then awarded it a guaranteed-maximum-price contract that put the company squarely at risk.

But despite lingering resistance to the construction-management method, conditions that argued for shortening the time between the start of design and the completion of construction (especially with double-digit inflation dramatizing the need for speed) were strengthening the case for Turner's new approach, and Barry Sibson knew it. In 1975 he heard about a bidding disaster on the new complex that had been designed for the County of Ventura in southern California, and he correctly sensed that he had found an ideal setting for advocating and applying the construction-management method to this public-sector project.

After years of planning and design by Ventura County and its consultants, bids had come in far over their $60 million budget. The County had fired its architect and a slew of consultants and was looking for a new direction when Sibson presented his proposal to manage the whole process. Turner was engaged to work with the architectural offices of John Carl Warnecke and Daniel Dworsky, first to provide preconstruction services during the design phase and later to manage the construction process itself. The program proved hugely successful, leading first to a series of additional projects for the County and then, in Sibson's view, contributing substantially to the widespread acceptance of construction management that would lie at the heart of Turner's success in California during the 1980s.

Almost simultaneously, Cabot, Cabot & Forbes, for whom Turner had done work back east, came into southern California with a contract for Turner to manage construction of a new high-rise office building on Wilshire Boulevard, putting Turner back in the high-rise business in Los Angeles for the first time since it had finished the Security Bank job there earlier in the 1970s. It would prove to be the beginning of a new and even more spectacular period of high-rise construction for Turner in the West.

The late 1970s and the early 1980s were good times for the company in most of its territories, but beneath the surface of some of these often dazzling successes there were occasional reminders of just how difficult it could be to maintain profitable dominance in a volatile and risk-intensive industry like construction. In fact, although Turner was certainly extremely well positioned during the late 1970s, things weren't quite as good as they seemed. Double-digit cost inflation and other factors had sometimes clouded the significance of the data, and although volume and earnings had indeed increased by about 40 percent and 60 percent, respectively, during the years since 1970, the dollar volume of all nonresidential construction in the country at large had increased by about 75 percent during that period. Turner's share of the national market had actually shrunk. And while Turner Development Corporation and Turner International had managed to keep their heads above water, neither had yet faced the harsh tests that would come their way during the decade that was to follow.

In addition, with an expanded and more decentralized staff managing an increasing variety of projects that now extended into twenty-six states, jobs that actually lost money were starting to surface a little more frequently and sometimes more severely than they had in the past. An occasional bad job had always been a fact of life at Turner, as it is in any construction company, and although its occurrence at Turner had certainly become less common since the days when a significant fraction of the company's work had been secured through competitive bidding, the occasional losing project had never entirely disappeared. Even the most profound strategies hadn't yet been able to eliminate the possibility that the cost of a complex construction project might exceed the prediction of even the most experienced cost estimators. Sophisticated risk-management systems were still a few years away, but as the size and variety of the company's work and interests increased, its risks were growing proportionately.

When Walter Shaw's term as chairman started, the contract for the first of the ill-fated pollution control projects in the Passaic Valley of New Jersey was still too new for Turner's management to realize that there was a potential for losses that would eventually reach $10 million, but the seriousness of that problem would soon be known. And it wasn't the only job that would trouble Turner during the waning years of the 1970s and the early ones of the 1980s. In Boston one of the most celebrated construction projects of the decade, I. M. Pei's splendid John F. Kennedy Library, was another. Don Denman, a senior Turner superintendent who had been with the company since he had received his engineering degree from Colorado State University in 1961 and who would be the job's field superintendent, had his first real sense of just how determined the company had been to get the contract when he heard that Turner's bid had been substantially lower than the bid of its closest competitor. It didn't take long for Denman to realize that this was a job on which a tight price had an especially strong potential for leading to serious trouble. His boss was Jack Greenip, Turner's project executive for the job, and Greenip's recollections of how things played out are vivid and not all pleasant. Methane gas had to be exhausted from the former garbage-disposal area on which the building was sited, and the process took longer than expected, driving the schedule for concrete work (which was being done by Turner's own forces) into one of New England's bad winters. Random debris long buried in the fill obstructed the driving of some of the precast-concrete piles, and an interpretation by the architect and his consultants required that Turner absorb the extra costs generated by having to abandon partially driven piles and drive new ones. It got worse. As soon as the building began to emerge from its foundations, its extraordinary role as a national monument of unique historical importance began to dominate almost everything that was to be done. Normally tolerated standards of workmanship that sometimes fell short of published standards would not be acceptable on this special and highly visible job, and a level of workmanship would be required that would be extremely difficult to meet and, of course, very expensive to maintain. Everything from the precast-concrete panels that enclosed most of the building to the drywall partitions that subdivided its interiors were rigorously controlled to ensure that not even the slightest departure from specified tolerances would be allowed. Thought was given by some of Turner's field staff to seeking financial relief to deal with the cost of meeting such extraordinarily high standards, but senior management in the company was resolved to do what had to be done without protest, and no request for relief was made. No expense was spared. By the middle of 1979, when it was understood that a grand opening of the library in the fall could be an asset in Ted Kennedy's campaign for the presidential nomination, Turner went on to subsidize premium costs to ensure that work on this already-losing job would be completed in time. When the library was dedicated on schedule in October 1979, and some of the donations that had made it all possible were publicly acknowledged, few in the audience realized that one of the largest of all the contributions might well have been Turner's unmentioned, involuntary donation of almost $1 million, its final loss on the project.

The Kennedy Library was far from the worst of the bad jobs of the period. That distinction went to the approximately $100 million skyscraper that Turner built for IBM in New York City, starting in 1978. The IBM job had come along at the end of what had been several years of relatively hard and worsening times in New York, and for Turner it promised to be the end of a downward slide in the fortunes of the New York territory. Financial problems had earlier in the decade brought the City of New York to the brink of bankruptcy, and although a rescue of sorts had been effected, the atmosphere that followed in the wake of the crisis had discouraged investors from going ahead with the kind of big commercial buildings that had become Turner's specialty.

IBM had wisely seen the late seventies as a good time for getting a low price on a new building, and they engaged Edward Larrabee Barnes to design a first-class divisional headquarters for them and for a few of their subsidiaries. Located at the corner of Fifty-seventh Street and Madison Avenue in New York, its cost would be more than ten times the cost of the Kennedy Library, but as things turned out, the two jobs would share a few important characteristics: Both the Kennedys and IBM had opted to select their contractors through a process of competitive bidding, and in both cases Turner would be dangerously eager to get the job. Otherwise, of course, they were entirely different projects, and the details of what generated problems for Turner illustrate the almost limitless variety of hazards inherent in the business of contract construction. In this case, Turner's price for the job proved to be extremely close to the price quoted by its nearest competitor, generating some unjustified confidence that it was an entirely safe bid, and the IBM award was celebrated in the Turner office as the beginning of better days for the New York territory. But what developed during the months that followed told a different story.

The bidding period for the IBM job, as for most such jobs, was brief and intense, and proposals from hundreds of subcontractors found their way into the offices of all the contractors bidding for the general contract. Unlike the controlled process in which a previously selected general contractor is able to ensure that every subcontractor is well qualified, the uncontrolled open competition on the IBM job allowed some subcontractors who wouldn't normally meet Turner's standards to enter the mix, and in an environment of intense competition and limited time it was hard to screen them out. The contractor who fails to integrate into his own bid the low, unsolicited proposal of any subcontractor risks the possibility of losing ground to every competitor who does use it, and while the price of using such bids can be high, the pressure to use them can be intense. In the fiercely competitive environment of New York in the late 1970s Turner found itself engaging subcontractors it would later wish it had never seen.

The first sign of serious trouble came even before much of the new construction had been put in place. The massive volume of earth and rock that had to be excavated and removed from a site that lay at the very heart of New York's commercial center proved to be too much for the subcontractor Turner had engaged for the work, and before that big task was anywhere near finished the subcontractor ran out of money. To avoid irreparable damage to the schedule, Turner subsidized what remained of the excavation work, at a cost that exceeded the amount of the original subcontract, and by the time the foundation work was completed, the cost of the IBM job had begun to exceed Turner's estimate. Later the electrical contractor failed, shattering another vital link in the process. This time Turner elected to replace the failed subcontractor with a stronger one. But by the time a suitable replacement firm could be identified and a new contract for the partially completed work could be established, a steeply escalating market had increased the price by several million dollars, drawing the job farther into the red. There were like stories for three other major subcontracts, each requiring that Turner absorb the much higher cost of a replacement subcontractor. It was impossible to prevent such events from slowing the progress of the work, and Turner slipped farther behind schedule, lower in the owner's esteem, and deeper into a financial hole. Exacerbating the situation, a torrent of changes in design to accommodate the owner's shifting objectives continued, slowing things further and contributing to a general decline of morale. By the time the work was finished, the IBM job had taken almost two years longer than Turner had estimated and the company had sustained an out-of-pocket loss that exceeded $14 million, the worst single loss in its history.

Over a period of the next half-dozen years there would be more of these serious losses, involving only a relatively small fraction of the company's jobs but averaging a total of almost $10 million per year.

The bad news about these and other troubled jobs worried Walter Shaw, and it came to him at a time when he was beginning to consider seriously a plan for identifying and grooming someone to succeed him in the leadership of the firm. Late in 1979 he made a move intended to address both those matters: He traveled out to the Midwest to meet with Herb Conant, who was senior vice president in charge of the Central Region, with the idea of bringing him into New York. Unlike Shaw, most of whose career had been spent on the sales side of the business, Conant was essentially a construction man. But Shaw had known Conant since his own days as territory general manager (TGM) in Chicago, when Conant was managing jobs there, and he'd followed his successful management of the Cleveland office after that, so he'd seen a good deal more than just a good construction man in him for some time. Conant had produced big volumes and superior earnings wherever he'd been and since 1975 he'd been running the Central Region as senior vice president. His style, influenced more by the job site than by the conference rooms in which Shaw had done most of his work, didn't always accord with the style that had characterized earlier Turner presidents, but in 1979 Shaw was becoming convinced that Conant was a promising candidate and that New York would be a good place to have a closer look at him. And besides, Shaw needed a top construction man at his side to address New York's recent spate of bad jobs and to restore the company's most active territory to good health. The timing for a trial run was good, and Shaw offered Conant the executive vice presidency of the company, with a New York base and responsibility for all domestic construction operations. By 1980 Conant had moved east.

Herb Conant had been opposed to the idea of Turner's securing new work by bidding competitively since his earliest days in the company, and what he found in New York strengthened his resolve to put an end to the practice. He simply felt that competing on the basis of price was not the way for Turner to get work. Everything Turner taught its people, he reasoned, flew in the face of the competitive-bidding approach. The company's strength lay in working with owners and architects from the very beginning, and its traditional objective in estimating cost was to ensure that there would be enough money budgeted to do what was wanted and needed, not to establish a level that would be low enough to underbid a competitor. Conant felt strongly that subcontractors needed to be screened for quality and perform-ance before their prices could be considered, and he saw that process as being threatened by the lump-sum bidding approach. If the company was going to con-tinue to see itself as the owner's partner, he argued, it should secure new work by selling its services, not by being the lowest bidder. Conant had no illusions about the discipline required to stay with such a policy through tough periods like the ones that had brought these bad jobs into the New York territory. His policy was to ride them out: hunker down, he advised, cut back, and wait until things get better. Turner would continue to submit occasional competitive bids after Conant went to New York, more often in some territories (and subsidiaries) than in others, but their frequency would diminish and, except in locations where the tradition was simply too deeply entrenched, Conant's arrival in New York would mark the begin-ning of a clear decline in competitive bidding in most of Turner's offices.

Of course, it didn't take Conant long, once he arrived in New York, to take the full measure of the situation there, and he took it head on. He assembled a new management organization for the region, one that was designed to complete quickly and cut losses on bad jobs that were already winding down and to revitalize the company's approach to bad jobs that hadn't yet unleashed their full fury. During his years in the Midwest he had come to know and assess Turner people across the country through interregional meetings the company regularly held to encourage information exchanges and the like. Now he reached out for a few of the men he regarded as being especially well qualified for what he wanted to do. He split the big Eastern Region into two parts, bringing in Al McNeill, a future chairman, from his job as TGM in Philadelphia to manage one of them and assigning Tom Gerlach, the previous Eastern Region manager, the job of running the other. McNeill's new region would at first include the troubled New York territory, as well as Pittsburgh, Philadelphia, and Boston; Gerlach's would include Washington, Miami, and a few subsidiary companies Turner had by then acquired in the South. McNeill had already established himself as a results-oriented construction man, well suited to the daunting problems in New York, and he'd soon have jobs like the IBM job reorganized to ensure that what was needed to get them finished would be effectively done in the least possible time. Within a little more than a year of his arrival at the corporate center, Conant would bring in Hal Parmelee, who had been TGM in Boston, to manage the New York territory itself. Step by step the problems were addressed, the losses were absorbed, and the hard work of getting these big and often nasty jobs built and finished went forward. Ten years later, McNeill and Parmelee would be chairman and president of Turner.

Conant didn't limit his management changes to the Eastern Region. He had soon extended some of them across the country. Chicago, normally seen as the center of the Midwest, had originally been made a part of the Western Region as a way of equalizing the annual volumes of the three regions, but by 1980 the Western Region had developed plenty of work of its own, and Conant shifted the big Chicago territory into the Central Region. He tapped Herb Church, who had at different times managed both the Chicago territory and the Western Region, to manage the Central Region.

Out in the Far West Conant selected Herb Pintard to be senior vice president in charge of the Western Region and Barry Sibson to replace him as TGM for the Los Angeles territory. Sibson, who had learned his civil engineering at Dartmouth and at Stanford's graduate school, had started with the company in Philadelphia and had been doing sales for Turner in Los Angeles since about 1971. Pintard, another civil engineer from Penn State, was a popular and well-regarded operations man who had started with Turner back east in 1942 and had come out to California with Turner's first contingent in the mid-1960s. He was almost ready for retirement at the time of his selection to run the region, and within a couple of years, when he did retire, Gene von Wening would step in to succeed him as manager of the Western Region.

Conant's decision to start by fielding his own management team solidified his control. He supplemented it by adding new systems and by refining others. He brought Bob Meyer with him from Cleveland, where Meyer had been regional financial manager for the Central Region and had raised the company's critical Indicated Outcome Report to a new level of effectiveness for anticipating and managing risks. This report, prepared approximately quarterly by each Turner office to define the real status of each job and to identify developing problems early enough to allow for remediation, had been in use in Turner for years but had been sometimes indifferently treated by territory managers and occasionally used by some to justify optimistic projections. Meyer, an engineer who had started with Turner in Philadelphia in 1964, had early on gravitated to the financial side of the work and had been especially effective at developing and analyzing material that provided the regional manager with a level of insight he needed to ward off trouble. Conant had seen Meyer's work as key to some of his own successes in the Central Region and when he brought him to New York he made him a vice president with responsibility for cost management throughout the country.

It wasn't long before things began to look better in New York, but before there was any celebration of a recovery, another large and prestigious job, New York's Museum of Modern Art, would show signs that it might rival IBM as a catastrophic loss. Ironically, this job hadn't been secured by bidding, but Turner had guaranteed its cost from documents that were too far from completion to justify the confidence

Turner placed in them. Between poor estimates that somehow escaped the notice of busy senior managers and poorly selected subcontractors, the job had added more red ink to Turner's books, further slowing the painful recovery from earlier disasters.

But eventually all these jobs would be completed and replaced by profitable new ones and the New York territory would begin to resume its role as a major contributor to the firm's volume and earnings. Fewer than ten years later, the New York territory would be at the center of the company's renaissance.

A few years earlier than all this, as part of an effort to increase the company's national market share, Walter Shaw had taken a closer look at the geographic pattern of its work and had been struck by its consistent failure to make a real showing in the South. There had been limited progress from the Atlanta effort, but greater success in Florida, where by the end of the 1970s Turner's Jack Woolf (still operating from a New York base) had established a modest presence for Turner. The Florida success had been achieved mainly through early work in the northern part of the state, some of it on a job for Disney at Lake Buena Vista, and later it would begin to include a share of the luxury housing that was at the core of south Florida's revival as a refuge for affluent northerners fleeing cold winters. But despite these jobs, Turner was at the end of the 1970s still in the process of seeking a significant foothold in the region and had not yet become a serious presence south of the Mason-Dixon Line.

In Turner's boardroom there had been consensus that the company was unlikely ever to penetrate the South until it abandoned its unyielding loyalty to the concept of a strictly union, closed shop. There had been a continuing national decline in union membership since the end of World War II, from about 35 percent of the national labor force to about 20 percent, and in the South in the late seventies union representation in the construction trades was a good deal smaller than that. Since its earliest days, Turner had employed only union tradesmen and had subcontracted work only to firms that operated on the same basis, so a change to an open-shop mode wasn't going to be easy. But it was decided that such a move was justified and that the time seemed about right. An effort was launched to find one or more well-regarded, open-shop general contracting firms in the South that might be available for acquisition. Such firms fairly regularly presented themselves to Turner for acquisition, but until 1978 the company hadn't been much interested.

The first of several such prospects came along in that year. Three partners in Temple, Texas, had decided to retire and were offering for sale the two general contracting firms that they had been operating successfully there for years. Their BFW Construction Company, which did the larger jobs, regularly operated in what was called an "area practice" mode that was largely open shop, and their Belco Construction Company stuck to a fully open-shop mode of operation. Between the two firms, they were doing close to $50 million worth of work a year; both were lean and aggressive, and both were accustomed to and entirely comfortable in a market where virtually every job was secured by being the low bidder, which was just what the company would soon be seeking to avoid. Their management had little taste for sophisticated control systems and the like, but they were succeeding in what they were doing and they looked like a couple of firms that had the capacity to function as a Texas profit center for Turner. The board decided to take a chance.

To ensure that such acquisitions as BFW and Belco would be able to operate entirely independently of what came to be called "Big Turner," the board in 1978 established a subsidiary it called TOS (Turner Open Shop) as a holding company to acquire the new firms, and it put New York's Ed Clarke in charge. Clarke, who had been with Turner since his Army Air Force days in World War II, had been managing some of the company's important work and he represented Turner on the AGC committee that was concerned with labor relations. He brought an especially appropriate and useful perspective to his new role. By the middle of 1978, TOS had acquired the two Texas firms, with an essentially laissez-faire policy of control intended to allow them to operate pretty much as they always had, and under their own management.

Less than a year later, while the Texas firms were settling into their new roles as Turner subsidiaries, Turner acquired F. N. Thompson Construction Company, a similar firm based in Charlotte, North Carolina. Thompson was an open-shop firm doing about half the combined annual volume of the two Texas firms, but a good share of its business was being secured through negotiation rather than through competitive bidding, and Thompson's management was generally more accepting of the control systems that Ed Clarke and his board needed for maintaining oversight from New York.

By the early part of 1981, the Texas and North Carolina acquisitions were contributing approximately as expected to the gross volume and earnings of the company, and a third company, the H. W. Pearce Company (with its subsidiary Universal Construction Company) of Decatur, Alabama, became available for purchase. Pearce was about the size of Thompson and, like the others, was a well-established, open-shop southern contracting firm doing its share of the good business of its area. Turner added Pearce to its growing southern organization.

With the Pearce acquisition in 1981, Turner was well along in its campaign to establish a southern presence. By 1982 the new southern holdings were contributing a combined annual volume that approached 7 percent of the company's gross business, together with modest earnings. The Pearce acquisition stumbled briefly about a year after the purchase when Pearce's son left, to be followed by his father a couple of years later, but its Universal Construction Company would continue as an effective and productive open-shop subsidiary.

In spite of their modest success, the southern acquisitions hadn't really achieved anything like the penetration that Walter Shaw and his board had been seeking. Turner's research had shown that there was almost as much open-shop work being done in the United States as there was closed-shop work, most of it in the South, and these small firms the company had acquired simply weren't big enough to capture more than a small share of it. Such a vast, untapped market was thought to be too big for Turner to ignore. What Shaw came to think would make more sense for the company was a big, open-shop firm of its own: not another acquisition, but an organization that Turner would generate from scratch and whose work would be on the same scale as Big Turner's work. What was needed, Walter Shaw decided, was a construction company that would resemble Big Turner in most respects but would employ non-union subcontractors.

Shaw consulted with Conant, Marshall, Gerlach, and others about the idea and there was consensus that it was a good one. There's some irony in such unanimous support, because only a few years earlier Big Turner had done poorly on a large open-shop contract it was managing for Duke University at its new hospital and medical school complex in North Carolina. On that job, which was just the kind of operation that Shaw was aiming for, Turner had been reminded almost daily of some of the less evident hazards of open-shop contracting on such a large scale, among them the absence of the traditional union hiring hall. On the Duke job, where the supply of skilled labor was inadequate and the progress of the work was unsatisfactory, it had been extremely difficult to recruit mechanics and virtually impossible to evaluate their qualifications even when they were recruited. Herb Conant describes Duke's nonunion electrical subcontractor as maintaining a work-force of 107 men that included only a small number who were thought by Conant to be qualified to do electrical work. Most of the rest, in Conant's view, were unskilled laborers who were simply called electricians. In contrast, Turner's own new open-shop subsidiaries were now operating on a much smaller scale in Texas and elsewhere, a scale that allowed them to know almost all the mechanics and to maintain a following of tested subcontractors who knew their own mechanics in the same way.

But sentiment for starting a big open-shop company was strong, and by 1983 a decision to do so had been implemented in Atlanta, where Turner established Trans-Con, with Vic Cestar, who had been brought in from Detroit, in charge. Cestar had come from the sales side of the business, and Conant buttressed him with Jim Houghton to run the new firm's construction. When Houghton died of cancer after only a short time on the job, Conant replaced him with Al Velco. The plan was that Trans-Con would seek big open-shop jobs, and although it was understood that these were most likely to surface in the South, there was no for-malized proscription against their being sought elsewhere.

Trans-Con would struggle from the beginning, and a good many factors con-spired against its success. Like any construction start-up, it would need time to

develop a following of its own subcontractors and to gain recognition and acceptance, and it would clearly need a fair amount of money to fund jobs that it felt it
had to take on at low fees while it was getting underway. An unfortunate idea that
this new Turner company could streamline itself to eliminate some of the reporting and control systems that were at the core of Big Turner's modus operandi
proved to be a seriously damaging one, undermining both control and quality.

During its first few years, Trans-Con was able to build annual construction volumes that approached $75 million, but there were no earnings; from time to time,
in areas where the union issue was becoming blurred, it found itself in conflict with
Big Turner. Soon Trans-Con was working on big jobs in widely separated locations,
and while its annual volume was rising sharply, its elusive earnings had begun to
turn to losses. Even the original justification for operating a big open-shop subsidiary had been weakened when the unions in some of the company's established
territories began to allow their members to work alongside nonunion workers.
When Big Turner found that it could integrate open-shop subcontractors into its
own jobs, the original justification for establishing an open-shop subsidiary was virtually eliminated. After a few years, the losses became much more serious and the
conflicts with Big Turner became more disruptive. In 1987, under a new administration, the company would accept defeat, electing to wind down Trans-Con's work
and to discontinue it. By then it had cost Big Turner $18 million.

These diversions, particularly the open-shop forays of the late 1970s and 1980s,
would have some individual, modest successes, but on balance they cost the company money during a period in which other reverses were beginning to put serious
pressure on its cash reserves. At least as important, they represented an investment
of time and energy by management that proved to be substantially disproportion-
ate to their earning potential. The total annual volume of business produced by
the four open-shop companies during the early 1980s was rarely any larger than
the volume generated by just a few of the big urban office buildings the company
was working on, and the earnings they generated were smaller. That applied to
Turner International as well. As recently as 1983, International had produced a
volume that was greater than $60 million, but it hadn't been able to generate earn-

ings that were consistent with a corresponding volume of domestic work.

Universal Construction Company, the Pearce holding that had survived the departure of its principals, was an exception, and it would still be a prospering and valued Turner open-shop subsidiary at the beginning of the new century. But the other open-shop acquisitions of the period would be gone by then. In 1985 the Texas subsidiaries would be combined into a single Turner subsidiary that retained the BFW name, but a few years after that a group within BFW would reacquire the firm from Turner. And the Thompson firm, which performed well, would continue as an active Turner subsidiary until about 1989, when it would be acquired by a joint venture of firms based in Alabama. After that, Thompson would occasionally join Turner as a joint venture partner on several jobs, the most notable of which was the successful contract for building a new stadium in Charlotte for the NFL's Carolina Panthers football team.

What had emerged from the acquisitions of the '80s was an increasing awareness that the company's prosperity relied essentially on the traditional, core construction business that had sustained it for almost a century and that had accounted for its continued growth and prosperity. By the end of 1983, the value of construction put in place in a single year by Turner had reached $1.7 billion, twice what it had been when Walter Shaw took over from Howard Turner in 1978, and its net earnings had tripled during those years. Such growth had outstripped anything that might have been accounted for by cost inflation, estimated at about 40 percent for the same period.

Every job had its own history, of course, but some histories were less predictable than others. Among the least predictable was one that started in 1980 in Turner's Houston office, under Tony Cucolo, a West Point–educated former army officer who'd been with the company since 1959 and had led the Houston territory through the extremely busy and profitable years of the oil boom. Cities Service, then the country's ninth largest oil company, had contracted with Turner to build a new corporate headquarters for it in Tulsa, a fifty-two-story monument to the fuel that had energized the country's prosperity and made Cities Service rich. The oil boycott of the 1970s hadn't done the American oil companies any harm, and Cities Service had plans to spend about $200 million on its building. Cucolo dispatched Roger Turnier, not long back from the Far East, to take charge in Tulsa, and Turner geared up for the big job. But only a few months into the work, it became evident to Cities Service that with the restored abundance of oil that had followed the end of the boycott, a decline in its price had acquired a dangerous momentum and that an end to the good times was in the making. The Tulsa job was suspended (except for a few trades) while Cities Service thought through its options. Turner and the project's designers searched for and found $100 million in cost reductions that reached into every corner, from foundations through superstructure, mechanical, electrical, and finish systems. The architects and engineers converted their original grand design to a much more modest, thirty-seven-story building, and Turner went back to work.

But what had happened proved to be only the first chapter in the story. While Turner forged ahead with construction, Cities Service became embroiled in a protracted takeover struggle, and by the middle of 1982 Roger Turnier began to see signs that even more serious trouble might lie ahead for the job. In December, his worst fears were realized when Cities Service, by then a wholly owned subsidiary of Occidental Petroleum, entered into a contract to sell the whole Tulsa project to a Texas developer who had his own ideas for it. By that time, most of what would be required to build the thirty-seven-story building had been contracted for by Turner, and a substantial fraction of it had actually been put in place, including almost 3,000 tons of structural steel. Turner shut down again, this time to address the intimidating complexities of determining the real cost of what had already been built or bought and then the corresponding complexities of what it would cost to finish the building for a new owner. This time it would be an eighteen-story, granite-clad commercial office building.

Within another year it would all be history. The developer had found a single tenant who leased all 740,000 square feet of the reduced building and Turner, having negotiated settlements with all the subcontractors and vendors, had finished its job.

In New York most of what remained of the bad jobs was finally being cleaned up and the volume of work in progress was again on the rise, led by a flurry of giant office buildings that included one for the venerable Irving Trust Company on Barclay Street, another for a group headed by Goldman Sachs on Broad Street, and some for other major clients as well. Each of the big new jobs represented more than about $100 million worth of construction, and some of the larger ones cost more than $150 million. But the biggest and in some ways the grandest of the new office towers to be built by Turner in New York during the 1980s was the one it would build for its old and valued client, the Equitable Life Assurance Society of the United States.

Monumental buildings of high quality had threaded through all of what was already the 120-year history of Equitable when it engaged Edward Larrabee Barnes in 1979 to design its fourth home office, as insurance companies like to call their corporate headquarters. Like most insurance companies, Equitable saw its buildings as exemplifying the very substance and reliability of the company itself, and there was no reason to expect it to settle for anything less than the same quality when it decided to replace with a new building the home office that Turner had built for it only twenty years earlier.

The earlier building, in which Skidmore Owings & Merrill had overlaid their contemporary perspective on the traditional monumentalism that had characterized other Equitable buildings, was one of the imposing towers that during the early 1960s had begun to bring to Manhattan's Sixth Avenue some of the corporate elegance that had started with Rockefeller Center on Fifth Avenue. Now the City wanted to push westward again, and it was offering zoning incentives that would induce Equitable to build. Equitable owned the whole block that ran from Sixth to Seventh Avenues and from Fifty-first to Fifty-second Streets, but its earlier headquarters building, which faced Sixth Avenue, occupied only the easterly half of the property. The plan was to acquire and demolish the buildings on the western half of the property, build an elegant new headquarters building there for itself, and then to fill the older building with new tenants at the high and rising rents that such choice buildings in New York were able to bring. By 1980 the plan seemed to be on track when the owner of one of the buildings that Equitable needed to demolish refused to sell for anything less than a price that Equitable was unwilling to pay. Equitable elected to proceed without it. Barnes produced a scheme that accommodated the continued presence of the small neighbor, and by early 1981 Turner, under Steven Simonfay (later replaced by John McIntire), had started the massive excavation that marked the beginning of new construction.

The noise and vibration of the rock excavation proved to be more than the owner of the troublesome building in the northwest corner had bargained for. His principal tenant was in the sound-recording business, and it wasn't long before the owner and Equitable had come to terms. That meant that the whole parcel of land was now available, but it also meant that the design of the building had to be radically changed, with wrenching effects on Turner's construction plan. With the job operating at full stride, Turner had to rework its entire construction plan, relocate its material and personnel hoists, rewrite its subcontracts, and address the job in dramatically new terms — construction manager's nightmare.

Equitable was undergoing severe changes of its own during this period, some of them generated by shifts in public attitudes toward some of the products it sold, and even these problems would have an impact on Turner's work. The explosive cost inflation that had characterized the economy during the 1970s had made people wary of long-term investments, and Equitable was adjusting its policies to suit. John Carter, a charismatic executive with eleven children, became its new CEO, and he brought along a set of new ideas that included radical decentralizing of the company. With the building fairly well along but not yet enclosed, it was decided about the middle of 1982 to assign the majority of personnel originally intended for the home office to other locations around the country and to limit Equitable's own occupancy to the top half of the new building, leaving the rest of the space to be leased to others.

The building had originally been conceived as a single-tenant headquarters, with a relatively small fraction of the space intended for lease. It had been designed with a cafeteria, a library, conference rooms, escalators and special elevators, and finishes appropriate to such occupancy. Now, only the upper floors would be designed for Equitable's special needs and most of the remaining space would be left as core and shell space to be developed for individual tenants. Difficult as that change would be for the architect, there was an aspect of it that made it at least equally difficult for Turner. Carter wanted Equitable's own offices at the top of the building to be ready first. That meant well-finished space, complete with special elevators to bring executives and visitors directly there, and an entrance system on Seventh Avenue. For Turner such a plan meant reversing many of its traditional construction processes: Sequencing of mechanical and electrical work had to be revised, subcontracts had to be rewritten to provide for new scheduling, and even the plan for erecting the building's enclosure had to be radically altered. But like all such difficult projects, this one was satisfactorily completed and would become part of the company's accumulated lore.

At the time the Equitable project was being finished, almost two-thirds of the construction Turner was doing across the country was classified as commercial, compared with about 20 percent when Walter Shaw had become chairman back in 1978. Shaw's board had changed too. John Burns and Herbert Johnson were gone, and in 1981 Howard Turner had retired from the board at seventy, still vigorous but having served the extra five years beyond his retirement that the board regarded as a reasonable limit for the chairman. Bob Marshall, among the last of his generation at Turner, had retired in 1983 after forty-four years' service, setting in motion a whole cascade of executive changes. Bob Kupfer took over Marshall's job as national director of marketing, relinquishing his own leadership of Turner International to Gene von Wening, who had by then settled into his new role as manager of Turner's Western Region. Urbane and broadly skilled in almost all the work of the company, von Wening was popular among its management people and especially well regarded by Conant as a potential candidate for even higher posts. He'd continue to manage both the Western Region and Turner International from his California base.

Replacements for retiring board members would now come entirely from outside the company, raising the majority of outside directors on the board to almost 60 percent. They included John Kircher, the retired chairman of Conoco; Edward McMahon, the retired president of St. Regis Paper Company; Gordon Walker, the

CEO of U.S. Industries; and Ellis (Bud) Gravette, chairman of New York's Bowery Savings Bank, who would a dozen years later become chairman of Turner.

By 1984 Walter Shaw had long since made his decision that his preference was to be succeeded in the presidency of Turner Construction Company by Herb Conant, and on the second of March of that year the board ratified his choice. Three months later, the stockholders approved a plan to establish a publicly traded holding company that would be called The Turner Corporation, as parent to Turner Construction Company and to the lengthening list of other firms that had been established or acquired. Soon afterward the new board would make Herb Conant president of the corporation as well as the company.

In the new corporate structure, which dramatized the separation between Turner Construction Company and the open-shop firms that would now relate to it only through their common parent, Turner Construction was able to distance itself safely from the open-shop activities that might threaten long-standing relationships in the company's traditional working areas. In addition, it was intended that the more or less independent and parallel status of each of the companies that would now be reporting directly to The Turner Corporation would encourage individual development and growth, and that such a revised corporate structure would free the management of Turner Construction Company itself to concentrate on its traditional and principal business, the construction of buildings.

According to Herb Conant's own reflections at the end of the century, he and the others were "riding the crest of a wave" when these sweeping organizational changes were made in 1984. And why not? The company was putting in place almost $2 billion worth of construction annually and its earnings after taxes were exceeding $12 million, about 20 percent of its corporate net worth. What's more, it had a backlog of work that was approaching $3 billion.

Conant and a few of the others knew about a dark place or two, of course. He had to be worried about Trans-Con's direction, but as bad as it was, he was able to see it as the kind of failed experiment that every risk-intensive company has to try from time to time.

And Conant was aware of problems in International too, but his responsibilities and attention as executive vice president had centered on the company's domestic work. He hadn't been involved in the details of the company's offshore activities. He knew that after years of struggle to establish a solid and suitably profitable base for itself abroad, TII was now building an approximately $100 million commercial office building in Singapore, and he knew about a dispute that had developed on the job there between Turner and its Asian client. But after all the disputes Conant had seen in his long career in the often contentious business of construction, it's unlikely that he would have imagined in 1984 that this dispute might at a later date be serious enough to threaten the viability of the company.

And although Conant sat on the board of Turner Development Corporation, it would probably have been reasonable for him in 1984 to view the burden that TDC was placing on Turner's increasingly strained cash reserves as little more than a transient inconvenience that would eventually be resolved by forcing TDC to sell off some of its holdings. Walter Schularick had by then been brought into Turner from Minneapolis Honeywell's real estate group to work with and later to replace Jim Griffis, and there was ample reason to believe that Schularick's sophistication in matters of commercial real estate could be relied on to protect Turner's interests. TDC was still reporting substantial holdings that were producing appropriate levels of income, so it seemed only a matter of enforcing Walter Shaw's recent, vigorous edict to Schularick to sell TDC's properties if he needed to raise cash. Neither Conant nor anyone else, in 1984, had reason to think that within a few years the earnings from these properties might shrink radically and that their book values would have to be harshly written down, imposing financial pressures on Turner at a time when it would be least able to deal with them.

In fact, all those devastating eventualities would materialize within only a few years. But there's no evidence that anyone at Turner was anticipating them in 1984.

14.

Conant

I t was hard to be anything but optimistic about Turner in 1985, when Herb Conant took over from Walter Shaw as chairman of the construction company and turned its presidency over to Al McNeill. There were a few trouble spots in view, of course, but Turner's was a big, far-flung, and risk-intensive business and couldn't be expected to be without problems. By the end of the year the company would complete almost $2.2 billion worth of work, up from about $1.7 billion during 1984, and earnings were good. There were 384 Turner projects underway that year, in thirty-two states and seven countries, and a backlog of more than $3 billion in other work that was waiting its turn to get started. In its eighty-third year, Turner would become a $70 million corporation, the country's leader among contractors specializing in building construction. Its annual volume of work was shown once again by ENR to be well ahead of comparable volumes of such vigorous competitors as J. A. Jones, Centex Rooney, Gilbane, and Fuller. The company had a full-time staff of almost 2,900.

Herb Conant's influence and control had been increasing during his five years at the corporate center in New York, and in 1985, when he'd been president of Turner Corporation for about a year, his impact on the company's management was unmistakable. He'd surrounded himself with some of the men in whom he had the greatest confidence, including Al McNeill as president of Turner Construction Company and Gene von Wening as executive vice president.

McNeill was by then probably about as close to Conant as anyone in the company's senior management. Like Conant, he was an engineer who had come up on the operations side of the business, a no-nonsense construction man who'd served as vice president in charge of operations as early as 1973 and had since then run the Philadelphia territory and later the new Northeast Group that included New York, Boston, Philadelphia, and Pittsburgh. Now he'd moved up to corporate headquarters in New York. Von Wening, also an engineer, had started his career in operations but had gravitated toward sales and had been a major figure in developing the company's western work. He'd been the first general manager of the San Francisco business unit and then senior vice president for the Western Region. Most recently he'd succeeded Bob Kupfer in the management of Turner International. McNeill and von Wening were in 1985 seen by Conant as his most capable and promising executives and indeed McNeill would within a few years succeed Conant as chairman. But von Wening, only fifty-eight years old in 1985, would soon be found to be suffering from esophageal cancer and by 1987 that terrible illness would take his life.

In 1985 McNeill and von Wening had plenty of capable company near the top. Bob Kupfer had taken on Bob Marshall's old job as head of sales in New York. The three regions into which the territories had previously been organized were for a brief period reduced to only two, with Al McNeill in charge of the East and executive vice president Gene von Wening in charge of the West. Individual territories, in turn, were for the most part linked together under newly designated vice presidents into groups that had natural dependencies on one another, while a few territories with no clear interdependencies (like Miami, Chicago, Houston, and San Francisco) were continued as independent business units under managers who reported directly to the head of the division.

In the Midwest, Chicago and Houston were a couple of the territories that continued to be independent of the groups, and their managers reported directly to Gene von Wening, the manager of the Western Division. Barry Sibson, who became a group vice president and was given responsibility for Los Angeles and a handful of its satellites, reported directly to von Wening too.

In the Eastern Division, Miami remained independent and reported to Al

McNeill, and three groups comprised all the remaining eastern territories. The Northeast Group under Hal Parmelee included Boston and New York; the Mid-Atlantic Group under Don Kerstetter included Philadelphia, Pittsburgh, and Washington; and a Central Group under Al Sanchez included Cincinnati, Cleveland, Columbus, and Detroit.

The new group vice presidents were a talented lot, and in some cases produced the next line of top management in the firm. Harold Parmelee, an especially popular and capable engineer who'd earlier been TGM in Boston, had first been brought down to New York by Al McNeill to manage the territory's difficult revival. One of the company's best-regarded executives, Parmelee had been educated in mathematics and engineering at Bowdoin and MIT, respectively, and had been with Turner in a broad range of roles since 1960. Within a few years he'd be succeeding to McNeill's job as president of Turner Construction Company when McNeill moved up to the chairmanship. Al Sanchez, educated in both engineering and law, had been with Turner for twenty-seven years when he was tapped to run the Central Group of territories. Barry Sibson, with degrees from Dartmouth and Stanford, had earlier succeeded Herb Pintard as manager in Los Angeles. And Donald Kerstetter, a civil engineering graduate of Drexel University, had been with the company since 1951, succeeding Al McNeill in 1980 as TGM in Philadelphia. Kerstetter had earlier served under McNeill there and had distinguished himself by bringing the Philadelphia Special Projects Division (SPD) to a level of success that made it something of a model for other such units in the company. Only a few years later he would play a seminal part in the company's difficult transition to the world of computer-based information systems.

These Special Projects Divisions (SPDs), which did relatively small, usually interior jobs that were occasionally but not often connected to larger projects being done by Big Turner, traced their origin to the old Plant Maintenance Company, an initially unwelcome subsidiary that had come along during the 1960s with the Twaits-Wittenberg acquisition in California. Plant Maintenance had functioned as a minor subsidiary doing small work, mostly interior, around Los Angeles. But the SPDs had come a long way since the 1960s, and by 1985, with a good many jobs (some as big as $5 million) under their belts, they were operating in ten territories around the country, accounting for almost 10 percent of the company's annual volume of business and generating earnings at a respectable rate. Largely through the support of executives like Tom Gerlach, who was a vigorous advocate from the beginning, the SPDs had managed to overcome the opposition of some in Turner who saw such small work as unworthy of Big Turner's efforts.

Donald Kerstetter had been especially successful in Philadelphia. Under McNeill, he'd been able to build on the base that Tom Gerlach had established during his time there, and he produced a wide variety of profitable SPD jobs that included not only interior work but a fair number of small, stand-alone buildings as well, sometimes under contracts that included their design. His successful Philadelphia SPD and others began to provide a bonus that was seen by some in senior management as being just as valuable as profitability: They were providing younger managers the unique experience of having full responsibility for entire projects from start to finish early in their careers, an opportunity unlikely to have come their way on major work until much later.

And the company's thirty-seven vice presidents in 1985 included their share of capable men too, some of them destined for positions of even greater responsibility in later years. Frank Basius, educated at Harvard, was the new TGM in Boston, and he'd later head the Northeast Group. Les Shute and Dick Manteuffel were a couple of Cornell graduates who'd been with Turner since the 1950s and 1960s, respectively, had each managed or was managing a major territory, and would continue in senior positions at Turner. Joe McCullough, who'd been with the company since 1955, had run the Cleveland office and would soon be at the head of the Central Group himself. Bob Fee, the high-rise builder who was by then managing operations in the New York office, was in 1985 only a little more than ten years from becoming president of the company.

By the time Herb Conant added the chairmanship of Turner Corporation to his chairmanship of Turner Construction Company, half-way through 1985, the problematic jobs that had been at the core of his move to the East in the first place had for the most part either been completed or had been brought under control, and the company's essential construction business was maintaining and increasing its already considerable momentum. Widening support for the idea that geographic diversity should provide an effective defense against disruptive variations in the workload encouraged the formation of new offices, and under Conant's leadership Turner's nineteen territories and offices would produce a dozen new satellites wherever new jobs and the promise of future work were thought to justify them. Of course, the promise of such growth didn't always materialize, and by the end of 1988 some newly established offices were closed. Twenty-eight domestic Turner offices were in place at the end of the 1980s.

The drive to broaden the company's base didn't stop with efforts to extend its geographic range, and during the period from about 1983 to about 1987 there were serious efforts to reach into markets that lay slightly beyond its traditional range. In 1983 the company turned to the business of furnishing and erecting finished granite and similar stone products throughout the country, and it brought in Malcolm Swenson, whose firm had been a major player for years in the cut-stone business, to establish a stone subsidiary called Ameristone. During the year that followed, Turner acquired a Florida firm it would call Turner Medical Building Services to design and build medical facilities smaller than hospitals, including physicians' office buildings, intermediate care facilities, diagnostic centers, and the like. And a year after that, Turner acquired Data Acquisition Sciences, a New York firm that would become the core of still another Turner subsidiary, Turner Power Group, established to build and own cogeneration facilities for companies whose power-consuming profiles suggested potential savings from cogeneration.

And the continuing drive to extend the company's markets or to intensify its access to markets it was already seeking didn't end there. A real estate consulting group was formed, and a failed effort was made to establish Turner Golf, which would have developed golf courses. Divisions were established within the company to provide expertise that would enhance sales and performance in such specialties as correctional and health care facilities and other special markets that were perceived as increasing. The overriding objective was diversified growth in areas that were reasonably congruent with the company's traditional business.

Growth was king in the mid-1980s. In Bermuda, in 1985, Turner acquired a 40 percent interest in D & J Construction Company, which had been doing hotel and similar construction there since about 1969, and a few years later it acquired Seaboard Construction Company of Key Largo, Florida, to enhance its south Florida presence.

In Ohio, Dick Manteuffel's Cincinnati territory reached out to make a couple of new acquisitions that were seen as potential contributors to the increase in market share that was the goal of every territory manager. The results were good but less than perfect. Hercules Construction Company had been identified as a worthwhile acquisition target in 1986, when Manteuffel went to St. Louis to look it over and liked what he saw. Named for its founder, Joseph Hercules (no relation to the Greek god), it had the look of a prospering general contracting firm that would provide just the access Cincinnati was seeking in St. Louis, a market that Turner had been unable to penetrate. After a conventional investigation, Manteuffel obtained board approval and Hercules was brought into the Turner family, but it wasn't long before he had second thoughts. Much of the work Hercules had on hand proved to be troubled, the firm's prospects were much less bright than expected, and the glowing references that had encouraged Manteuffel turned out to have been based more on fondness and sympathy for the company's locally popular principal than on merit. The Cincinnati group, increasingly busy with a surge of hospital and other work, simply pushed on and eventually closed Hercules down, folding its assets into a new office that Turner was creating in Kansas City. Nothing ventured, nothing gained.

The acquisition of Lathrop Construction Company in Toledo was an expansion effort that produced the opposite result: an entirely worthwhile move that had originated with Al McNeill when the Lathrop people themselves approached Turner, seeking to be acquired. Even older than Turner, Lathrop brought along a well-established clientele, largely industrial and firmly rooted in the automobile manufacturing industry, and a first-rate staff that would turn out good work and generate profits.

In fact, Cincinnati's growth would probably have been pretty well assured even without any of these new acquisitions. Manteuffel had taken charge there in 1983, after almost twenty years of solid experience in operations, and his elevation to the new role occurred at just about the time Cincinnati was beginning to get its share of the vigorously expanding national market in hospital construction.

The growth of hospital work had started back east with the historical inevitability that forced most of the older eastern cities to replace their aging hospitals, and it was substantially accelerated by the political changes that pushed government into a major role in paying for what had to be done. Then the expanded availability of health insurance came along to ensure that an aging population would be able to pay for using the new facilities, and when new technologies rendered even fairly modern hospitals obsolete, the demand for new construction soared. By the 1980s the building of hospitals was regularly accounting for almost 25 percent of Turner's annual work volume, second only to commercial building construction, and the company was ranked first in hospital construction by Modern Health Care.

Cincinnati exemplified the new direction. During the 1980s Turner was building the city's Good Samaritan and Jewish Hospitals, at about $67 million and $55 million, respectively, and it was finishing its Miami Valley Hospital, which cost about $42 million. One of Dick Manteuffel's early jobs as territory manager was to travel to Nashville to sign contracts for what would become about $88 million worth of hospital work at Vanderbilt University, where Turner had already done a good deal of such work earlier. The Vanderbilt project became the basis for establishing a branch office in Nashville, and by the time that job was finished in 1989 Nashville had become a fully fledged Turner territory of its own.

Hospital construction was a natural specialty for Turner, and the company's dominance of the national market wasn't surprising. Most of the jobs were big, and virtually all were technically demanding. Where there were phased replacements or additions to existing hospitals (as there almost always were), they usually required complex scheduling and deft management. Turner was able to bring to such jobs a depth in personnel and a high level of technical experience and capability that were less easily found among smaller, local firms, and its position in the health care sector reflected such strength.

Throughout the rest of the Midwest and the East, Turner's hospital work continued to be a major element in its volume. At times the company had construction underway on as many as 100 separate major hospital projects in a single year, and during one period in the 1980s, in New York, it was simultaneously building four of the country's largest hospitals, with a total completed construction cost of almost $500 million.

The company was less successful in its early efforts to penetrate the hospital construction market of the Far West, where much of the work was smaller and was still being done by local general contractors. It hadn't done much hospital work in the West before the 1980s, but its success in the management approach to construction was by then well known there when Ed Quimby set out to convince local officials that the construction-management approach could be effectively applied to hospital work. Quimby was a seasoned Turner veteran who had started with the company in Boston in 1969 and had moved up through a variety of business development positions, and although this task would take a while he was ultimately successful. Within a few years Turner would begin to provide construction management for some of California's big new hospitals, and Quimby would go on to establish and manage a new Turner office in Orange County, as a satellite of the Los Angeles office.

As big as the hospital sector was for Turner, it was still only about 25 percent of the approximately $2.5 billion in construction that the firm was doing every year during the mid-1980s. And although most of the rest of the company's volume comprised commercial office buildings and the like, not all of it did. The largest single project Turner had ever done came along in September of 1983, when United Airlines engaged it to provide preconstruction services (and later full construction-management services) for the huge terminal complex it was preparing to build at the world's busiest airport, Chicago's O'Hare.

Architect Helmut Jahn of Chicago's Murphy/Jahn had produced a futuristic postmodern design for the UAL complex that included a couple of parallel buildings with glass and steel roofs that were reminiscent of the grand railroad stations of Europe. Each building would be a third of a mile long and would be connected to the other by a large underground concourse. The plan was to build them on a site then occupied by O'Hare's obsolete International Terminal.

UAL was estimating that the whole job, including special systems like baggage handling, might cost as much as $350 million in 1983, and that it would be built in phases that would be completed by the end of 1988. In fact, the cost would prove to be closer to $500 million, but it was indeed completed in 1988, as planned. Turner's Bob D'Alton, who was about ready to retire, stayed long enough to manage the preconstruction phase, but in 1984, when UAL added the construction phase to Turner's contract, the company brought in Bernie Newton, the former Marine Corps officer who had by then headed up his share of Turner's most important Chicago jobs. Newton took charge as project executive with Bill Sowa, who'd started with the company twenty years earlier as a field engineer on the big Krannert Center in Illinois, as superintendent. They'd build a terminal that would cover an area half the size of the Chicago Loop.

Right from the start of caisson work in the cold winter of 1984-1985, the job was a massive logistical and production challenge: very big, often complex, and dominated by an unforgiving, phased schedule. The site was quickly enclosed by a mile and a half of security fencing and a 1,000-car parking area for the exclusive use of construction personnel. UAL had decided that its job should have a Turner officer resident at the site, and to satisfy that preference the company brought in Shelby Reaves, a vice president who had worked on or managed projects across half the world as an engineer and had more recently served as executive vice president of Turner International. Reaves, educated in engineering at Duke University, was no stranger to big jobs, having spent several years as project manager on the ninety-nine-building Mei Foo job in Hong Kong. The son of Col. George Reaves, the distinguished West Pointer who had managed his own share of Turner's biggest projects, Reaves was a good fit for the job.

Right from the start, the UAL job was going to demand some additional, more subtle skills of Reaves. He would be taking over a major project that was already being well managed by an entirely competent contemporary. It couldn't have been easy, but within a few weeks Shelby Reaves and Bernie Newton had worked out an accord that satisfied both of them and, from all accounts, worked smoothly and effectively. Reaves, as "officer-in-charge," handled the complex administrative side of the sprawling project, and Newton, as project executive, handled its actual construction. As it turned out, the arrangement proved to be even better than the intelligent compromise it had at first seemed to be. The job was so big and the problems of administering and building it so complex that in fact it took every bit of the capacity of two senior executives to manage it effectively. Before long, the work went to a six-day week and disbursements reached $16 million a month. The pace was so fast that it began to outstrip even UAL's considerable ability to keep up with its cash needs, and a $10 million fund had to be put at Turner's disposal to ensure fast payment to vendors and subcontractors whose timely performance was considered critical to maintaining the schedule.

But by the time the UAL job drew within about nine months of the deadline for completing the first of the project's two phases, the broad range of problems that can impede progress on even the best managed of big jobs had begun to threaten Turner's ability to meet its completion deadline. Turner's staff of managers on the job already exceeded 100, but what was needed was additional senior level supervision that could be strategically distributed to each of the critical areas of work while there was still time. At about that time Reaves learned that senior operations manager Ralph Johnson was in town. Johnson, the longtime Turner man who had recently been made the national manager of operations, was another member of that elite group who had earlier worked in Cleveland under Conant, and he was chairing a Chicago conference of operations managers from all over the country. Reaves brought Johnson and his conference guests out to the site for a day to show them what was going on at O'Hare, and within a week of the outing he began to see the results of his hospitality: Johnson had reached out to Turner's network of senior field men across the country and rounded up a dozen or so of its best men, dispatching them to the UAL site. They did what had to be done to ensure meeting the deadline.

By summer 1987, twenty-nine of UAL's planned fifty-two gates were operating, as had been promised, but it had taken a monumental effort. During the three months that immediately preceded the opening of the first twenty-nine gates, the job had gone to a seven-day workweek, with 2,000 men working, and John DiEgidio, a vice president who'd been with the company for more than thirty years, had been brought in from Cleveland to buttress the supervising staff. When the first phase of the work was finished, Newton and Reaves moved on to other Turner jobs and John McIntire, who was operations manager in the Chicago office, took over supervision of the second phase of the work. By the end of 1988, all fifty-two gates were operating and the project was finished.

Halfway around the world, in Singapore, things hadn't been going as well for Turner. Ever since the successful job at Changi Airport, Bob Kupfer and his Turner International group had been seeking a widening of Turner's role in the development of the region, and by 1983 they had reason to believe that they had finally found themselves in the right place at the right time. The dramatic emergence of the Pacific Rim as an area of economic vitality had made Singapore an international commercial center, with new construction almost everywhere, and Kupfer's very good relationship with a powerful Singapore businessman named S. P. Tao was in the process of producing what was thought to be a major new construction opportunity for Turner. Tao was a distinguished personality who had been born into a privileged Chinese family before the Second World War, had worked as a laborer on the Burma Road during the war, and had since become one of the region's most successful developers. Earlier in the 1980s, when the average rental price of new, high-quality office space in Singapore had risen to four times its 1977 level, his investment syndicate had engaged I. M. Pei to design Singapore's premier office building: an approximately 1.4-million-square-foot pair of gleaming, thirty-seven-story towers that would be called The Gateway. It was estimated that the towers would cost a little over $100 million.

Bob Kupfer was still the top man in Turner International, although soon afterward, when Bob Marshall retired, he would take over Marshall's job as corporate director of sales, marketing, and planning and turn over his own leadership of International to Gene von Wening. But in 1983 Kupfer was working toward securing a contract to build The Gateway for Tao's group, and he had finally won out in a hard-fought competition with Japanese and Korean competition.

The good news ended there. Although Kupfer had for years resisted fixed-price contracts in any of International's work, he had felt obliged on the Gateway job to agree to sign one. It was a decision that set the stage for events that would prove costly for Turner. The new structure itself was to be built on reclaimed land, and before engaging Turner, Tao had contracted with another firm to drive sheet piling needed for foundation work and that would, in fact, be in place when Turner started work at the site. Not long after Turner got underway, deficiencies in the sheet piling began to appear, and over the ensuing months, as they became more serious, Turner looked to Tao for relief. But Tao's response held that Turner would have to participate in the cost of any required corrective work, a view that was opposed by Turner, and the basis of what would become a long and difficult dispute was established. Construction and discussions continued apace, with Turner doing some essential remedial work along the way to ensure safety but refusing to underwrite the several million dollars' worth of work needed to replace the sheet piling.

The dispute intensified and broadened as the work proceeded, resisting negotiated resolution. Early in 1984 the engineers responsible for inspecting fieldwork became increasingly captious in their criticism of Turner's other work at the site, at one point demanding the removal of elevated concrete slabs on the unprecedented grounds that although the upper surfaces of the slabs met specification requirements for level, their soffits didn't. The rejected work was used as a basis for withholding substantial amounts from progress payments that were due, and the relationship between Turner and its client worsened.

Something else was happening in Singapore that's thought by some to have had a defining impact on the impasse. The real estate boom had abated, and new office space wasn't renting well. The rental price being fetched by space like Gateway's had declined by about 25 percent in a single year, and the owner's incentive to finish The Gateway any time soon had virtually disappeared.

By the middle of 1984, Tao had stopped making any payments at all to Turner, and by the end of the year Turner had shut down the job. At that point, with one tower up about three stories and the other up about eight, Tao owed Turner $5.2 million in certified progress payments and was withholding another $1.4 million. Even more ominously, Turner had by then contracted for the purchase of millions of dollars' worth of products that were in the process of being fabricated in plants around the world, and the company was of course obligated to pay for them.

Turner's vulnerability to crippling loss was exacerbated by its legal situation. An attempt to recover through litigation was seen as an extremely risky course with a very low probability of success, requiring proceeding as a foreigner against a well-regarded local figure in a Singapore system of modified British law. The Gateway in 1985 represented as severe a threat to Turner as the company had ever seen.

Turner personnel who'd been working at The Gateway were reassigned to other locations abroad and in the United States, and the company itself became persona non grata along the Pacific Rim. Perceived as a villainous outsider in a dispute with a fellow Asian, Turner was effectively cut off from new jobs in the region. Efforts were made to move toward resolution through negotiation, but they were largely unavailing until the middle of 1987, when I. M. Pei's intervention brought the parties closer together. With some improvement in the real estate climate in Singapore, a plan for resolving the construction issues was worked out, and there was guarded optimism that new faces at the negotiating table might encourage a settlement. Turner's Ralph Beck was brought in to take charge of its negotiating team, together with a small, carefully selected staff that included Doug Bennett, a Harvard-educated MBA who had been working in corporate management at Turner. While legal teams on both sides came to within days of court proceedings, negotiations led at almost the last moment to an offer that came tantalizingly close to acceptance. Turner offered to accept shares in the ownership of The Gateway in lieu of the cash shortfall that had made an earlier Tao proposal unacceptable. But Tao's response proposed a quantity of shares that would have been insufficient to provide for settling a very large claim from the curtainwall manufacturer. Turner rejected the response and prepared to go to court, but things changed radically when Tao surprised them by announcing that he had made a separate, direct arrangement with the curtainwall manufacturer that would insulate Turner from its claim. An inclination to settle the long and costly dispute had by then been growing in the Turner camp, encouraged and facilitated by Bob McAllister. As Turner's project executive for The Gateway, McAllister was in the important and unique position of enjoying the continued goodwill and confidence of S. P. Tao, and he was able to broker an agreement in which Turner would accept a combination of cash and shares. After securing concurrence from the affected subcontractors to accept the offer, Turner settled with the Tao group, construction was resumed, and by spring 1990, the work had been completed.

A few years later Turner would sell its shares in The Gateway to the Tao group for about ninety-five cents on the dollar. It had been a terrible and expensive experience, dramatizing at an especially difficult time in Turner's history the inherent volatility of an industry in which serious risk is a continuing companion, even for the most substantial and conservative practitioner. A later irony that somehow underlines the ongoing acceptability of such risk is that only a few years after The Gateway was finished, Turner would do another, similar job for S. P. Tao in Sri Lanka.

The Gateway episode was probably only one of several factors that induced Herb Conant, in 1985, to reexamine the relationship between the personalities and operating styles that attached to the newer and farther-flung activities of which Turner International was a part and those that were inherent in the company's traditional, mostly domestic core construction activities. By now it had become apparent that the company's interests were moving in two diverging and largely independent directions, each with its own focus and objectives, and Conant moved to separate them into two companies, naming a different president for each. He named Al McNeill president of what would be called the corporation's Construction Group, and he named Bob Kupfer president of its Diversified Services Group.

The Construction Group was intended to focus on the kind of work the company had been doing for eighty-three years, but the Diversified Services Group was something else. Here, under Kupfer, would be consolidated all Turner's newer activities, those that were at varying distances from the beaten path and that were still largely untested, and they would include Turner International, Turner Power, Turner Medical, Ameristone, Turner Development Company, and the real estate consulting firm that would be called Turner Real Estate. A little later in 1985, as the new Diversified Services Group was developing, its newest member, Rickenbacker Air Industrial Park, was just coming into view.

The Rickenbacker episode may in some ways have been the inevitable product of a period of rapid expansion in the company, characterized by widening corporate interests and increasingly decentralized management at Turner. The Columbus territory had by 1985 done a few small jobs developed by a Columbus lawyer named Bill Eachus, who had made a name for himself as a linebacker for Ohio State University and was locally well regarded. Rick Lombardi, a capable and ambitious Princeton-educated civil engineer who had served his Turner apprenticeship in New York and then managed some of the company's big Pittsburgh work during the late 1970s, was by then a few years into his job as manager of the Columbus territory and as eager as any territory manager to expand his volume. When Eachus came along with a development plan for Rickenbacker Airport that was several times the size of any of the earlier work that Turner had done for him, Lombardi was an interested listener. In this plan, Flying Tiger Airline, the air cargo firm that had been started after the Second World War by survivors of the legendary Flying Tiger Squadron, was going to lease a big, state-of-the-art air cargo facility that would be built for its exclusive use at Rickenbacker Airport. A local authority had been established to manage and facilitate the process and to provide some of the needed funding, and a sponsor was being sought to finance, build, and own the facility and lease it to Flying Tiger.

The county that owned the 1,600-acre airport had by early 1985 failed in its first effort to implement the plan with a favored local developer and now turned to Eachus, who had a following of wealthy investors from whom he intended to obtain financing for the project. He was committed to Turner for the construction. From the beginning there was a little uncertainty about the financing, because Flying Tiger was understood to be financially weaker than a prudent investor might have liked, but there were aspects of the proposition that were thought to offset the tenant's weakness. The principal offsetting factor was a combination of available investment tax credits and accelerated depreciation scheduling that attached to the proposition, benefits that would offset substantial tax liabilities for the high-earning investors that Eachus would be bringing onboard, and those potential tax benefits would make an increased level of risk more acceptable.

But there was a potentially serious flaw in the plan too. The regulations that would provide the tax relief were to expire at the end of 1985, and for the investors to derive their benefits, the $48 million building and a related approximately $16 million worth of airport improvements would have to be completed by then. It was already late spring, there was a substantial amount of work to be done, and Eachus didn't yet have his financing in place.

With the project in jeopardy, the county stepped in on the first of July with its own large share of the project's cost, and Turner decided to accept it and gamble on Eachus's ability to produce the rest of the money. By the afternoon of the day on which the county's $12 million check was received by Turner, the first 200 cubic yards of foundation concrete were in place, and a pace was established that day that never slackened until the end of 1985, when the whole $64 million project was finished.

But the balance of the financing never materialized. After half a dozen profitable quarters, FlyingTiger in October of 1985 reported a huge quarterly loss, and Eachus's investors disappeared. By then Turner's own investment in the project had reached $14 million. Conant and McNeill elected to seek their own financing, with a plan to do whatever was necessary to get Flying Tiger into the building and paying rent. For as long as necessary, Turner would become the owner.

Coming on the heels of the trouble at Gateway and other problematic jobs, the developments at Rickenbacker were about the last thing Turner needed in 1985. For a company like Turner, the option of simply abandoning the project could never even be considered, so it simply faced up to making the best of things. Bonds were issued with Turner's own guarantee, and by the end of December1985, at virtually the moment the work was being finished, the long-term funding for the project was put in place. Turner had by then completed $64 million worth of work in six months, a prodigious achievement, but its troubles had only started. Although acquisition of Flying Tiger by Federal Express would later ameliorate some of the problems, the severely disadvantageous financing plan that had finally been required to raise the money would impose continuing and almost prohibitive costs on Turner for years to come.

For the most part, there was little knowledge or discussion of these massive losses within Turner except in the privacy of the boardroom and in the highest reaches of corporate management. Of course, people who were directly involved knew all about them, but the great breadth and intensity of the firm's traditional construction work during the 1980s tended to obscure the bad news or to reduce it to something that seemed to most people to be more like an irritating distraction than something to worry about. The volume of work the company was building in the United States and elsewhere was still larger than the comparable volume of any like firm, and it was increasing by leaps and bounds toward an annual value of $3 billion, with profitability sufficient to maintain and occasionally to increase the uninterrupted payment of dividends to the shareholders. It was an immensely busy period for Turner in which there were almost always more than about 350 jobs at one stage of activity or another, and it wasn't unusual for at least thirty of those to be larger than $50 million, with half of those thirty often larger than $100 million.

In addition to the continuing volume of health care construction, Turner during the 1980s was building hotels for Hyatt, Marriott, Radisson, and others; college and university buildings for Cal Tech, Cornell, Princeton, Rutgers, Wesleyan, Yale, and others; and sports facilities in Detroit, Denver, and in Charlotte, North Carolina. The exuberant growth in the number and geographic distribution of projects had the effect of extending the company's experience to include almost every imaginable building type. There were prisons in California, Connecticut, and Ohio; airline terminals in California, Illinois, and Tennessee; large convention and exhibition halls; museums; theaters; department stores; and a host of other special building types distributed throughout most of the country. There was even a resurgence of Turner's old special capability in industrial construction, and during the 1980s the company worked on the construction of new plants or the renovation of existing ones for Boeing, Chrysler, Kellogg, Martin Marietta, and others. In California, Turner built an American headquarters for Honda, where the dedication ceremony featured a rare American appearance by Soichiro Honda, the founder of the company.

Even with such a broad distribution of work, most of what Turner built during the 1980s was commercial office buildings, many of them the spectacular new high-rise towers that were beginning to fill in the skylines of the country's largest cities. There was nothing new for Turner about spectacular office buildings, as the company had been building them for years, but except for the virtually continuous array that Turner had been building for the Galbreath interests since the 1950s, most of the big office building work of earlier years had been done for the country's big corporations. For the most part, those had been jobs in which Turner's had been more the role of general contractor than construction manager. Turner's big corporate clients knew what they wanted, told their architects what it was, and then engaged Turner to build it. The buildings normally provided extremely high-quality space and in many cases presented to the public just the corporate image that was being sought. But the owners of the buildings were companies that derived their income from the goods or services they produced, not from the office buildings that Turner built for them, so there was usually a good deal less pressure to ensure that what was built would be economically optimal.

John Galbreath and others like him had another agenda, and Turner was a part of it from the beginning. The buildings themselves were Galbreath's product, and his earnings depended entirely on the production of space that would generate a return on his investment. For these buildings the design of the space, the materials that were used, and the time and money needed to put them all in place were essential elements in the profitability equation. It was in that context that Turner's special capability for managing the process from the beginning of design until the completion of construction flourished. Although Turner had been engaged for years in one form or another of what would come to be called construction management, that modus operandi had only really begun to gather momentum in the late 1960s. It grew through a number of variations during the Galbreath years that followed, and by 1980 it had become Turner's predominant basis of contracting for its services.

By then the country's economy was expanding vigorously. An aging John Galbreath continued to play a role in his firm, but by the 1980s his son Dan had taken over as CEO, bringing Turner along for construction of large urban projects across the country. Of course, the Galbreaths by then had some strong competitors themselves and many of them were becoming important Turner clients too.

Gerald Hines was one of them. An electrical engineer himself, he'd been a successful entrepreneur in Houston in the early 1970s, when he developed Shell Oil Company's headquarters there. Like his competitors in the still relatively young field of upscale development work, Hines was committed to the idea that by producing buildings of extraordinarily high quality he could attract very strong tenants who would be able and willing to pay the high rents he'd be charging, and he started by hiring the best architects and the best builders he could find. In Chicago, where Shell Oil Company joined with him to finance his Three First National Building, an approximately $85 million, fifty-seven-story office building, he commissioned Skidmore Owings & Merrill to design the project and he brought in Turner to build it.

Three First National would prove to be an immensely successful project for everyone involved except Turner, for whom it would be a financial disaster. Hines had brought an approach to contracting for the work that was unique, and its potential hazards escaped Turner's full appreciation until it was too late. In the Hines approach, the construction manager committed in the beginning to a price that included the cost of building the basic structural shell, occasionally including the elevators and some other core components but always including the cost of managing what was estimated to be the entire project as well as a fixed fee. It was stipulated that subcontracts for work not yet provided for in the base contract would be added without any increase in Turner's price beyond the net amounts of the subcontracts themselves, and it was intended by Hines that whatever Turner had provided for managing the work and for its fee would remain fixed. Under this plan, Hines's staff negotiated directly with subcontractors for the rest of the work, with varying degrees of participation by Turner, and awarded subcontracts that were added to Turner's contract without further markup. Such added, aggressively negotiated subcontracts sometimes generated problems and costs that Turner felt hadn't been anticipated in its contract with Hines, and the results were uniformly painful. At Three First National that contracting approach (together with the impact of blizzard) proved to be especially damaging for Turner, and the company suffered an out-of-pocket loss of several million dollars.

The company took its lumps, continuing to regard the Hines people well but resolved to evaluate the subtleties of the new approach more thoroughly. By the time the 1980s came into view, Turner was wiser and more capable of working out a (marginally) more generous arrangement for the next Hines job, a splendid high-rise office building in Houston that would be called Texas Commerce Tower. Designed by Turner's old friend I. M. Pei, at seventy-five stories it would be one of the tallest buildings west of the Mississippi River. Turner's Dick Corry, one of the seven future Turner leaders who as younger men had managed the work at Erieview Tower in Cleveland during the 1960s, took charge of the job, and by 1981 construction history had been made in Houston.

Texas Commerce Tower was a graceful, slender reed of a building more than a thousand feet tall, with a structural frame that was a blend of cast-in-place concrete and structural steel that challenged the builders from the start. Corry first experimented with a couple of approaches to building it, but early on he elected to import from Australia a superbly effective jacking system for raising his formwork from floor to floor, and he made a decision to pump all the superstructure concrete the full seventy-five stories to the roof. The system was disassembled every night after the day's work had been finished and rebuilt in time to resume pumping the following day. Before long, Corry had found a rhythm that produced a new floor every three days, a rarely matched performance that Engineering News-Record reported in detail and featured on its cover. Of course, Corry was by then one of the company's elite high-rise builders, having previously built the sixty-four-story U.S. Steel headquarters in Pittsburgh, but little of what he had done or would do during the rest of his thirty-nine years with Turner would match the Texas Commerce job.

Once Texas Commerce was substantially completed, Corry went on to build Hines's Republic Bank tower in Houston. A fifty-seven-story jewel designed by Philip Johnson and wrapped in a thinly sliced red granite imported from Sweden, it's remembered by Corry as a textbook job that was built profitably and virtually without a problem. Later, in 1988, Corry would succeed West Point-educated Tony Cucolo as manager of Turner's Houston-based Southwest Territory.

By the mid-1980s, what Turner was doing for Hines was approaching the scale and style of the Galbreath work that had been at or near the center of Turner's urban construction since the 1960s, and while the relationship between Turner and Hines was unlikely ever to reach the extraordinary closeness that had characterized the company's relationship with the Galbreaths, it had become an extremely strong one. By the time the Houston work was finished, Turner had started construction for two more spectacular high-rise towers for Hines in New York, at a combined cost that exceeded $200 million, both designed by architects whose prominence matched Pei's and Johnson's. Over the next dozen years the company would put in place more than a billion dollars' worth of work that was owned or controlled by the Hines Company.

The renaissance of the big cities was bringing along a whole new breed of sophisticated developers to replace the conservative insurance companies and banks that had sponsored much of the urban development of earlier years. John Galbreath had been in the vanguard of the new developers, but by this time he was in his eighties and although still consulting on such work (and still bringing Turner into his projects wherever appropriate), his most active years were well behind him. Within only a few more years both he and his son Dan, who had succeeded him as CEO in 1980, would die within seven years of one another, John in 1988 and Dan in 1995.

There were other important, upscale developers. In New York Robert Tishman and his son-in-law Jerry Speyer had split off from the old, publicly owned Tishman

Realty and Construction Company to do development work on their own as Tishman Speyer, and when they were brought in by Equitable in 1983 to supplement that company's own staff on the project Turner was building for Equitable in New York, Tishman Speyer and Turner got to know each other. In 1986 Tishman Speyer engaged Turner to build the $67 million office building at 375 Hudson Street that would later become Turners' own corporate office, and a long and loyal relationship between the two firms followed. At around the same time, the Pittsburgh-based Oliver Tyrone group, headed by a scion of the old Oliver Steel family of Pittsburgh, was developing high-quality buildings of its own and engaging Turner to build its National Steel Building in Pittsburgh, its Diamond Shamrock Building in Cleveland, and its 1234 Market Street Building in Philadelphia under a contract that enabled Turner to do simultaneous centralized purchasing for major trades for all three buildings.

Out west, where Turner had by the 1980s established itself as the region's leading builder, another crop of large-scale urban developers was emerging, and Maguire Thomas Partners in Los Angeles was among the most successful of the lot. Maguire was a former banker with a flair for architecture and Thomas was a former trial lawyer, and they shared with Galbreath and the others an idea that well-designed buildings in the country's urban centers made good investments. By the later years of the 1980s Maguire Thomas Partners and Turner had become close and interdependent friends, having built the two huge Wells Fargo Centers that Skidmore Owings & Merrill had designed in Los Angeles and having gone east together to build I. M. Pei's big Commerce Square project in Philadelphia. But it would be Pei's First Interstate Building in Los Angeles that would become the most widely known of all the Turner-built Maguire Thomas buildings.

First Interstate was a seventy-five-story story steel-framed tower in a region so vulnerable to earthquake that it was designed to survive a shock of Richter magnitude 8.3, and would comprise almost 2 million square feet of the kind of office and retail space that characterized the elegant architectural vocabulary of I. M .Pei. To build it, Turner brought in another of its high-rise stars, Doug Meyer.

It's probably fair to say that Meyer had been preparing for the First Interstate job for most of the thirty-two years he'd already spent working for Turner. He was another of the Cleveland Seven, the men who had worked together on the Erieview Tower job in Cleveland during the 1960s and had all later moved on to executive rank at Turner. He'd worked under Corry on Turner's U.S. Steel job in Pittsburgh and been head man for Turner on the sprawling complex of buildings that Philip Johnson designed for IDS in Minneapolis at the beginning of the 1970s. In 1973 it was Meyer who was brought out to the Rocky Mountains to build a world headquarters building for Johns Manville near Denver, and later it would be Meyer that Turner would bring to San Francisco to build the great Moscone Convention Center, with its six-acre, column-free, below-grade exhibit space. He started building the First Interstate building in Los Angeles in June 1987, and by early 1990 the tenants had begun to move in.

As Turner moved into the latter part of the 1980s its annual volume of construction was moving ever closer to $3 billion, an amount sufficient to sustain its position as the largest of the big American contractors who specialized in building construction. The scale of the company's work was by now so vast that even a huge project like Texas Commerce or First Interstate, which could normally be expected to take two to three years to complete, would each represent during the years in which they were under construction less than 2 percent of the work Turner was doing.

But there had been other things going on at Turner since about 1980 that would, by the closing years of the decade, begin to take their toll of the firm's prosperity. When Walter Schularick had taken over for Jim Griffis at Turner Development Corporation during the early eighties, he had accelerated its shift away from residential development to a focus on commercial development. For a while the shift appeared to be working well. Banks and insurance companies had been authorized to spend limited fractions of their resources on the acquisition of such properties and for a while they represented a good market for the kind of buildings that TDC was developing. It was a process well known to Schularick, whose earlier work as development manager for Honeywell had been similar. He brought a lively energy to the task and had soon relocated TDCs principal office from Chicago to Tampa, Florida, which was thought to be the center of a potential expansion. Within a year or two TDC had developed a staff of more than 100, and there were active TDC projects in a dozen cities around the country. Turner had invested something like $40 million in the operation. Although by 1983 Turner's annual reports were still showing only modest sales and modest earnings for TDC, hopes were high.

But the expected increase in the pace of sales didn't materialize, and that failure began to impose a new pressure to which Turner was entirely unaccustomed: The company was starting to run short of cash. Each TDC project required new money that couldn't be recovered until the project was sold, and as the number of unsold projects increased and as the big network of TDC salespeople continued to bring new projects into the system at a fast rate, the amount of Turner's debt and the extent of the cash that had been invested in TDC projects increased. Turner's bonding companies were beginning to consider the need for limits that would inhibit the company's core construction business.

And that wasn't the worst of it. Accounting and reporting conventions in the new business weren't always exactly like the straightforward rules to which Turner was accustomed in its construction work, and it soon became evident to the board that earnings projections that had been the basis for establishing high estimated asset values for the properties had in some cases been dependent on compliance with leasing guarantees and other uncertainties of a softening marketplace. In practical terms, optimistic sales projections had been the basis for property valuations, and the net effect had been an overstatement of Turner's own corporate net worth. Walter Shaw tried to stem the flow of cash by instructing Schularick to discontinue the creation of new projects until he had accelerated the sale of completed properties, but between a softening of the market itself and what appeared to some to be Schularick's own eagerness to start new projects and to retain for Turner as much ownership in the completed ones as possible, Shaw's effort was largely unavailing. Schularick retired and was replaced by John P. Arthur, who would do what he could to implement Shaw's directive, but of course by then TDC and its network of properties already had a considerable momentum of their own.

As late as 1986 there were still twenty-one projects under development, aggregating almost 3 million square feet of space, and in that year Congress ratified damaging changes in the tax law that reduced even further the value of properties that TDC owned. Between an already weakening demand for space and adverse changes in the tax law, the net realizable value of properties that TDC was trying to sell plummeted, and Turner's annual report would have to tell the story. A severe write-down was the unavoidable next step, and its impact on Turner's financial statement exacerbated the fears of the bonding companies. What had not many years earlier seemed an entirely reasonable and prudent course of action for this traditionally conservative company had now become a threat to its very survival.

By 1987 even the continuing profitability of the company's core construction business wasn't enough to offset the monumental impact of what was happening in TDC and elsewhere in the Diversified Services Group, and Turner had its first losing year since the Great Depression, only the fourth in its eighty-five year history. Between the damage imposed by the Gateway project in Singapore, by the Rickenbacker project in Ohio, by TDC, and by mounting losses in the company's open-shop subsidiary, TransCon, Turner's late-twentieth-century flirtation with enterprises outside its traditional business scope had lost its appeal.

The loss that showed up in 1987 shook top management to its roots, and it was followed by some drastic changes. TDC moved quickly to terminate plans for new starts and began the serious business of liquidating its existing holdings, although commercial prudence inhibited the pace of liquidation and the process would spill over into the 1990s. Trans-Con's work was folded into Big Turner's to allow Trans-Con itself to be discontinued. Bob Kupfer retired from Turner to take a senior position with Turner client Tishman Speyer, which was starting a development program in the Far East, and the separation between Construction and Diversified was discontinued. Al McNeill, twenty-eight years into his career at Turner but not long into its presidency, braced to lead a battle for the company's survival.

15.

McNeill and Parmelee

Not many of the almost 3,400 people who worked for Turner in 1987 were able to remember a losing year. There hadn't been one since the $2 million Freedomland disaster twenty-seven years earlier, and before that it had been another twenty-five years since Turner's brush with the Great Depression. Good and regularly increasing volume and earnings had by 1987 become so commonplace for Turner that the $22 million loss the company reported that year could certainly have been expected to shock and upset anyone who was paying attention.

But in fact most people below the level of the company's senior management didn't really think much about the news, at least at first. Company executives and managers worried about it, of course, but most other people at Turner were so thoroughly absorbed in the massive volume of construction the company was doing at the time that even such awful news didn't immediately get the attention it deserved. In most of the thirty-seven locations where Turner's business was being done in the United States and abroad, attention was for the most part focused on managing almost $2.8 billion worth of construction that Turner put in place during 1987, and to some extent on another almost $4 billion in backlog that would be carried forward into 1988 and 1989. Outside the Diversified Services Group, almost every job had remained profitable, the serious problems having for the most part been concentrated in the TDC properties and in what was being done by some of the newly established or newly acquired subsidiaries. It would still be a while before the real impact of the bad news would make itself felt among the rest of the staff, and before the long, sometimes arduous, but ultimately successful effort toward recovery would begin to show results.

At sixty-five, Herb Conant reached the mandatory retirement age for chairmen in 1988, and during that year what would effectively become an office of the CEO would begin to take shape under Al McNeill as the incoming chairman and Harold Parmelee as McNeill's replacement as president. The poor financial setting of 1988 was an especially inauspicious one for a new management team, but it was a stroke of good fortune for Turner that McNeill and Parmelee were the natural heirs to the top jobs. Both were consummate Turner loyalists with long histories in the firm, and both were smart and technically competent. At least equally important, the temperamental balance between the two of them was ideal for a combined management approach.

McNeill was no stranger to troubled situations, having almost a decade earlier come to New York from Philadelphia to rehabilitate a spate of problem jobs and to put the region back on its feet, tasks to which he was able to bring the effective if sometimes prickly authority of a man who was accustomed to being in charge. He'd been president since 1985 and had reorganized the New York region into several business units that included, but separated from one another, markets that had previously been ineffectively submerged in a single New York territory. Parmelee, the cerebral and more reserved Connecticut Yankee whom McNeill had brought down from Boston in 1983 to run New York, had by 1988 risen through a group vice presidency to become senior vice president for the Eastern Region, and he brought along a capacity and enthusiasm for detail that would make the pair of them a supremely effective team. Both were steeped in the Turner culture, the deeply embedded sense of extended family that had characterized the place for eighty-five years, and both were ready to do what had to be done to lead the company through a period that would prove to be even more difficult than they imagined when they started. Fifteen years later, contemporaneous accounts of their period of management would describe it as one in which there was a continuing and successful effort by both of them to ensure that the each was as capable as the other of managing the company's business.

Their management quickly focused on a variety of objectives intended to achieve three goals: stemming the losses to ensure survival of the firm, enhancing the company's cash liquidity, and increasing profitability.

They started with the urgent task of stemming the losses, immediately putting a stop to any further development by TDC and focusing on the completion and sale of its holdings. But the momentum that had already been generated by that troubled subsidiary made the goals elusive. TDC had been far from alone when it entered the business of developing nonresidential properties back at the end of the 1970s and in the early 1980s, with prospects of significant earnings in a promising market. Pension funds had by then begun to invest some of their abundant resources in such properties, strengthening an already growing market, and in 1981 the Economic Recovery Act had further enhanced the market by providing attractive incentives for individual investors as well. Under its provisions, an investor was able to write off depreciation of its properties over short periods at sharply accelerated rates, effectively rendering much of the income generated by them (and by other, unrelated investments) free of taxes. It was possible in those years for wealthy businesspeople and professionals to invest in such properties at relatively low rates of return, largely in order to shelter big incomes that were being generated elsewhere, and during the freewheeling days of the early 1980s such high earners invigorated a burgeoning market that looked as though it knew no limit. Between 1981 and 1985, just when TDC was most active in its development work, funds invested in projects like TDC's increased by almost 500 percent, flooding the country with new commercial real estate.

By 1985 all this exuberance had produced a good deal more commercial space than anyone needed or wanted. With completed buildings on its hands and others at various stages of development, it was no wonder that TDC was having trouble complying with Walter Shaw's earlier edict that it should be selling off some of its holdings to raise cash. And the bad news didn't end there: In 1986 the federal government, recognizing that its earlier goal of stimulating construction had been well achieved, reversed its ground by enacting a new tax reform bill in which the accelerated depreciation features of the 1981 regulations were repealed and by mandating that it would no longer be possible for a "passive" investor (one not actively engaged in the work) to use losses incurred in such projects to offset gains earned elsewhere. Those changes quickly discouraged virtually all investment in such ventures and harshly reduced the values and prices of buildings that had already been completed. The new regulations became a major threat to the solvency of some of the investors and institutions that had become involved in these once-attractive properties, and they had a devastating effect on TDC, which would write down more than $60 million in the value of its holdings over the next few years.

Turner's management, saddled with a portfolio of properties that would prove extremely difficult to sell except at destructively low prices, was for the most part forced to retain them and to continue paying interest on debt that by 1988 had grown to more than $200 million. Over a period of about the next half-dozen years, while the company struggled to sell off the properties, the burden of paying that interest would be a stubborn and continuing obstacle to profitability for Turner, and the task of stemming losses in such a setting would prove to be a slower and more demanding one than anyone expected.

TDC was by far the worst of the loss generators that had to be addressed by the new management, but it wasn't the only one. The troubled Gateway project in Singapore was at its most vulnerable stage in 1988, shut down and awaiting resolution that was then still more than a year away. And although the immediate impact of the almost simultaneous disaster at Rickenbacker had by then been recognized and addressed, the long-term aspects of its resolution required Turner to continue to absorb losses over the remaining years of a new lease. Trans-Con had been discontinued; its obligations and $18 million loss transferred to Big Turner, but its troubled jobs had to be finished.

The task of eliminating or at least reducing losses wasn't limited to the big and high profile Turner enterprises. Other activities of the now defunct Diversified Services Group were for the most part losing money too, and stemming the company's losses required addressing those activities as well. Turner Medical Building

Services, Inc., had been established by Diversified to develop small ancillary buildings for hospitals, including medical office buildings, ambulatory clinics, and the like, and had in fact done a little work, mostly in Florida and out west. But on balance, it was an unprofitable operation and was discontinued as a development subsidiary almost as soon as the drive to eliminate losses took hold, remaining active for a few years to wind up its affairs and to provide consulting services to health care institutions planning new construction. Turner Energy Systems was another subsidiary that had been established under the Diversified Services Group, this one to build cogeneration facilities for clients seeking to level out their demand for electrical energy they were obtaining from public utilities or to protect themselves from power shortages and outages. Here was an enterprise that might have been a decade or two ahead of its time, but in the late eighties, when Turner Energy was predicting a billion dollars in annual sales within another year or two, it languished with few contracts and no profits. It was discontinued. Turner Golf, Inc., was a Diversified component that had been established to build golf courses, but although some money had been invested to organize and develop the operation, none of its prospects had ever reached the construction stage. Like Turner Energy Systems, it was discontinued.

Ameristone, Inc. was among the largest of the Diversified companies. It had been established to operate as a natural stone subcontractor, furnishing and erecting finished stone mostly for the new high-rise commercial buildings on which high-quality granite or limestone facades were being specified. To manage Ameristone Turner had brought in Malcolm Swenson, an experienced former stone contractor himself, and during the late 1980s the company had done the stone work on some of the country's most prestigious new high-rise buildings, including high-rise towers in Chicago, New York, and elsewhere. But furnishing and erecting stone for urban buildings can be a risky business, and losses plagued the new company. Worse yet, the big office building market effectively disappeared during the 1980s, and competition for the few jobs that survived became very difficult for Ameristone, whose losses mounted. By 1988 Turner had pretty much phased out Ameristone's domestic operations, but through an association with the

British W. E. Grant Company, it had taken on some stone work in Great Britain. That Grant-Ameristone joint venture would continue for a few years but was ultimately terminated without any significant recovery.

Turner International Industries (TII) was another major component of the Diversified Services Group that wasn't producing profits in the difficult days of the late 1980s. In spite of that, its future seemed a little more secure than the futures of its sibling firms. With its relatively small number of widely scattered jobs, even intermittent profits for individual projects were proving to be insufficient for offsetting the cost of managing and administering such a far-flung organization. But Turner's management was at that time inclined to tolerate some level of deficit because it attributed to TII an ability to support Big Turner in other ways, perhaps by providing U.S. clients with insights into the mechanics of getting construction done abroad, even when it wasn't going to be done by Turner. It wasn't a unanimous view, but it had enough support to keep TII going.

By 1987 Bob Nilsson had replaced Frank Voci as TII's CEO, and during that year Nilsson attended a meeting of the World Economic Forum in Switzerland that would affect TII's future and Turner's as well. On his trip to Switzerland, Nilsson visited Peter Steiner, whom he had first met during the 1970s when young Steiner had worked briefly for Turner in the United States in search of exposure to American construction methods. Steiner's father had headed Karl Steiner AG, one of the largest construction firms in Switzerland, but by the time Peter Steiner and Bob Nilsson got to socializing in Switzerland in 1987 young Steiner had inherited his father's job.

Over the next year or two Nilsson and Steiner interacted from time to time, mostly at subsequent sessions of the World Economic Forum. TII was still struggling for profitability, nurturing a variety of opportunities that included several in Great Britain, where it had entered into a joint venture with the British firm R. M. Douglas to manage construction of the $166 million Birmingham (England) Convention Center, and where it was about to join with Douglas again to build a big plant for Honda in Swindon. Although none of those projects produced the profitability that was being sought, prospects for TII were bright enough in 1990 to induce Peter Steiner to propose joining forces with TII to seek construction contracts in Europe, an idea that got the enthusiastic attention of McNeill and Parmelee, who made several trips to Europe to discuss it. By late 1990 an agreement had been put in place to establish a jointly owned firm for doing construction in Europe as Turner Steiner Europe (TSE), leaving TII itself free to continue independently its pursuit of work elsewhere around the world.

Meanwhile, the events of the late 1980s had left Turner itself short of cash for the first time in its long history. The formation of TSE would bring modest relief, but between the continuing demands of TDC's debt and the lingering effects of unsuccessful ventures, a company that had always discounted its bills, and that had always had more cash available than it really needed, was starting to pay a good deal more attention to its cash balances than it ever had paid before.

What is sometimes characterized as the Turner culture may have exacerbated the cash problem. In most companies engaged in hard-edged businesses like construction, maintaining staff is seen as being among the more elastic of costs: When times are good they hire all the people they need, and when times are bad they lay off anyone who can't earn his keep. But the concept of a lifetime career at Turner had from the company's earliest days been an essential (albeit unwritten) part of the employment compact. There had always been some attrition during about the first five years of employment, when some new hires who probably should never have gone to work for Turner in the first place would leave the company, but after that early winnowing, almost everyone at Turner was likely to remain with the company for the rest of his working career. Every year hundreds of retirees with twenty-five years' service (or more) still gather at annual dinners in the country's big cities to relive their working days, and even among these sometimes hard-bitten construction veterans it's difficult to hear anything but the fondest recollections of their relationships with their colleagues and with the company. Early in 1992 it probably didn't surprise anyone who knew Turner well to hear that, in spite of the hard times that had come along since 1987, the company's staff had shrunk very little.

Preserving such a culture can be expensive. Turner people who performed poorly in one area or whose responsibilities in an area had ended for one reason or another were sometimes transferred to other jobs, rather than laid off. And older employees close to retirement were sometimes assigned tasks that were only modestly productive but that would ensure their continued employment until their actual retirement dates arrived. It was all part of a management style reminiscent of an earlier time, and it bred fierce loyalties that were difficult to quantify in terms of profitability. But in the short span of time that was increasingly becoming the metric of the 1990s, it was inevitable that such a style would be seen by some as one that obstructed the company's effort to regain meaningful profitability. Before long, differences between those who sympathized with such a view and those who opposed it would have to be addressed.

McNeill and Parmelee were both products of the culture themselves, and their commitment to it would effectively forestall significant layoffs for another few years. They addressed the cash problem in other important ways, but although they were able to produce some improvement, it would be1996 before cash availability would be anything less than a serious problem for Turner. A heightened awareness of the importance of cash was basic, and they saw to it that rigorous cash-management plans were established and maintained in the business units. Whatever had to be done to husband cash was done: Collection of invoices was accelerated, and payments made by Turner slowed a bit. From time to time, during the years that immediately followed the big write-down, incentive bonus programs were suspended for a year or two at a time, and salary increases became much less frequent, especially among the highest earners. Austerity was the watchword, and for the most part the loyalty of the staff made it less difficult than it might have been.

Not every increase in available cash was the direct result of the company's efforts to enhance its liquidity. Al McNeill had never been entirely comfortable with some of the open-shop acquisitions that his predecessors had made a dozen or so years earlier, reasoning that there had been nothing in Turner's existing trade relationships that would have precluded its right to do open-shop work in most areas anyway, and that such acquisitions were unnecessary. In addition,

McNeill was a practitioner of strong central control and consistent performance among the Turner business units, and he had never been entirely happy with the lingering independence of some of the acquired subsidiaries. In 1989 he sold the F. N. Thompson Company of Charlotte to an Alabama-based group that included a combination of Finnish and American investors. Over the years that followed, Turner and Thompson would join as co-venturers in a number of successful projects that would include building the big stadium in Charlotte for the newly formed Carolina Panthers football team. A couple of years after the Thompson sale, McNeill sold the BFW Company to a group from among its own management.

The sale of Thompson and BFW left two of the most successful and prized of the 1980s acquisitions firmly within the Turner family: Universal and Lathrop. Universal had been the sole survivor of the H. W. Pearce acquisition, whose other component companies had either left when various members of the Pearce family left Turner or whose operations had simply been discontinued. But Universal, which had already been a prospering Alabama general contracting firm when it was acquired with the other Pearce holdings in 1981, blossomed even further under Turner and would go on to do some of the most important work in the region, sometimes with participation by other Turner units and sometimes without it. Lathrop, like Universal, had already become a major force in construction in Ohio when Turner acquired the company in 1986. Based in Toledo, Lathrop was actually a few years older than Turner, had a generally similar culture and clientele, and by 1986 had built some of the most important buildings in the state and more than 100 bridges along its federal highways. When acquired, Lathrop was being managed by David Morgan, but he retired soon after the acquisition and was succeeded by Robert Maxwell, an exceptionally capable manager who had already been with the company for almost twenty years. Lathrop's already broad range of construction capabilities included an increasing volume of industrial work for manufacturing firms that were locating or expanding plants in the Midwest, and within a few years the company would twice win the Turner Flag for improvement in its performance. Both Universal and Lathrop shared the problems that the recession of the nineties was visiting on Turner itself, but like Turner they were staying the course and would recover within a few years.

Other strategies to improve liquidity were fashioned too. In 1991, when the company's lease at 633 Third Avenue was expiring and the landlord who had replaced John Galbreath in that building proposed a radical increase in rent, the company moved its New York office and its corporate headquarters downtown to a slightly less conveniently located building Turner had recently completed for Tishman Speyer at 375 Hudson Street. It was in a neighborhood that was gaining favor as a downtown office location and was just across Houston Street from a huge concrete-and-brick building that Turner had built for Western Electric seventy-one years earlier. The new building at 375 Hudson wasn't a bit less sound and attractive a place for the company's corporate headquarters than 633 Third Avenue had been, and it provided enough space for integrating most of the departments that had previously been separately housed in various locations, all for a cost that didn't exceed what the company had been paying. And McNeill was able to induce the new landlord to fund a substantial volume of tenant improvements as well.

In the same year as the move to Hudson Street, Turner curtailed its long-established and abundantly overfunded defined-benefit pension plan in favor of a new defined-contribution plan, a change that had the effect of increasing the company's book value by about $30 million and materially strengthening its balance sheet. What was more important was that a few years later a "cash balance plan" evolved, allowing the company to use some of its accumulated excess to pay premiums and freeing up cash that would otherwise have come from earnings, providing more of the increased liquidity it had been seeking.

There were other cash-generating strategies of varying size and effectiveness, including the sale of shares to the retirement plan and to the officers, but the biggest and most effective cash generator of all proved to be less the result of a well-planned strategy than an accident of history. A little over a year into the life of the new Turner Steiner Europe venture, Peter Steiner approached Al McNeill with a proposal to expand the Steiner interest beyond its 50 percent position in Turner Steiner Europe to include 50 percent of Turner International itself, creating Turner Steiner International. The subject of such a substantial further acquisition by Steiner had in fact surfaced during the earlier discussions that had led to the formation of Turner Steiner Europe, but McNeill had been wary, favoring a period of what he would later describe as living together before committing to marriage. But now that the TSE venture was a little over a year old, McNeill was ready to talk about expanding it, and he and Parmelee explored it with Peter Steiner and his group and then with the Turner board. In the negotiations that followed, an even broader and more favorable agreement was struck that established Turner Steiner International, jointly owned by Turner and Steiner, and more significantly, provided that the Steiner interests would acquire for cash a large block of Turner Corporation convertible securities. In exchange for $15 million, under this new agreement Turner would issue securities to Steiner that when converted to common shares would give the Steiner group control of almost 22 percent of Turner itself. It was a welcome milestone in the effort to restore the operating capability that had characterized the firm's long history, but the underlying risk of lost control would later figure in decisions critical to the company's future.

Gradually, some of the losses were being stemmed and a degree of liquidity was being restored, but the battle was far from over. Earnings that in earlier years would have been considered acceptable were being eroded by recurring losses and by the annual cost of servicing what remained of the debt that the McNeill-Parmelee administration had inherited, and the company's annual figures continued to oscillate between small profits and small losses. Even with the slowing of the loss rate and the gradual restoration of liquidity, Turner was still going to need to address the third of Al McNeill's basic goals: an expansion of profitability sufficient to restore the pattern of growth that had characterized the company's history from its earliest days.

One aspect of profitability, of course, was simple operating efficiency, and although steps had been taken at the corporate level and throughout the business units to ensure that the overhead was well controlled, there really wasn't much ground to be gained there. Quaker-driven forces had from the earliest days tended to steer Turner away from excess, and although there was some tightening down, the culture continued to militate against staff contractions that would have had more impact. An aspect of increased profitability that clearly needed to be addressed now was construction volume itself, and a vigorous effort to increase it was made during the late 1980s and the 1990s.

Unfortunately, it was a time when the tide of history was running against Turner. The national economy was slipping into recession toward the end of the 1980s, and the approximately $144 billion in new nonresidential building construction that was put in place by contractors throughout the United States during 1990 had by 1991 declined by almost 20 percent and would remain depressed until 1995. Worse yet, the fraction of that shrinking national market that Turner regarded as its own target, one that was dominated by the major urban and institutional projects that had been at the heart of the company's work for years, had been reduced even more. Just maintaining its previous share in such a distressed market could at best promise only modest earnings, and even achieving that would be no easy task in an economy in which competition had sharpened and fees had fallen. The administration hunkered down for the struggle.

A strategy that seemed likely to help in the preservation of market share, and that might even have the capacity to increase it, was one in which the company identified specific market segments in which Turner had some special advantage, and then intensified its sales efforts within them, sometimes at the expense of less promising targets. One such market that attracted Turner as sales volume began to slip included big public work and publicly funded private work. Here in the public arena was a market that included a great deal of the very large and often demanding work that not many construction firms could handle, and although it was by no means a new market for Turner it was one the company hadn't cultivated for years. But now public projects presented a new problem to Turner: Whenever such publicly sponsored projects required the builder's committing to a guaranteed cost, they also required that performance and payment bonds be provided, and obtaining such bonds, never a problem for Turner before the 1980s, wasn't going to be easy in this troubled period. As the condition of the economy worsened, the requirement for bonding increased, spreading beyond publicly funded projects to some in the private sector as well. Bankers, sensing weakness among some of their big developers, were starting to require bonds from them for the first time, and as a result, some private developers were starting to require bonds from their builders. The resources of the bonding companies themselves were finite, of course, so between troubled times and increased demand, bonds became more and more difficult to get.

One of Turner's responses to such new pressures was to develop strategies for reducing or eliminating the extent of bonding it was required to provide. For major subcontracts and for some others, it was able to obtain bonds from its own subcontractors that would bring a measure of protection to its clients, nominally reducing the need for Turner itself to become bonded, but it soon became clear that even with such strategies it was going to be necessary for Turner to increase its own bonding capacity if there was going to be any effective progress against the tightening of sources.

Federal Insurance Company, the Chubb subsidiary that had been providing Turner's performance and payment bonds for half a century, had been having its own problems with mounting contractor failures and was determined to stand fast on its existing bonding limits. Federal had, in fact, been considering reducing its limits at just the time that Turner was seeking an increase, and its resistance to increasing Turner's limit solidified Turner's resolve to seek additional, reliable relationships with at least a couple of other surety companies.

Between Turner's own recent financial reverses and the stresses the bonding companies themselves were feeling, it would have been hard to find a worse time to seek new sureties, and the task of getting it done fell to Hal Parmelee. Some of the dozen or more big companies he would approach to discuss bonding had been unsuccessfully seeking Turner's business for years, and in some cases they were understandably reluctant to consider it now that the shoe was on the other foot. But others who knew the company's reputation recognized a chance to build a foundation for substantial future business, and in some of those cases procedures were set in motion for monitoring Turner's financial recovery as a basis for justifying confidence. Parmelee established routines that would keep potential bonding sources regularly informed about earnings targets and achievements, in some cases even bringing rival insurers into joint meetings to hear about and discuss what and how Turner was doing. In time, the confidence the insuring companies were seeking began to develop, and signs that Turner's bonding problem might be approaching resolution began to appear.

Aetna, later acquired by CIGNA, was especially resistive at first. But in an early meeting with senior Aetna officers Parmelee had sensed the interest of a rising young executive, and he continued working with him toward Aetna's participation for several years before the big insurer would decide to take a chance. Liberty Mutual hadn't even been in the surety sector of the business before this period, but it was an old friend of Turner's, having provided the company's general insurance for years. When it had discovered a provision in its own charter that authorized it to write bonds, it had come to Turner in search of advice about the industry. Parmelee worked closely with them, and once Liberty made a decision to broaden out into the bonding business, Turner became one of its early customers. With Aetna and Liberty, Turner had developed two substantial additional sureties to supplement Federal.

As a result of the company's regained bonding strength and the progress that had been made in stemming losses and improving liquidity, there was now guarded optimism that volume, the essence of profitability, could be improved too.

Even early in 1991 there weren't many people below the senior level in Turner who had any real knowledge of just of how bad things had been or how bad they were. And it was understandable: During the years from and including 1987 through 1990 the company had put in place an annual average of more than $3 billion worth of construction, more than it had ever done before, and everyone responsible for getting that huge volume of work built had been fully engaged in doing it. It was, after all, construction that was the company's business, and on its jobs and in its offices people were simply so fully absorbed in getting the construction done that the condition of the national economy and the burden of the company's debt just didn't get much attention. Of course, Turner's senior managers were keenly aware of the problems, and they weren't alone. The Turner people responsible for securing new business were seeing them every day as the backlog declined.

By 1991, with the national recession deepening, the annual volume of new sales at Turner had fallen below the average of its preceding four years by 15 percent, a decline of almost half a billion dollars a year. That disturbing reduction was even sharper in the Northeast, where it had fallen almost 30 percent. Even in the usually stable central and western parts of the country almost every business unit saw annual declines of more than 10 percent. Turner's market share held fairly steady, but that was little consolation where real earnings were critical. The work simply wasn't there, and it wouldn't start to return for a few more years.

Such a turn in market conditions couldn't have occurred at a worse time for Turner, and it took its toll. Soon there had to be some weakening in the company's long-standing resolve to preserve staff jobs at almost any cost. There would be more layoffs, together with a broadening awareness of the company's problems. In the boardroom, where a general awareness of losses generated by high-risk ventures was still fresh, difficult times began to exact a toll too. Some directors wanted an even more vigorous contraction of staff, and some urged a commitment to zero-risk contracts, neither of which was acceptable to McNeill or Parmelee. Controls on spending were intensified, few strategies for securing new work were overlooked, and the company began to settle into an operating mode that would continue the vigorous pursuit of new and profitable work while it rode out the awful storm of the early 1990s.

The alignment of business units that managed work across the country had by then reverted to a three-region plan, with Tom Gerlach heading up the Western Division; Al Sanchez heading the Central Division; and Don Kerstetter, the former manager of the Philadelphia unit, heading the Eastern Division. In 1993 that structure would give way to an eight-region plan in which McNeill and Parmelee themselves would each take senior responsibility for a single region, McNeill for Washington, D.C., and Parmelee for New York and Boston. In the new structure, Sanchez would manage Cleveland and New Jersey plus several subsidiary companies, and Don Kerstetter would manage Philadelphia, Miami, Orlando, and Atlanta. Barry Sibson, who had been running the Los Angeles office, would replace the retiring Tom Gerlach as manager of the Western Region, which included all the West Coast offices; and Joe McCullough would take over a group that included Chicago, St. Louis, and Texas. Dick Manteuffel would take over a group that included Cincinnati, Nashville, Columbus, Pittsburgh, and Detroit. Joe Vumbacco would be brought over from his legal duties in the company to manage the Connecticut region.

These early 1990s were a difficult period for almost everyone in the construction business, and Turner was no exception. Between 1991 and 1995 the total volume of work in what Turner regarded as its own markets never rose to a level that was more than about 80 percent of what it had been in 1989, and the company would have two losing years during the period while showing negligible earnings in the other years. Of course, putting in place an annual average of even $2.8 billion in construction in each of those five years would still be a daunting task, and the work that was done was every bit as important and distinguished as the work the firm had been doing before. There just wasn't enough of it to compensate for the continuing drain imposed by earlier problematic ventures that were still taking their toll, or to pay the continuing deficits of the international group.

Bob Fee, who'd been working his way up through the Turner system in New York since the sixties, and who'd been running some of its biggest and most important jobs there since the seventies, had moved into the company's senior management in 1986 as vice president and general manager of the New York territory. But by 1991 it would have been hard to think of that once eagerly sought job as a plum: Between the national recession and the virtual collapse of the commercial office building market that Turner had dominated in New York for years, the annual construction volume that the company had seen as its own market there had shrunk by almost a third, and the territory that had for years been at the very center of the company's prosperity was struggling. Annual sales that had exceeded $500 million only a few years earlier were down to $250 million, cancellations weren't uncommon, and short-term prospects were poor.

Of course, the New York office was then emerging from a period in which it had done some of the city's most spectacular new buildings, many of them under

Fee's own supervision. Not the least of such recently completed projects were a few that had been brought to New York from Texas by Turner's good friends at the Hines Group. Almost simultaneously Turner had built Hines's thirty-story CBS Building (later renamed for E. F. Hutton and still later for Deutsche Bank) on Fifty-second Street, and nearby at Fifty-third Street and Third Avenue, it had built the thirty-four-story Hines-owned office building that would inevitably become known almost everywhere as the Lipstick Building because of the extraordinary lipstick-like shape that architect Philip Johnson had given it. And soon the company would be working on what had to be the most complex of all the Hines jobs, the granite-and-glass office tower that Skidmore Owings & Merrill had designed for construction above the old eight-story U.S. Post Office at 450 Lexington Avenue. It was as a part of that project that Turner relocated the operating elements of the busy Grand Central Post Office and then scraped out its remaining innards, bracing and preserving in place its landmarked exterior walls. Under Bob Fee's general supervision, with Gary Nebrycz and Jim McKenna providing project management, Turner next threaded massive new foundations down between and under the tracks of the busy railroad that operated below the building's lowest basement. By the time the company had built an office tower above the level of the old roof and restored the post office to its home quarters, a little more than three years had elapsed, and Turner had attracted a great deal of attention and widespread praise. But conditions in New York would still be such that more time would have to pass before the prosperity of earlier years would return.

New York had no monopoly on such complex work during this period. Out in the Westwood section of Los Angeles, where the decline in construction volume was beginning to look almost eerily like what was being seen in New York, albeit less severe, Turner had been doing work that was every bit as difficult as the post office. The company had taken on a contract to build an approximately $42 million office building that would occupy almost every square foot of a tiny, congested site at one of the country's busiest traffic intersections, the corner of Wilshire Boulevard and Veteran Avenue. The job comprised a seventeen-story office tower with eight levels of underground parking below. Although it was fraught with the usual problems of burrowing deeper into the ground than its immediate neighbors, the job really didn't appear on its face to be much more difficult than a good many other urban structures the company had built. What made One Westwood so complex were three underground watercourses that crossed the small site, threatening the stability of the very deep excavation and complicating the problem of ensuring the stability of adjacent structures. And exacerbating that combination of challenges was the unwillingness of adjacent owners to allow Turner to extend essential tie-backs under their buildings, making a reasonable and economically feasible solution increasingly difficult to find.

But a solution was found that made the job something of an engineering milestone. To facilitate dewatering and to ensure the stability of the adjacent buildings without the usual tie-backs, Turner elected to enclose the site with a 104-foot-deep, below-grade perimeter wall that would function as both a cofferdam to keep the water out and as the new building's eight-story foundation wall. The complex strategy for doing it was to install alternating sections of the perimeter wall in a deep perimeter trench, using first a bentonite slurry and then displacing the slurry with tremied concrete and doubling back to fill the empty sections until the wall was complete.

Hazardous and difficult as such an approach was, it was only the beginning. The design of the building itself required construction of a five-foot-thick reinforced concrete mat below the lowest parking level to support the building's columns and to resist hydrostatic pressure imposed by groundwater. But installing such a mat about 100 feet below grade was still a long way off when the construction plan was being hatched, and both the structural mechanics of bracing the new perimeter wall during construction and the economics of the project's schedule argued against such a delay.

Under project executive Charles Koch, Turner opted for a difficult plan that simplified the bracing scheme and reduced the original job schedule by months. The building's interior steel columns were welded into long sections and carefully lowered by crane into deep vertical shafts that Turner had excavated as much as seventy feet below the lowest parking level. Once in position, the columns' lowest sections were concreted in place to give them the properties of friction piles. Now the structure had a reliable, well-supported column system in place in advance of the installation of its supporting mat, and Turner was able to proceed with the remaining excavation of the site. As the difficult excavation process inched its way down between the new columns toward the mat level, the steel-and-concrete parking decks were put in place one by one with access openings left for excavating and removing the material that remained below. The reward for such tedious work was to be a big saving in time, but another departure from established procedure was going to be required before the full reward could be realized: As the work progressed below grade, a second set of crews in each trade was moving up into the seventeen-story tower above, setting steel, placing concrete, and ultimately completing the enclosure of the tower's superstructure at about the same time as the last cubic yard of concrete was being placed in the structural mat below. It was in every way an extraordinary process that attracted national attention in the industry and in much of the contemporaneous trade press, which labeled it the "up/down" method of construction. By the end of the century four other such projects would be done in the country, and three of them would be done by Turner.

Extraordinary as the Westwood job was, it was only one of many in the Los Angeles territory, which by the mid-'80s had become second in volume only to New York. But by the time another year or two had elapsed, the national recession would be asserting itself in the West, too, and it became a factor in determining where and how Turner would find new business. The surge of high-rise office buildings that had been at the center of its Los Angeles market had begun to wane, and Barry Sibson, who had become manager of the Western Region after Gene von Wening's untimely death, was beginning to cast a wider net for new work.

The San Francisco territory, in a sense the northern frontier of Sibson's Western Region in those days, was poised for its own growth spurt. In 1990 it had just earned the Turner Flag as the business unit showing the greatest improvement in sales and performance, and by the early 1990s it was seeking to capitalize on the momentum of the Moscone project, where its construction-management approach had established Turner as the construction-management force to reckon with in the Bay Area. Local authorities had pretty much completed the technical and political planning required for restoring and rebuilding many of the public buildings that had been damaged in northern California's 1989 earthquake, and they brought in Turner to manage construction of some of the bigger and more difficult post-earthquake jobs.

But by then the receding national economy was beginning to cast its shadow across San Francisco, too, and Turner's continued prosperity in the area was going to require reaching beyond the city and its immediate neighbors. By 1990, under Bob Wilson and Paul DeMange, the territory had begun to spread its wings, successfully reaching up into Sacramento and the surrounding towns for new work to replace some of the recession-inspired local decline. But even with its success in the Sacramento area, nothing the San Francisco territory would do in the early nineties would be more important to the Western Region's growth than its dramatic expansion into Oregon and Washington.

There had actually been a significant Turner presence in the Northwest since the 1970s, when the company had contracted with the federal government to manage construction of its $66 million Western Regional Center for the National Oceanic and Atmospheric Administration (NOAA) near Seattle, a job that included vast site development and harbor work as well as construction of 400,000 square feet of new buildings. Other big work in Washington and Oregon had followed during the 1980s, including (among a fair amount of other work) the Portland Justice Center, a big office building in Portland to accommodate the government's Bonneville Power Administration, and an expansion of the Portland Airport. For a good part of the 1980s it looked like Oregon was going to emerge as the center of new business for Turner in the Northwest.

But as promising as the Oregon work was, in the 1980s there was nothing in the Northwest that could rival the imposing Boeing presence in an around Seattle, and when the great airplane builder decided in 1988 to expand its manufacturing plant there, its choice for construction was Turner. The idea of a full-scale business unit in the Northwest had been given a good deal of thought by Turner's management, even before the Boeing job came along in 1988, especially in 1987 when Turner was awarded a contract to build the $105 million, 1.7-million-square-foot Two Union Square office building in Seattle for a development affiliate of the University of Washington. Two Union Square was a state-of-the-art high-rise office tower to match anything the company had done in California, awarded just when the market for such projects appeared to be collapsing, and destined for national prominence because of its pioneering use of ultra-high-strength concrete. But it was still the $85 million Boeing job (and the preference of Boeing's management) that convinced Turner's own management that Turner's future in the Northwest demanded an independent Turner office in that region, and that Seattle was where it should be.

The company's campaign to compensate for the decline in some of its western markets wasn't limited to its expansion into the Northwest by any means. Ed Quimby had come out west a few years earlier to see what he could do to bring the Western Region into the big health care market that was providing so much work in other parts of the country. He set up shop in Orange County, where he became general manager of the office. There was then still a certain novelty in the idea of concentrating a whole sales program on a selected building type, although Bob Nilsson had done the same thing for Turner's health care efforts back east and Bob Levine would soon be doing it in the Midwest. It was an approach that had received sporadic attention since the days of Bob Marshall, but it was one that was just coming into its own now with the enormous increase in attention being given to health care throughout the country. What made it especially appealing to Turner, which had by the mid-1980s established itself as a national leader in the field, was a growing awareness that the company could often shift capability in such a specialized area as health care from one location to another. The jobs were often big and complex and required preconstruction and construction capabilities that smaller local contractors were unlikely to have, and new ways of delivering health care and new ways of paying for it were radically altering the construction needs of the institutions providing the care. Out west, Quimby was able to offer Turner's broad-based hospital building experience and reputation to hospital boards that badly needed it, and little by little, the firm gained a foothold that would not many years later become virtual dominance in health care construction in the West.

What proved to be an especially important factor in establishing such a role for Turner was the rise of the health maintenance organization as an institution for delivering health care services. Kaiser Permanente, one of the earliest and probably the best regarded of the HMOs, was California-based, and in the mid-1980s, when Quimby was launching his campaign to expand Turner's role in health care construction, Kaiser was beginning a major expansion program of its own. A relationship between the two firms began to develop when Turner's bids were low on a couple of big jobs at Kaiser's Fontana complex, and once those projects began to play out, Kaiser became convinced of the usefulness of an approach in which the contractor's budgeting and production insights could be made available during the design period, optimizing and shortening the whole process. Before long, Kaiser had begun to engage Turner as its own construction manager and to rely on the company for a significant share of Kaiser Permanente work in California and elsewhere.

The concept of focusing on individual construction specialties wasn't new, of course, but in the early 1990s it was, for the most part, still more a sales approach rather than an operational one. At that time Turner was still a few years away from what would become its much more substantial and deliberate commitment to address important market segments through independently managed, specially qualified business units, each staffed not only for selling such projects but for managing their construction as well.

There was plenty of evidence that it was a good idea. Changes in the needs of the population and growth in the capacity of an increasingly affluent society to meet them were generating promising new construction markets of their own, and by the mid- '90s Turner was beginning to identify itself as an exceptionally qualified builder in some of the new specialties. Although it would still be a few years before what it was calling its "niche" approach would give way to the comprehensive process of dedicating selected business units to single market segments, it was a productive early step.

Laboratories for doing some of the country's most complex research, and sophisticated facilities for producing pharmaceuticals that hadn't even been imagined a few years earlier were beginning to show up among the company's new projects. Sports facilities that could only be built by companies of Turner's great size were surfacing with increasing frequency too, many of them with public profiles that were proportionate to their size and to the vastly expanded public interest in professional sports. Where television was generating big revenues, the major teams were especially eager for new facilities, and Turner was the choice of more than a few. In basketball the company built arenas for the Cleveland Cavaliers, the Portland Trail Blazers, and the Charlotte Hornets, and in 1996, in a joint venture with its former F. N. Thompson subsidiary, it would complete construction of the $150 million state-of-the-art football stadium for Jerry Richardson's Carolina Panthers, which would set a standard for a whole generation of NFL stadiums to follow.

The nature of work on almost any construction project, especially the very big ones that Turner was doing, is such that the task at hand is normally complex and demanding enough to absorb pretty much all the attention of the people working on them. Most of the approximately 3,000 men and women who were working on Turner jobs during the early 1990s were probably aware by then that business wasn't as good as it should have been, but few of them realized that the company was struggling. Although most of the company's projects were individually profitable, the debt that had been inherited mainly from the errant ventures of the 1980s was still imposing financial burdens that would inhibit the company's return to prosperity for a few more years.

There sometimes seemed to be no relief from forces that operated against a return to reliable profitability. The outbreak of the Gulf War brought new work almost to a standstill for the early months of 1991, and the savings-and-loan crisis had an effect on the real estate market that was so chilling that it rendered practically impossible the sale of TDC holdings at prices anywhere near Turner's original cost. At the same time, a radically tightened credit market was discouraging much of the commercial construction that had been at the core of Turner's

market for years. By 1991 many of the company's markets had sunk to new low levels. For Turner, even maintaining its former share of a declining market wouldn't
be enough to produce the earnings it needed to offset the burden of inherited
costs and losses. To make things worse, the very nature of its contracts was making
it even more difficult. In its new risk-averse posture it was doing much more construction-management work than it used to do, and its fees for such work were
smaller than they would have been for a like volume of traditional, at-risk general
contracting work. What was needed was a new strategy for expanding earnings in
a difficult period, and a variety of approaches evolved in different Turner territories.

In Chicago, where Turner had during the 1970s and the early 1980s been the
preeminent builder of high-rise, commercial office buildings, the market for such
work had by the later 1980s begun to shrink. The territory's emphasis had been
shifting to the low-rise buildings that predominated beyond the city's center, and
to the interiors work that had intensified when the demand for renovated space
began to exceed the demand for new space. By then the concept of establishing
special project divisions (SPDs) to do interior tenant work under separate contracts had begun to gain favor in a number of Turner territories, and some of them
began to recognize that such smaller work was best managed in a model that was
different from the Turner standard. Chicago had, in fact, established an SPD of its
own as early as 1976, using a scaled-down approach in which project managers
managed their own jobs, did their own cost estimating, and functioned as their
own client interface. It was a model that replicated to a great extent the modus
operandi of the general contracting firms against whom they would have to compete, and it proved effective. Of course, the new SPD had its problems competing,
but it adapted to the rigors of lean competition, probably derived a certain advantage from its relationship to Big Turner, and was pretty much able to hold its own.
By the end of the 1980s Chicago's SPD was doing $80 million worth of work a year,
and not long after that it would be doing almost as much work each year as its parent was doing.

And that wasn't Chicago's only strategy for shoring up its earnings. In 1988 it branched out to establish a satellite office in Kansas City, where Turner had almost half a century earlier built a 5-million-square-foot aircraft engine plant for Pratt & Whitney. A rising Turner star named Rod Michalka was tapped to manage it, and Kansas City soon became one of the most productive of the company's offices, becoming the operating base for a new territory that in 1991 included Missouri, Kansas, Iowa, and Nebraska.

Chicago's emphasis on its SPD was repeated in other locations, including Texas. There, where the collapse of the OPEC oil cartel had depressed the economy of the region in the 1980s, it was the SPD's interiors work that sustained the territory until the early 1990s.

Another strategy that evolved in the demanding environment that attended the economic recession of the 1980s and 1990s brought Turner into the business of building public elementary schools and high schools. Of course, the company had been doing construction for many of the country's colleges and universities almost since its earliest years, but building public elementary schools and high schools had, in most places, been a different and generally unattractive business for contractors of Turner's stripe. Until about the 1980s, such work had often been a financially hazardous activity in which contractors of sometimes widely varying ability and substance competed contracts exclusively on the basis of price, and the consequences were often economically and politically disastrous for the school districts. As the need increased for getting such schools properly built within tight budgets of time and money, several Turner territories began to contract with school districts for managing the whole process from the beginning of design through the completion of construction. In some cases, as in New York, Turner most often contracted to manage the work of a small number of large prime contractors for each school, while in others, as in Columbus, it usually managed a large number of small contractors who, in a conventional setting, would have been subcontractors. In both those cases (and elsewhere, including Connecticut and Illinois) Turner as construction manager started at the beginning of the design process with preconstruction services intended to ensure constructibility, cost, and value, then managed the soliciting and evaluation of publicly opened bids, and finally supervised the construction itself, often for multiple projects in the same school district.

On one contract in the 1990s a school district in Ohio engaged Turner's Columbus office under Rick Lombardi to manage a troubled school project that was already under construction and had become mired in destructive conflicts and claims among its prime contractors. Once Turner took control of the job as construction manager, it was able to restore order and progress. But it secured peace among the prime contractors only when it agreed to the unanimous stipulation of the contractors themselves that Turner agree to continue supervision of the project through its completion.

As other new strategies evolved, Turner's role in the previously peripheral area of school construction took it into other public work as well. During the 1980s the company had established a Justice Facilities Division for providing construction-management services for new prisons, courthouses, and the like, and in 1985 it brought in Jack Chapman, who had represented Turner's client on the Portland Justice Complex, to contribute his substantial experience in this specialized and changing field. By the mid-'90s Turner had become a major contender for such work and was adding an average of a dozen new justice facilities to its construction volume every year. Within a few years it would be doing more such work than any other firm in the country.

During this same period the company was entering into an increasing number of joint ventures with design firms around the country to take on the design-build contracts that were gaining favor in the industry and that were a special interest of Hal Parmelee. Although some of them tended to be relatively simple building types, they weren't always. In Miami, Atlanta, and in Middletown, Connecticut, for example, such joint ventures produced elaborate justice complexes that included jails and courtrooms, work that fit especially well with the company's new interest in such building types. In Minneapolis such a design-build contract linked Turner with the distinguished architectural firm Kohn Pederson Fox (KPF) to produce a spectacular, nationally acclaimed (if painfully unprofitable) new federal courthouse.

Optimistic expectations that the Turner Steiner association might energize Turner's international operations and bring profitability to them during the early 1990s didn't materialize, and Turner's international work continued to be another economic drain on the company during that period. Neither Bob Nilsson in TII nor some in Turner's own senior management relaxed their advocacy for International on the grounds that it could provide capability the company's big corporate clientele might expect from Turner. But by the end of the century there was evidence that support for that view had virtually disappeared.

By the time Turner entered the mid-'90s, it was still working hard to reduce its debt burden and to restore a reasonable and consistent level of profitability. There had been some further reduction of staff, but a significant fraction was still being achieved by a process of normal attrition. It was increasingly understood by then that conditions weren't good, but even at that relatively late stage of what had become a prolonged period of hard times there was plenty of evidence of Turner's continuing vitality, and most of its employees continued to think of a Turner career as one that under any but the most terrible circumstance was likely to continue until retirement.

The annual Turner dinner, before the Second World War a gracious black-tie, stag affair attended by the company's senior managers, now had a more contemporary look. By the '90s the company had become too big for a single dinner, so each business unit held its own affair, sometimes attended by one or more representatives of New York's corporate hierarchy and certainly by all the unit's local staff members and their spouses. Once-mandatory formal dress had long since given way to casual business clothing. Smaller luncheons for members of the venerated Quarter Century Club were still being held regularly in different parts of the country with undiminished enthusiasm.

In New York, Turner's Stuart Robinson was producing the Turner Index, a widely respected indicator of construction costs regularly monitored by publications and organizations interested in construction economics. Karl Almstead was still a few years from succeeding him. In 1993 Ben Palagonia, who in 1966 had become the fifth in the series of artists who had since 1910 maintained the annual tradition of displaying as a single composite drawing all the current work of the company, was preparing his twenty-seventh Turner City. It would be another year before his son, John Palagonia, would join him in the work, and still another four years before the younger Palagonia would take over from his father. And 1993 was also the year in which the Council on Tall Buildings published a list of the world's 100 tallest buildings, attributing nineteen of them to Turner.

By the '90s there had been some profound changes in Turner's demography. Of the company's approximately 3,000 employees, about 28 percent were now women, compared with about 17 percent just after the Second World War. Some of these women were now employed in managing the construction itself, whereas in earlier years they had all been employed on the administrative side of the business. Statistics showing the incidence of nonwhite employment in the early years are elusive, but it's likely that it was extremely small, while in the mid-'90s nonwhites represented about 14 percent of the permanent staff. Equally significant, the company was, by 1993, a quarter of a century along in its own vigorous campaign to encourage black entrepreneurs in construction and to encourage the training and employment of black mechanics in the trades. Turner's role as an Equal Employment Opportunity advocate had begun in 1968, when it became the first construction firm to establish an EEO department, and its efforts had continued since then under Cleveland's Hilton Smith, a Turner vice president. In the early 1970s Turner's joint venture with black-owned Trans-Bay Construction Company in Oakland began a series of such partnerships that would later include a joint venture with black-owned Santa Fe Construction Company for doing major hospital work in New York, a relationship that was still active and vigorous at the end of Turner's first century.

Demography wasn't the only thing that had been changing at Turner during the 1990s. There were important technological changes in progress too, none of those more striking than what had been going on in the area of information systems. The computer had first appeared at Turner's home office in the late '60s, entering slowly and fairly tentatively as a UNIVAC mainframe in New York, mostly for handling the increasing burden of financial reporting. Tony Sanfilippo entered the company's developing Information Systems Group at about that time, and he's one of the few who survived the radical changes in that critically important sector over the years and was still in authority there at the end of the company's first century.

Sanfilippo remembers that while the business units themselves entered the computer world sporadically during the 1970s they were individually too small to justify having their own mainframes, so they began by renting time on big equipment at local service bureaus, gradually developing more capability of their own but without much standardization or control from New York. Toward the end of the '70s the company began centralizing the system in New York and building a more substantial department there around two big new IBM mainframes and a growing information technology staff. The remote business units took turns availing themselves of New York's capability.

But between the explosive growth of the technology that emerged during the 1980s and the simultaneous expansion of the company's own work, it didn't take long before there would a need for a major upgrading of systems. Unfortunately, it was an expensive and difficult need that announced itself just when the fortunes of the company had begun to sag, and it would become even more difficult when a decision to move Turner's headquarters from its Third Avenue location in New York to 375 Hudson Street was made later in the 1980s.

Turner's Don Kerstetter had been given the job of heading a new board that had been organized to oversee the development of information system technology and to manage what had by then become an Information Systems Group that was approaching 100 persons. Richard Schell was recruited from a government agency to head the Information Systems Group itself, with Tony Sanfilippo as his operations manager. When word was handed down by senior management that there would be no room in the new building for the big mainframes that had been at the heart of the company's information technology, Kerstetter's board and the Information Systems Group knew they had their work cut out for them.

But this time history was on Turner's side. The personal computer had announced its arrival in no uncertain terms, and by the time of Turner's move to

Hudson Street, Microsoft had developed its revolutionary new Windows operating-system software. PCs were appearing everywhere, and by 1988 Kerstetter had brought in Peoplesoft, a creative young consulting firm headed by Dave Duffield, to develop the special systems needed to satisfy the extremely complex demands of salary and payroll processing. By the time of the move to Hudson Street, the company found itself able to leave its mainframes behind and to achieve a radical reduction in the size of its information technology staff.

While the work of bringing in new computer-based technology and new perspectives was for the most part eminently effective in the area of information systems, it wasn't always as successful in other areas. During the early 1990s the concept of Total Quality Management (TQM) gained a great deal of favor in industry, and Al McNeill saw it as a chance to improve the quality of what Turner did in ways that would raise morale and encourage the growth in volume that was being sought. This was a time when shrinking markets were not only reducing the volume of work that was available to the company, but also were making it increasingly difficult to maintain market share in what remained, and the idea of demonstrating a clear superiority of product was preferable to competing on the basis of already extraordinarily low fees. TQM was an approach in which each worker in the system was urged to examine with new rigor and depth his own role in the process, viewing himself (as the system's guidelines suggested) as both the internal customer for services and as the internal provider of services. Systems for facilitating and encouraging such efforts had earlier been developed in other companies and by independent advocates of TQM, and Turner's Frank O'Connor was put in charge of introducing and implementing them. Anderson Consulting was brought in to provide training, with individual Turner personnel designated to head up programs in individual territories. The program was given an aggressive trial during the period that followed its introduction. TQM did attract more than a few committed supporters, but it was difficult to gauge its precise effect on the company's performance. By later in the 1990s, under pressures of intense workloads and changing company management, it appears to have lost favor.

In the early '90s, the central focus of the directors and managers of Turner remained the restoration of growth and prosperity in what continued to be a dishearteningly shrinking market. There was increasing talk of "right-sizing" and "reengineering," euphemisms for laying off staff and for outsourcing, and in 1993 the board established a reserve of $8.5 million for costs expected to attend the layoffs and outsourcing that had been resisted but had finally been accepted as necessary and inevitable. There were increasingly widespread layoffs that by 1994 would reduce the salaried staff of the company by a devastating and demoralizing 30 percent. Some administrative functions were consolidated, and others, over time, were subcontracted to outside vendors By 1995 the concept of a probable lifetime career at Turner had become a casualty of the times. Worse yet, things were destined to become even worse before they got better.

In fact, although there had by then been signs that bottom might have been reached in Turner's markets, it would still be a few years before meaningful recovery occurred. Risks that had been taken during periods of shrinking markets and harsh competition were beginning to produce discouraging and sometimes alarming results with increasing intensity and frequency, making recovery an even more elusive and distant goal. A series of ventures that had eluded corporate management's control produced a stunning loss that the company places at $15 million. In 1995, even as the national market that Turner considered its own was beginning to recover, another loss was reported for the Minneapolis courthouse job that further delayed the return of the long-awaited profitability the firm had been seeking. As late as 1996, when for the first time since the 1980s Turner would do more than $3.5 billion worth of construction, old burdens and new losses would continue to plague it and to deny it a profit.

By 1996, the struggle for renewed prosperity at Turner had been going on for so long that antagonisms had begun to harden between the board of directors and Chairman Al McNeill that might never have survived in better times. The board was becoming increasingly impatient with what it perceived as McNeill's reluctance to implement policies it felt were essential to recovery. It had even begun to question his management style, reasoning that the hands-on approach that had characterized it from the beginning had inhibited his ability to analyze and address serious functional deficiencies that were the rightful concern of the chairman. And the philosophic gap between those who (like McNeill) thought of the Turner culture as the sacred and irrevocable center of the company's existence and those who thought of it as an insurmountable obstacle to the company's survival was never far below the surface of many of the issues that had come between McNeill and his board.

When, in August 1996, the directors were told that even further massive and unanticipated losses on the Minneapolis courthouse job had surfaced after they had been assured by McNeill as recently as two months earlier that the worst was over, resentment that they had not been kept sufficiently informed was overlaid on the deepening conflict, and they voted to replace McNeill as CEO. On the morning of August 9, after two of the directors had met privately with McNeill and informed him of the decision, he resigned from Turner. By the end of the day he had gathered his personal effects and vacated his office at Hudson Street.

16.

Gravette and Fee

I t was Friday morning of the second week in August 1996 when Al McNeill's thirty-eight-year career at Turner ended, and the news spread with the speed of a prairie fire. By noon it was known and being discussed throughout the company and wherever else there were Turner people, with reactions that ranged from profound surprise to outright shock, occasionally mixed with the sort of anxiety that often comes with unexpected change. There was an occasional Turner veteran who professed to have seen it coming, too. After almost a decade characterized by reverses and disappointments in the company's long struggle to regain its prosperity, there were some who thought the tenure of the man in charge was bound to be in some jeopardy.

McNeill was a third-generation construction man who'd spent his entire adult life working for Turner, starting in the field right out of engineering school at Lehigh and spending more than half his career running big construction jobs or managing the men who were running them. And then he'd spent another fifteen years in corporate management, the last eleven as CEO. His roots and friendships in the company were deep and strong, and after thirty-eight years he had accumulated loyalties almost everywhere. Barbara McAllister, who'd been with the company since 1972 and was working in marketing in New York in 1996, burst into tears when she heard the news of his resignation. For her, McNeill was what Turner was all about: a good man with enough mud on his boots to qualify him for leading a great construction company and with the wisdom needed to manage its affairs. It would take her a while to understand and appreciate the reasons for the change. Pat Knowles, who'd been McNeill's executive assistant for seventeen years, cried more than a few tears of her own when the news broke that Friday morning. She'd started with Turner in 1971, and after a few years in purchasing had become McNeill's administrative assistant when he was managing the Philadelphia office. When McNeill went up to New York's corporate center in 1985, Pat Knowles had gone with him and had been working as his executive assistant ever since. Like her good friend Barbara McAllister, she'd need some time to understand and accept the legitimacy of such an end to the career of a man about whom she cared so much. It was extremely difficult for anyone in Turner to imagine that after all those years Al McNeill wouldn't be around anymore.

But although shock and sadness abounded, there were restrained reactions from some McNeill loyalists who were more circumspect in the matter. The years that had led up to 1996 had taken their toll, and even among his most committed supporters there were some who had come to worry about the company's survival and had begun to wonder privately about whether there might be some merit to the idea of change at the top. A few years later, one especially reflective Turner executive would recall the painful combination of sorrow, guilt, and guarded optimism he had felt in the late summer of 1996 when he heard the awful news about his good friend Al McNeill. Sorrow, he remembered, because of what he saw as the overriding injustice of firing a man who, after inheriting problems that he hadn't created, had shepherded the company through some extraordinarily difficult years. There was plenty of guilt, he remembered, because he knew and regretted that although he and others had failed to provide McNeill the support that might have saved his job, McNeill was gone and he was still there. With it all, though, was his guarded optimism; he addmitted that maybe such a change in leadership might provide a solution to the company's stubborn problems after all.

McNeill's successor as CEO was Ellis T. (Bud) Gravette, an urbane, Washington State native in his early seventies who was as thoroughly experienced and capable in matters of corporate finance and in the management of big companies as he was inexperienced in matters of engineering and construction. Of course, he wasn't the first man to lead Turner without the benefit of an engineering education, that distinction having gone to the founder's own son, Chan Turner, whose exemplary leadership as president and chairman had extended from 1947 to 1970. And he wasn't the first man to do it without ever having spent any time in construction, either. Chan's younger cousin Howard Turner, who had brought the intellectual appetite and profound discipline of a trained scientist to the company's management, hadn't ever been more than an occasional visitor to a construction site before he began his own thirteen-year term as president and chairman.

Bud Gravette was nothing less than a professional and expert businessman, a man who understood and had mastered the subtleties and sometimes harsh realities of managing a large corporate enterprise in the 1990s. His reputation for being able to bring that special expertise to troubled corporations had become nationally known and respected by 1996. And although he had never had any mud on his boots, Gravette was no stranger to Turner, having been recruited to its board fifteen years earlier by Walter Shaw, when the two of them were serving together on the board of New York's Bowery Savings Bank just before Gravette became the bank's CEO. He had been an active and effective Turner director ever since.

Although wide and ultimately divisive differences had by 1996 developed between Gravette's thinking and McNeill's about what would be best for Turner, the two men were curiously alike, with styles that were aggressive and direct. There was even more than a little physical resemblance between the two of them, although Gravette was half a generation older, and they had until only a few months before McNeill's resignation been good friends. But during the spring and early summer of 1996, as McNeill's relationship with the board deteriorated, Gravette had become increasingly convinced that Al McNeill wasn't going to be able to lead the company back to prosperity. Gravette became a vigorous advocate for change, and once the directors had made their decision to request McNeill's resignation, he had agreed to serve as interim chairman until a successor to McNeill could be found.

It was no small challenge, even for the tough-minded, seasoned Gravette, who had already begun to adapt to a life of semiretirement in California. But one aspect that promised a measure of continuity at the operations level was Hal Parmelee's continuing as president. After years of having the firm's top management characterized by McNeill as an office of the CEO, with "Hal and Al" having interchangeable responsibilities as co-managers, the board of directors had at first been inclined to make a simultaneous clean break with both McNeill and Parmelee. But Gravette had successfully urged against requesting Parmelee's resignation, advocating his continuation in the presidency with an understanding that he would be among those who would be considered for later selection as the permanent CEO.

It wasn't at the operations level that Gravette's concerns about Turner were focused, but rather at the management level, and there he needed no such buttressing to ensure continuity. He had been monitoring and advising about managing the company for years and had come to his new role with a clear vision of what he felt was wrong and what had to be done to correct it. He had been especially unhappy about what he perceived as McNeill's reluctance to shed the vestiges of his years in the field and with his inclination in some cases to become personally involved in the solution of problems that Gravette felt would have been more effectively delegated to others. McNeill and Parmelee, in Gravette's view, had taken on massive workloads for themselves that effectively denied them the time and capacity to address in a productive way some of the difficult and subtle problems that were impeding the company's recovery.

By the Saturday morning that followed the upheaval of August 9, Gravette was already busy sketching the outlines of a new organizational structure to implement his concept for managing Turner, and by the beginning of the next week he had presented it to Hal Parmelee with a request that Parmelee fill in the names of those he recommended for filling the key positions. The new structure was conceived to reduce to only five the number of persons who had been reporting directly to Parmelee and McNeill and thereby to broaden and strengthen the management base. And it promised another, less obvious benefit as well: The five executive vice presidents who would now report to Parmelee would become highly visible to Gravette and to his directors, just what Gravette thought was necessary to optimize the evaluation and selection of successor management.

Parmelee, a thirty-six-year Turner veteran who knew and was genuinely liked by virtually everyone in the company, selected Barry Sibson, Dick Manteuffel, Stuart Robinson, Bob Fee, and Glenn Little for the top jobs, and Gravette rounded up the five of them for his first directive. He instructed them to divide up the company's senior responsibilities among themselves. Sibson ended up with the West Coast and Texas, Manteuffel with the Central Region, and Robinson with most of the East except for New York, New Jersey, Philadelphia, Pittsburgh, and Detroit. Those exceptions were left to Bob Fee, who would have responsibility for those territories and for Turner International, Turner Caribbean, Turner South America, and for D & J Construction. Glenn Little was placed in charge of national sales and marketing. Gravette made no secret of his view that failure to set ambitious goals and to achieve them wouldn't be tolerated, and the business of putting in place what by late 1996 had become a slowly increasing volume of new business went forward with relatively little disruption.

Bud Gravette knew the company's strengths as well as its weaknesses. He had never had any doubt about its ability to do construction work effectively, and his realigning of senior management was essentially a way of redistributing the workload to optimize performance. What really worried him was the array of conditions and events that preceded, attended, and followed the construction process, the risk-intensive activities that had little to do with the construction itself but that had in the past wrought havoc with the company's profitability. He was committed to an idea that the restoration of profitability at Turner would depend as much on the company's ability to manage its risks as it would on anything else.

It would be unfair to suggest that a disciplined approach to risk management hadn't been established earlier, starting in a serious way under Howard Turner, continuing under Shaw and Conant, and receiving heightened attention under McNeill and Parmelee. But under Gravette, the concept of risk management was elevated to an even higher level of importance, and it became a compelling influence in almost everything the company did. Gravette lost no time in addressing it wherever he saw evidence that it needed attention.

Close to the core of an intensified approach to risk management was the Contract Review Committee (CRC), which was charged with responsibility for reviewing and approving new contracts. Under the previous administration, the CRC had been inclined not to pay much attention to contracts that were smaller than about $25 million, and few of the contracts that it did end up reviewing were rejected. For the most part, new contracts were negotiated by the company's sales-people, whose eagerness to sell the work may in some cases have impaired their judgment about provisions to which Turner was being asked to subscribe. In a relatively unaggressive review process, few of these potentially dangerous contracts were ever caught. In other cases a cultural predisposition to allow significant autonomy to local business units had become a factor that favored CRC's approval of contracts that might otherwise have been challenged. Not long after the new chairman's emphasis on risk management became understood, the CRC would begin to increase the range and number of contracts it examined, and its reviews would become much more rigorous. There was a marked increase in the number of contracts being sent back for revision or actually being rejected, a first step in a process that would become even more effective over time.

The new emphasis on risk management spilled over into Turner's handling of its legal problems. In spite of its large annual work volume, the company had never maintained anything but a very small legal staff, and it was a staff that was more focused on internal procedural matters than on initiating or defending against claims. During the litigious years that had immediately preceded the 1990s, when there was a proliferation of claims against Turner, the managers of business units across the country had become accustomed to retaining their own lawyers, with results that for the most part were expensive and time-consuming and often only modestly effective. Now Bud Gravette turned to the law firm of Peckar & Abramson for an intensified program of preventive legal oversight in which very early reviews of questionable contracts were undertaken before they were signed and in which business-unit managers were encouraged to seek counsel as soon as the earliest signs of potential disputes surfaced. The results quickly began to reduce both the number of claims and the cost of dealing with the ones that survived.

Cultural changes that had been integral to Gravette's having been selected in the first place and that were now at the center of his management approach were nowhere more evident or controversial than in the area of personnel. If risk management was the foundation of his approach, accountability was its cornerstone, and his commitment to a policy of rigorous accountability allowed little tolerance for failure. That inevitably meant that some underperformers at Turner would lose their jobs, and some of those who would suffer were bound to be people with long histories of service in the company. By late 1997 two of the five new executive vice presidents and the man in charge of Turner International were among a fair number of Turner veterans who had been induced to retire early.

This had to be an extremely difficult period for Hal Parmelee, who was still president. After thirty-seven years with the company, almost half of them in positions that brought him into close contact and friendships with Turner people all over the country, firing longtime employees was something he found extremely hard to do. Bud Gravette, committed to the chairman's task of ensuring the company's solvency and nurturing its return to prosperity, had the luxury of being relatively new to most of the company's operating leadership. He had few relationships in Turner that would have imposed the problems being faced by Parmelee, and the sometimes harsh impact of the dismissals opened a gap between the two men that would widen over time.

Bud Gravette's vigor in opposing underperformance was matched by his boldness in identifying people he thought understood and were ready to implement his ideas about how the company had to be managed, and only a few months into his first year as chairman he began to focus on Bob Fee. Fee was in some ways a Turner maverick, a well-tested and popular member of the old guard but not an entirely committed believer in the sanctity of the Turner culture. After thirty-four years with the firm, Fee understood and in large measure shared Gravette's idea that running the company as an extended family at the end of the twentieth century was unlikely to succeed, and his own reputation as a senior executive who had himself risen through the ranks measurably enhanced his ability to translate such a view into management policy.

Fee was born into the business. His father had been a vice president at the venerable Starrett Brothers & Eken Company, builders of the Empire State Building, and young Fee had been working in construction since his student years. Educated in business at Iona College, he had prepared himself with some engineering at the City College of New York before starting with Turner as a field engineer in 1964. Within a few years he was managing interior construction work on the fifty-four-story office tower that Turner was building for U.S. Steel on Trinity Place in New York (One Liberty Plaza). In the years that followed he would work his way up the project management ladder that by 1978 would make him a project executive. At that senior Turner level Fee would have responsibility for some of the firm's most spectacular urban work, including high-rise towers for Goldman Sachs, E. F. Hutton, Irving Trust Company, and others. By the time Bud Gravette began paying special attention to him in 1996, he had spent eight years as vice president and general manager of Turner's New York business unit, and another couple of years as senior vice president in charge of a region that included South America as well as New York and New Jersey. In 1996 he was an executive vice president with responsibility for New York, New Jersey, Philadelphia, Pittsburgh, and Detroit, and with executive responsibility for all Turner's international work as well.

Gravette saw Fee as a superb, previously undervalued executive, and in December 1997, he made him president of Turner Construction Company. At the same time, he assigned to Hal Parmelee the critically important but clearly less attractive job of resolving half a dozen major and potentially very damaging claims against Turner that had resisted resolution for years. Fee had been based in New York for more than thirty years when he became president, and his positions of increasing responsibility had, during his most recent months there, brought him into the company's highest center of authority, so there was no time needed for adjusting to a new environment. Within weeks, his imprint was being felt throughout the company, and that was certainly no surprise to Bud Gravette.

Fee's views about individual accountability and about the importance of managing the company's risks were even more focused than Gravette's, and during his months at the chairman's right hand in New York he hadn't made any secret of them. He'd felt for years that most of the company's problems originated long before anyone in the field had anything to do with the work, that most of its troubles had started with flawed cost estimates, poorly written contracts, or unwise purchasing, and that although there were occasional jobs on which deficiencies in fieldwork had exacerbated problems, money that was going to be lost was usually gone before the projects ever got out of the ground. And Fee had been equally outspoken to Gravette and to the board itself about his idea that everyone in the company had to be held strictly accountable for everything included within his or her scope of responsibility. He made no bones about his view that although poor performance had in the past generated harsh words and occasional demotions and transfers within the company, it had rarely produced dismissals. Fee advocated getting rid of persons who weren't performing well and rewarding those who were performing exceptionally well with salary increases and bonuses, and by early 1998 many of his views had been translated into policy and action.

That wasn't all. It was Fee who intensified and implemented Bud Gravette's campaign to enhance the effectiveness of the Contract Review Committee, which had years earlier been created to evaluate and approve proposed construction contracts. Fee started by reducing the minimum size of contracts the committee would review to $2 million and then he reduced it to $1 million, effectively ensuring that virtually every new contract being considered by the company would have to survive the scrutiny of the committee before it could be signed.

Roger Lang, an exceptionally perceptive Turner executive, had earlier served as CRC chairman under Parmelee and McNeill, and he continued under Bob Fee. Lang had been struggling to improve the committee's effectiveness, but the burdens of other pressures had prevented McNeill or Parmelee from giving its work the energy it needed from them. Under Fee, Lang was able to bring the committee to a new level of effectiveness. Bob Meyer was another capable senior executive whose judgment was brought to bear on the matter of risk management. Meyer was a corporate vice president whose special focus was on matters of cost control, and when his unsettling Earnings Erosion Report confirmed and documented Fee's thesis that most of the problems that plagued the company had originated long before any dirt had been moved, the CRC began to be appreciated as the company's first line of defense against avoidable risk.

Under the new regime, the CRC became an increasingly powerful control. The number of jobs it rejected rose from fewer than 1 percent to about 4 percent of the number submitted to it. More importantly, the managers of the business units gained an awareness of the increased attention their proposals were getting in New York and became much more careful about what they submitted for approval. In some cases, when the CRC saw a contract that was potentially sound but that it felt was beyond the capability of the business unit that had proposed it, strategies for strengthening local capability were recommended or mandated by the committee as conditions for approval.

Turner had for many years relied on what it called its Indicated Outcome Reports to provide an early warning system for anticipating troubled jobs that were in progress, but their effectiveness had been limited by sometimes casual or misleading reporting. Under Fee, the reliability of the IOR system was quickly improved, and within a year the rate of delinquency in submission of the reports had been reduced almost to zero and the quality of the information produced had been substantially improved.

Fee's term as president had started with changes he felt needed immediate attention, and inevitably some positions within the company were lost and more than a little pain was felt. But history once again began to turn in Turner's favor, and by 1998 the markets that the company regarded as its own had begun to show sustained growth, and Turner's own volume was increasing along with them. Revenues generated by ENR's top 400 contractors had risen by almost 14 percent since 1995, and Turner's own 1998 volume of a little over $4 billion would make it the fifth most active of ENR's top 400 firms. Its volume was exceeded only by three huge industrial builders and by a national firm specializing in large-scale housing development. More important, the company's net earnings in 1998 showed their first significant improvement in years, rising to almost $20 million, and its backlog of new work exceeded $4 billion.

Continuity in the ranks of the company's most senior operating managers was especially vital for the still relatively new administration of Gravette and Fee in 1998, especially in such a promising market, and after the early realignments it became clear that the transition had gone fairly smoothly. Reporting directly to Bob Fee by 1988 were executive vice presidents Dick Manteuffel out in Cincinnati and Stuart Robinson in Connecticut, a couple of solid Turner executives with broad experience and long histories in the company; Dick Dorais, who had under Fee replaced Barry Sibson as manager of the Western Region; and Ed Quimby, who had taken over responsibility for sales and marketing.

Manteuffel was still the center of solid management in the Midwest, an increasing and reassuringly stable resource after his many years with the firm. His responsibilities had by then broadened to include all the Lathrop work, several major Midwestern business units, and the growing Universal unit in Nashville, and they now included Texas as well.

Stuart Robinson, a Turner manager who'd been with the company since graduating from engineering school at Lafayette College in 1968, had by some accounts been Bob Fee's most serious competitor for the presidency in 1997. He'd earlier managed some of Turner's most important jobs in New England. In 1988 he'd taken over as manager of the struggling Connecticut territory, which under his leadership would by 1993 be awarded the Turner Flag as the most improved business unit in the company. During Fee's presidency, Robinson's responsibilities were significantly broadened to include the rest of New England as well as Washington, Atlanta, and the increasingly successful Florida territory, which would still be managed at the business-unit level by Mike Smith.

Dick Dorais, now emerging out west as one of the company's brightest stars, was the vigorous and personable veteran not yet out of his forties who had taken over Barry Sibson's role as manager of the Western Region. Fresh from running the San Francisco business unit, Dorais had been attracting his share of attention in the West and back east at the corporate center in New York as well, where some in the company likened him to a younger Bob Fee. His appointment as regional manager when Sibson left couldn't have surprised many people. He'd started with Turner in the early 1970s, and after a few years in the Midwest had in 1977 gone out to San Francisco to work on the landmark Moscone Convention Center project. That was a fortuitous posting for young Dorais, whose engineering credentials and special knowledge of emerging computer-supported management techniques had the effect of making him the first Turner engineer on the new job. He started out as part of a group that would manage the scheduling and planning of the whole, complex array of events that needed to be coordinated before design and construction could begin. Then he had continued through preconstruction tasks that centered on cost estimating, scheduling, and purchasing and that eventually placed him close to the managing center of one of the most spectacular construction projects of the period. Six years after starting at Moscone, Dorais would be the last Turner man to leave the job, and by 1998 he was running the whole Western Region.

On the financial side, Don Sleeman had been brought up by Bud Gravette as senior vice president in 1996 to serve as chief financial officer. Sleeman was a thoroughly experienced financial man who'd come to Turner in 1987 after ten years in the respected Coopers & Lybrand accounting firm, and he'd held a variety of increasingly sensitive financial jobs in the company since then. He was seen by Gravette as another unusually capable man who had a good understanding of the new approach to risk management. Before much time went by, Sleeman would reorganize staffing to ensure that financial managers at the business-unit level reported to regional accounting managers, who then reported directly to the corporate center.

The depth of experience among managers just below the most senior level in 1998 could reasonably be characterized by most standards as extraordinary, even for a construction firm as strong and far-ranging as Turner. Few of the company's competitors could match it for depth at the senior vice president level, where Turner had almost a dozen men who averaged thirty years' service. Here, men like Roger Lang and Bob Meyer were especially noteworthy for special skills that were getting increasing attention in Turner, now that its focus had shifted from an earlier emphasis on the actual performance of construction work to its management. Although Lang and Meyer had each put in his time on the operations side of the business, by 1998 they had both become key figures in formulating and implementing the company's risk-management strategies.

Of course, the core of Turner's business was still very much management of the actual construction process itself, so seasoned builders like Ralph Johnson, who had been with the company since getting his engineering degree from Valparaiso University in 1959, were critical to the execution of the work. Johnson had become a vice president at the unusually early age of thirty-six in 1973, when he was made operations manager for the Cleveland office, and by the 1980s his special capability for managing the big jobs that were at the heart of Turner's work was what controlled his assignments. That would come to mean that he could expect to find himself at almost any location where the company had major construction problems to address, and his career included tours as operations manager in Cleveland, Columbus, Detroit, and Washington, as well as interim operating management assignments in San Francisco and New York. Under Hal Parmelee, Johnson had become national operations manager for Turner, with responsibilities that took him anywhere in the country where problems were surfacing or where there was a need to harness his skills to avoid them.

By 1990 Johnson had begun to add a more public aspect to his work. In that year he represented Turner as president of Albany-based General Building Contractors of New York State (GBC), the state's ranking building contractors' organization. Ten years later he would go to Washington to assume the presidency of the prestigious Associated General Contractors of America (AGC), the ranking national organization of U.S. construction contractors.

Shelby Reaves was another senior executive with a long and colorful history of managing big jobs for Turner, many of them a long way from U.S. shores, and by the late '90s he had added the management of a couple of Turner's Florida business units to his career. At that point Reaves was on his way to managing construction of the big stadium that Turner would build for the Cincinnati Bengals football team, a glorious last hurrah before becoming the second in his family to retire after long and distinguished careers at Turner.

Strong operations backgrounds (increasingly mixed with business development experience) continued to be important in the selection of persons to run the regions and business units from which senior corporate officers were most often recruited. Rod Wille stood out, having already managed the business unit in Newark and later the big Midwestern region that included Chicago, where he had been able to guide that once-dominant business unit through the difficult transition that followed the virtual collapse of the urban construction market in the city itself. By 1998 Wille was running a big and geographically diverse group of business units that included Chicago, Kansas City, Denver, and Texas, and after that he'd add Washington and Atlanta, while giving up Chicago. Wille was a fellow regularly described by colleagues as a man who was clearly headed for even greater responsibilities in the company.

Changes at the corporate level had been well absorbed by 1998, and in an environment of restored markets and growing earnings, attention became increasingly focused on what was proving to be a promising younger generation of managers at regional and business-unit levels across the country. Tom Gerlach Jr., son of the distinguished Turner executive who had retired as executive vice president in 1991, was by 1998 attracting a good deal of favorable notice up north in Seattle. Like Dorais, Gerlach was a Moscone veteran, having spent a few of his earliest Turner years there learning the business under one of the company's preeminent builders, Doug Meyer. Since then he'd done a little of almost everything in Turner, including running the Chicago SPD unit, doing some successful business development work in California, and even doing a turn for Turner Steiner International in Europe. But it was his 1996 selection as manager of the young business unit in Seattle that was destined to bring Gerlach to national attention in the company. By the time of his 1996 move to Seattle, the business unit there had done some significant work in the region, including a spectacular fifty-six-story office tower for a subsidiary of the University of Washington (Two Union Square) and a 1-million-square-foot production facility for Boeing. But the Seattle work had lacked the continuity and growth that had been expected in the burgeoning

Northwest, and it remained for young Gerlach to change that pattern.

What would make things a little easier for him than they might have been otherwise, was a growing record of Turner successes in building big sports facilities. In 1994 the company had finished construction of the $200 million Gund Arena in Cleveland for the Cleveland Cavaliers, and at the time of Gerlach's arrival in Seattle about two years later, Turner was winding up work on the $150 million Ericsson Stadium in North Carolina, a joint venture with its former subsidiary the F. N. Thompson Company, for the Carolina Panthers football team. Only a few months later the company would complete work on the $165 million Arthur Ashe Stadium, which it was building in New York for the United States Tennis Association. With those and other such major sports-related jobs already in its backlog, Turner had during the early '90s become a major player in the small group of firms qualified to build the country's huge new sports complexes, and Gerlach had arrived in the Northwest in time to ensure that Turner wouldn't miss out on an especially spectacular one that was being talked about for Seattle.

Only a few months before Gerlach's arrival, Turner's Seattle business unit had finished work in nearby Portland on the $200 million Rose Garden Arena that the Paul Allen interests had developed for the Portland Trail Blazers basketball team. A 21,600-seat arena project designed by Ellerbe Becket for basketball and hockey, it included parking structures for almost 2,000 cars, a restaurant, several bars, and an office building. It had been built in a joint venture with Drake Construction Company, a local firm. The project had been run by Turner's Gus Sestrap, a young western native who had earlier built the Union Square tower in Seattle, and it had been smoothly and successfully executed. Now Paul Allen's people in Portland had become Turner believers, and they had bigger fish to fry about 150 miles away, near Seattle.

What they wanted to build there was a new stadium for the Seattle Seahawks football team, and when Gerlach arrived in 1996, their project was still in the talking stage. Turner had already done cost studies for some early concepts, but during the year that followed, Ellerbe Becket would be brought onboard in place of the original architect and work would go forward in earnest. New strategies and cost estimates were produced by Turner and modified to reflect thinking that was emerging from a joint forum that included Turner, Ellerbe Becket, and the Allen Group. Over the course of about the next year solutions would be found for the architectural, structural, and political problems inherent in an estimated $420 million project that would rely on a blend of private and public financing. By June of 1997 the voters had approved the project by public referendum. Within a few days of the vote, Turner-Drake was awarded a contract to build the big complex in two phases, and a program of formal design and preconstruction services had been launched. By Labor Day of 1998, design work reached a stage that allowed construction of the first-phase exhibition center and garage to go ahead, with October of 1999 scheduled for completion. Under Turner's Gus Sestrap, by then a project executive, the schedule was met and within days of the dedication, Sestrap's work on the big stadium phase itself was underway. In March of 2000 viewers across much of the country watched on television screens as the stadium that Turner would be replacing with a giant new one was demolished by implosion in a little over ten seconds, and the big job itself was underway in earnest. Twenty-seven months remained for producing the huge 72,000-seat stadium in which the Seahawks would start their 2002 season.

The West wasn't the only part of the country where this late-twentieth-century generation of Turner managers was getting itself noticed. In the Midwest, where the company's Lathrop subsidiary in Toledo had been a continuing success ever since its acquisition by Turner in 1986, Robert Maxwell's personal style and his effectiveness in running the business unit had brought him into the ranks of the company's senior managers. Maxwell had come along with Turner's acquisition of Lathrop, when he was already almost twenty years into his own construction career and four years into his work as executive vice president of Lathrop. The ease with which he was able to settle into Turner's management probably surprised some in a company that was accustomed to developing its managers from within its own ranks. But by the late 1990s, earnings in Maxwell's Lathrop unit, exceeded only by the huge business units in New York and Chicago, had made believers of everyone who understood them. It was seen as an extraordinary achievement when the sizes of the markets in those two very large cities were compared with the market that the Lathrop unit was able to address from its base in Toledo.

During the early months of Bob Fee's presidency, the country's midsection had started to regain its share of the rising national prosperity, and Turner's regional and individual business-unit managers were focused on what was developing in their individual territories. Almost ten years earlier Jim Mitnick, a thirty-eight-year-old Purdue-educated engineer then two years along in a Turner vice presidency, had been placed in charge of the company's once-thriving Pittsburgh office, and within a few years it had begun to prosper again. By the later 1990s Mitnick's responsibilities had been expanded under Fee to include Detroit, Cleveland, Buffalo, Philadelphia, and New Jersey, and by 1998 he'd be seen by some as on his way to higher office in the company. John DiCiurcio in Chicago was another Midwestern manager who was making a name for himself during the increasingly prosperous days of the late 1990s and was attracting the attention of corporate management. Educated in engineering at Rutgers, he'd gone from early engineering and cost-estimating work at Turner into business development, and by the 1990s he was managing an emerging Chicago satellite in Arlington Heights. Only a few years later he'd succeed Rod Wille as manager of the big Chicago business unit, gaining a reputation there as an exceptionally capable manager who was ready to promote promising young people in his unit, raising the energy level of the place and producing annual earnings that would restore Chicago to its former leadership position among the company's territories.

There were other effective and successful managers in the Midwest, of course, but by the late 1990s few of them were attracting more notice at the company's corporate center than Rod Michalka in Kansas City. The son and grandson of construction men near Pittsburgh, Michalka had learned engineering at the University of Pittsburgh and had worked his way through the usual variety of Turner jobs in Pittsburgh and Chicago before he was recruited for a task that would influence the rest of his Turner career. Joe McCullough at the Chicago business unit had tapped Michalka for help in his effort to establish a satellite to expand Chicago's market base, and between the two of them they had picked

Kansas City, Missouri, about 500 miles from Chicago, a town with a stable economy, a promising future, and a town with only one significant potential competitor for Turner. Michalka had taken on its management, and in short order he had been able to secure for Turner a consulting contract to guide the city through the complex process of planning for and building an approximately $115 million addition to its convention center. By the time the job was finished, a Kansas City satellite would be well established, with respectable earnings and a growing volume of other new work, and by 1995 Kansas City would be a fully fledged, profitable business unit.

By 1997, Denver would be added to Michalka's responsibilities, with spectacular results. The company was already a candidate to build a new stadium there for the Broncos. The project was a joint enterprise of the privately owned Denver Broncos football team and a political district that had been fashioned from counties in and around Denver. Michalka put his own considerable energy behind the campaign to get the job, and by January of 1998 the Broncos had selected the architectural/engineering firm of HNTB to design the stadium and Turner to build it.

But there was a catch: The owners couldn't promise to pay HNTB or Turner for any of their work unless and until a public referendum scheduled for November of 1998 had authorized the project, and it was estimated that by that date HNTB and Turner would have spent something in the range of $4 million to $5 million. If the referendum went against the stadium, HNTB and Turner would forfeit everything they'd spent, and that was a risk that no one was willing to take.

Michalka devised a hedging strategy he felt was prudent, and it worked. Turner and HNTB joined forces as a single design-build venture, and together they secured an insurance policy from Lloyd's of London that promised to reimburse them their preconstruction investment if the referendum were to reject the stadium plan, all in return for a premium of about $1 million. Michalka arranged with the Metropolitan Football District of Denver to reimburse the premium if the referendum approved the stadium. In fact, the public did approve the project and construction was underway by early 1999.

Left: Walter B. Shaw, chairman from 1978 until 1985, when he retired after 44 years with Turner. Right: Herbert D. Conant. He succeeded Shaw and served as chairman until 1988.

Left: Alfred T. McNeill, chairman from 1988 until 1996, a period in which he and president Harold J. Parmelee effectively shared many of the duties of the office. Right: Ellis T. (Bud) Gravette, a board member since 1981, became chairman in 1996 and served until 1999.

Left: Thomas C. Leppert, who leads Turner at the time of its hundredth anniversary, has been chairman since 1999. Right: Robert E. Fee, a veteran of 38 years with the company, has been president since 1997.

*The Mei-Foo housing
project in Hong Kong, built
by Turner during the period
from 1966 to 1978,
comprised more than
13,000 housing units in
99 high-rise buildings.*

This dark green and glass skyscraper on New York's Madison Avenue was completed for IBM in the early 1980s.

At 1,000 feet, Turner's Texas Commerce Tower in Houston was in the early 1980s one of the country's tallest buildings. At the upper right its emerging steel frame appears, and it is shown again in the photograph at the lower right. The middle photograph shows the finished building.

When Turner topped out this Pittsburgh building in 1982, it was being built for U.S. Steel. But the Mellon interests acquired it during construction and it became One Mellon Bank Center.

*Construction of the two
37-story towers that
comprised The Gateway, in
Singapore, was fraught
with difficulties, but it was
successfully completed in
1990.*

This exceptionally large terminal complex for United Airlines at O'Hare International Airport was completed in 1988.

First Interstate Building in Los Angeles, completed in 1987, is a 75-story tower built to withstand extraordinarily severe seismic forces in California.

*450 Lexington Avenue,
New York. During the early
1980s, Turner preserved
the landmarked exterior
walls of the post office that
occupied the site while
building this 32-story
office structure between
and above them.*

The Vanderbilt Medical Center, a complex of buildings constructed by Turner in Nashville during the 1980s and 1990s.

New York was still the largest single producer of revenues and earnings in the company, and by the late '90s it was developing a rising star of its own. Peter Davoren had barely turned forty when Bob Fee became president of Turner in 1997, and like Fee at his age, Davoren had spent most of his career honing his insights into the unique marketplace that exists for a big construction firm in the New York region. By then he'd worked on many of the big jobs that Turner had done in town, starting with the ill-fated IBM job on Madison Avenue and going on to a spate of the company's other spectacular high-rise office buildings. By 1992 he was running the New York Interiors group, a hard-edged unit within the New York territory that had succeeded New York's SPD. In the Interiors operation, where Turner had to face aggressive competition for its share of an estimated 40 million square feet of demanding, fast-paced interior work every year, Davoren made his mark. By the time Fee became president, Davoren's group was averaging more than $200 million worth of moderately profitable work annually, a higher annual volume than many of the company's business units were doing, and Fee tapped him to run the entire New York unit. Three years later he would be a regional vice president in charge of the New York, New Jersey, Philadelphia, and Pittsburgh units.

How much of the hard-earned growth that occurred in the company's volume of work and in its earnings between 1995 and the end of 1999 reflected a general improvement in economic conditions in the industry and how much of it reflected changes in the way the company was being managed isn't easy to gauge with absolute certainty. There had been an improvement in the national economic climate, but there was also a dramatic improvement in performance within the company. The troubled jobs had, for all practical purposes, been cleaned up and no new disasters had surfaced since policies that stressed risk management and tighter controls had been put into place. Things were going very well at Turner. Morale and energy levels were high, and there seemed more than a little justification for a general view that the new management and the new approach had a lot to do with it.

As activity and profitability in the company's operations continued to increase during the late '90s, there was a corresponding increase in activity in the CEO's office and in the boardroom. By then there had been some talk about the possibility of restoring Turner to a form of private ownership that would be more like what had obtained during the years before it had become publicly owned. Back then, when the still closely held company was from time to time buying back its shares from persons who were leaving the firm or who wanted to redeem them for other reasons, it had authorized the public offering mainly to provide an independent marketplace in which the shares could be fairly valued. Now Bud Gravette and others argued that the original distribution of the company's shares to the public had long since achieved its original purpose and that there was really no longer much justification for the company's remaining public. Gravette himself felt that the benefits of public ownership in a company like Turner simply didn't justify the burdens that attached to sustaining it, and even before his elevation to the chairmanship he had advocated a number of strategies for returning the company to private status. But most such strategies required bringing in powerful outsiders who were expected to bring along an element of reduced company control, and many of the company's officers and some members of its board were sufficiently concerned about the implications of reduced control to prevent any of the strategies from being accepted.

Even as Gravette and others on the board were exploring and pursuing options for privatizing the company, they elected to make the best of public ownership while it lasted, petitioning for being listed on the New York Stock Exchange instead of the American Stock Exchange. That effort, facilitated by the company's improved financial condition, succeeded during 1998 and broadened the market for Turner's shares.

One aspect of Bud Gravette's continuing eagerness to encourage privatization of the company was the $15 million worth of debentures that had been held by the Steiners since 1992. The agreements that controlled the destiny of these debentures provided that in 2002 they would either have to be redeemed or converted to common shares that would have given the Steiner group the largest single interest in the company's ownership. Gravette regarded both these eventualities darkly.

An option for Turner's gaining its own control of those debentures or at least for placing them in the hands of friendly interests whose objectives would be more nearly congruent with Turner's own objectives was what Gravette and a few of his colleagues on the board were seeking as the beginning of the new century drew closer. But their efforts to bring in substantial private-sector interests were unavailing. There was lively interest in the capital market, but there was a continuing feeling among some of Turner's own senior managers and among some of its board members that whatever advantages might accrue from such a change were likely to be offset by the threat of unanticipated control from new principals.

Things began to change early in 1999 when Bud Gravette became aware that the chairman of the very large and distinguished German construction firm HOCHTIEF was interested in meeting with him to discuss matters he thought would be of interest to both of them. HOCHTIEF was the largest construction firm in Germany, with a long history dating back to 1873, almost thirty years before Turner was founded. In 1998 HOCHTIEF was doing almost half again as much construction work as the approximately $4 billion annual volume of business that Turner was doing. A large and powerful firm that was equally comfortable in building construction and heavy construction, HOCHTIEF was organized to perform a very high fraction of its work with its own forces, and in 1998 it was employing almost 35,000 persons. In some ways, it represented what Turner might have become by 1998 if it had not years earlier begun to veer away from the practice of performing most of its work with forces in its own employ and toward the management of construction instead.

In an early March meeting in New York with Hans-Peter Keitel and Harald Peipers, who were, respectively, HOCHTIEF'S CEO and a former member of its executive board, Bud Gravette and Bob Fee weren't surprised to learn that HOCHTIEF'S interest had been attracted by news that the Steiners were arranging for a public offering of their Turner holdings. HOCHTIEF had several relatively minor construction holdings in North America itself, including a 35 percent interest in a construction company in Arizona, but it had decided that its strategic interests would be best served by a larger, major presence in the United States, and its board had been exploring the possibilities of either establishing such a presence by creating a new construction company or by acquiring an American company whose substance and style would fit with its own. The potential for acquiring the Steiner interest in Turner looked like a good start.

In fact, once the two sides held further meetings that were expanded to include Turner's chief financial officer Donald Sleeman and HOCHTIEF'S Hans-Wolfgang Koch, Bernhard Buerklin, Hanno Bastlein, and Busso Peus, a potential for a much larger and more aggressive acquisition began to take shape. By April it had become clear that the negotiations might well lead to HOCHTIEF'S acquiring all of Turner. The Turner board was brought into the process in April, and by the end of the month HOCHTIEF had submitted a formal offer to purchase the entire company for about $270 million.

It wasn't enough. Bud Gravette may not have known a lot about setting steel or pouring concrete, but he was expert in his understanding of the currents of commerce, and he knew that the real market value of a company like Turner depended as much on its history, its staff, its clientele, and its potential for profitability as it did on its current balance sheet, and he stood firm.

HOCHTIEF took another look. Over the months that followed there were further meetings in the United States and in Germany to intensify the insights of each of the companies into the business of the other. HOCHTIEF made further offers, and some consideration was given to a possible joining of the forces of the two firms, but there was no resolution until the middle of the summer. On July 30, 1999, Gravette informed HOCHTIEF that a special committee of Turner's board had voted to accept HOCHTIEF'S offer of about $370 million to acquire all of Turner's shares and outstanding options. Their offer had been based on a purchase price of $28.625 per share, almost twice the average price at which the shares had been traded on the New York Stock Exchange in 1998. On August 16, 1999, Turner and HOCHTIEF signed a formal merger agreement, and by September the acquisition proposal had been ratified by the requisite majority of Turner's shareholders. Thomas C. Leppert, a Harvard-educated businessman and well-regarded expert in contemporary commerce, who had only a little more than a year earlier been personally recruited for the Turner board by Bud Gravette, replaced Gravette as chairman on October 1, 1999, and the work of merging the interests and operations of the two firms went forward.

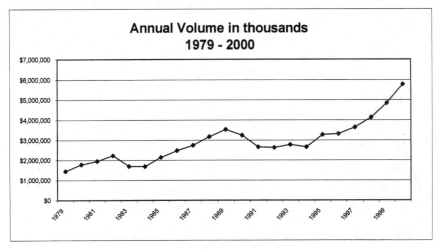

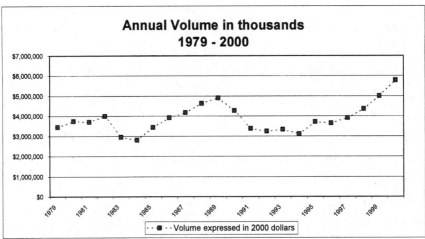

17.

Leppert and HOCHTIEF

A t the end of the twentieth century, having rallied and strengthened Turner and built a bridge for leading it into the new millennium, Bud Gravette retired. He left it to Tom Leppert to ensure an orderly landing and deployment on the far shore.

Like Gravette, Leppert was a westerner. He'd been raised by a widowed mother near Phoenix and had graduated in 1977 from Claremont McKenna College in California, where he'd been president of the student body. Smart and ambitious, he was by the time of his graduation from Claremont McKenna worldly enough to know that a postgraduate education in business at either Stanford or Harvard would immensely facilitate his progress, so he applied for admission to both. His family wanted him to stay out west, of course, but it was economics that would determine his decision: Both schools accepted him, but Harvard offered a full scholarship that a young man already severely burdened with debt couldn't afford to refuse.

It wouldn't take Leppert long to feel the impact of an education at the Harvard Graduate School of Business. As soon as he graduated in 1979 he was tapped by McKinsey & Company, the distinguished sixty-year-old firm that dominated the rarified world of high-level domestic and international strategic planning, and he'd spend most of his next seven years in its Los Angeles branch, ultimately becoming one of the firm's youngest partners. McKinsey was well known as a breeding ground for the wunderkinder who would dominate American commerce and industry during the rest of the century and beyond, providing strategic planning to some of the world's most powerful firms. During the 1980s and later it was difficult to find a list of major corporations that didn't include at least a few that were headed by McKinsey alumni, and firms like American Express, Celanese, Delta Airlines, Dun & Bradstreet, IBM, Morgan Stanley, and PepsiCo led the way. For Leppert, McKinsey became a stimulating, real-world laboratory for applying what he had learned at Harvard to an array of complex problems ranging from industrial production to finance and corporate turnarounds. And it was all done in a setting populated by colleagues who were as well educated and fiercely competitive as he was. It was a heady environment for a young man not yet out of his twenties.

But those early years would bring another, equally broadening component to Tom Leppert's growth. In 1984, while he was still with McKinsey, he and eleven others from all over the country were selected from among 3,000 well-qualified applicants for a year-long fellowship in the Reagan White House. The White House fellowship program had been established under Lyndon Johnson during the sixties as a way of exposing exceptionally qualified young men and women to the work of government at the highest levels, and it already numbered among its alumni a lengthening list of distinguished Americans that included Colin Powell and the now-retired chairman of CNN, Tom Johnson.

In 1985 McKinsey granted Leppert a year's leave of absence for the assignment, and it proved to be everything he'd hoped for. The White House fellowship would provide the public-sector exposure that had been missing from his earlier work at Harvard and McKinsey, and it would add to his already maturing views of the private sector a privileged insight into what made things work in government. He'd spend about half his time in the office of the secretary of the treasury, where he'd find himself near the center of cabinet-level decision making, and he'd spend the other half in the White House itself. Threaded through the year was travel that included an information-gathering, government-managed tour through the Soviet Union and other countries of eastern Europe that took him to the very heart of the period's international affairs. Toward the end of the year, some of Leppert's McKinsey colleagues had begun to wonder whether he'd ever return to management consulting after his White House days, but he surprised them, returning in 1986, broadly educated and on the lookout for a senior position where he could put his skills to work.

The years that followed didn't disappoint him. He left McKinsey to become a "national partner" in Trammel Crow, the Dallas-based developer of commercial real estate, and after that he went out to the central Pacific to run Castle & Cooke Hawaii, a big firm that developed, owned, and managed real estate and resorts. In the mid-1990s, his reputation for being able to manage large assets attracted the attention of Hawaii's Campbell Estate, which recruited him as trustee to manage its $2 billion portfolio.

It was while he was with Campbell that an old friendship from his early McKinsey days resurfaced to change the course of Leppert's career. A dozen years earlier, during a consulting assignment for McKinsey, a big industrial client whose management strategies were being explored had simultaneously engaged Bud Gravette to evaluate some of its senior staff. The two men worked together closely and developed a friendship that continued into the late 1990s, when Gravette was beginning a search for a successor to his own job at Turner. By spring 1998, he had decided on Tom Leppert, but Leppert wasn't sure. He saw Turner as a first-class organization with a distinguished history and good prospects, but by now he was well along in his own successful career and he wasn't convinced that moving to Turner would be best for him. Gravette suggested joining the Turner board for a while, where he'd have an intimate view of the company and where he'd be able to decide with confidence whether or not it was likely to provide the future he was seeking. Leppert joined the board on that basis, and in short order he liked what he saw. Turner was everything Gravette had described, and Leppert believed it had the potential for significant further growth. It was agreed that when Gravette retired in 1999 Leppert would succeed him.

It would all work out in time, but during the months between Leppert's decision in 1998 and his becoming chairman late the following year, events would change the setting. By early 1999, with the U.S. economy performing well and much of what Gravette and Fee had done driving Turner to even greater volumes, the nature of what was awaiting a new chairman was changing. Not long into 1999 the board made a decision to move the company's corporate headquarters from New York to Dallas, a location it saw as being more accessible for a truly national firm whose interests were evenly distributed throughout the country. The decision to move to Dallas was something that appealed to Leppert and it would be implemented before the end of the year.

But nothing that happened between his joining the Turner board in 1998 and his assuming the chairmanship in late 1999 would have the impact that the HOCHTIEF merger would have. Instead of assuming the chairmanship of a publicly held corporation that answered to its shareholders, Leppert would become chairman of a wholly owned subsidiary of HOCHTIEF.

Just who this new parent company really was is something that was then well known only to the small number of people (including Tom Leppert) who had participated in the merger activities. It would be a while before it would be as well understood by the rest of Turner's people. Almost everyone knew HOCHTIEF to be the distinguished 124-year-old construction firm that was the largest in Germany, but as in any such change, there were bound to be lingering uncertainties about exactly who and what lay behind the nameplate.

HOCHTIEF had been founded near Frankfurt, Germany, about 1873, when Henry C. Turner was still an infant, by a couple of brothers named Philipp and Balthasar Helfmann. For a while Helfmann Brothers remained a relatively small contracting firm, but before long it had begun to grow and prosper, and by the closing years of the nineteenth century it had incorporated and was becoming a substantial player in the region's construction.

The early part of the twentieth century saw a good deal more growth in volume and scope, with contracts in many parts of Germany and abroad. Much of the firm's work went beyond building construction to include bridges and other civil engineering structures. But World War I and its aftermath were difficult for Germany, especially when the victorious Allies imposed confiscatory reparation penalties that stifled postwar economic recovery and nurtured resentments that would have a significant role in the terrible events of the decades that followed.

The depression years of the 1930s were just ahead, and what had become a blue-collar complement of 4,000 in HOCHTIEF shrank to about 500. It was still a substantial organization, doing a respectable share of whatever buildings and engineering structures were being designed, but times were hard and prosperity was elusive.

What came next was the terrible period of Hitler's National Socialism in Germany, when HOCHTIEF and the rest of German industry lost control to the government. Construction activity accelerated sharply during the late 1930s, and during the war years that followed the company would do a tremendous volume of construction, often as lead contractor in consortia established for vast projects that would have been too large for a single contractor.

The war left Germany in ruins, with almost 20 percent of the country's housing and commercial buildings destroyed and vast numbers of people without shelter or food. HOCHTIEF had lost all the building sites and equipment it had maintained outside Germany, and in what would become East Germany under the Russians, but after a period dominated by contracts for debris removal, recycling, and some reconstruction, it managed to restore the vitality of a few of its branches. By 1947 things had improved markedly, and HOCHTIEF had enough work to employ almost 8,000 blue-collar workers and almost 1,000 white-collar workers. Its earlier momentum was returning, and by 1952 the company would become profitable for the first time since the war years.

By the 1980s, HOCHTIEF had long since become typical of what has been called the economic miracle of postwar Germany. It was by then a powerful construction presence in the home country and abroad, building dams, power plants, bridges, airports, factories, and landmark civil works that included the Tarbela Dam in Pakistan and the Bosporus Bridge in Turkey, as well as a fair number of the spectacular new buildings that were beginning to punctuate the skylines of Germany's principal cities.

In 1992, Dr. Hans-Peter Keitel, who had come to HOCHTIEF in 1988 after a successful career in engineering, became chairman of its board. He brought with him an interest in diversifying the company's activities even further while preserving its core capability as a builder. He favored accelerating the development of turnkey work in a variety of modes and encouraged broadening the scope of the company's project development work.

By then, HOCHTIEF had invested in or developed a portfolio of construction-related holdings around the world, including two in the United States. One such American investment was an approximately 35 percent stake in the Kitchell Corporation, a mid-size construction firm based in Phoenix, Arizona. A second American investment was Dames and Moore, a prominent engineering firm, but HOCHTIEF had sold that holding profitably when Dames and Moore became listed on the New York Stock Exchange in 1996.

By the time of the acquisition negotiations with Turner, HOCHTIEF was employing more than 37,000 persons, and its gross annual revenues were exceeding $8 billion dollars (US). Adding Turner's 1999 revenues of almost $5 billion would make HOCHTIEF the second-largest construction company in Europe and the sixth-largest in the world.

By the accounts of participants, negotiations between Turner and HOCHTIEF didn't fit the traditional pattern. At the outset, they were less about price and earnings than they were about ensuring a solid match between the two cultures. Representatives from both firms started by probing one another's thinking as to matters of ethics and management philosophy, and as soon as they were entirely satisfied, the plan advanced smoothly. Support for the acquisition plan among Turner's senior management was especially critical to Turner's board — and to HOCHTIEF too. Turner executives at or above the level of senior vice president were canvassed, and the favorable consensus that emerged quickly cleared the way for ratification.

When the new millennium dawned in 2000, Turner was for the first time in its history the subsidiary of another firm, a status that was expected by some to require some wrenching adjustments. But in fact the transition proved to be exceptionally smooth and, for the most part, easy. Business proceeded almost exactly as it always had at Turner, with little or no impact from the merger felt anywhere in the company. Within only a few months, peers in the two firms had been connected by e-mail and would later begin visits to one another's offices, while half a dozen especially adventurous managers and staff from each company took the option of relocating across the Atlantic for periods designed to last up to three years. A natural exchange of information about procedures and systems followed, and within a year the two firms had put in place processes designed to intensify and expand the exchanges and to exploit the synergies that the originators of the merger had anticipated.

The immediate postmerger period was an extremely good one for Turner. The volume of private-sector nonresidential construction, the core of the company's work, had been rising steadily in the United States, increasing by almost 40 percent after 1996 alone. By comparison, Turner's annual revenues during the same period had almost doubled, significantly increasing its market share. By 2000 any uncertainties about whether Bob Fee would be able to make the big change to senior corporate leadership from his years in the management of operations had long since disappeared. Tom Leppert had taken control of the corporation, and although it was still too soon to determine with any certainty how successful he'd be, the signs were good. The positive momentum of earlier years had returned.

The early months of the new century also brought changes that were independent of the HOCHTIEF acquisition, all initiated by Turner. For years the company's business units had been organized rigidly around their geography, but under the new administration some new business units were established to focus instead on selected market segments. It was a radical escalation of an old approach the company had once called "niche marketing," which was, in essence, a relatively superficial concentration concerned with sales. Now Turner was creating full-fledged business units, not just for securing contracts in special segments of the market, but for implementing them as well. The idea was that the market-segment unit would identify and seek projects in its own special field, wherever it found them, and that it would then join forces with local business units to build them. The objective was to use Turner's broad national network and its enormous experience to enhance its competitive advantage in selected market segments. It was an evolution in the company's business plan whose time had come. Now that the scale

and character of the work were changing, the geographic silos that had characterized Turner's organization had begun to impede its ability to coordinate between
units.

In the new approach, business units dedicated to single specialties were going
to require unique staffing that often meant recruiting outside Turner, a practice
that was still new to a company in which senior executives had almost invariably
come up from the ranks. But cultural changes now made bringing in specially
qualified staff from outside the company less difficult than it had been in the past.
Even the spectacular growth in the breadth and volume of the company's work
favored the success of the market-segment units. Turner's profile had become so
high, and its capacity for doing big and complex jobs anywhere in the country had
grown so large, that it was a natural candidate for almost every major project that
came along.

Rod Wille was the senior vice president who was given charge of the new market-segment program. Ken Leach, who had been building pharmaceutical and
biotechnical facilities for thirty years, was recruited from outside Turner as vice
president in charge of the business unit for that sector, an area in which the firm
had already done substantial work. In 2001 ENR listed Turner as the country's
leading builder of such projects. Aviation was another sector to be identified as a
market-segment business unit, and Bob Fee flew into Washington, D.C., to interview and hire Jayne O'Donnell to run it. O'Donnell, educated mainly in architecture, would bring along twenty years' experience in aviation-related construction,
the last ten in managing some of the most important airport projects in the country. Big sports facilities had been part of Turner's work almost from the beginning,
but the scale of new facilities was becoming so extraordinarily large that the
company again moved outside its own ranks to recruit Dale Kroger. He'd been
managing a big sports construction program for another national contractor and
brought to Turner the level of special competency that was being sought.

There were other specialized units waiting to be developed too. Late in 2000
the company added a business unit that would concentrate on construction of
prisons, jails, and courthouses. Other market segments being addressed were

health care, education, and technology.

At the beginning of the company's hundredth year, other groups were surfacing at Turner that were as different from the traditional business units of the past as the market-segment groups were, and each was intended to broaden the base of Turner's business. One was Turner Logistics, which Turner's Mike Raftery ran. Logistics was becoming the focal point for using procurement to leverage the benefits of Turner's large volume. It would coordinate large-volume purchase of products and materials across the entire network of Turner projects. It started as a centralized procurement facility for purchasing the special mechanical and electrical equipment that had in the past usually been bought as unidentified components of mechanical and electrical subcontracts, at the local business-unit level. Now Logistics was buying that equipment, sometimes at a discount generated by multi-project purchasing, often simply to ensure that what was being provided would be satisfactory to Turner and that delivery commitments would accord with Turner's scheduling. And as the new centralized procurement system began to take hold, there was talk of extending its application to other equipment and materials. By the end of 2001, the logistics business unit was beginning to do purchasing for clients other than Turner. Even farther from the company's traditional base was Turner Casualty and Surety (TCS), an insurance subsidiary formed to provide the big insurance policies that protect Turner and its subcontractors from job-related liabilities, managed by vice president Rod Michalka.

If there's a single element that's common to almost all enterprises of the twenty-first century, it's information technology. By 2001 Turner's emphasis on, and the company's investment in, that central component of contemporary commerce exceeded anything seen or imagined earlier in the company's history. A new computer-based education program called Turner Knowledge Network was being developed under Jim Mitnick to provide an education resource for its far-flung staff. Under the program, employees will be able to study at their own pace and on their own schedules without traveling the long distances that had been required in earlier programs. Inherent in the concept is a plan to make TKN products available outside Turner to subcontractors and others in the industry.

In 2002, one business unit after another was being signed on to a new computer-based project-management system designed by a former Turner employee. In the new system, called Prolog, everyone from the field superintendent to the project executive has instantaneous insight into the status and rate of progress of every element of the work. Recognizing the importance of moving to a universal and consistent project-management system, Turner acquired a minority stake in Meridian, the company producing Prolog. In Dallas, meanwhile, other important information technology work was moving ahead in a campaign designed to ensure the seamless exchange of information among all the business units.

Turner's evolution in the new century showed signs of other significant change as well. The company had for years been aggressively but not very effectively seeking minorities to fill professional positions, and its efforts to hire females at the that level had been even less effective. But early in the new century, half the new recruits were minorities or females, and by the time of the company's hundredth anniversary there were six female vice presidents.

Few large firms had survived the often harsh vagaries of construction for as long as Turner had, and in the late summer of 2001 not many of them were likely to be as pleased about things as Turner was. But the company had good reason for optimism. In its hundredth year, with a staff exceeding 4,500 and an annual volume of work that would exceed $6 billion, there was little but good news.

That benign perspective was shaken to its roots on the morning of September 11, 2001, when two airplanes were flown into the Twin Towers at the World Trade Center, killing more than 3,000 people, destroying 15 million square feet of buildings, and damaging a like amount of construction nearby.

Turner's New York office on Hudson Street is less than a mile from the site of the World Trade Center, and Turner was the port authority's "on-call" contractor. The company had already been providing ongoing construction services at the site and maintained a small staff in the basement of one of the towers. Within minutes of the first strike, Peter Davoren, Turner's senior vice president in charge of the New York region, had been notified by telephone that what was thought to be a small plane had accidentally slammed into one of the buildings. But that illusion would be brief. From his office near Davoren's, Bob Fee would moments later see the gigantic ball of fire that suggested something much worse, and by the time Davoren and Fee had begun their effort to verify the safety of Turner's people, a second plane had struck. The real horror of the disaster was now apparent.

By later that day, all Turner's personnel at World Trade Center had been found safe. About midnight, Davoren received a call from New York's Office of Emergency Management (OEM), requesting Turner's help in search and rescue. At eight in the morning on the twelfth, Turner and four other contractors were at the site, working out a strategy for identifying and dividing the work to be done. Firemen and others would do the searching and rescuing, but the contractors would provide the men and equipment needed to get the debris out of the way, load it onto trucks, and remove it from the site. Everything would be done on a round-the-clock schedule, seven days a week, until the work was finished. Each contractor was assigned a work area, and Turner's was the northerly sector, which included the ruins of Building 7 and the bridge that connected it to its neighbor.

Surrounding the World Trade Center was a ring of buildings that had been badly damaged by debris from the collapses. Most of their glass had been broken, their once-elegant facades had been damaged or destroyed, and the buildings themselves were filling with ash that was being deposited by smoke. One badly damaged building was the fifty-three-story tower at One Liberty Plaza, which Turner had built for U.S. Steel in 1972 and on which Bob Fee had been superintendent. One Liberty Plaza's owner engaged Turner to restore the building, and for months afterward Bob Fee monitored progress on the job himself. Along another edge of the Trade Center was a row of badly damaged buildings that were part of Battery Park City, a complex of commercial and residential buildings that had been designed by some of the world's most eminent architects and built during the seventies and eighties to bring a special grandeur to the lower end of Manhattan. The present, private-sector owner of those buildings, a longtime Turner client, engaged the company to restore, and in some cases to rebuild, the affected structures.

With thousands of people relocated to temporary quarters, pressures to complete as soon as possible were intense, of course, and Turner was able to do what it promised. By January 2002, its removal work was finished, and both new construction and restoration work on the surrounding buildings were proceeding apace, with a late 2002 completion date as a target.

No one who worked among the ruins of the World Trade Center emerged unscathed. It was a disaster of such horrific proportions that it penetrated the consciousness of everyone who came near it. But as Turner's work advanced, evidence began to appear among people who had roles in the grim task of debris removal or restoration that they were glad to be part of the business of setting things right again. The work itself began to symbolize recovery, and the shock of the tragedy began to recede as restoration and new building work went forward.

In New York and elsewhere around the country, Turner was building some of the largest and most demanding projects in its history, and the pressures that characterize such work had never eased. Soon ENR would publish its annual rankings, and Turner would again appear as the largest building contractor in the United States. With a backlog that promised even busier times ahead, and with a workforce now approaching 5,000, the company turned to its second hundred years.

Index

retirement of, 16, 274
role after retirement, 280–281
Rosenburgh (Carleton) and, 214–215
San Francisco office and, 256
successor for, 241–242
as successor to J. Archer, 12
at Swarthmore, 93, 101
Turner (Howard S.) and, 277
Warren and, 214–215
Wilson and, 189
Turner, Howard, 25, 93–94
Turner, Howard S.
Altom and, 295
appointment as chairman, 16
appointment as chief executive officer, 16
appointment as director, 212
appointment as president, 16, 242
board of directors and, 216–217, 309, 310
career of, 14–15
computers and, 221
Creelman and, 262
education of, 14
foreword by, 12–16
Hong Kong and, 282
leadership of, 273, 274, 277–278, 280–281, 401
regional organization and, 286, 302
retirement of, 16, 309, 339
risk management and, 403
sales volume under, 335
Sears Tower project and, 261
Shaw (Walter B.) and, 277, 285
Turner (Chan) and, 277
on Turner Concrete Steel Company, 91
U.S. Steel project and, 273
Turner Index, 393
Turner International Industries (TII), 281, 283–285
under Gravette's organizational structure, 403
Kupfer and, 302, 352
Nilsson and, 307
as part of Diversified Services Group, 355–356
problems for, 340–341, 393
Reaves as executive vice president of, 350
regional plan of, 286
Shaw (Walter B.) and, 311
status of, 322, 372–373
volume of work, 334–335
Von Wening, and, 339, 343
Turner, J. A. (Jeb) III, 304
Turner, J. A. (Jerry) II, 304
Turner, James R. (called J. R.), 25, 93
Turner, J. Archer Jr. (Jerry), 14, 294
Turner, Jim, 93, 154
Turner, Joseph Archer (Archie), 25
after Second World War, 176
appointment as chairman, 14
appointment as president, 168
on board of directors, 169
construction company of, 13
death of, 14, 186
as executive vice-president, 14
letter from Navy Secretary Forrestal to, after war, 176
marriage and family of, 14
on postwar planning, 178–179
request for reduction of responsibilities, 181, 185

son of, 304
as successor to Henry C., 12
Turner Concrete Steel Company, 67, 90, 91
Turner Construction Company and, 93, 130, 133, 136
Turner Forman Concrete Steel Company and, 58, 59
Turner, Katherine, 93, 182
Turner Knowledge Network, 430
Turner Logistics, 430
Turner, Marlee, 15
Turner Medical Building Services, 346, 356, 370–371
Turner Power Group, 346, 356
Turner Real Estate, 346, 356
Turner, Rebecca Sinclair, 26
Turner, Richard Sinclair, 25, 93
Turner, Richard Townsend, 23–24, 33
Turner, Richard Townsend Jr., 24–25
Turner South America, 403
Turner Steiner Europe (TSE), 373, 376–377, 393, 412
Turner Steiner International, 376–377
Turner, Tom, 9, 302
Turner, Virginia Melick, 274
Turner, Walsh, Fuller, and Slattery, 229–230, 236
Turner, William W. (called W. W.), 13, 23, 25, 58, 59, 67, 90, 91, 93, 130
Turnier, Roger, 252, 281, 282, 336
Twaits, Ford J., 244
Twaits-Wittenberg Company, 244–245, 253, 344
Two Union Square office building, 387, 412
T. Y. Lin, 319

Uhlinger, J. P., 90
Uhl, Louis, 289
UNDC (public-benefit corporation), 308
Union Bank Building, 246, 247, 248
Unions, 108, 150, 190–191, 247, 330–331, 333, 334
    See also open-shop
United Aircraft, 157, 219
United Airlines (UAL), 349–351, 352
United Engineering Center, 240
United Engineers, 119
United Nations project, 191–192, 231
United States Tennis Stadium, 413
Universal Construction Company, 332, 335, 375–376, 409
University Hospitals of Cleveland, 291
University of Pennsylvania, 109, 314
University of Pittsburgh, 110
University of Washington, 412
"up/down" method of construction, 385
urban housing, 256
urban renewal, 248
urban skyscrapers, 198–199
U.S. Army Supply Base (Brooklyn), 86
U.S. Gypsum, 116, 184
Usilton, L. H., 87
U.S. Leather Company, 28
U.S. Rubber Company, 66, 128
U.S. Steel Corporation
    Cor-Ten, 258, 272
    Dravo Building and, 317–319
    Galbreath project and, 203
    Galbreath-Ruffin group and, 270
    headquarters building for, 272–273
    One Liberty Plaza and, 406, 432